Ardent Spirit

Ardent Spirit

A fictionalized biography based on the true story of the Odawa-French Fur Trader Madame Magdelaine Marcotte La Framboise.

J. K. Royce

ARDENT SPIRIT
Copyright © 2017 by Julie Katherine Albrecht Royce

Cover Design by Bob Royce, Sheila Bali, Jay Horne, and Mathew Medina

Front Cover Picture by Sheila Bali

All rights reserved. No part of this book may be reproduced, scanned, or distributed in any printed or electronic form without the express written permission of the author.

The **quotations** that begin the chapters of this novel are believed to be genuine and accurate. They come from a variety of sources, and cannot be verified with certainty.

For Bob

Without your constant support as I worked in front of a computer for hours, days, months and years, this book would not exist. I will always be grateful for the blind date of 8/8/88.

                                      And for Bonnie Albrecht

Acknowledgements

My first debt of gratitude is owed to the business owners and residents along the Lake Michigan shoreline. In countless conversations, they insisted Magdelaine La Framboise was a woman shortchanged by history. Their curiosity and opinions inspired me to write this novel.

It is a tricky endeavor thanking individuals. I was given assistance from more people and institutions than I can possibly mention. Inevitably I will overlook some who were critical to this book's existence. To them I offer my apologies and sincerest appreciation.

Librarians are unsung heroes and heroines of historical research. I availed myself of their knowledge at Central Michigan University, the Michigan Historical Library (Lansing), Mackinaw City Library, the Grand Haven Library, the Muskegon Library, the Hackley Library, the Mackinac Island Library, the Burton Library, the St. Joseph Library, and the Wisconsin Historical Collections.

The staff at Ste. Anne's Church, including Brother Jim Boynton, Heather May, and Amy Pavlov, generously offered time and information during my visits to the church and in the emails we exchanged.

I am indebted to Mary McGuire Slevin, Susan Jurkiewicz, Maureen Scully, Charles Pierce, Bonnie Albrecht, John McDowell, D. Michael Dudley, Michael Marcotte, Martha O'Kennon, Kenny Neganigwane Pheasant, Steve Brisson (Director of Mackinac State Historic Parks), Robert M. Candey (National Aeronautics and Space Administration), Dr. Keith Widder (Michigan State University) and Valerie van Heest (Michigan Shipwreck Research Associates). Each offered a way to improve the story: a new fact, or a suggestion and encouragement.

Courtney Phillips and Ofer Elitzur provided the quiet haven of their home for me to write. While they were at work, and my two adorable grandsons were at school, I had no interruptions from phones, housekeeping duties, or the internet. It was just me and a working draft.

I thank Jes Phillips for playing devil's advocate. At many steps of my writing journey he offered advice—always helpful, sometimes painful.

I appreciate the many comments and editing suggestions of Violet Moore, Margaret Lucke, Margie Lampel, Julaina Kleist-Corwin, Anne Koch, Elaine Schmitz, Sharon Svitak, Jordan Bernal, Sheila Bali, Sally Kimball, and George Cramer, as well as those of my other critique group members: Neva Hodges, Paula Chinick, Lani Longshore, and Vee Byram.

And finally, more than to anyone else, I thank my long-suffering husband, Bob Royce, who played chauffeur, computer support team, cover designer, and therapist. God knows, he's as thrilled as I am that the novel is finished.

To everyone who helped, I say *Miigwech*, or thank you.

Table of Contents

1. Sacred Space 1
2. Magdelaine La Framboise: Looking Back 3
3. Destiny 5
4. An Uneasy Choice 7
5. False Witness 11
6. Josette 23
7. Wintering in the Country 32
8. A Daughter's Death 40
9. Father Gabriel Richard 51
10. The Ugly Trade 64
11. Lucy and the Story of the White Indian 70
12. The Anishinaabek 83
13. Rix Robinson Takes Over Magdelaine's Trade .. 95
14. Sugar Camp 108
15. Beaumont, Heartbreak, and Tanner Returns ... 125
16. The Winds of Change 140
17. Ferry Opens a School and Betsy Marries 157
18. Religious Discord and Betsy Returns 168
19. Death of George Schindler 186
20. Word from a Son 192
21. Dreams 199
22. Reconciliation 209
23. A Storyteller 219
24. Crooked Tree 227
25. Wild Strawberries 237
26. Wampeme 247
27. History and Treachery 257
28. Death of Love 271
29. Mazzuchelli, Mosquitoes, and de Tocqueville . 284

30. Gathering Storm	301
31. Saying Goodbye	313
32. Mackinac Heartbreak	324
33. Preparing to Go Home	338
34. Startling Revelation	348
Postscripts	355
Glossary	365
Visualizing Magdelaine	371
Selected Bibliography and Further Reading	376
Genealogy Charts	386
Background Notes	408

Chronology

1530 to 1761   **The French dominate the fur trade in the Great Lakes Region for two centuries.**

1720   Jean Baptiste Marcotte is born in Cap Santé, Canada (the Upper Country).

1724   Charles Langlade is born.

1740   Thimotee Neskech (Marie Neskech Marcotte) is born.

1760 to 1797   **The English Dominate the Great Lakes Fur Trade.**

1761   Although taken by the English a year earlier, mainland Fort Michilimackinac remains under French possession until the British Commandant, George Etherington, arrives in 1761.

1763   The fur trade falls into British hands at the end of the Seven Year's War. The French lose Canada.

         Chief Pontiac's War begins. The English are attacked at Fort Michilimackinac (Mackinaw City).

1776   The Revolutionary War begins. Americans declare their independence from Britain.

1779   The North West Fur Trading Company is formed.

1780   **Magdelaine Marcotte is born in St. Joseph.**

         British Commander Patrick Sinclair moves the mainland fort at Mackinaw City to Mackinac Island where it can be more easily defended.

1783   Jean Baptist Marcotte is murdered.

         Treaty of Paris acknowledges American victory and turns over Mackinac Island and the fort to the Americans.

1783-84	The Mackinaw Company is established.
1784	John Jacob Astor arrives in Baltimore from Europe.
7/13/1787	The ordinance for the government of the Northwest Territories is drafted. It includes the geographic area that becomes Michigan.
1790	Blue Jacket and Little Turtle defeat U.S. General Josiah Harmer.
1792	American General Arthur St. Clair is defeated by the Great Lakes Coalition, a confederation of Native American tribes with support from the British for control of the Northwest Territory during what is also known as the Northwest Indian War, Little Turtle's War, and by other names.
1794	Magdelaine Marcotte marries Joseph La Framboise à la façon du pays.
1795	By the terms of Jay's Treaty the British give up possession of Michilimackinac.
	General "Mad" Anthony Wayne defeats indigenous force at Fallen Timbers.
9/24/1795	Josette La Framboise (Pierce), daughter of Magdelaine and Joseph La Framboise, is born.
1796	**The Americans take official possession of Michilimackinac ushering in American control of the Great Lakes Fur Trade.**
1803	President Thomas Jefferson, unable to stop the forward progression of settlers, suggests the First Nations people be relocated.
	The Louisiana Purchase adds 828,000 square miles to the United States, doubling the country's size. The purchase price is $15,000,000, or about five cents an acre.
7/11/1804	Joseph and Magdelaine La Framboise marry before a Catholic priest on Mackinac Island.

3/1805	Joseph La Framboise, son of Magdelaine and Joseph La Framboise, is born.
5/14/1805	Lewis and Clark Expedition sets off from Camp Dubois. The possible expansion of the fur trade is one purpose for the "Corps of Discovery."
1806	Joseph La Framboise's murder leaves Magdelaine a widow.
1809	The American Fur Company under John Jacob Astor establishes its headquarters at Mackinac Island.
1811	Prophet's Town is destroyed by William Henry Harrison.
1812	The War of 1812 breaks out between U.S. and British.
7/17/1812	The British land on north side of Mackinac Island and take possession of the Island.
10/5/1813	Tecumseh is killed at the Battle of Thames.
2/18/1815	Treaty of Ghent orders Fort Michilimackinac (Mackinac Island) returned to the Americans.
1817	Josette La Framboise marries Benjamin Pierce, brother of future president, Franklin Pierce. The wedding takes place in the home of Elizabeth and David Mitchell on Mackinac Island.
1820	Josette Pierce dies from complications of childbirth. Her infant son, Benjamin Langdon Pierce, dies a few days after his mother.
1821	Magdelaine La Framboise retires from the fur trade and sells her interest to Rix Robinson.
1822	Dr. William Beaumont begins his famous experiments and observations of human digestion after he saves the life of Alexis St. Martin.
1830	Andrew Jackson adopts the "removal policy" to relocate all eastern Native American tribes west of the Mississippi River.

1832	Black Hawk's War begins.
1833	Bodwe'aadamiinh clans forced to relocate west of the Mississippi.
1834	John Jacob Astor retires from the dying fur trade.
	Ramsey Crooks becomes president of American Fur Company.
1/26/1837	Michigan is granted statehood.
Fall 1838	Bodwe'aadamiinh at Twin Lakes are removed west.
1841	William Henry Harrison, the newly inaugurated president, dies in office.
4/4/1846	**Death of Magdelaine La Framboise.**
1850	Michigan's new constitution grants full citizenship to "civilized" Odawa.
1984	**Magdelaine Marcotte La Framboise is inducted into the Michigan Women's Hall of Fame for her achievements in business.**

Above is Father Otto Skolla's rendering of Madame La Framboise's home and Ste. Anne's church during rendezvous, circa 1843, published 1848. The original engraving was from a painting by Father Skolla, and both engraving and painting were discovered in a monastery in Hungary. Neither has survived. We know of their existence because of reproductions in several books published in the early twentieth century, including Antoine Rezek, *History of the Diocese of Sault Ste. Marie and Marquette* (Houghton, 1906). Below is the scene redrawn by Sheila Bali for the background on the front cover.

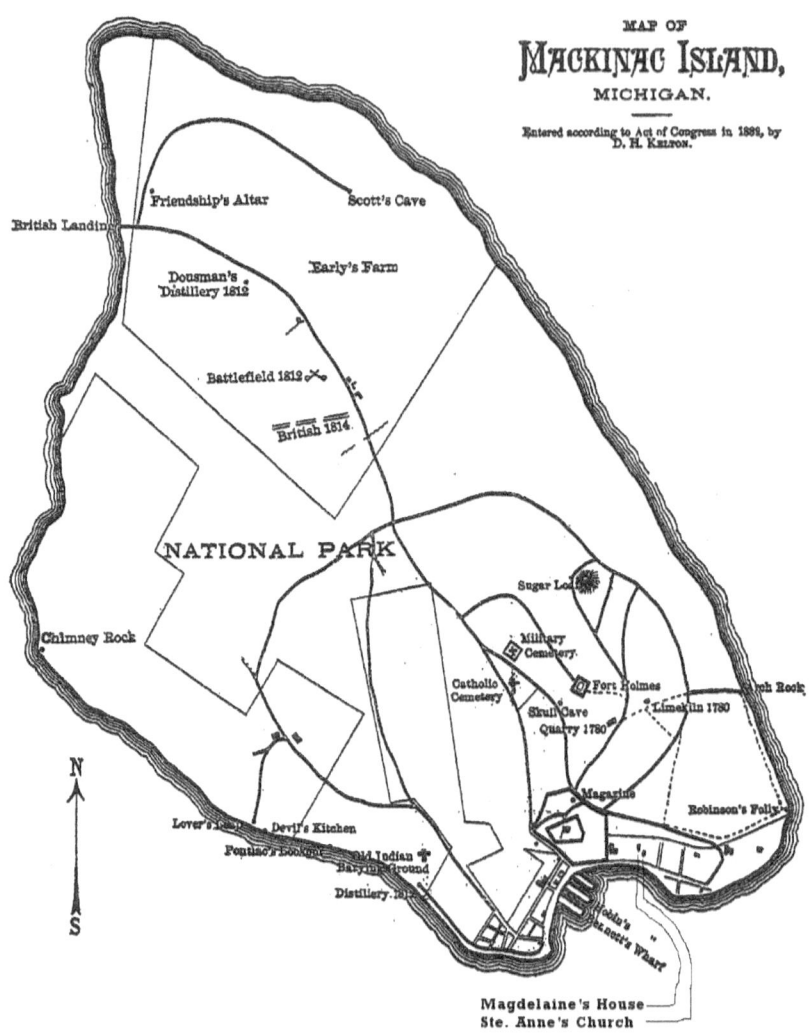

Magdelaine Marcotte La Framboise called it Mishi-Makinaak. It was the island-heart of the Great Lakes fur trade. In 1780, the year Magdelaine was born, the British Commander, Lieutenant Governor Patrick Sinclair, moved the English fort from the Michigan mainland to the mystical splendor of the two-by-three-mile island in Lake Huron. The fates of the remarkable Madame La Framboise and this magical place were interwoven with threads of peltry, religion, greed, and war.

1.
Sacred Space

"You have to look deeper, way below the anger, the hurt, the hate, the jealousy, the self-pity, way down deeper where the dreams lie. Find your dream. It's the pursuit of the dream that heals you." **Billy Mills, Oglala Lakota**

My Odawa mother described sacred space as the instant between exhalation and inhalation, that speck of time when you breathe out the life-sustaining air Mother Earth provides, and your soul opens to receive the wisdom of spirits.

Sixty-six years of living would embellish Maman's words and teach me that the seconds between breaths were sufficient to change the very core of life.

1806

My husband, Joseph, and I had stopped at Gabagouache[1] with our two canoes and twelve engagés. We would spend the night there on our way to our winter fur trading post at Crockery Creek. It was late fall, and the air smelled of campfires, pine trees, and a crispness that suggested approaching winter. Scarlet and orange leaves, unable to cling to branches that no longer nourished them, floated on the afternoon breeze and became part of the colorful carpet that crunched beneath our feet. The village of my childhood welcomed me home.

Children swarmed about us like flies at a church picnic. They squealed and laughed and grabbed for Joseph's hands as he passed out maple sugar candy. To the men, he offered a gill of rum. Social niceties smoothed the way of the fur trade. Ardent spirits were as critical as the beaver.

White Ox stepped forward and offered Joseph a rare white beaver pelt in exchange for a bottle of rum. Once a powerful man in the tribe, White Ox had succumbed to a craving for alcohol. His fur was worth far more than he demanded. I locked eyes with Joseph and shook my head. The movement was so slight, none but my husband noticed it. Joseph nodded agreement.

"Tomorrow morning, my friend," Joseph said. "Bring back this fur before our canoes shove off. We will talk." White Ox narrowed his unblinking, bloodshot eyes. He reeked of the poison that ravaged his body and confounded his senses. His nostrils flared, his rage was as palpable as the air before a vicious tornado strikes. Cursing under his breath, he stomped away.

The incident, quickly forgotten, did not mar the remainder of our evening. We listened to the gossip of friends, held and kissed babies born since our last visit, and ate spit-roasted venison and rabbit. Francois played his fiddle, and we watched fireflies dance to his music. Some soared so high their sparkle seemed one with the stars.

When night fell, Joseph reached for my hand, and I followed him inside our wigwam. Before retiring to her separate tent, our servant, Angelique,[2] had spread our sleeping rolls and set out a cup of fresh water for each of us.

Joseph took a sip, then knelt beside his bedroll, crossed himself, and clutched the small silver cross he wore tucked beneath his shirt. I slipped down on my knees next to him, bowed my head, and thanked God for the day's blessings.

I have no memory of a noise...a footfall...a disturbance, but I have keen hearing and an even keener sense of surroundings. I had an awareness—nothing more specific—something was wrong. I half opened my eyes. A gun pointed at Joseph's back. I followed the barrel of the long rifle from a hand—a finger on the trigger—to a face so crazed I scarcely recognized White Ox.[3] My mind did not register what I saw, but in that moment between exhalation and inhalation, I heard an explosion, saw a burst of flame. My eyes darted to Joseph who slumped forward. Dead.

2.
Magdelaine La Framboise: Looking Back

"We will be known forever by the tracks we leave behind." **Dakota Proverb**

1846

I started with that story of Joseph's murder when Josephine Marley came visiting during the winter months of 1846. Josie, as I called her, had been ten years old and motherless when her father dropped her at my home like a stray puppy for which he had no purpose. I took in a dozen or so children during the years of my widowhood, but Josie laid claim to my heart more surely than any but my natural children. Now grown to womanhood and married, she still called me Maman.

As my health declined, Josie came each morning on her way to her teaching duties at our Catholic school. She said my life was Mackinac Island's history, and she hoped I would share it with her. She argued it was a way to leave behind a piece of myself. I suspected she needed memories—mental pictures—to comfort her after I was gone. Other than the affection I had shown her, she had not known an abundance of love.

There was no shortage of time for reflection during the days that I weighed Josie's request. My body lay tethered to its deathbed. God and my impending demise vied for my thoughts.

Many Indians do not believe in death, only different worlds. The Great Spirit does not threaten his children with eternal damnation. Perhaps that is because by the time Indians die, they have done their suffering.

But I am also a Catholic. We believe in a hereafter, heaven or hell. I have heard it argued that the Christian God is more vengeful and wrathful than man can contemplate. His price for one unrepented false step is everlasting hellfire. I have stumbled often, but I do not fear the moment I face my creator. I believe he is more gracious and forgiving than we either imagine or deserve.

As I waited to depart this world, my pondering, by turn, either tortured me or brought me peace. Death, my companion, peered from every crevasse and corner of my bedchamber, unaware it could stand bold in the daylight. I welcomed its seductive promise of seeing Josette again, of meeting Benjamin Langdon, of letting Elizabeth Mitchell and Maman comfort me, of thanking Joseph for being my teacher.

I once supposed the Almighty wronged me, and I harbored my grudge as armor to protect me from my own anger. That was before I accepted that how I lived my life was my responsibility, not God's.

I wanted to grant Josie's request, but the sun rose and set three times before I began parsing out snippets of my past. My hesitancy sprang from an uncertainty of where to begin. My heart urged me to start with a tale of love, but what mattered more were the choices I had made. Looked at from that vantage point, my decision grew clear. I heard my maman say, "During your earthly sojourn, you will need the wisdom of spirits that comes in those split seconds between breaths. It will guide your choices." In Maman's words I found my voice and my starting point as Josie's storyteller.

I did not expect to recount a lifetime in the short space of hours I shared with Josephine Marley, but I promised myself the stories I told her would be the truth. I was not painting the portrait of a saint, but of a woman, who, as the Odawa would say, tried to walk through the world in a good way.

Magdelaine La Framboise look-alike? Drawing by artists Missy Horne and Sheila Bali. See Visualizing Magdelaine, p. 371.

3.
Destiny

"Everything on earth has a purpose, every disease an herb to cure it, every person a mission. This is the Indian theory of Existence." **Salish (Mourning Dove)**

September 1789-1794

I had met Joseph La Framboise in 1789, during the season when waves grew high along the Misigami shoreline, and men insisted the sky changed color as often as a woman changed the feathers in her hair.

As the French measured time, I was nine years old and played a coy game with growing up. Some days I amused myself with cornhusk dolls, others I longed to give birth and hold my own babies.

Joseph was twenty-three that fall. The older women of my clan described him as successful, sturdy, clever, and even pleasant-looking. I saw a grizzled Frenchman who bathed too infrequently and smelled almost as bad as the pelts of the dead animals that caused his canoes to sit low in the water. At his chin and above his lips, straggly red hair sprouted and did nothing to improve his appearance. His height was disappointing for a grown man. Boys half his age towered over him. There was nothing about him that made me wish I were of marriageable age.

Joseph came to Gabagouache, the village of my childhood, to exchange needles, knives, blankets, kettles, and guns for our furs. He and his men barely stepped ashore before a crowd gathered to examine his goods. I watched him from a line of trees that I believed shielded me from notice. He looked past those who thronged about him like players around a game of dice. He ambled in my direction. When he was within spitting distance, he offered me a piece of rock candy and a bright blue ribbon. He had honest, sincere eyes set in a sun-weathered face less handsome than any man in our tribe. I clutched the gifts, then backed away, whispered, "Miigwech," and escaped into the woods. I paid him no more heed than any other fur trader who happened by.

Joseph returned every year. With each visit he eyed me more closely. The candy and trinkets he offered me increased in size and value. Five years after our first meeting, he arrived at our village wearing a blood-red capote too warm for the season. It hung open, unsecured by either button or leather strings. An unstained white chemise peeked from beneath it. The seams of his jambieres faced outward. They were fringed and held in place by a wide sash. Preening like a rooster among hens, he wasted his efforts on me. I was, by then, fourteen years old and unconcerned with a man who had already used up half of his life. I schemed for the attention of Wampeme,[4] who was close to my age and stirred feelings I had never before known.

The first night of Joseph's September 1794 visit, he took his dinner with my family. He smiled too much, eyed me too often, and after dinner crowded to the far side of our longhouse where he huddled with Uncle Kinochausie. It took a nudge from my older sister to convince me that it was my fate being discussed.

When Joseph and his engagés packed up and left our encampment, I went with them, married in the custom of the country, *à la façon du pays* as the French called it, to a fur trader who would provide valuable connections for my people. I was less sure what the agreement provided me.

4.
An Uneasy Choice

"What is life? It is the flash of a firefly in the night. It is the breath of a buffalo in the wintertime. It is the little shadow which runs across the grass and loses itself in the sunset." **Crowfoot, Blackfoot**

Fall 1806

In the twelve years before his death, my husband transformed me from a wide-eyed woman-child into a shrewd fur trader. I learned to assemble an outfit,[5] became adept at bending the American rules so our business flourished, and knew how to control the alcohol we offered the Indians as a token of good will. I understood even better than Joseph the dangers of drunkenness.

My husband paid with his life when we misjudged White Ox. The night of Joseph's death, my screams rent the suffocating night air. Our engagés and Angelique rushed into my tent. I remember mumbling, "White Ox." I remember Angelique trying to pull me away from where I hunched over, holding Joseph's head in my lap. I would not let anyone move the body. The only other thing I remember before she and my men backed away, is asking to be left alone.

I prayed for God's guidance. I prayed for Joseph's soul and the future of our fatherless son and daughter. I prayed that by morning I could shape a plan.

I looked into my husband's face, laid my cheek against his cold forehead, then placed our best woolen blanket next to him and rolled his body onto it, gently wrapping it about him. Lying next to

Joseph for a last time was both comforting and disturbing. His soulless presence emphasized how alone I was.

Four paths were open to me. I could remain in Gabagouache. Uncle Kinochausie would assume responsibility for me. A woman was always welcomed in her family's lodge. It made no difference how many children she brought with her; an extra rabbit or a bit more corn was thrown in the kettle to feed them.

If I preferred, I could return to the little cabin Joseph had built for us on Mackinac Island. There I would enjoy the company of my sister, Therese, and that of my friend, Elizabeth Mitchell, who became a second mother to me when my own maman died of the pox years earlier. The profits Joseph and I had accumulated from our years of trading would provide a comfortable life. I could add to my wealth by selling our business to traders eager to expand. If I sought an easy existence, this was a reasonable option.

If I decided against either of those courses of action, I could marry another Frenchman. Joseph and I had twenty posts along Misigami's shoreline.[6] A trader who married me would gain bourgeois status. I would tender my financial interests to him, carry out wifely duties without complaint, work like a beaver from sun up until our evening bowl of sagamité, and my efforts would make him rich. If he married me in the Catholic Church, I would have the Black Robes to enforce our contract. Otherwise my husband would incur no moral obligation should he tire of me. He could abandon my children and me and take our wealth with him. If I chose carefully, however, little Joseph, Josette, and I would be treated well, and life as we had known it would scarcely skip a heartbeat.

I found this the most unappealing choice.

I considered my alternatives in the light of the rules my religion placed on a woman's behavior. I wondered if my fourth—my final—choice would gain God's approval.

With the first rays of morning sun, I gathered my voyageurs. The questioning looks on their faces told me they awaited my decision on what came next. They were unsure whether I would remain in Gabagouache with my uncle or return to my island home. They would get me settled before they attached themselves to other traders for the wintering season.

I scrutinized the assembled group. Francois shifted his weight from one foot to the other. Pierre twisted his hat in his hands. I asked myself if they would respect me as their boss.

"Francois and Pierre, please construct a box for Joseph's body. We will bury him with proper words before we head to our winter post. Jacques awaits us there." My future hinged on their reaction.

"The winter post?" Francois asked. "Are you not staying here?"

"Or returning to Mackinac Island?" Pierre asked.

To them I must have appeared addled.

"No, we will go to Crockery Creek. I am able to trade. If you are willing, I will have your help."

Without a word my voyageurs answered. They set about work according to my instructions. We buried Joseph. I thanked him for his kindness. His patience. For giving me two fine children. I promised to watch after them as he would have. I asked God to take my husband into his care and give him the rewards he deserved.

Pierre thanked Joseph for being both a boss and a friend. Francois said he was grateful that my husband appreciated his fiddle and had taken him on as an engagé when there were stronger men looking for work.

I had been with Joseph for nearly half of my life, and in those years I made myself an eager student. Now came the test of what I had learned.

Before we left the Crockery Creek post near the end of wintering season, I got unexpected visitors. Three Indians from Gabagouache stood outside my door, one on either side of a third who was trussed, hands behind his back, feet tied loose enough to let him shuffle. My knees weakened as I faced White Ox.

"He is yours to do with as you please," said one of his guards.

If there was an appropriate response to the offer, it escaped me. I gripped the doorframe. The men stood as rigid as three great white pines. White Ox wore an angry countenance, the other two looked merely stoic. I glanced through the door behind me at Angelique, who hovered inside by the fire. Her hands flew to her mouth, and her eyes bulged wide as if she expected me to pick up a knife, slit White Ox's throat, and leave her to clean up the mess.

I turned back to White Ox. "I cannot be your judge and executioner. Your sentence is for God to mete out. Seek God's forgiveness and live the remainder of your life in a way pleasing to him."[7]

The two men holding White Ox turned to each other. One shook his head, the other scratched his chin. Both avoided looking at me.

"Joseph honored our Catholic God, and I must honor Joseph. He would not seek revenge but rather urge forgiveness. I do no less."

White Ox did not blink. I was unsure whether he was afraid I would change my mind, or whether I had assaulted his dignity, refusing to let him die like a man.

The two Indians released their captive. I think it was shame, not fear, that gave White Ox the wind's speed.

Our bateaux stopped at Gabagouache on our return to Mackinac that next spring. My men exhumed the box with Joseph's remains for transport to the island and a proper burial in the Catholic cemetery on Market Street next to Ste. Anne's Church.[8]

I asked about White Ox, hoping he had redeemed himself, but was instead told a tale that furthered the tragedy. Shunned by the village, he had plunged his hunting knife deep into his breast. He was found dead in the underbrush of the nearby forest.

5.
False Witness

"You must speak straight so that your words may go as sunlight into our hearts. I will not lie to you; do not lie to me." **Cochise, Apache**

June 1820

"Zhaawan Kwe.⁹ Zhaawan Kwe. Madame La Framboise… Magdelaine."

I do not know how many times Wampeme's younger wife, Kimama, called my name that morning before her shrunken, mouse-like voice penetrated the clamor coming from the makeshift summer village along Mackinac Island's shore.

I turned at the sound of my Christian name. My about-face gave her no time to halt. Her fragile body collided with my sturdier frame. She tripped backwards. I grabbed her shoulders and kept her upright. Pox marks pitted her cheeks. A healed gash traced a vicious path across her forehead. The scar unnerved me, but it was her eyes, filled with terror and black as a starless night sky, that forced me to turn away from her fixed stare.

She sagged against me, her words muffled by my bosom. She smelled of sweat. Not sweat from racing to catch me, but the rancid magnified sweat that accompanies fear. "They will kill him."

"Who?" I shook her, though I already knew the answer.

"Wampeme." Her breathing was ragged, and she battled for the next words. "You must help him."

I pushed her away. Guilt knotted my stomach. "Then Wampeme should approach me." Even as I said it, I was grateful to be facing only his lesser wife.

Kimama fingered the worn fringe of her buckskin tunic. "Wampeme would never beg a favor from you."

I considered my history with her husband and nodded.

"I have no pride," she said, "if it will save him."

"Then you best tell me what has happened." I led her off the path near the blood-stained cockfight pit. She slumped against the trunk of a gnarly-rooted oak. I squatted, keeping between us a distance that evidenced we were not friends.

Kimama clutched her scrawny arms across her chest and inhaled several deep breaths. "An Englishman came to our longhouse the day before we departed for Mackinac Island. He eyed Wampeme's stack of furs."

Through clenched teeth, I asked, "The Englishman's name?"

"Jacob Wilson." She paused, perhaps to gauge my reaction.

I knew the man from my trade. He would sooner cheat an Indian than trade honest with him. Wilson issued threats made more frightening by the silver-filigreed, single-shot pistol he carried in the inner pocket of his wool frockcoat. He had a habit of opening the garment often so no one missed the weapon's menacing silhouette.

"He offered a bottle of devil water and asked to buy our pelts. Wampeme doesn't touch ardent spirits. He told Wilson we'd trade the furs at rendezvous." Her tremors had lessened, but her fingers flitted about, landed, and dug at crusty edges of a nasty-looking scab on her forearm.

At my best, I am not a patient woman. "Go on."

"Wampeme invited Wilson to share our evening meal of corn soup. The trader spit on the floor. He twisted his lips and snarled like a rabid dog. 'It is an insult to refuse to drink with me.'

"Wampeme wanted no trouble. 'Have an extra gill for me,' he said. 'Rum troubles my stomach.'

"Wilson cursed Wampeme and added, 'You're a filthy, thievin' savage.'"

Savage. The white man's name for us. I swallowed hard, sensitive to the taunt, but hiding my anger. If my bitterness distracted me, it did not halt Kimama's account.

"Wilson swore he'd make a complaint to Samuel Abbott here at the trading company. Said he'd see to it that no one bought our furs."

"And Wampeme did nothing?"

"Nothing..." She coughed and cleared her throat, paid no attention to the blood that oozed from the sore she had opened. "Until Wilson took the bottle of rum and poured it over our beaver pelts. My husband balled his fists tight. Took two slow steps toward Wilson, pushed him out of the longhouse, followed him outside and shoved him again."

I saw where the story headed. Then, too, I knew Wampeme. "Is Wilson dead?"

She registered no surprise at my question. "Wilson was many pounds heavier than Wampeme, but the fur trader's weight came from rich food. It slowed him rather than give him an advantage. He picked up a rock and rushed toward my husband. Wampeme landed a powerful blow to protect himself. Blood gushed from Wilson's nose. Two yellowed front teeth flew to the ground. He stumbled into the fire. He raised his hands to protect himself...or maybe to plead mercy. If Wampeme noticed, he gave no sign. The Englishman's face twisted like that of a madman. His screams were so fierce I feared they'd reach the next village. He ran, but the flames followed him...fed on his clothes...ate his flesh...until he dropped."

I saw satisfaction in her faint smile. "What of the remains?" I asked.

"They fueled the blaze...it feasted on a dead fir tree, tinder and what was left of the vile man."

The Englishman was of no concern to me. If the matter ended there, Kimama would not sit, cowering, an arm's length from me. I worried that what she wanted from me would both trouble my conscience and offend God. "What causes you to seek my counsel?"

"A friend brought me a warning this morning. Her cousin, Ahanu, told Abbott of the incident. The head clerk promised an immediate investigation."

I closed my eyes for a moment. Blackness did not make the problem disappear or give me a promising resolution. "What does Wampeme say about all of this?"

Her breath came as if from lungs choked on panic. "I did not share my friend's news with him, but instead came looking for you." She wiped tears with the back of her forearm, leaving a streak of blood on her cheek from the now oozing wound. "We've seen the white man's answer to Indian problems. Without your help, Wampeme will not see tomorrow's sun. You know I speak the truth. Abbott is said to be a man who shuns violence, but once the story spreads, someone will feel honor-bound to seek revenge for Wilson." She bent forward, covered her face with her hands and sobbed.

"Stop." My compassion would have been greater, caused me to reach out to wipe her face of the blood and tears and make promises that all would be well—if she were not Wampeme's wife. My heart beat so fast I feared it would spring from my chest. "Stop wailing. Do you hear me?" The words I wanted to hurl at her remained buried inside me. *I hate you for bringing this matter to me. I hate you for ignoring the position it puts me in. And I fear for my soul, knowing I hate you most because you sleep next to Wampeme.*

"Return to your tent," I said. "Say nothing of our conversation. I will come later."

I wanted to rush home, hide myself under the freshly beaten feather-tick coverlet of my bed, and let its heat rid me of the chill that crawled like ants over my skin. Instead I retraced my steps in the direction of the trading post to find Samuel Abbott.

I regretted that the short walk provided me time to revisit the past.

I had been of marriageable age when Wampeme traveled to L'Arbre Croche after his parents died. My family migrated with the seasons from St. Joseph to Mackinac Island, but the place called Crooked Tree captured my heart. The first time I saw Wampeme, he wore a breechclout and ran along the shoreline of Misigami. By the way Frenchmen measure time, twenty-six years had passed since that day, but heat coursed through me, and my womanly parts tingled as I recalled the image. *God forgive my unchaste thoughts.* Wampeme's lithe, well-muscled body had moved like a panther, and I wondered if he, like the fierce cat, was dangerous. For days, I followed his habit and put myself at a restrained distance from his path, pretending to dig wild onions, carrots or herbs when I expected him to pass.

My heart pounded a strange beat each time he approached. I imagined conversations: *Do you think the summer crop will sustain us during our hunting season? Should we fear the Americans? Do you believe the American Great Father, George Washington, is better than the French and English before him?* I had no end of questions to begin our conversation. No end of questions to make me sound wise and older than my years. But the first words between us were his. "Does your life consist of anything other than harvesting what you find along my morning trail?"

"I knew this spot before it was yours." Then my mind emptied of rational thought. Maybe it was for the best. We walked without conversation, enjoying the sounds of the whippoorwills and watching the sandpipers snatch sand fleas from the beach.

Days later, he presented my mother the choicest rabbit from his day's hunt. He shadowed Uncle Kinochausie and offered to help set traps.

It was that season, on the first night that rain turned to ice, that Joseph La Framboise came to the wigwam of my uncle and contracted to marry me. I had asked God to rid me of impure desires for Wampeme and teach me acceptance.

Reliving the past solved nothing. I hurried my steps to the trading company. I wanted to catch Abbott before the citizens of Mackinac Island riled themselves to a frenzy over the charges. Wampeme's word was worthless. If the offense charged was against a white man who traded with John Jacob Astor, the word of a savage carried even less weight.

As I reached the corner where the American Fur Company headquarters stood, the noon Angelus rang.

From years of habit, I closed my eyes, stopped, and made the sign of the cross. *God, it is a mortal sin to bear false witness, but my heart forces me to help Wampeme. Please forgive me.*

I stepped into the building. Several traders haggled over the price of their furs. Samuel Abbott stood off to the side overseeing the activities. "May I see you in the back room for a minute?" I asked. My stomach roiled as though I had eaten an animal too long dead. "It is a private matter."

"Madame La Framboise, you look flushed." He motioned me through a door and to a wooden chair. "Are you feeling poorly?"

I sat. He ladled me a cup of water from a barrel kept next to a small teak dining table that served as his desk. "No, I am fine." I took two long sips of the water to keep it from sloshing over the rim onto my unsteady hands.

He scrutinized me, his face clouded with questions. "What is it I can help you with?"

"I have come from speaking to Kimama, the younger wife of Wampeme, a member of my tribe."

"I know the man. I should think you'd disapprove of him. Two wives and all, but I sense that isn't why you have come."

I nodded, but said nothing. *What exactly had he heard?* It seemed information vital to the story I concocted.

"I assume you are here because of the allegation floating about town. The one—sworn to by a member of Wampeme's own tribe—that your friend murdered Mr. Jacob Wilson? Then the killer set out with his family for this island."

Abbott, darker than either of his English parents, could himself be mistaken for a mixed-blood Indian if he swapped his waistcoat for animal skins. A clerk's beaver hat covered short straight black hair. Only his icy blue eyes seemed wrong for an Odawa face.

"The rumor reached my ears. You can imagine the distress such a falsehood causes me."

"A falsehood?" His mouth turned down more at one corner than the other. The look made me feel ten years old. My older sister, Charlotte, shot me that expression when she caught me in a lie.

I tapped my fingers against the cup I held, then looked up and locked eyes with him. "Yes. A falsehood. I was in L'Arbre Croche when Mr. Wilson arrived. I had landed my canoes there three days prior. I spent time with friends. I traded a few furs with Wampeme. He wanted to keep the rest of his stack to trade here on the island. Kimama needed needles and a special calico, and I had none remaining in my outfit." I slipped into falsehood, and the tale took on its own life.

"How is this important to the death of a respected trader who does business with the American Fur Company?" Abbott stretched out his legs, crossed them at the ankles. He appeared relaxed and ready to pounce on my first word that lacked the weight of truth.

"I saw Wilson. He, too, wanted to trade for Wampeme's remaining furs. But as with my supplies, Wilson had little merchandise remaining, and Wampeme was not interested. The trader drank a gill of rum and was given a roasted partridge before continuing on his way. The night turned angry as a nor'easter rolled in. I hope the gentlemen met with no harm."

"Can you prove that Wilson left, or that he didn't return at a later time?" Again that lopsided scowl, but this time it bothered me less.

"I saw him depart. He is a lone trader, no engagés. He was hard to miss as he struggled to get launched." I piously folded my hands. *God forgive me for I sin.* It had turned into a day I needed a lot of absolution.

As though reading my thoughts, Abbott said, "Madame La Framboise, you are a woman of God. I know you would not burden your everlasting soul with an intentional lie."

Was he toying with me?

He continued. "Seeing Wilson leave doesn't account for whether he returned."

I measured my response. "What I am willing to swear is that the next morning, as you have noted, Wampeme and his family departed in canoes for the island. I remained two additional nights in a wigwam next to Wampeme's vacated longhouse. Any sign of trouble or Wilson returning, I would have known it, and Wampeme was on the island when I arrived. My engagés, my companion Angelique, and I left on the third day."

"Your men will so attest?"

"They will."

"And your slave, Angelique?"

"*Mais oui.*"

"And all you've told me…you'll swear it on God's holy book and the souls of your Catholic priests?"

"If you wish." My Odawa loyalties and Christian values warred with one another. I hoped Abbott would not make me take such an oath. I touched my mother's crucifix, which hung around my neck, and promised God I would make amends.

"I hope that old Wilson paddles into camp soon and puts speculation to rest." Abbott slapped his hands against the table as though concluding the matter.

"I pray the same. If he has met with misfortune, I hope the circumstances make clear it was accidental."

As if an afterthought, he said, "I can't figure why someone—a friend of Wampeme's, no less—would fashion such a fabrication."

"To gain favor with you, I suppose…maybe give him a trading advantage. He may have thought you would think he is a good Indian, willing to come forward with news, even if it hurts one of his own. But if you bring whoever told you this vicious tale into my presence, I will challenge him in front of you." My growing courage carved a course unhampered by rational consideration.

"It won't be necessary. Your word is enough for me. The matter is settled."

I trudged home, my heart heavy with sin. Instead of thanking God for the perfume of lilacs and the warm breeze kissing my cheeks, I begged forgiveness for a trespass I regretted, but one I would repeat a thousand times under like circumstances. The Black Robes preached a God who cared as much for his red children as his white. He promised to be with me every moment. He promised to answer my prayers. He promised paradise at the end of a faith-directed life. Maybe my lies had cost me those beguiling promises. The next visit from a Catholic priest to our island, I planned to ask how a believer earned forgiveness for an unrepented offense against God.

When I reached my cottage, I collected gifts for Wampeme's family. Odawa tradition required I not arrive at his tent without tokens of friendship.

I walked the trail that paralleled the beach and connected my cabin to the shops of Mackinac. To my right, the afternoon sun settled like a benediction over Fort Mackinac. On a limestone bluff overlooking Lake Huron, the whitewashed and vigilant fortress stood in contrast to the temporary Indian encampment on the other side of the path. My eyes searched huddled tepees and settled on eagle feathers that hung above one entrance flap, a sign of Wampeme's totem.

I picked my way through the fires, half-starved dogs, and naked, unwashed children. The previous night's frolic left an undercurrent of excess—alcohol and the sickness that followed its overindulgence. The scent of evergreens mingled with smoke and masked the stench. Odawa women sat cross-legged near open fires where sagamité simmered in cooking pots, adding a more appetizing aroma that was familiar and comforting, but at the same time repugnant to me.

I spotted Kimama sitting on the ground, a blanket around her shoulders, close enough to the fire to stave off the late afternoon chill. I crouched near and handed her a mocock of sugar and a rawhide pouch of pemmican. I spoke in a whisper. "I come to tell you it is taken care of."

"Are you—"

"Is that Zhaawan Kwe I hear skulking about my tent?" Wampeme's honey-smooth voice interrupted his wife. He stuck his head through the flap. "I hope you didn't plan to sneak off without a word to me? Come inside. Sit. We'll talk."

His smile was maddening. "It would violate appearances," I said.

"You don't worry how your gifts make me look when I have none to offer in return, but you fear our friendship will cause gossip?"

I followed his eyes as they traveled the sparse interior about him. He grabbed a knife from a sheath at his waist and from his shirt cut the rawhide string that attached a bead as brilliant and blue as Mackinac Harbor on a sunlit afternoon. He pressed the bauble into my hand. I resisted the urge to hurl the glass ornament back at him. Custom did not permit such an insult. I fumed at his rebuke, but in spite of the years that had passed, his words, the glare he fixed on me, the warmth of his nearness, returned me to the tongue-tied girl with whom he had walked the beaches long years ago.

I had a stop to make before I returned home. I slipped into Ste. Anne's Church knowing I would be alone. No priest lived on the island. French voyageurs and Indian converts entered the house of worship only on Sunday morning, when one among them led a discussion aimed at honoring God. All other days, if the Holy Spirit was present, he enjoyed no company.

I sat in the back pew considering my situation. I had defused Ahanu's allegations. My falsehood had not been the first lie to ever escape my lips, but truth is what God commands. Honesty is easier than keeping straight the tangled threads of deception. No one suggested God judged dishonesty by degree. Yet I never supposed he would thrust me into the fires of hell for telling my dear friend, Elizabeth Mitchell, that she looked lovely in her newest black frock, the exact same as all the others her seamstress stitched for her. I repented these petty falsehoods and imagined the Almighty winked and said, "I understand, Magdelaine, but try harder to keep these fibs to a minimum." Could I justify my deception to Samuel Abbott as an untruth birthed of necessity, or was such rationalization self-deception?

Self-deception—the worst lies. Wilson died. My lie allowed Wampeme to get away with murder. Who was I to believe I could ration out justice?

I rose and shuffled to the altar, my feet as heavy as the rock anchors we used to hold our canoes in place. I dropped to my knees and begged God's forgiveness. He seemed to ask if I would make amends by telling the truth to Samuel Abbott. My answer remained "no."

A week later I purchased copper kettles, wool blankets, and French hunting knives that my engagés would collect later for our winter trading outfit. My business finished, I walked home from the fur headquarters. Building materials littered my property where the skeleton of a much larger home grew around, and overshadowed, my cottage. The sun's unseasonable heat warmed the day enough that I passed to the shaded side of the path, where maples flaunted fresh buds. As I angled to my yard, I noticed Ahanu crouched like a predator.

I drew close. I had taken a step beyond him before he said, "You have no greeting for me?" A simple question turned sinister by the guttural way he spat it.

I had accused this man—though he was innocent—of the very sin that burdened my conscience. I wanted to hurry into the safety of my dwelling and bar the door. "Why do you hide yourself by the roadside like an animal on the hunt?"

"Hide? That is how you see it? I want to talk." He aimed slow, deliberate words that challenged my courage.

"I am listening."

He picked up a twig and slowly, methodically, swept pine needles into a pile in front of him. "People of my village believe the myth that Magdelaine La Framboise— Zhaawan Kwe—is an honest woman."

"I never sought to be described—"

He cut off my response with a vehemence that shook me. "And yet, you are." He smashed his fist through the pine needles he had gathered, scattering them in all directions. "Samuel Abbott calls me a liar. Says my furs are no longer welcome for trade. He won't be bothered by Indians he cannot trust. Amusing, isn't it? It's me he doesn't trust."

"I am sorry."

"Sorry enough to admit to Abbott you know nothing of the matter?"

My fingers skimmed Wampeme's blue bead, which I had threaded onto a leather string. It dangled from my neck, nestled next to my crucifix. I offered no reply to Ahanu's question.

"Or just sorry that my family will go hungry this winter?"

"Sorry enough to buy your furs."

"Spare me your charity. It doesn't restore my honor."

"The honor of betraying a friend? Your treachery would have cost Wampeme's life."

"Betrayal and treachery? Harsh accusations uttered from your mouth. Reserve your judgment until you know the truth."

"The truth? Tell me."

His face contorted in a look that could turn the flames of hell into Mackinac's winter icicles. "Abbott has ordered me off the island. If I stay, he'll have Magistrate Puthuff arrest me for obstructing the peace. My own people shun me. Look me in the eyes. Remember this face. May it prove a ghost-like apparition that forever haunts you." He opened his mouth as if to say more, but instead he rose and shuffled away like a man defeated.

6.
Josette

"The warrior, for us, is one who sacrifices himself for the good of others. His task is to take care of the elderly, the defenseless, those who cannot provide for themselves, and above all the children, the future of humanity."
Tatanka Lyotake, Sitting Bull

September - October 1820

I stood in front of my cabin amid the advancing construction efforts and watched the hive-like activity. After several minutes, I spotted Josette and Harriet, my daughter and granddaughter, making their way toward me from the fort. They picked up their pace, and I hastened in their direction. The moment they were within reach, I threw my arms around them. In a month, I would depart for winter camp, and I relished my remaining time with family.

Though a head shorter than me, Josette had inherited my oval face. Our eyes were an identical coal black, but hers were soft, mine hardened by life. She stood tiptoe to plant a kiss on each of my cheeks. "Benjamin[10] wanted to be here to discuss house details with you," she said, referring to her husband, "but he's busy with soldiering business."

I stooped and covered Harriet's face with kisses. "I love you as much as the distance from where we stand to the country from where Grandpapa Joseph's family came." I raised my right arm and pointed in the direction of France.

Enjoying a three-year-old's sense of humor, Harriet giggled, stretched her arms high over her head, and added her half of our ritual greeting, "I love you to heaven and back, so I love you more."

I rose and brushed my daughter's wavy, dark hair from her forehead. "I always value time with my son-in-law, but I understand."

"I should hope so, since every spare minute he doesn't spend on the cursed English business, he devotes to ordering supplies and planning this grand house of yours." Josette's eyes sparkled with playfulness. Laughter layered her words as we stepped onto my property. "He oversees each detail of construction as though his continued existence on this earth depends on it. When I am hard-pressed to find my husband, I seek him traipsing about in this mayhem."

I rubbed my forearms to ease the morning's chill. I clasped hands with Josette and Harriet, their fingers cold against my palms. We picked our way about the debris littering the yard. My current modest dwelling would remain the center of the spacious home being constructed around it. I favored the idea that the cabin Joseph built for us—the place where our children were born—was the heart of my lavish new residence.

"Will the money I set aside for the project last until I return next spring?" I asked.

"Quite, Maman. With the ample funds you left, we could build a house twice the size you've instructed."

"Twenty-five years trading furs and I will never lack for earthly pleasures…if there is anything you or Harriet or Benjamin need, I hope you know—"

"I know, Maman, but our needs are well taken care of by Benjamin's allotment."

I stepped around stacks of lumber strewn in our path. "When I was your age, Harriet, I shared wigwams and longhouses with many relatives." I paused inside the frame of the burgeoning structure before again addressing her mother. "Perhaps this new house will be too grand. It looks big enough for our whole clan."

"It is perfect. It will have rooms enough for all of the grandchildren Benjamin and I will give you. Joseph's, too, when my little brother is old enough to marry."

I released hands that had become warm in my grip. Harriet cradled her pale, blue-eyed porcelain doll, murmuring to it as if it were a live baby. Josette knelt next to her daughter as I walked the length of the addition, examining the frame for the door, touching the transom casement, feeling pleased that not even my tallest friends would be forced to stoop to enter. *God, prevent my admiration from becoming sinful pride.* "You and Benjamin have done a fine job overseeing the work. I am grateful."

"Grateful enough that you'd let Pierre handle the wintering this year so you could stay on at Mackinac?"

I smiled and tramped back toward my daughter. "I find winter camp harder each season. I dread leaving you and Harriet behind."

"And I hate that you endure long months in dreary camps."

"They are not dreary. They take me back to the villages and my people." An image of Ahanu, defeated and angry, flashed through my mind. *My people.* I chased the thought away, unwilling to let it spoil the day. I stood in front of Josette and offered a hand to pull her up. "Still, there is not much to amuse me there. I am happy to have Angelique's company. I reflect on my life, talk to God and daydream about Harriet's mischief."

"If you stay on the island, Harriet will keep you busy. I'd rest easier knowing you are safe."

"You tempt me…cold months in front of a crackling fire…telling stories to Harriet…my own bed."

"Oh, Maman, can you stay at Mackinac? Benjamin believes it's only weeks before the house is finished. You could spend Christmas with us." Josette rose and led us through an opening between timbers and let her fingers rest on the sill for a window that would arrive any day. "Look at the view you'll have of the harbor. Maman, please stay."

"Another year, maybe two." I entwined my fingers with Harriet's to prevent the child from climbing about the sawhorses or touching the tools that lay unattended on the ground. At the property edge, voyageurs turned summer construction workers ate lunch under a huge elm and watched us.

"One year." Josette tilted her head and grinned at me. "Promise me, only one more year." She followed me inside. "We'll have a huge frolic, the likes of which this island has never seen, when my maman returns from her last winter at the posts."

By mid-October, Josette's tawny skin lost its glow. She ate little and nausea plagued her. I suspected that a new life sapped my daughter's energy. When Josette confirmed my suspicions, I tempered my joy with prayers for her health.

One afternoon, a week before I was to depart for winter posts, I entered Josette's chilly rooms in the officer's quarters. I saw my daughter through the open door to the bedroom. Harriet sat cross-legged on the bed next to her mother, playing with a set of paper dolls, a gift from Great Aunt Schindler.[11] As soon as the child spotted me, she bounded in my direction.

"Maman's resting." Harriet threw herself into my arms.

"I see that." I fingered curly, cherub-like tendrils of hair and then pulled her into a hug.

"I hear you, Maman. So watch what you say."

"What I say is that you might do well with a cup of tea." I lifted the kettle from the hook over the hearth. It was full and hot. I dropped mint leaves into a mug that sat on the table and poured water over them.

Josette propped herself up and wrapped slender fingers around the steaming cup I extended toward her.

"Drink. It will settle your stomach." The noon Angelus bell chimed three times. I dropped my head, thanked God for his mercies, and asked him to be with Josette. I then looked up and opened my eyes.

"I'd drink hemlock," Josette said, "if you promised it would give me back my strength."

"You joke, but boiled hemlock needles are a good spring tonic." I did not admit I knew herbs that would relieve Josette's body of the child she carried. I wondered if I would consider them if my daughter's condition worsened, and I feared for her life. I hoped it never came to that. I had already invited God's wrath for the harm I caused Ahanu.

Josette tipped her head and stared at the brew. "I hope this isn't really hemlock."

"No, I promise it is not."

She took several swallows.

"I am thinking of staying this winter. I could care for Harriet and help you with the new baby."

"Maman, besides Benjamin and Harriet, I have Aunt Schindler, Catishe, Marianne and Betsy.[1] How many do you think it takes to watch one small woman and help a baby into the world?" Harriet climbed back onto the bed and lay her head on Josette's shoulder. "I'd love having you stay, but it isn't necessary that you remain on my account. You have expressed a desire to winter another year before retiring."

"That was before I knew you were with child." I placed fingers to my daughter's forehead. The churning of my stomach calmed when I confirmed Josette suffered no fever. "You look pale."

"You can blame that on Papa and my French blood." Josette leaned over and set the cup on the chest of drawers.

"You make light, but you do not look or act yourself of late."

"Are you suggesting I am limp and pallid as an over-laundered dish rag? It must be your intent to protect me from the venial sin of vanity." When Josette grinned, she looked more like Harriet's older sister than her maman.

My countenance stiffened. I refused to drop the matter. "A mother worries about her children, even grown, married ones."

"Then fret over my little brother. He's two thousand miles away. Surely that provides fodder for your worry."

"Montreal may be a far distance, but Joseph[12] stays with his aunt. He studies hard and according to the reports I receive does well.

---

[1] Catishe is the daughter of Magdelaine's slave, Angelique. See Background Note 2. Marianne is Marianne La Salliere Fisher, daughter of Therese, niece of Magdelaine. Betsy is Marianne's daughter, Elizabeth Fisher Baird.

Next year he will apprentice himself to a fur trader. That will be soon enough to worry about him. For now, it is the circles under your eyes that cause my heart sorrow."

"Maman, you see more than is there. You walked in on me taking a nap. A woman in my condition suffers a lack of vitality. It's nothing more. I've delighted in having you here this summer, but it is past time for you to go. You have never before stayed until October. If you don't leave soon, the winds of November will chase you downlake. If the water's edge freezes, your canoes will be forced far from shore, and it'll be me who worries—over capsized canoes and a drowned Maman."

"It is not too late to change my plans."

"We've been over that. Your outfit is purchased. Your engagés expect you to travel with them."

"They can handle the posts without me." I looked at the crucifix above Josette's bed. God will watch over my daughter, I thought, but it might not hurt to offer him help.

"It isn't necessary. If it was your choice to quit this year, I'd be rejoicing your decision. You made it clear you need an additional year to settle your affairs. Go. Take care of your obligations. I'll watch for your canoes to arrive early at rendezvous. You can spend next winter with the children and me."

"That is a promise…if death does not claim me from the consternation you cast on my frail constitution."

This brought a hearty laugh. "You, frail? Maman, I've heard you described many ways but never frail."

I lifted her hands and kissed the tips of her fingers. "I will pray for you every day."

"I know you will, and God will hear your prayers."

When I walked home that afternoon, turbulent dark clouds hovered. Some clashed and sent thunderous roars to accompany me. The Catholic God forbade listening to false idols, but I could not escape the feeling that Chebbeniathon, the Odawa sky-god, was sending an angry warning. In light of that message, Josette's assurances brought little comfort.

I departed Mackinac Island on a morning so cold that a thin scum of ice covered the lake near shore. Josette mustered enough strength to dress herself and Harriet. They accompanied me to the harbor. A handful of traders pushed bateaux and canoes into the water.

My engagés shambled about, good-naturedly punching one another and skipping stones, while I said long goodbyes. Our outfit, trade goods, and supplies for the wintering season caused the bateaux to sit low where they had been anchored.

"I need to give you enough kisses to last until next summer," I told Harriet. The child's arms clung tight around my neck. I set her on the ground so I could indulge myself a proper embrace of my daughter. I made no mention of the tears that glistened in Josette's eyes as she turned to walk away.

I watched as she and Harriet shuffled back toward the fort, and when they were only a silhouette, I signaled for my men to carry me to the boats. As we paddled toward open lake, giant elm and maple, stripped of summer leaves, shrank to the size of saplings and whispered, "Godspeed."

My thoughts turned from the promise of a new grandchild to the realities of the fur trade. My Métis[13] blood secured for me the trust of the Indians along Misigami's shore. The tribes preferred trading with me rather than the agents sent by John Jacob Astor. The great man's wolves could nip at my ankles, but they could not turn my people against me with bribes of higher fur prices or more trinkets.

Josette was right. It was time for me to retire. I had enough money to sustain me if I lived to be a hundred, and still I would leave a pleasing sum for Joseph and Josette and Ste. Anne's Church. I wearied of the American Fur Company's treachery and its tactics to push out the independents. I struggled to hold my own. Astor's main agent, Ramsey Crooks, a friend in normal situations, had turned against me and collected affidavits charging me with selling illegal alcohol during the course of my business. He knew it was the way of the trade. He and other Astor men did it too.

Jesus, I know you commanded us to love our fellow man, even the difficult ones. But John Jacob Astor is a loathsome little worm with scruples that mark him a poor excuse of a man. He and his puppets hope the evidence they offer will be my undoing. I halted my thoughts. Astor's actions were no worse than mine, nor did they excuse my misdeeds.

Crooks might believe he had achieved his goal and brought me into the Astor fold, but I convinced myself that my contact with the fur company was on my terms. This season I would operate a small station on assignment and risk for Astor on the Sowanquesake, the river with the forked streams, but I would continue to maintain my own posts at Flat Rock, Crockery Creek, and Muskegon Lake.

One more year, I told myself. Time to get my men well-placed and ensure that someone reliable would trade with my people. Then I would quit.

Ramsey Crooks
Public Domain

John Jacob Astor portrait by John Wesley Jarvis, circa 1825
Google Art Project, Public Domain

A wall from Magdelaine La Framboise's original home remains
visible inside the lobby of the current day Harbour View Inn.
Photo courtesy of Bob Royce

7.
Wintering in the Country

"The soul would have no rainbow, if the eyes had no tears." **Tecumseh, Shawnee**

January 1821

Winter camp suffered long days filled with too little activity. Minor annoyances that would have disappeared in the sunshine festered inside closed doors struggling to keep out the season's icy wrath. Visits from friends and fellow traders broke the monotony. Guests brought news and spiced an otherwise bland existence.

January roared in with snowstorms, one following on the coattails of the other. Inside our little two room cabin, my six men grumbled and groused. On good days, when the weather cooperated, I had them accompany me to the village of Moccottiocquit, where we traded pots and pans, knives and guns, and scissors and shoes for the furs his tribe had collected. This occasional bartering was not enough to keep boredom at bay.

At breakfast one morning, Pierre and Louizon reached fisticuffs over which of them got a larger portion of corn soup. I ordered them outside to cut wood though we had a pile high enough to see us through the moons of ice and snow and well into the next season. They needed fresh air, and I hoped physical labor would settle them down.

Another day Francois, who was as good-natured as God ever created a man, lamented being trapped indoors. "My jobs are to paddle bateaux and lift bales of fur. Sitting inside and watching spiders spin webs is no pastime for a man." He plunked his cup down hard enough that coffee splashed over the rim onto the table.

I picked up an axe standing next to the front door and handed it to him. "Since you wish to paddle, you can free the bateaux from the ice with this. If the blowing snow does not stop you, you can chop a few feet in each direction of the boat, then climb in and row back and forth to your heart's content…or until the river freezes over again."

Francois slapped his thigh and let out a hearty whoop. He reached for his fiddle and offered no further complaints that day.

I remembered those incidents for their ordinariness…their normalcy. Normalcy I would soon yearn to recapture. They were the last moments of levity before, just a day apart during that winter of 1821, two men lumbered through the backwoods to my post. The arrival of neither carried joy.

If the desolation of camp burdened me with daydreams of Wampeme, never did I wish for the temptation of his company. Yet he came.

"Perhaps you'll be less worried about the appearance of impropriety here than on your fancy island," he said.

I expected Wampeme to challenge me, or even make suggestions that would blaze my cheeks bright with embarrassment. That day, however, his tone struck me, heavy and serious.

"Let's walk," he said.

"It is too cold. Angelique will bring you vittles, and we can talk here at the table." I distrusted myself alone with him.

"Since when have you turned into a fragile flower, hiding from a few flakes of snow?"

Our stares, direct and piercing as arrows, battled more honestly than our words. "The darkened sky predicts another winter storm, and the wind has picked up in the last hour."

"You'd prefer I spoke my piece in front of Angelique?"

If Wampeme's clenched jaw did not send me for my cape, beaver hat, and gloves, his narrowed, angry eyes did. I followed him outside and down the slight embankment to the river's edge. I thought he would reach for my arm to guide me. He did not. We walked many minutes on the iced-over river, me a step behind, following his lead. Neither of us spoke. Snow crunched under our feet. Blue jays squawked displeasure at our intrusion. My better judgment warned me not to attempt light conversation.

After we passed the first river bend beyond my post, he turned back to me and stood, motionless as a deer that hears a hunter's approach. His face contorted, his expression cold and hard as the air biting exposed skin. His lips pressed so tight not a sound squeaked through.

I took one step closer to him before I realized he had stopped. His breath warmed my face. I avoided his intense eyes, hooded as they were by long, thick lashes. I feared they could be my undoing.

Finally he said, "You are the first woman to whom I gave my heart." There was sadness in his tone, but also something dangerous. "I never asked for it back. There is nothing I wouldn't do for you."

"Enough. You are a married man. Your talk offends God."

"Truth offends that Catholic God of yours? How about your betrayal? Does that offend him?"

How dare he say such things? I had jeopardized my reputation, committed a crime by my lies, and offended my God, all to save him. I glowered, and fury—maybe even something akin to hatred—replaced my earlier, more scandalous emotions.

"I have never betrayed you. I avoid you as appropriate, but never betray you." I inched away from him. "What provokes this attack?"

He studied his moccasins as though their contact with the ground offered a sight more compelling than me. After several moments, he raised his eyes again. "How could you go to Samuel Abbott and tell him lies?"

I gasped. I expected no gratitude, but it would have been more appropriate than a rebuke. "I did it to save your life. I did it because Kimama asked me to. I did it because—" I stopped myself from adding *because I care what happens to you.*

"I never sought your help, and Kimama had no right to ask on my behalf. I've chastised her. Her motive I understand. Yours, I do not."

"You are my friend." It sounded weak and far from the whole truth.

"Ahanu has left the Michigan Territory and headed to the Red River Settlement of Ojibwe, where he faces a harsh life. It is a poor band. He took with him six children and a wife suffering of ague."

"I did not know."

"Does it change things?"

"No."

"Ahanu is a good man. He did not go to Abbott because he is otherwise." Wampeme grabbed my hand and jerked me closer. "I killed Wilson. I would have admitted the act if Abbott asked me."

"And gotten yourself killed." I struggled to break free of his grip, but he held tight.

"If need be, yes, die as a man."

His anger frightened me, but his rough grip stirred baser feelings. I stopped fighting.

"I am not without enemies, one of whom seeks power. He knew what happened to Wilson and was aware that Ahanu witnessed the fight. This enemy would have been disgraced...called a traitor...if he carried the news to Abbott. Instead he forced Ahanu to do the deed: 'Tell Clerk Abbott that you saw Wampeme kill the fat old trader, or I will tell the chief clerk that both you and he struck the fatal blows.' Ahanu came to me with the threat. I advised him to go to Abbott with the truth. I'd heard the chief clerk was stern, but fair. I waited for Abbott to visit my tepee, but I didn't go in search of trouble. It wasn't until later, when Ahanu returned to L'Arbre Croche, that I learned what you had done."

"Kimama mentioned none of that."

"She didn't know. You had no right to argue unbidden on my behalf. You created falsehoods without knowing if I'd agree to your scheme. I hold to the tunics of neither you nor Kimama. I would go to Abbott even now and right things for the lot of good it would do."

"He would be even angrier at Ahanu, and after my story, he would believe nothing you say. There are local traders who would come after you and consider it an act of courage to end your life."

"My soul is already dead from the shame you cause. My body goes on living because my wives and children need me to hunt and trade…to provide for them."

"Why does Ahanu leave the village? Surely you have cleared his name with your tribe."

"No. And I will not. That is his request. I see his reasoning and must honor it."

"I do not understand."

Wampeme shook his head, clenched his jaw. For several long seconds, I wondered if he would explain.

"Everyone heard that Ahanu reported me to Samuel Abbott. Ahanu argues that if we make the true circumstances known, the circle around which the story travels will grow larger, and the details will work their way back to the clerk. As you note, Abbott will be even angrier at Ahanu, though my friend is without guilt. I'd be hanged or thrown in prison if an angry mob didn't come for me first. My family goes hungry either way. Before your interference, I hoped to plead my case to a man I thought might believe Wilson provoked the attack. Your lies poison Abbott's mind. He will believe nothing either Ahanu or I say. He will certainly lose respect for you. Your reputation will be made a mockery."

"I cannot undo that which is done."

"Exactly what Ahanu said. He worries that reopening the matter exposes my enemies to punishment, and they in turn, will harm his family. His words to me were, 'You are cleared and safe. I am happy for that. My life changes either way, but at least I remain a free man.'"

Wampeme's glare held no warmth. "There is no way to restore Ahanu's honor without risking further harm. The least I can do is respect his request to let the matter rest."

As I considered a response to soften his heart, he turned, walked away, and left me standing alone. He never looked back. I wondered why he had traveled from L'Arbor Croche to my camp in the midst of winter to confront me. He could have waited until my return to Mackinac took me through his village in the spring. I concluded his anger was too great to keep inside until then. I crumpled to the ground and wept. Snow clouds opened and blanketed me in a white shroud.

The distress of Wampeme's visit paled by comparison to the devastating message my second caller delivered a day later.

I did not attempt to suppress my pleasure when I answered the knock on our trading post door to find Rix Robinson standing there shivering from the cold. I liked the tall, bearded trader. I judged him a decent man who, unlike Astor, was able to get along with everyone: employees of the American Fur Company, independent traders, and the Great Lakes Indians. I intended to quit the business, and I favored selling to someone like Rix.

"Come in before you catch your death of pneumonia."

Robinson entered, pulled off fur-lined gloves, stuck a reddened, rough hand into the pocket of his buckskin britches, and withdrew a crumpled letter.

"You carry news of Josette?" I expected the letter informed me of my grandchild's birth.

My stomach clenched when my friend's face paled. He placed a hand on my shoulder and moved me back far enough to shut the door to the frigid air behind him. He guided me to the table where I collapsed into a chair. He took a seat next to me.

"Would you open it and read it to me please?"[14]

Robinson read the words that my son-in-law had written. When he finished, he laid the sheet of ivory paper between us, sat a small bottle beside it. "Laudanum will ease the pain."

I clutched the medicine with one hand and ran the fingers of my other over the letter. Dead. Josette was dead. My grandson was dead.

I would never hold Benjamin Langdon, kiss his soft head, smell his sweet baby smell. My daughter, the daughter who had seemed my reward for marrying a Frenchman instead of following my heart, was lost to me forever.

I thought about Joseph. He knew nothing of his sister's death—would not until I returned to Mackinac and had Marianne send him a letter. I wanted to embrace my boy, insist he return home so I could keep my remaining child safe. I knew I would not do that.

After several moments, I stood. "Thank you for suffering last night's storm to reach me. Please forgive me if I am less than hospitable."

I turned to Angelique. "Please fetch Mr. Robinson some food." Tremors rippled through me, I looked back to my guest. "If you would care to stay the night, we can make room for another blanket roll on the floor."

I fought the urge to bolt, to open the door wide and outrun the wind. Outrun God's decision to take my daughter, or if nothing else, outrun Rix Robinson's telling me of it.

Instead I withdrew to a tiny space cordoned off with rough lumber to afford my single bed privacy. On the east wall of the cubbyhole, a pane of glass, barely the length of my forearm, had been mudded into place the year prior. "I want to always see the sun," I had told Pierre when he cut a hole in the cabin's frame. Now, from a short rod above the makeshift window, I draped a deer hide to shut out the light I had once welcomed. I slumped onto the straw-stuffed mattress, clasped my rosary, closed my eyes.

I leaned against the wall for support and tore the letter into bits no larger than the oversized snowflakes that had covered our camp the previous night. Piece by deliberate piece, I ripped, hoping the pointless task might halt my racing thoughts. I let the scraps flutter to the floor, carrying the shards of my shattered heart with them. I should have seen my daughter's condition was more serious than she admitted and prepared the herbs to relieve her of the child. If she refused, I should have sneaked them into her tea. A mother must do what is best for her child. Surely God would understand that.

Voices intruded from the other room, muted chatter like the buzz of mosquitoes.

I feared I would never find strength to rise again. I remembered Josette when we had hugged on the shore before I departed Mackinac in the fall. It had been one of her better days. I ached to hold my daughter—feel her warm living body—one more time.

I uncorked the tincture that Robinson had provided and swallowed a gulp. I fell into a fitful sleep where Josette was alive and happy. When I awoke the next day, the illusion disappeared. I fought my thoughts, but still imagined her last hours. In my mind, she died again and again and again, as though there were no limits to the number of times she could leave this world.

On the third day, I sipped broth that Angelique insisted I drink. I argued with God, challenged his wisdom, demanded to understand why this happened. During the best moments of those days, the tragedy numbed my brain. During the worst, it created a crisis of faith. I aimed my anger at God, but that did nothing to squelch my hope that Josette and Benjamin Langdon were in his care.

My men stayed away to let me grieve. Only Angelique dared bring water and bits of food to my bedside.

After several days—I lost count of how many—I arose before sunrise, drew an overcoat tight about my tunic and slipped outside. *How dare the sun come up and pretend the world had not changed?* I sprinted, stopped, sprinted again. I stumbled, started over until the last ounce of strength drained from me. I collapsed and sobbed until crying brought no more tears. When I returned to the cabin, no one spoke of my loss.

"God," I prayed, "You can have the new house, all that I own, and I will do anything you demand. Please, please, God, let the letter be a mistake."

I got no answer from God. My daughter and grandson, unlike his beloved son, had not risen from the dead.

8.
A Daughter's Death

"They are not dead who live in the hearts they leave behind." **Tuscarora saying**

May 1821

We entered the protected bay of Mackinac Island where the sight of the village looked as cold as my thoughts. Mothers die before their children. That is the natural order of things—a God-given mercy. I was no stranger to death. It had raged into my life before, bloody, mean-spirited, ugly. The backside of life. But how could the loving Christian God ask me to accept the death of my child? Odawa gods believed a child's death threw the world out of harmony. My eyes should close forever, my last breath should be drawn, and my heart cease beating before my daughter left this world.

My pain, like a pebble tossed into still water, rippled until there was no place free of it. Things would never be the way they had been. Why had God sent the universe teetering out of balance?

Seagulls squawked and dove close to the canoes, eyeing us for scraps of food. The birds added their "aw-uck, aw-uck" to the engagés last refrain,

Alouette, gentille alouette,
Alouette, je te plumerai.

Songs that set the rhythm for rowing generally soothed me, but this day my distress was too great to be calmed. Pierre directed his full attention to arrival and tested the water's depth with his paddle.

We had survived the wintering season without serious damage to the fragile bateaux bottoms, and he would not risk bashing them on rocks this close to Mackinac's shore. He held up his hand. At the signal to stop, the rear steersman in each of our three vessels dropped a stone anchor overboard.

I scanned between wigwams and campfires for Therese and Harriet. They did not know when our crew would paddle into the harbor. I could little expect them to spend their days sitting idly on the rocks awaiting my arrival. Still, so strong was my desire to embrace my granddaughter that disappointment prickled the nape of my neck.

My men created four-handed, locked-wrist seats to carry Angelique and me ashore. As they sloshed through knee-deep water, I issued orders. "Louizon, deliver our personal effects to the house. Pierre, take the other men and secure the furs at the trading post. Get them counted. Tomorrow I will barter a price for our bales." My engagés set me on the ground as though I weighed no more than the fluff of a dandelion.

Angelique and I trudged up the beach and turned toward the imposing white frame structure of my new home. The sight of it sickened me. "Its dormers stare like unwelcoming eyes that question our presence." I shifted my gaze back to the water and avoided closer inspection. "It reminds me of how things have changed."

"It is empty," Angelique said. "Wait until a fire warms the rooms, and the smell of rice sweetened with maple syrup escapes the pot. If that doesn't make it feel like home, Miss Harriet's shenanigans will bring it life."

As we drew close, I saw two small, hand-carved wooden crosses marking a spot in the southeast corner of my property. The ground that encircled them had not yet sunk to the level of the surrounding yard, and no grass covered the exposed dirt's raw nakedness. My palms turned sweaty, and I wiped them on my leggings. I gestured toward the grave. "I need time. Go inside, put away our things when the men bring them. Take stock of our needs."

"*Oui*, Madame." Angelique patted my arm and walked toward the front door.

I called after her. "I need to see my sister and Harriet. It may be a while before I return."

I found Therese in her kitchen grinding dried corn into meal. She let out a shriek that brought Harriet running to see what excitement caused her great aunt's outburst.

"Nookomis! Nookomis!" Harriet dropped her cornhusk doll and swooped toward me.

"Can this big girl be my Harriet?" I knelt and scrutinized my granddaughter. "I have missed you more than you missed me." I gathered her close and gave her hugs and kisses.

She pushed back from my tight embrace. "I have missed you almost as much as I miss my maman."

My stomach lurched. "That is indeed a lot of missing." I drew a deep breath and forced a smile.

"Maman and Benjamin Langdon are with God. Papa and Auntie Schindler say they can't come back."

Therese gestured toward the front room. "Take Harriet and sit. I'll join you in a minute when I finish my work."

I guided my granddaughter to the main room and dropped onto the worn divan that had been mine before my new one arrived last season. Harriet climbed onto my lap and continued chattering. "Papa lets me stay here with Auntie Schindler. I like it. I get to play with Betsy.[15] Sometimes Madame Biddle[16] brings Sophia over. Betsy and I watch her. Sophia's learned to walk. Auntie Schindler says the little scoundrel finds trouble quicker than we can say 'Sophia, no.'" Harriet leaned forward and turned so she could look me square in the eyes. "Now I can come live with you, right?"

"Of course."

"Betsy too?"

"When she wishes. And your papa can visit you every night when he finishes soldiering, or finds himself with extra time."

"I used to live with Papa and Maman."

"You did." How much did a four-year-old understand about death, I wondered.

She read my thoughts. "That was when Maman watched out for my tomfoolery. The fort is no place for a girl without someone to keep track of her."

For a moment my smile turned genuine. "Is that what you think?"

"That's what Papa told Auntie Schindler." The child rocked back and forth. Her thumb found its way to her mouth.

I removed a string of red and yellow beads from around my neck and handed it to her.

She clutched the sparkly glass necklace between her fingers. "Did you make it, Nookomis?"

"No, I traded a pound of coffee for it. It is perfect for my favorite granddaughter."

"You're teasing me. How can I be your favorite if I'm your only granddaughter?"

I tied the gift around her neck. "If I had a million, you would still be my favorite."

Therese entered the room, wiping her hands on her apron. "Harriet, run along and let Catishe give you lunch. She made cornbread, and I know there's honey in the cupboard. It's my turn to talk to your grandmaman for a few minutes."

"But…Auntie…" Therese's stern-set mouth stopped the child's protest. Harriet's lips curled into a pout. She scuffed moccasined feet against the planked floor as she left the room.

"What is so important, Sister, that you chase away my granddaughter?"

"Good news. News I expect will fill your heart with joy."

"You assume that anything other than Harriet can do that?"

"I do." Therese let the words hang. When she got no response, she raised her eyebrows. A smirk replaced her usual serious countenance. I refused my sister further comment.

Therese could contain her secret no longer. "Father Gabriel Richard will arrive on our shore any day."

"That is good news for Catholics waiting for a baptism or marriage. It is of no concern to me." My response so lacked warmth that it chilled the room. My throat tightened. I weighed the difficulty of maintaining a Christian attitude in front of a priest when my mind was embroiled in battle with God.

"It is indeed good news for you. He wrote several months ago to announce his visit. I had Marianne write back and tell him he'd be welcome to stay with you."

"You thought such an invitation was not presumptuous?"

"You could use his company…and his counsel. Every year you have hoped for his return. Now he comes."

I believed my sister's intentions were pure, but that did nothing to soothe my irritation. I raised my voice. My tone, like my words, carried a challenge. "You had no right to offer my home. Let him stay with you."

"Magdelaine, what turns your nature sour? My house is too small. Catishe, Marianne, and Betsy share a room. We haven't an extra bed. With George[17] taken ill with apoplexy, an extra body would prove a hardship. You and Angelique and Harriet cannot possibly use all of your space."

Space that Josette had promised to fill with grandchildren. I stood and paced the room. From the window I looked across the distance to my house. I then pivoted with such swiftness the movement felt like a confrontation. "You have placed me in an awkward position. Pray do not expect my gratitude, do not expect my good humor. Above all, do not expect me to play God's humble maidservant to Father Richard."

I called Harriet. As I waited, I whispered, "You have invited a guest to my home who is neither appreciated nor welcome."

The last remaining swallow of the laudanum helped me through the lingering afternoon hours. Nightmares passed for sleep. When I awoke I determined a course of action.

The calm of the purple and pink twilight sky could not quiet my dread as I returned to my sister's house. I had no need to explain my behavior of earlier that day. Sisters understand. She opened the door, and took me into her arms. We stood for several moments, my need to be touched, to be held, so great I could not break the embrace.

When she stepped back, I fingered Wampeme's blue bead. Quickly I released the glass bauble and clutched the crucifix Maman had given me when I married Joseph. Even now, my faith trampled by doubt, first thing each morning I drew the crucifix over my head.

"I need to know…" My voice quivered.

"Some things you are better spared." Even as children, Therese had understood my thoughts before I spoke them. She hugged me again.

With her arms still around me, I asked, "Will you come with me to the fort?"

"You are sure you want to do that?"

"No. I'm not sure I want to, but I am sure I must."

She held my hand as we walked to Benjamin's quarters. I knocked, and after several seconds, my son-in-law opened the door. His uncombed hair, his unshaven face, his swollen red eyes, all bespoke suffering equal to mine.

"Benjamin," I said, "I have missed you."

He kissed me on the cheek. I smelled whiskey on his breath when he said, "I am glad you are home safe." He pulled a kitchen chair close to the table, sat, and studied the liquor in his square-footed English drinking glass. He did not offer us a seat, but Therese and I joined him.

"I will come see Harriet tomorrow," he said.

"She will look forward to seeing her papa." My words brought the slightest smile to his face. It disappeared when I added, "The reason I come has nothing to do with Harriet."

He did not ask my meaning, but lowered his near-empty drink to the table and waited.

"Since Rix Robinson brought me your letter I have not slept a night without visions that put me beside Josette's death bed. I imagine her words, her anguish. I see her die so many times."

Perhaps Therese had been right. I might be better off not knowing. Still, I could not let it go.

"If I am to be tortured, help me at least fashion the nightmare with accuracy." In the seconds that I paused, Benjamin's eyes moved from his glass to confront me with the same question that Therese had asked: Did I really want to know?

I offered him the same weak explanation I had given my sister. "When I see every detail of that night, perhaps the nightmares brought by not knowing may be conquered. That is my hope."

For several minutes we sat in silence, numbed by common tragedy.

Benjamin broke the quiet. "I still hear Josette's cry. I do not know how Harriet continued to sleep in her little bed on the other side of the room. My wife's shriek pierced that moonless night with such violence I believed the end of the world was upon us." Tears welled in his eyes. He stopped for a moment and cleared his throat. I heard his barely audible, "Perhaps for me it was." He collected himself and went on. "I grappled for a tinder to light the oil lamp. By then Josette had bolted upright. Her hand covered her mouth as though to mute her screams. Her ragged breathing…her flushed face…I knew the situation was dire."

Therese reached over and grasped my hands with hers.

Benjamin looked away from us. "Josette said, 'It wasn't like this with Harriet.' She clutched her belly and with a gush, her blood soaked our bed. The commotion brought Dr. Beaumont from next door.[18] He let himself in, came to the bedroom guided by my wife's moans."

Benjamin rose. He staggered to a pine cupboard above the washboard and opened a door. Next to plates and cups stood a half-empty bottle of whiskey. He brought it to the table and set it down before picking up where he had left off.

"If the situation alarmed the doctor, he masked his concern. 'Benjamin, leave us,' he said. 'The baby is coming. I will do everything possible to deliver the infant and your wife back to you healthy and safe.'

"I picked up my sleeping daughter and withdrew to this room. My words trailed behind me. 'I'm running to the village to summon Therese. I'll leave Harriet at the Schindler house.' I didn't wait for an answer."

"I came back with Benjamin," Therese picked up their account. "By daybreak Josette's contractions came in regular, short intervals, but the baby made no progress. More hours passed. Josette's labor ceased and she fell asleep. When the pains started again, they were spaced closer together and sharper."

My sister chewed at a broken fingernail, then stopped and dropped her hands to her lap. "By the second day Josette was delirious. I sat by her bedside. Dr. Beaumont urged her to take sips from a cup he offered. He said it was a mild sedative of crushed evening primrose, a concoction he learned from you." Therese nodded toward me. "I agreed it was good medicine, but too weak to soothe her or relieve her distress."

From the small west window I saw the sun had dropped behind the horizon. Neither Benjamin, Therese, nor I lit a candle. In the dim light I made out the grim set of my sister's mouth. "The doctor said I might be right, but Josette was dehydrated and needed the liquid." I soaked cloths in a pan of water, wrung them out, and placed them on Josette's forehead. I mumbled that I wished there were a priest on the island to offer comfort. Josette whispered, 'I'll be fine, Auntie. God will grant me time, and if he doesn't, he won't hold it against my admission to heaven that we had no priest.'"

Benjamin crossed his arms on the table and laid his head, face down, on them. Therese added details. "By night the primrose did nothing to ease the pain. Dr. Beaumont said he had no laudanum available and was awaiting a new supply for his soldiers. He resorted to opium he had made from poppies grown in his garden."

I considered the laudanum Rix Robinson had delivered to me, and wished it had gone instead to Josette. I had abandoned her and did not deserve to have my torment blunted.

Therese said, "Minutes before midnight, Josette managed a weak push and the doctor wrenched the baby boy from her body. Beaumont put his ear to the child's chest and listened for a heartbeat, smacked the infant's bottom, got a listless whimper in return. The doctor handed the newborn to me and turned back to Josette. Her breathing was shallow and uneven, her eyes unfocused. She took my arm, but her grip lacked strength. She told me she could not die…it could not be God's time for her. I felt a slight pressure from her fingernails where they touched my skin."

I cried without making a sound. Tears streamed down my sister's cheeks. Between mournful-sounding gasps, she said, "I leaned near Josette and whispered, 'Dear God, please hear my niece's prayer and add mine. I beseech you to make her well and spare her life. She is needed to continue her work on this earth.'

"Josette's hand went limp. Within minutes she was dead."

Benjamin raised his head, poured whiskey into his empty glass and took a gulp.

I laid my head on Therese's shoulder. We each struggled for composure. I thought about asking her to stop. I had heard enough. But something perverse inside me said, *you have come this far, hear the whole story.*

"Beaumont took the ashen-colored baby—the child hadn't yet been named—opened its mouth, inserted a finger and removed mucous. When the doctor finished, he returned the little one to me. I swaddled the child in flannel blankets and moved into this room where Benjamin sat at the table, as he does now."

Benjamin interrupted. "She's being Christian. I slumped at the table, where over the past twenty-four hours I'd finished a bottle of Kentucky whiskey. I'm sure the reek of alcohol drifted across the room to meet your sister. Dr. Beaumont was steps behind her. He told me he'd lost my Josette. There was nothing he could do.

"I asked about the child. I looked at the bundle in Therese's arms and then glanced away. If I let the baby into my heart and lost him thereafter, it would be more painful than never meeting him.

"Beaumont told me my son's breathing was labored. He said prayer was the only medicine. Therese would not let me avoid the child." Benjamin's eyes confronted my sister. I could not tell whether the look was an accusation or expression of gratitude. "She brought him close and pulled the covering away from his face. I stared at the tiny miracle and prayed harder than I had ever prayed in my life."

Benjamin rubbed his eyes, took a deep breath before going on. "I touched the baby's wrinkled face and told Therese that Josette and I had chosen Benjamin Langdon for a boy's name."

"I considered it a good name," Therese said. "We both hoped the baby would be strong like his namesake, John Langdon.[19]

"He asked to see his wife. I prevailed on him to allow me time to prepare her," Therese said. "Benjamin's body shook as I put the tiny bundle in his arms so I could attend Josette.

"In the bedroom, I washed my niece before inching the soiled sheets from beneath her body, and in the same manner replacing them with fresh linens. I searched the chest's drawers for suitable clothing and dressed her in a soft-blue smock she had ordered before learning she was expecting a child. When the garment arrived, Josette had held it against her growing body, laughed and said she would have to save it for the baby's christening because it wouldn't fit her for months. None of us dreamed she'd be buried in that dress.

"Unable to bear my niece's vacant eyes, I touched my fingers to her eyelids, and drew them down. I combed her thick hair and arranged it like a black halo on the pillow about her face. I then walked back into this room and took Benjamin Langdon from his father."

"I sat beside Josette for a long time, holding her cold hand," Benjamin said. "I let my fingers caress her cheeks. The suffocating air in our small bedroom carried a trace of lavender from her hair.

"When I staggered back, Therese pretended not to notice my puffy eyes. I'm sure I looked nothing like the Commandant at Fort Mackinac, or the staid military man I am supposed to be."

"There was nothing more we could do," Therese said. "Benjamin asked if I would take the child until he could make arrangements. I agreed and secured a wet nurse, but your tiny grandson seemed unable to take nourishment. I thanked God for the time he gave us to have George[20] baptize little Benjamin and for the many hours he gave me to rock the baby and tell him how much you—all of us—loved him. Several days later, our precious child stopped battling. I believe he chose heaven with his mother to the continuing struggles here on earth."

Their story finished, I stood and stepped behind my son-in-law. I patted his shoulder and thanked him. Therese and I reached the door before Benjamin spoke again.

"I waited to compose a letter telling you of Josette's death. I hoped to temper the tragedy with news that Benjamin Langdon was thriving. Instead I had to tell you that he, too, was gone. Prayers had not proven the remedy Dr. Beaumont hoped they might be. I ordered my men to use pickaxes to dig graves on the frozen ground of your property. I knew you'd want your daughter and grandson close."

Benjamin stiffened with another gulp of liquor that emptied his glass. "Every day I wish I could bargain to change the will of God."

9.
Father Gabriel Richard

"You say there is but one way to worship and serve the Great Spirit. If there is but one religion, why do you white people differ so much about it? Why not all agree, as you can all read the book?" **Red Jacket**

July 1821

Father Gabriel Richard was a skeletal man. Years of serving his flock at Ste. Anne du Detroit and traveling to Catholics in the harsh backcountry had stripped his bones of extra flesh. When he arrived at my door, he looked as though a strong wind might blow him to the heavens. I would not have been disappointed if he had departed for paradise in such manner. My "Welcome, Father" sounded insincere, even to my ears.

I left the priest to unpack his bags in the room I had prepared for him. When he finished that task, he joined me at the kitchen table where Angelique had laid out cheese and fresh strawberries. My silence prodded him to speak.

"I wish I had been here to give Josette the sacrament of Extreme Unction," he said, "and see her remains committed to the earth."

Perfect sentiment from a priest to a grieving mother, like a response learned in seminary. Resentment bubbled in my stomach at how casual it sounded. I sat stock still except for the tic in my right eye. I could not quell the twitch any easier than I could muster an evenhanded response.

"Do you remember?" Josette was my first baptism on this island."[21]

"And you wish to have provided comfort, last rites, and then buried her as well?" I clenched my hands into fists that hid beneath the table.

"It is a priest's duty...his honor...to—"

"A mother should offer comfort to a dying child." I turned away from him, away from the crucifix that dangled from his neck. "I do not know if I am angrier at God or myself. I cannot forgive God...for taking her...or myself for wintering in the country and not being with her when she died."

The priest spent his first week on Mackinac Island visiting the homes of French Catholics, where he offered much-awaited counsel. He prepared for marriages and baptisms in a congregation too long without benefits of those sacraments. In his spare time he read scripture and his Breviary.

"By next week I want Ste. Anne's ready to begin offering daily mass," he said.

Each night, he dined with me in my new kitchen—triple the size of my cabin's original. A newfangled cook stove went unused for most meals. Angelique preferred cooking over the flames of the massive stone fireplace. Finely crafted maple shelves, lined with cast-iron pots and pans, gave the room a welcoming look. Trappings did nothing to mask the tension created by Josette's hovering ghost.

One evening before Father Richard blessed the food, I opened the backdoor to let a cool breeze pass through the house. I prepared for the verbal maneuvering that came with every meal. We avoided talk of death, shared only mundane details of weather and politics, each in our own way dancing around conversational dangers.

"Patrick Sinclair[22] was no English fool choosing the most beautiful spot in the entire new world for his fort," Father Richard said. "He was reckless, perhaps even despised by many, but no fool."

I had no idea where this prattle headed and cherished no desire to contribute to it. I moved dishes of roasted chicken, Mackinac potatoes, and last season's preserved pickles closer to the priest, but said nothing.

"The Lieutenant Governor held no love for French-Catholic voyageurs, Odawa converts, nor even our Catholic God, but the man recognized the importance of all three to the fur trade. He'd have been reckless to relocate his new fortress to the bluff on this island without bringing along his best insurance for keeping the French controlled."

Politeness forced me to feign mild interest. "What was this powerful weapon?"

"Ste. Anne's Church, of course." The priest helped himself to more chicken. "I've had dreams about Angelique's spit-roasted chicken."

"The little wooden church was disassembled and carted across the ice from the mainland the year I was born. My father helped move and restore it at the corner of Market and Hoban." I stopped, sensing talk of Ste. Anne's might veer the conversation in an unwelcome direction.

"Your church began as the small mission of Father Marquette. It was moved to St. Ignace, then transported to Mackinaw[23] on the mainland. Ste. Anne's is your spiritual rock. It was God, not fate, who connected your life to the church and the island."

I did not respond. During the lull, the priest's expression barely masked his discomfort as he shifted to a more neutral topic. "This year's late spring thaw was bad luck for traders, but lilacs still bloom. Their scent drifts through your door, one of God's many gifts…a pleasure I hope carries on in heaven."

I relaxed at inconsequential talk of flowers. "Survival of both my purple and white lilacs was a condition of building my new house. The white are my favorite of all flowers. I insisted the builders not disturb them."

"I am told that an early missionary priest brought the first bushes to this island."

"That may be true, but the English take credit, as they do for any other good that has found its way to our shore."

"However they got here, they are a gift."

"If mine are either a blessing or a gift, I have Elizabeth Mitchell to thank. When I came to the island, one of the many things she taught me was to prune my lilacs properly."

"Then I will thank the gracious lady the next time I see her."

He had tried mightily to engage me, although it was my house and conversation my duty. For the first time since Father Richard's arrival, his efforts were endearing and his company almost comforting.

A few days later, the temperature soared and the heat invited an afternoon break. Father Richard returned from Ste. Anne's, where he had spent the morning. He joined me in the parlor. Angelique poured us each a cup of tea, set the teapot on the mahogany sideboard along with a tray of sweet biscuits, and disappeared. The priest sat at one end of the couch, and I took the Windsor chair near him.

"I had planned to leave the trade this year," I said. "But I am reconsidering."

His stark black robe and emaciated features gave a harsh appearance to a man gentle by nature. "Are you not happy on the island?"

"With Josette's death, I wish to keep busy…spare my mind time to think."

"Busy is good. Our Saint Benedict taught that idleness is the enemy of the soul. A Catholic could do worse than follow his example." Tiny spectacles, attached by leather straps, perched on the priest's forehead. He pulled them down when he read his Bible, but, now, propped on his brow, they gave the illusion he possessed two sets of eyes. "I've always imagined it was tedious at winter posts…waiting for Indians to show up with furs." He studied the cookies, reached for a second one.

Part of me wanted to end the conversation, but another part of me wanted him to understand. "My mind is not made up. I am considering returning to the business for another season."

A fly lit on his long beaky nose, and he swatted it aside. "You have suffered a grave tragedy, but do you not have happy memories here?"

I paused and considered his question, trying to understand my own feelings before passing them off to him. "My grief is fresh. Every thought of Josette reminds me I cannot bring her back. Solitude is too painful, but sitting all day, playing whist or bridge with Mrs. Mitchell, Therese, and Agatha, seems too frivolous."

"Wintering is more meaningful?"

"In winter camp, I am sometimes cabin-bound, but other times I travel to the villages and help in small ways. I carry food and prepare dinner for a family afflicted by illness. I take medicine and help with minor injuries." I thought for another moment and then added, "Maybe it is not simply being busy. Maybe it is being useful."

"Here you have little Harriet. Her father has no time to attend a child and take care of military affairs." Cookie crumbs sprinkled his somber habit. He brushed them into a cupped palm and dropped them on his empty plate.

"I cannot predict the future. What if Benjamin remarries or sends my granddaughter back east to his people?"

"You want guarantees? There are no guarantees. You are blessed. God gives you a strong son, friends in numbers so great you probably can't count them, a grand home on this special island, and a granddaughter who keeps you young and brings joy to your life. God will take care of you and provide."

"Like he took care of Josette?" I bowed my head, the disapproval in his sunken eyes difficult to face. "I want to be grateful for God's bounty." I choked on my words. What I really wanted was to curse God, dare him to punish me further, but I could not share those feelings. My voice became soft, and I realized I was shaking. "I no longer feel God's presence...am no longer certain what I believe."

He reached over, tilted my chin up, forced me to look at him. "You cannot shut God out of your life."

"Father, you and the other priests taught me that God answers my prayers."

"He does."

"I prayed mightily for a rosy-cheeked, robust grandchild and a healthy Josette. Therese and many others prayed for their well-being. God did not hear our prayers. Why did my daughter die when we all prayed to keep her?"

"God doesn't always answer prayers the way we want. To you, her suffering seemed without end, but compared to the everlasting glory she now enjoys, it was but the briefest blink of an eye."

"Even if that were true…"

"It is true."

"…it makes no sense. We needed her."

"You have to trust that God knows all. He loves Josette and knows what was best for her."

"Dying was not best!" I slammed the arms of the chair with my fists.

"Perhaps he needed Josette, or maybe he wanted to save her from a more dreadful fate. It could be a million reasons we mortals cannot understand, but you have to believe that God heard you and answered in the way he knew was best, even if his reasons aren't clear."

"I am not sure I can love a god who takes my only daughter."

"God understands your distress. You need to ask him to help you through this difficult time. The agony of death seems too much to bear, but Josette and Benjamin Langdon are free. They are happy. Some day you will be reunited with them."

"I wish I believed that."

"You do, my child, but pain clouds your thinking."

"Why would God test me this way? Take the one thing I could not bear to part with?" I looked about me, all the expensive furnishings ordered from Paris to fill the rooms of my new house. Each day brought an additional delivery. Yesterday a box of porcelain arrived, and I left it in its packing carton. I gripped my hands tight, one in the other, and resisted the urge to walk over to the box, lift it as high as I could manage, and smash it to the floor. "I expected I would love this house, but I hear footsteps or a knock and think it will be Josette. Such moments are cruel hoaxes. I want back the time I missed spending with her because I wintered in the country."

"You cannot reclaim time. But God gives you the opportunity to direct your future. For every story Josette never heard, Harriet will be there to listen. God will give you strength when you count the blessings that remain—Harriet, your sisters, Mrs. Mitchell, your church. You will experience joy again. With time, you will treasure the memories of Josette without being engulfed in sadness. Accepting that God has plans for you will help."

"Father, I have watched death take those who were not ready. I have held their hands and whispered false hope. I thought I had mastered death. But I deceived myself. I am no longer brave in its presence. A mother is never ready to lose her child. It leaves a hole that forever remains empty." The sultry air was dense with my accusations, and we fell into silence.

I thought of Joseph. By now my son had received the letter Marianne sent telling him of his sister's death. With his Montreal education, I had hoped Joseph would enjoy an elevated social status like Josette. I imagined him a clerk for the fur company, a teacher, maybe even a lawyer. Whether by choice or opportunity, he followed the fur trade like his father, his mother and his grandfather before him. I gained little comfort from a surviving child who distanced himself, apprenticed to Joseph Rolette, in the far reaches of Minnesota. I loved and missed Joseph, but as much as I tried to deny it, he could not fill the void created by Josette's death. Josette was my first born…her mother's daughter. Born the year after I married Joseph, she eased the lingering sadness of leaving my childhood village with a stranger twice my age. Joseph was his father's son. Uncomfortable feelings for favoring one child over the other would not change that.

After several long moments, I relaxed my hands and spoke again. "I was taught that God would take care of me. When Odawa women married Catholic men, the church insisted our husbands honor their unbreakable bonds and never abandon us. Indians accept a hard life. Believing in God makes it easier."

"So you believe in God for what you think he can do for you?"

"You make it sound awful."

"You feel he's gone back on his promise because he didn't spare Josette when you asked him to?"

"He ignored my prayers."

"I tell you again, he did not. He took care of Josette in his way. You do not get to determine how God acts."

The responses he hurled like barbed accusations, made me wish to remind him he was a guest in my house and he should stop. I had been taught deference to priests, and I could not go that far.

"What do you expect from God? You wish to order his actions? See his plan and be given a say in it?"

The priest's words only made me angrier with God. I needed Josette here on earth, Benjamin and Harriet needed her. If God decided not to grant my prayers that he spare her, then he owed it to me to help me understand why, not just leave me flailing and rudderless.

Father Richard shifted his gaze as though to avoid my harsh glare, then he turned back to me. "God has not forsaken you."

"Is he punishing me for my sins?" I closed my eyes, waited for an answer.

"Anything God does, he does from love. Sometimes he sends punishment on those he loves—to turn them back to the paths of righteousness. Why do you think you have angered God?" Father Richard fastened his gaze on me and waited for a response.

I rose and paced toward the window. I considered my words. "To the Odawa, evil is not a personal transgression, rather it is a wrong that causes the world to be askew. Indians attack the disharmony without morally condemning or punishing the individual."

"The Catholic Church requires personal accountability. That is God's law." Father Richard's stern voice said my explanation carried no weight with him.

"Yes." I spoke softly, hesitantly. "God judges his children for their sins." *Sins.* I thought about Wampeme, the lie, Ahanu. Had God taken my daughter because I wronged Ahanu? Or had I angered God by a greater sin? One that could not lay claim to an honorable intention. A sin that brought tragedy and despair to my people. The possibility that my offense angered God, and he took Josette to return me to the path of righteousness was intolerable.

Keeping my back to the priest, I stared at the harbor. I saw a canoe hauled ashore and wished I were working and not a captive of this man who asked disturbing questions. When I could avoid Father Richard no longer, I said, "I spent hours in the solitude of my winter post, door closed, on my knees until they ached, asking myself how I lost God's favor."

"What did you conclude from your introspection?"

"My sins are so grievous that God cannot forgive me. He took Josette to show me I am beyond saving."

"Whatever you've done, I promise God loves you. Nothing—absolutely nothing—damns you to hell, if you ask forgiveness. Josette's death was unconnected to your transgressions, it wasn't to punish you. God does not take an innocent life to show you the light. It concerns me that you believe you have committed sins so heinous that you merit God's wrath. Magdelaine, what have done?"

"You are my priest, and a man who honors his word. I fear that if I confess my sins, you will excommunicate me. Maybe I would not care if you did. At this moment, I do not trust my feelings. Suffering hell seems an appropriate punishment. I would endure it, if it brought Josette back, or even if it merely tempered my own anguish and guilt."

Father Richard ran crooked fingers over the diamond-shaped tufting on the arm of my red sofa. In those long seconds when he seemed lost in contemplation, a look of disappointment crept over his face. Without my admitting it, I saw that he knew. The rumors he had heard about me were true. I prospered—grew rich—in a business where I sold liquor to my people.

A grimace tightened his thin lips. "You know in your heart that God exists. Perhaps you have offended him. We all offend God. It is the human condition. We have to recognize our sins and change. Whether or not God punishes you, calamity can help you reconsider your course."

"It will not bring Josette back." I leaned forward and clutched my stomach to ease the sick feeling.

"You need to make amends. That is how you get through the pain. It won't happen overnight. The reason I threaten to excommunicate traders who barter alcohol is the same reason you are burdened with shame. It destroys God's children. It takes men and women who mean to live good, decent, God-fearing lives and shackles them to ardent spirits. They sell their souls for the powerful drink."

As much as I knew the priest wanted to comfort me, his position on the issue stopped him from offering more. "It was the way of the trade, Father. That is not an excuse. But traders who refused alcohol were not traded with."

"Magdelaine." The tone with which he spoke my name carried harsh rebuke. "Of all God's children, you have perhaps suffered the most from the ugly reach of alcohol's claws. It was responsible for your husband's death. It was responsible for your father's death. Now, in some distant way, you believe it responsible for Josette's death."

His words hardened with his growing disapproval. "You have seen men here on this island drink themselves into the devil's stupor. They court all kinds of mischief. More than one has stumbled about, fallen into campfires, sustained unimaginable injuries and become a useless burden to his family. The men are not alone in their depravity. Women waste their days in a trance, unable to attend their children. The only thing they have left, after the suffering they bring to pass, is their taste for the poison."

"I convinced myself I was fairer with the Odawa than the other traders. I gave them more for their pelts. I offered gifts with real value, guns, knives, not trinkets and beads—"

"Magdelaine." Father Richard spoke my name again, and his voice sharpened as he thrust words with his spiritual sword. "There was no justification. If others offend God, does that give you leave to do the same?"

My eyes skittered the room like a trapped beaver. "Will God—or my people, or you—forgive me?"

"You already know God will forgive you. It is not for me to condemn those who turn from their sinful ways. But you need to make amends. The same St. Benedict who instructs us to stay busy offers more wisdom that you might consider. Our blessed saint said, 'Listen, and attend with the ear of your heart.' Your own wisdom, given by God's grace, will lead you from the darkness that threatens you."

"It is hard, Father."

"I expect so. Until your faith is strong, act in accordance with God's commandments. They're a good set of rules for everyone. Act as though you believe, attend church, or when there is no priest, attend meetings held to discuss religious matters. Say your Angelus thrice daily. Pray before meals, before bed, when you need help. Talk to God as though he is your friend. Act as though you believe, and your heart will follow."

The priest set his teacup on the side table. "Let me tell you a story. It isn't about sin or redemption or even about punishment. It's about changing direction.

"I came to Baltimore in 1791, during the French Revolution. I, and three other Sulpician priests, labored under threat of death in our homeland."

"What had you done, Father?"

"It wasn't so much what we had done as what we possessed. The church owned most of the land in France. If the church was discredited, the debts people owed it might be forgiven. The movement to destroy the Catholic Church grew strong. God directed our escape to this new country as surely as if he had sent a host of angels to carry us over the seas and drop us safely on these shores.

"By 1805, the year your son Joseph was born, I ministered in Detroit. Napoleon and Pope Pius the Seventh had reconciled, and I believed the situation in my homeland had changed enough that I prayed for God's blessing to go home.

"In June of that year, before I could set sail, a horrific fire destroyed Detroit. Flames consumed hundreds of buildings. Only two structures survived. More than forty people died, many wandered homeless and hungry. They trudged the scorched ruins, begging for water and food and blankets."

The priest paused. Perhaps to allow me reflection. Perhaps to allow me to add to the conversation. If he hoped his story gave me understanding, it would have disappointed him to read my thoughts. Those poor homeless souls had undoubtedly sent prayers for help and, like me, must have wondered why God was both deaf and blind to their plight.

Seeing that I intended to remain quiet, the priest continued. "God had a new purpose for me. I needed to help the people of Detroit rebuild. I needed to give them hope. I needed to heed God's plan for my future.[24]

"What I'm telling you, dear child, is that you can show God your remorse for past transgressions. Your life can find new direction from the tragedy of Josette's death."

Father Gabriel Richard
Photo from *History of the Diocese of Sault Ste. Marie and Marquette*, published 1907, Public Domain

10.
The Ugly Trade

"It is a story of all life that is holy and is good to tell, and of us two-leggeds sharing in it with the four-leggeds and the wings of the air and all green things; for these are children of one mother and their father is one Spirit."
Black Elk

July 1821

The night after my conversation with Father Richard, a dream ambushed me and sucked me into a hell where I believed the Great Spirit voiced that he, too, was displeased with me. The Odawa listen to their dreams. Whether mine came from God, the Great Spirit or my own shame, mattered less than the message.

I stood in a strange village amid rows of tired, sad-looking longhouses with broken poles and sagging roofs. I called the greeting, "Aanii." No one answered. Clouds half hid the moon, but I recognized White Ox as he crawled from beneath dense underbrush that had been his grave. He stood and shook off twigs and dead leaves.

"The world is off kilter," I said. "It is how I imagine alcohol would affect my view."

He ignored my comment, stepped so close I felt the chill from his body. "Why?"

I inched backwards. Pretended I did not understand.

"Why?" he repeated.

I willed my feet to run, but they had turned into giant boulders. My hands trembled. Fear, sharp and cutting, bit at my skin. I tried to scream. My voice was no more cooperative than my feet. *Father God, help me.*

For the third time, White Ox asked, "Why? You spared me. Left my punishment to the Great Spirit." His glower turned to a sneer. He raised his eyebrows and asked another question. "What shall your punishment be?"

"I killed no one."

"Neither your God nor mine believes that."

The breath that carried his words was so hot it set the village ablaze. Flames engulfed the empty dwellings, engulfed White Ox.

"I can explain," I shouted at White Ox's charred body.

From the corpse came his strong voice. "Explain it to your God. Persuade him of your innocence." Each word he spat set another fire. "Were bales of beaver pelts worth the four American dollars you received for them? Were they worth destroying Indians with alcohol to increase your profits?"

"How dare you? You wanted it. Indians would not trade with us if we did not offer ardent spirits."

The blackened bones of his arm reached from the blaze. "Tell yourself that." He pulled me into the inferno. "You are the only one you can convince."

I slapped at embers that seared my legs and fouled the air with the stench of scorched flesh.

A Frenchman descended from heaven. "Leave her alone." He offered me the handle of a canoe paddle and pulled me from the pyre. "Marry me," he said. "Your land is full of four-legged furry wealth. We shall be rich."

When I hesitated, he said, "Don't worry. White Ox can't hurt you."

Before I could argue, a spit-polished soldier in red uniform crept up behind the Frenchman and slashed the poor fellow's throat. The soldier then held out his hand to me. "Forget him. We all die. I can make you richer than the Frenchman. I pay more for your furs."

I grabbed at the Englishman. He pulled me close, reached inside his breast pocket, extracted basswood cord, and shackled my stone-like, blistered feet. Before he finished, another soldier, this one wearing a blue waistcoat and a yellow trimmed hat, leveled a musket at the Englishman's head, and the Englishman fell next to the Frenchman who had fallen next to White Ox.

"Pay none of them heed. We have learned well from you. We slithered through thickets on our bellies. We hid behind trees so bullets could not reach us. We shot the British as they pranced in neat rows on battlefields. This is our country now. We are your great fathers."

"No! No one owns the land. It was given to all red men to use as brothers." I hoped that if I shouted loud enough he would hear.

"You are a fool, but what can I expect from a savage?" The American spoke slowly as if explaining to a child. "Land is for the smartest, cleverest, bravest, strongest. Americans are your only hope for survival."

I reached out, still seeking a way to rise from this hell. My efforts were thwarted by the dead Englishman, the hole in his skull mending itself as he rose from the ashes. He clutched my ankle. "We will not go without another fight," he said. "My king won't give up this land. He lives across a great water on a small island. He needs space to relocate his subjects, space for them to build houses, barns, picket fences. Space in a new country. We'll reserve land for your people. Swamp lands, desert lands, barren lands. Leave to us this rich place where the bones of your fathers are buried."

The Englishman released me and climbed into a boat manned by fellow Englishmen. "If you are a smart squaw, you will hide in the distillery while we attack the Americans at Fort Mackinac. When it is safe, we will fetch you, and you can begin packing."

I strained to understand his fading words.

"First you must gather your tribe's warriors to help us run off the Americans."

On raw, oozing feet, I hobbled in the direction of Mackinac to warn Therese and Elizabeth. I took no more than a dozen steps before a mountain of dead animals—decaying, maggot filled beaver, muskrats, mink, bears, otters—blocked my path.

Rain poured down. Red rain. Blood. It squelched the flames. I lost my footing on slippery carcasses.

An animal chorus sang. "It is our blood, it is our blood."

"You cannot talk." I struggled to stand.

"You are wrong. We have made your sins known to the Great Spirit," said an otter.

"He was already aware of her wrongs," said a shaggy bear.

"There was a time you respected me," an elk said.

A beaver picked up the accusations. "She believed the Frenchman when he told her beavers have no soul. She believed the Englishman when he told her God put the four-leggeds here for her pleasure."

The charges came so fast I could not keep track of who hurled them.

"You trade fishing hooks and calicos for our skins."

"You stopped asking our spirits to forgive you when you claimed our bodies."

"You no longer work to fill your children's empty bellies, but to grow wealthy. Wealthy from our slaughter."

"When the pale-skinned newcomers came to this country, the Odawa believed the Great Spirit dwelt in each blade of grass and every pebble along the shore."

Before I could defend myself, an animal from the back of the pack chanted, "How great is the widow-woman's need? How great is the widow-woman's greed?"

Others joined in and they sang it over and over and over. I covered my ears.

When it was quiet, a furless beaver said, "You didn't honor us. You left our meat to rot."

A bear drug his claws up my naked leg and my blood mingled with his. "See, we all bleed. We all feel. We are all one blood. When did you forget that?"

"I have not forgotten."

A beaver's front teeth ripped my arm as though fashioning a sapling for his dam. He chewed. Chewed and spat out what was left of my flesh.

Other beavers rushed forward, and took turns gnawing. They devoured my legs, hips, stomach, face, until all that was left of me was a skeleton with a beating heart and coal black eyes. The beaver spewed my skin, my hair, my fingernails, onto the heap of body parts, bloody and useless.

"Why? Why did you do it?" The beavers sounded like White Ox.

Their words were drowned out by the flapping of wings. Crows surrounded me in such numbers they blacked out the rising sun. "We are your friends," they said. "We appreciate your work." Each bird wore a tiny black robe.

I shrugged my shoulders, looked down at my moccasins.

I felt life leave my body, and I drifted above the flocked crows to a place from which I watched the mayhem.

Frenchmen killed Englishmen. Englishmen killed Frenchmen and Indians. Americans killed anyone who got in their way. And everyone killed the four-legged creatures.

From beyond the fray, I realized I no longer suffered. Instead of rejoicing, I was angry. Angry at those who laid blame. Angry because they would not tell me if this place was the spirit world or heaven. Angry because I could not escape my self-imposed hell.

I woke drenched in sweat. The nightmare's images taunted me. I remembered only one other dream that had left me as weak and empty. The seed for that earlier dream sprang from a children's game of stickball played on a sweltering summer afternoon.

Our tribe had settled outside the gates of Old Fort Mackinaw. Everyone—white and red children alike—looked for a way to pass the time until cooking pots provided dinner.

An English boy said, "We can beat the savages at a game of ball."

Everyone cheered the suggestion. We picked up sticks. Mine was smooth and straight. The children sorted themselves into two lines, Odawa in one, English in the other. I stood alone at the side of the grassy clearing, clutching my strong birch bark stick. Neither side made room for me.

I was eight years old the summer I began having a recurrent nightmare, where I saw myself slump to the ground and fight back tears as the other children played. Remembering that childhood dream was like diving deep into Lake Huron and swimming through clear water toward the sunlight. Only everything was upside down.

I had my answer. It was my time to quit the trade. I would heed Father Richard's advice and search a new direction to make amends.

11.
Lucy and the Story of the White Indian

"Humankind has not woven the web of life. We are but one thread within it. Whatever we do to the web, we do to ourselves. All things are bound together. All things connect." **Isna la wica, Teton Sioux**

August 1-15, 1821

Twice in the span of a week, a dream troubled my sleep. If the first nightmare helped me resolve the issue of quitting the trade, the second was less helpful. I did not know what to make of it.

I eased my body from under the quilts, but the vision of Josette lingered. I fought the urge to smash the crucifix that hung above my bed—render it impotent and discard it with the rest of the household refuse. Fear of waking Harriet, who had taken to sleeping with me, reined in my sacrilegious impulse.

On my way to the kitchen, I smoothed my buckskin tunic and straightened my braids. I had never embraced wearing fussy European dressing gowns that wrinkled while one slept in them.

"Good morning, Father." I joined Father Richard at the breakfast table and poured a measure of tea through a silver strainer into a porcelain cup.

A half-eaten plate of eggs and bacon remained in front of the priest. He closed his Bible and said, "I hope you enjoyed a restful sleep."

"I am still adjusting to Harriet thrashing next to me, not that I am complaining, mind you." I broke off a piece of biscuit and nibbled it, no hungrier than I had been the prior day when melancholy directed me to Arch Rock.[25] I had sat there and stared out over the soothing waters of Lake Huron at the sacred place the Odawa believe Gitchie Manitou[26] first breathed life into man.

I bit a morsel, chewed with deliberation, and swallowed. "Father Richard, do you believe God counsels us in dreams?"

The priest scratched his head near his bald spot. He looked back at his Bible before answering. "It is not for me to tell God how to make his wishes known."

"When the Odawa need spiritual guidance, they choose a quiet place for reflection and fasting."

Father Richard pinched the sides of his nose, then rested his hands on the table. "Our God, too, has made his intentions known through dreams, but you need to make certain you are hearing God's voice and not that of false idols."

"Of course, Father…but it is difficult to distinguish between the two." I shoved aside my small plate with all but the two bites of biscuit remaining. I had not invited the prior night's dream, but neither did I want to ignore Josette's warning: *If Benjamin sends Harriet to live with his family in New Hampshire, her Odawa-French blood will be an embarrassment. She will become estranged from you.*

"I am here to listen to your concerns and help you navigate perilous spiritual waters." The priest dabbed egg yolks onto his biscuit and continued eating.

"I take comfort in that." It helped to be back on Mackinac Island in the company of Therese, Elizabeth, and Harriet. I was even pleased that Father Richard stayed with me, though I had no intention of admitting that to my sister. God meant too much to me; I could not let go of my faith without a struggle. I told myself the dream reflected my own fears, not communication from Josette or even an omen from any god.

My maman had brought God to my life through stories. Her version of Catholicism came from my papa and the black-robed priests who visited our village. As a child, I no more questioned God's existence than I questioned that strawberries tasted sweet, fire burned, or the sun warmed Mother Earth. I took pride in knowing more about the Catholic God than other children in our village. My faith was simple and trusting.

With Josette's death I needed more.

The loss of my daughter weighed both heavy and wrenching. My heart, still a gaping raw wound, had only begun to heal. With time, I hoped the pain would soften. I had to believe that. I did not want to lose God, just understand him. Understand how or why he took Josette. Or at least accept he did it from love. I did not expect an easy journey would deliver me to such a conclusion.

Father Richard finished the last of his eggs and pushed his chair back. He straightened his black robe so no more than his ankle-high black boots showed beneath the neatly stitched hem.

After allowing me time to ask more questions if I had them, he smiled and stood. "I believe I've dallied long enough. God's work isn't done by laggards." He shoved his chair back under the table. "I need to prepare the altar and clean the church. Even traders who respect their house of worship leave a testament to their presence. After last week's rain, muddy tracks crisscross the wood floor. I'm not unhappy about that, you understand. I am grateful they come."

I rose and smiled back at him. The priest was not a tall man; his full height brought him to the bridge of my nose. What he lacked in physical substance, he made up in energy and passion.

On impulse, I said, "Father, let me help make preparations for tomorrow's baptisms. I can do the dusting and sweeping." The advice he had offered days earlier seemed sensible. Going through the motions might strengthen my convictions. If not, I would at least have the satisfaction of doing something useful.

"What of Harriet? Don't you need to attend to her?"

"She wants to pick wild raspberries with Betsy and Angelique this morning."

"Then by all means, I welcome your company and your service."

"Let me grab the broom, rags, and oil so we can give Ste. Anne's a proper cleaning." I rummaged in the pantry off the kitchen.

Father Richard relieved me of the supplies and moved back to let me exit the house before him. Our morning shadows lurched ahead of us along the weeded path. As we neared the church, my eyes settled on a solitary figure peering through one of the building's three side windows.

"Do you know her?" Father Richard motioned toward the woman, who scurried behind Ste. Anne's and disappeared.

"Not well. Before coming to Mackinac, she lived with the Ojibwe a far distance away in the interior of the continent. Her family shunned civilization." *It is the place to which I have banished Ahanu.* "She is the mother of our sweet Lucy, the child Therese adopted."

"Twice in the scant time since I have been on the island, I've seen her loitering about the church." Father Richard opened the door, and I entered. "Yesterday in her haste to flee, we nearly crashed into one another. She averted her eyes and hurried away without a word."

"She is a troubled one." I picked up the dusting rags, poured on a trickle of oil, and began polishing the front pews. My response left the priest's question poorly answered, so I added, "She is trying to find her spiritual path. Maybe in that way, she and I are not so different."

Midway to the altar, Father Richard paused and turned toward me. "Should I be concerned for her soul?"

I regarded the priest, then dropped my cloth and stopped work. "Sorrow fills Miskwabunokwa."

He nodded as though to say he already knew that much. "After our near-collision, I called after her. She picked up her step…hastened away…but not before I saw her vacant, joyless eyes." The priest cocked his head, encouraging me to explain. "Tell me her story and that of her dear Lucy."

"I first met Miskwabunokwa when she paddled to our shore a year ago this month…it was before I left for wintering. She was with John Tanner—the one they call the white Indian—and their family.

It is he who caused her problems and remains the source of her misery."

"Then tell me about this Tanner fellow so I may understand both his heart and that of the woman."

"That will take some time." I rubbed a mosquito bite that welted on my wrist and wondered if I wanted to share a tale that raised uncomfortable questions for me. After a few seconds I said, "It starts more than thirty years ago."

"I have all morning, and nothing better to do than listen as we clean."

I resumed dusting. Father Richard began arranging the altar for the sacraments he would perform the next day. He stood sideways to his work, watching me.

I gathered my thoughts, figured where the Odawa storyteller in me should begin. "James Tanner, a stranger to my family, brought details of a tragedy to our small hut in St. Joseph the year before my husband's murder. The customs of the Odawa, and the French as well, lean toward generosity with God's bounty. We invited him to share our sagamité dinner. James was traveling through the Ohio and Michigan country appealing to Indians, soldiers, traders— anyone who would listen—to help him find his older brother, John."

"John was lost?"

"Kidnapped." I doused the cloth with more oil and cleaned with a ferocity appropriate to the account. "John Tanner was born the same year I was. James pieced together his brother's story from details their parents repeated often as he was growing up. It was fleshed out by news that filtered back over the years, and eventually was made whole by the white Indian himself. Tales like John's circle campfires on winter nights when to fill the long hours the village shares news and rumors."

The priest finished the altar. He picked up a rag and began working alongside me. I pushed the oil in his direction without interrupting my account.

"The brothers were the sons of an Episcopalian minister who had brought his brood to the Ohio River—territory made dangerous by Indians resentful of white interlopers. The father worried that the family's move from Virginia might be ill-advised. He feared for the safety of his three small children, but the lush, fertile valleys proved a temptation he could not resist.

"The preacher worked hard clearing a space for a house. Neighbors, delighted to have another white man living close by, especially one who could also minister to their spiritual needs, helped the newcomers settle."

The open church door invited a feeble breeze to freshen the stale air around us. A dog stuck its head inside, barked to see if we would invite him in. I shooed the animal with a "get out of here" and a wave. It whimpered and backed away.

After the lull, Father Richard said, "Men of God hope for a warm welcome and are rarely disappointed."

"Yes, even stray dogs see you are good company." The smile curling the corners of his mouth assured me I had not offended him. I considered the circumstances that brought the priest to my home. Maybe, I conceded, he was my sign that God had not abandoned me.

I continued my story. "The Tanner children were warned not to go beyond their clearing. Their father drilled into them fear of unfriendly Indians who filled the woods. One afternoon, the parents left John to watch his baby brother, James, and younger sister, Martha, while they planted corn. They were distraught to return and find John had disappeared.

"John was only nine at the time. According to details he later provided, he was irritated with his runny nosed baby brother. He wanted a few minutes of peace out of earshot from James's whimpering. He had not intended to go far.

"At the edge of the Tanner property stood a walnut tree. John convinced himself that James and Martha would not suffer if their big brother slipped away for a few moments. Standing under the tree, John removed his straw hat and gathered as many nuts as it could hold. It is unlikely he heard a footfall, snapping twig, or any other warning before unfamiliar arms seized him from behind."

The priest let out an audible sigh. "I can imagine his horror, looking into the face of a painted wild Indian."

I had mentioned nothing about war paint, but left the priest to his conclusions. "John's Shawnee captors knew the territory and the trails through the country. They made good time returning to their home camp far to the north in the Saginaw Valley.

"All that remained to tell what had happened was that small pile of nuts in John's hat, and moccasin prints.

"An alarm went out to the settlers of the area. Eager to assist, and knowing it could have as easily been one of their children, they took up pursuit. After several days, they abandoned their efforts. The kidnap began the transformation of John Tanner into the white Indian."

"Tragedy for both young Tanner and his family." The priest sat, propped his elbows on his knees, and supported his head with his hands while he awaited more detail.

"The Shawnee beat John. Gave him little to eat. Several times he believed death was imminent. Eventually John was traded or sold to an Ojibwe woman who had lost her son. She loved John as her own, although not everyone in her tribe was as accepting of the white child. His life remained a series of hardships until he grew to manhood and proved himself an able hunter."

I lack the skills possessed by the best Odawa storytellers, but the priest appeared riveted. "My family promised James we would do everything we could to help him find his brother. We made inquiries among the Odawa and Ojibwe bands with whom we came in contact. Years went by. Rumors abounded, but none strong enough to reunite the stolen son of Reverend Tanner with his family.

"Two years ago while I wintered near Gabagouache, a trader I did not know wandered into my camp. He had run across James Tanner in Detroit. James was on his way back to Kentucky. He asked the trader to let me know James had found his brother. John had agreed to make a trip to the old family homestead in mid-summer. James expected his brother to make a stop at Mackinac

Island and asked that Therese and I offer any assistance to John and his family that we could."

"It's a dire tale. I don't expect you will provide me a happy ending."

I grinned at the priest. "Father Richard, it was you who told me that answered prayers are not always what we hope they will be."

He rose, moved back a row, and picked up his rag. "You listen well. I heard a soft snort, then he turned serious again. He seemed impatient for me to provide more details. "I haven't yet been told why the one you call Miskwabunokwa looks shattered. She is the wife of this Tanner fellow?"

"Yes. Wife à la façon du pays. Twelve moons ago, John pitched a wigwam here on the beach. Therese, as is her nature, set about to learn who the new people on the island were. It was late in the season for regular voyageurs to arrive. My sister stuck her head inside the wigwam and saw a woman—Miskwabunokwa—lying on a mat. Poor thing looked two breaths away from meeting the Almighty. Therese asked if she could be of help to her. John Tanner introduced himself. 'She will be well in a few days," he said. "She gave birth to my daughter the day before yesterday and is tired from rowing.'

"Therese, mindful of our promise to James, returned home and accumulated food and other supplies for the family. In addition to Miskwabunokwa, John, and the newborn infant, there were two other sons and another daughter. None looked like they had eaten regularly.

"Father, I do not mean to sound prideful or arrogant, but Miskwabunokwa's family seemed crude, shabbily dressed, and their language hard to understand. We tried to be charitable as Christ would have us be."

"I'm sure you were." The priest's tone made me feel guilty for my judgments, and I wished I could swallow them whole.

Our dusting efforts put us in the last row of pews. Father Richard sat back down to listen to the remainder of the tale.

"The day after Therese met the family, John Tanner burst through the front door of her home. Knocking was not a politeness he had learned in the back country. She eyed him carefully. The garments he wore were certain to cause amusement wherever he went, human nature often being cruel and looking to laugh at someone else's expense. I suppose James had given his brother clothing he hoped would let John pass without notice, but James was six inches shorter than John, if the distance of white flesh between where John's pants ended and his moccasins began was any indication. James had failed to leave a pair of shoes. The sleeves of the hand-me-down coat did not reach the taller man's wrists. John seemed as oblivious to the shortcomings of his dress as his brother would have been to the proper way to wear an Indian breechclout or leggings.

"Neither Therese nor I could assist John with better-fitting clothes. I have had no husband in twenty years so no man's wardrobe to visit. George Schindler, my sister's husband, is a slight man whose clothes would rip at the seams if Tanner tried to squeeze into them.

"I was at Therese's house when John burst in. We attempted to determine what he wanted of us." I doused the rag with oil for a few last swipes of our cleaning effort.

"And what was it?" The priest's impatience denied me a pause.

"Miskwabunokwa felt out of place on Mackinac Island and resisted the trip to Kentucky. The union between her and John offered no outward signs of affection or feeling, but when Miskwabunokwa became stubborn and insisted she would return with her youngest child to their Indian village, John grew agitated. He would not permit her to take the baby and desert him. As a compromise, he asked that Therese or I keep the newborn. He proposed that he would return to fetch the child when the youngster was three years old.

"It was more than I wanted to undertake. I was still wintering in the country and had no man to carry on the trade while I played nursemaid to an abandoned infant. Therese's husband George suffered apoplexy, and she did not need the additional burden.

"The situation reached loggerheads, which were broken when Therese, out of Christian charity, consented to adopt the child. Marianne would help her mother raise the little girl. I would assist when I could. Miskwabunokwa agreed to remain for one year to nurse the baby before returning to her own village. Paperwork was drawn up describing the custody agreement, and since Therese was a dutiful Catholic, her husband, George Schindler, presided over a lay baptism, which we hoped sufficed to satisfy God until you could perform a proper Catholic baptism.[27] We named the child Lucy."

The priest rested one arm along the side of the pew and leaned back. "I hope the mother will see the similarity of that situation to her marriage. The country marriage sufficed, but now it is time for her to submit to the church's formal blessing of her union."

"It would make Therese rest easier."

The dusting complete, I laid aside the rags and oil. I sat in the same pew as Father Richard, though several feet separated us. I brushed specks of dirt from my buckskin tunic. For a brief second, I compared Miskwabunokwa and me. My dress, more heavily beaded and in better shape, was still animal hide. I rarely dressed in the clothing a seamstress had created for me from calicos or silks available at the fur company headquarters. I had believed Miskwabunokwa's inability to commit to the Catholic faith made us different, but now, as I stitched together my own fragile convictions, patching them piece by piece, like scraps of a worn but warm quilt, I was not so sure.

I raised my gaze again, level with that of the priest. "After George baptized the child, Tanner took down his wigwam and the family separated. John Tanner hired a man to handle the paddle vacated by Miskwabunokwa. He set out with his older children for Kentucky and the spot from which he had been abducted those many years earlier."

"Miskwabunokwa has now been here the promised year?" the priest asked.

"Yes. She indentured herself to a local family and does general housekeeping. The family was more moved by Christian charity toward the poor woman than by hope she knew how to properly clean a house."

"And is she ready to return to her tribe?"

"I suppose that is why you see her looking mournful. Therese—and even I, last summer—did our best to convert her to the Catholic faith. She listened and at times overcame her superstitious nature and accepted the true God. But, just as often, she changed course—like an elk eluding a hunter—and decided to return to her tribe...the old ways...the old gods." *Perhaps the difference between Miskwabunokwa and me is that since Josette's death, I have trusted no gods.*

"If she goes back to the Red River Country, she gives up contact with Lucy?" The priest asked it as a question, but his sad eyes acknowledged it as a fact.

"Yes." My lips tightened, but I went on. "Miskwabunokwa nursed her daughter for the year. Separation will not be easy. Therese and George also love Lucy as their own child. In a selfish way, even I would be saddened at the loss of a beloved niece."

"What does the woman feel for this John Tanner? Would she like to reunite with him?"

"That is Miskwabunokwa's wish. John refuses to marry her in the Catholic Church—a necessary condition we impressed upon her, if she wants God's salvation. We told her God sent his son to pay for her sins, but living with John in an unholy union prevents true repentance. She cannot profess regret for her wrong and at the same moment continue the offense."

I thought about Wampeme and Ahanu. Like Miskwabunokwa, I had not figured out how to gain God's forgiveness for a sin I would gladly commit again. I wanted to ask Father Richard about my own absolution, but feared the answer. "In her heart, she believes she is his wife, and she mourns his absence."

The priest's eyes closed for a few seconds. He steepled his fingers, bit his lower lip, and then asked, "Do you think I can talk to her?" A slow smile crept to his mouth and suggested that the possibility of a conversion pleased him.

"You can try. But I fear it is John who needs convincing. I have no reason to believe he will be any more amenable to a Catholic marriage when he returns than he was before he took leave."

"Why is he set against it?"

"A year ago I would have said stubbornness, Father. Pigheaded stubbornness." I shrugged my shoulders. "I am no longer sure."

John Tanner. Also known as the Falcon
and Shaw-Shaw-Wa-Be-Na-Se
From *A Narrative of the captivity and adventures of John Tanner*, by
Edwin James, London, 1830.
Public Domain

Recreation of Ste. Anne's church (church of Ste. Anne de Michilimackinac) as it looked when it stood within the walls of Fort Michilimackinac. The original church was disassembled and transported to Mackinac Island where it was reconstructed at the corner of Market and Hoban.
Photo Courtesy of Mackinac State Historic Parks

12.
The Anishinaabek

"We are the Anishinaabek. We are the people of the Three Fires Confederacy, the Odawa, the Ojibwe, and the Bodwe'aadamiinh people. Our oral history traces us back to the Eastern Coast of Turtle Island where our spiritual leaders told us that we should travel to the west until we found food growing on the water. Our people traveled until we found wild rice growing on the water and we knew we were home." **Unknown**

August 15-31, 1821

I sat on a slatted wooden chair on my front porch and watched Elizabeth Mitchell's calash swerve and sway at the whim of the dogs pulling it toward my house that Friday afternoon in mid-August. I loved Elizabeth and her husband, Dr. David Mitchell, like a second set of parents. David Mitchell, a proud Englishman, had been a surgeon at Fort Mackinac when the British occupied the garrison. He was well-known and respected until the Americans defeated the English. As one of the vanquished, he fled to Round Island, where he built a second family home. Elizabeth remained at Mackinac and traveled to see her husband when convenient.

Twenty years older than I, Elizabeth cast a shadow twice the width of mine, but she carried her size with the stride of royalty. Neither the beaver cap she wore even in the summer heat, nor store potions she bought to smooth her aging skin, rendered her face more than pleasant. She possessed features I became used to and associated with a kind spirit, although others might not describe them as adding womanly grace and loveliness to her appearance. A pure blood Ojibwe, Elizabeth traded furs and kept company with the French who dominated the business. I came to know her after my marriage to Joseph. My first rendezvous, she watched out for me like a mother bear protecting its cub.

Elizabeth addressed me this August morning in her odd language that none, but those who knew her well, understood. It combined Ojibwe, French and English in no discernible pattern. "Oh, *ma chère*," she said, "tonight a dinner. Kenawwaw come to my wigwoman. My cook prepares au de kawmeg, au sawway, ozawominog, et miskouminog. You join us, *oui?*"

I did not answer her invitation with an enthusiastic, "I would love to join you," but with a more evasive, "It all sounds delicious. The whitefish you serve is superb."

"*S'il te plaît, viens.* Even the charming company of those I've invited won't make *la fête* a success if you do not come. Your spirits will be improved with a night of gaiety."

A night of gaiety was precisely what I preferred to avoid. Elizabeth's parties were as famous on the island as she herself was. She rarely spoke at such events, but managed to assemble guests who created lively conversation. At the last party I attended, more than a year ago—prior to leaving to winter and before Josette's death—Samuel Abbott was seated next to me. "Now that Missouri has become the twenty-fourth state," he asked, "do you think the Michigan Territory will be soon to follow?" Always uncomfortable in Abbott's company, I merely shrugged. Statehood was not likely to influence the lives of either Indians or French fur traders.

Elizabeth's invitations might be cherished, but the thought of an evening in her house—the house where Benjamin and Josette were married—surrounded by the rowdy, high-spirited Mitchell clan was more than I could endure. I did not need to be reminded with every word, every morsel of food, every intriguing comment that my grand house, where I once believed I would hold dinners to rival Elizabeth's, was without my children. The sin of jealousy looked to enter my heart, and I had no intention of obliging it by providing easy access.

I managed a cough and dabbed at my nose with a handkerchief. "I would love to join you, but Harriet has a case of sniffles, and I think I am catching her illness."

Elizabeth cast me the dubious glance of the unconvinced.

"In fact, I was about to go inside and lie down when I saw you approach."

After a sigh as sincere as my cough, she turned and called behind her as she trudged to her cart, "*Si vous* feel better by eight, come. We set an extra place."

The David and Elizabeth Mitchell House
Market Street, Mackinac Island
(The house has since been torn down.)
Photo Courtesy of Mackinac State Historic Parks

I drew the window blind to oblige my charade. I had slumped into my favorite chair, picked up my mending basket, and threaded a needle before Benjamin knocked. From his countenance I guessed a serious matter occupied his mind. If I entertained doubts about quitting the trade, they vanished with the news he delivered.

"Walk with me, Mother. It is still light. Harriet is asleep, and Angelique is here should she awaken."

At my front gate, I steered our stroll toward Arch Rock and away from the Mitchell home so I would not be spotted appearing to feel much better than I had pretended. We had taken only a few steps on the packed dirt path when Benjamin spoke. "Have you decided whether you'll continue trading this winter?"

"I am done with the business."

"I assume you've given it clear thought? The fur trade has been your life. Traders speak the name Madame La Framboise with awe."

"It was my life, but no longer." I studied grass sprouting from the hard-packed dirt as though wisdom lay hidden in the blades I trampled. "I wish I had made that decision before we lost Josette."

"I don't know if I will ever accept life without her." He took a deep breath. Tears glistened in his eyes. I turned my head away to spare him embarrassment. If he had nearly lost composure, he got his emotions under control before adding, "What will you do with your time?"

"Spend it with Harriet. In the country, my heart ached for Josette and Harriet. Josette is gone. My granddaughter is four years old and growing fast. I cannot bear to be without her another season."

He seemed to study me, and then he nodded. "Harriet loves spending time with her grandmother."

"Not as much as Nookomis enjoys spending time with her."

"I won't argue with you, if leaving the trade is what you've decided." His smug countenance flashed approval. "Still, I don't want Harriet or me—or even Josette—to be the reason for your decision."

"Benjamin, no one is responsible for my decision but me. I am forty-one years old and tired to the bone."

"Who will take over your posts?"

"There is a good fellow over in the Grand River Valley. You know him. Rix Robinson. He brought me the news of Josette's death at my post where the Sowanquesake meets the Grand. I met him again to talk business before I began my voyage home. He is fair to my people. He will help me this next season by purchasing my remaining merchandise and honoring my contracts with the tribes. He will pay me a fair price."

"They speak highly of him at the Company."

"Rightly so. He gets along with everyone. He is loyal to the American Fur Company, but he does not abuse the Indians—at least not as much as some." *Perhaps not even as much as me.* Spasms clutched my stomach. I wished for a clean slate to start over, but even God could not grant me that.

"If they don't like him, they won't allow him to continue trading in their villages." He tapped his long fingers against the trouser leg of his crisp military uniform. "Your decision makes what I'm about to tell you easier. On the seventeenth day of July, Spain ceded Florida to the United States. I've asked for a transfer from this post. My request has been honored. I'll be sent to Florida to keep the Seminole in check."

It took a few seconds for me to grasp his news. "Oh, Benjamin." I reached out and clutched his forearm. Standing nearly as tall as he, my eyes fixed on his. "Can I convince you to reconsider?"

"The decision is made. I depart in a fortnight."

I remembered the dream that had troubled me a few days earlier and thought of him taking Harriet from me. "But I—"

"I'd like to leave Harriet here with you."

Less than a week later, Harriet and I stood on the rocky beach as my son-in-law bade us farewell. I felt silly in my Paris bonnet, and it did little to keep out the sun's penetrating heat. I believed Benjamin preferred a mother-in-law dressed European style to one who looked ready to stir sagamité over a campfire.

"I leave my daughter in your capable hands." Benjamin kissed me on the cheek. "Each night after her prayers, as she readies to climb into bed, remind her that her papa loves her and will see her soon." He crouched and gave Harriet a long hug. "Mind your nookomis, Little One." He stood again and faced us as he marched backwards, turning for furtive glances to avoid missteps, until he reached the canoe that would paddle him to the schooner.

I grasped Harriet's small sweaty hand. The Angelus bell rang three times. I closed my eyes for a short prayer, but Harriet's soft whimpering interrupted. I knelt and kissed her tear-dampened face.

"I do not want Papa to leave me."

"I know, but you cannot follow him to Florida." I pulled a tatted handkerchief from the sleeve of my dress and patted her eyes. "Your papa is a brave man. He will help the governor fight the Seminole. When the battle is done, he will return to you."

"Will Maman be with him?"

No matter how many times I told Harriet that her maman was not coming back, she seemed unable to understand. The taste in my mouth soured. "No, sweet girl, your maman is with God."

"She had to go to watch after my brother?" Harriet clutched my skirt with her free hand and buried her face in the soft material.

My hands shook. "That is right. Benjamin Langdon needed her."

"But I needed her. Did she love him more?"

"You must not think that. Your maman wanted to stay with you, and keep Benjamin Langdon with her too, but God decided he needed them more."

"I hate God."

I pretended not to hear her blasphemy. We watched until the schooner was no more than a black dot on the horizon. Harriet waved a last time. Yawns replaced her earlier mewling sounds. I scooped her up and headed home. "Maybe we should have a maple sugar treat before your nap."

That brought a smile to her face. "I get to choose the piece I want?"

"Of course."

At the white picket fence in front of my home, I set Harriet on the ground and watched her totter toward the door. My granddaughter's gait was woozy and slow. She stopped at the flower garden beside the porch, studied the roses and bleeding hearts, and plucked a daisy. She handed it to me. "Can you give this to Maman?"

"I cannot do that, but your maman can see us from heaven. She knows you picked this for her, and she is smiling. We will set it in a vase of water, and when we look at it, we will think about her." As a rule I never brought flowers inside. Torn from their roots, they withered, died, and left me feeling I had disrupted Earth's balance. This was a day to break rules.

Inside the foyer, I bent to loosen the strings and removed Harriet's bonnet. I smoothed her long, curly, brown hair. "The piece of candy I promised, then that nap."

Harriet chewed with deliberation. When she swallowed the last of the candy, she said, "Can I sleep in your bed? And will you tell me a story?"

"You would have made a successful trader, granddaughter. You could charm your way to fortunes."

Harriet returned my grin. "The story about us." She reached for my hand as we climbed the stairs to the bedroom.

"You mean the Anishinaabek?"

"That's it. The story about the Shinaabee."

"Anishinaabek." I repeated the word, pronouncing each syllable. You and I are Anishinaabe Kwe, Odawa women."

"What does that mean?"

"The Anishinaabek are the Great Spirit's special people."

Harriet lifted her arms so I could help her remove her pinafore. Clad only in a petticoat, she climbed onto the big quilt-covered bed. "Will you lie down with me?"

"How else could I tell you the story?"

She curled close to me.

"At the beginning of time, our people lived along the Atlantic coast of North America, the place we named Turtle Island. We were called 'those who came down from the sky.' That is what Anishinaabek means. Our dwellings were like wildflowers on Mother Earth. Our numbers were great as the stars that light the evening skies."

"More than the houses on Mackinac Island?" she asked.

"So many more. You could not count them."

Her eyes widened as she contemplated such a number.

"A thousand years ago, the Great Spirit came to our people and brought them a warning: light-skinned strangers will appear on your shores."

"Was that bad?" she asked.

"The Great Spirit was not certain. The new strangers might be good for his people. But they might also bring destruction."

"Like the Red Coat monsters?"

"The Red Coats are not monsters like in Odawa stories. But they were light-skinned strangers. You are right about that part."

Harriet's thumb found its way to her mouth, a habit she had reverted to since her mother's death. "Papa told Maman that the Red Coats were thievin' murderers. Isn't that monsters?"

"Is that what your papa said?" My granddaughter was too young for my version of that story. Someday Harriet would be told the oral history of her people's attempts to drive out the light-skinned intruders, starting even before our most respected leader, Obwandiyag. I wondered about Benjamin's current mission to keep Indians from what had been their lands. At least the Seminole were no friends to the Odawa.

I chided myself for disloyal thoughts about my son-in-law. Harriet tugged on my sleeve. "Nookomis, did you think I fell asleep? Tell me what the Shshsh...nebik did?" Her tongue still failed to get around the word.

"The Great Spirit told them to divide. Half of them remained along the coast to greet the new people like friends or family, and the other half prepared for a long trip west in case the invaders were not friendly."

"Were the new people nice?"

"Well, it would be a while before anyone could say for sure. The Great Spirit told the Anishinaabek who stayed behind that the light-skinned newcomers might wear the face of friendship, but in their hearts they might be enemies. 'Be careful,' he said. 'Even if the new people appear harmless, do not rush to judgment. Until all doubt is removed, and it is as clear as the moon in the winter sky that they come in peace, you must remain vigilant.'"

"What is vigilant?"

"It means that the Great Spirit's children should watch to see what the strangers did. They would know by actions, not just words. They should give the new people time for the spirits of their hearts to show."

"Were the strangers good?"

I laughed at her earnestness and kissed the top of her head. "You hurry the story. The Great Spirit said, 'If you find the strangers come in friendship, the knowledge they bring from their world will combine with the Anishinaabek's spiritual wisdom to create one people, mightier than the world has ever known.'"

"Did that happen?"

"I have told this story too many times. You know the ending."

"No, no, I don't." She sat up, her eyes wider. "Tell me what comes next."

"Well, to the Anishinaabek setting out for distant lands, the Great Spirit explained, 'If the wish for a mighty people joined in friendship proves but a false hope, and the light-skinned newcomers wear the face of death, a time of great calamity will befall the Anishinaabek. Then the only hope for survival rests with those who travel far inland and begin a new life.'

"The Anishinaabek did as the Great Spirit directed. Some left the homes they loved. They filled ten thousand large canoes and traveled inland along the St. Lawrence River, to the Ottawa River, to Lake Nipissing, and then to the Great Sweetwater Lakes. They stopped along the way at the place where water rushes over a high cliff along the Niagara River and at the point we now call Detroit. The Great Spirit told his people to search for a place where the food grew on water."

Harriet put her hand up to stop me. "That's not right. Food doesn't grow on water. It grows in gardens like those of Madame Biddle and Madame Mitchell."

"Ah, but it did grow on water. Just like the Great Spirit promised. When the travelers reached the land of the big lakes, they stopped and explored rivers and smaller lakes, and they found wild rice, what the Odawa call pagwadjanomin or manoomin growing on the dark waters."

Harriet laid back and clutched a piece of quilt in her fingers. "And they stopped?"

"Yes. They camped at places with names that would tie your tongue in knots."

"Tell me."

"Manitou Island, Sault Ste. Marie, Duluth, Chequamegon, La Pointe, La Baye, and down the coast of Lake Misigami to L'Arbre Croche, Gabagouache, and St. Joseph." I paused after each name and let her try to repeat it. "They found wild rice at all of those places."

"Nookomis, is this a real story or a made up one?"

"The Odawa pass the story down from grandmamans to mamans to children. The children tell their children. The great storytellers of our people tell this story. It is our history, and it is true."

"Can I read about it when Papa sends me to school?"

"Our past is not written down. We keep it in our hearts and share it only with those we love.

"We were originally one people, but we divided into several tribes. The Council of Three Fires included the Odawa, the Ojibwe and the Bodwe'aadamiinh tribes. We were sometimes called the People of the Three Fires, the Three Fires Confederacy, or the Three Brothers. The Ojibwe were the older brothers and the keepers of the faith. They were the hunters. The Odawa were the middle brothers and the keepers of the trade. The name Odawa came from the word *Adawe* which means to trade."

"Like you are a trader?"

"Like I was a trader."

Harriet yawned. "Now I stay here with you." When her eyes were almost closed, and I thought she was seconds from sleep, she asked, "Who was the other brother."

"They were the Bodwe'aadamiinh, or the younger brothers and the keepers of the fire. Mishi-Makinaak Island was the meeting place for the Council of the Three Fires. It was chosen because it was the center of the bands that spread throughout Lower Canada and the Great Lakes."

She seemed to have revived, so I went on. "In the early days in their new land, the tribes that had lived together on Turtle Island, divided and fought each other."

"That is bad, Nookomis."

"You are right. Fighting is not good. It is not how we should live with each other." White men did not have a monopoly on fighting each other. Indians had done it for years.

"During one battle the Odawa captured a young wounded Ojibwe warrior. The Odawa spared his life and carried him back to their tribe. The nookomis of the warrior who captured the young man nursed the Ojibwe back to health. The grandmaman had lost a son in battle and adopted the young Ojibwe. She was amazed that they understood nearly every word the other spoke. It made the grandmaman believe they came from the same tribe in a long-ago time. The grandmaman took the young man to the tribal elders and convinced those wise men that they should drop their bows and arrows, hatchets, and war clubs and embrace all Ojibwe as brothers. Both the Odawa and the Ojibwe respect their elders and listen to their advice. The chiefs heard the story, smoked the pipe of peace, and the tribes began treating each other as brothers again."

"The grandmaman made them stop fighting?"

"I think the Great Spirit sent grandmamans to earth to bring love and peace."

Unknown artist's portrait of Benjamin Kendrick Pierce
Painted for his wedding, circa 1815
Public Domain

13.
Rix Robinson Takes Over Magdelaine's Trade

"The first peace, which is the most important, is that which comes within the souls of people when they realize their relationship, their oneness, with the universe and all its power, and when they realize that at the center of the universe dwells the Great Spirit, and that this center is really everywhere, it is within each of us." **Black Elk, Oglala Sioux**

September 1821

The black night gave way to graying dawn. A rosy glow marked the sun's advance on the horizon. I watched an extravagant burst of pink and scarlet rays turn the waters of Lake Huron purple as I traipsed the few rods to Therese's home. To my right, along the beach, bony dogs nosed through waste and yelped to discourage gulls, rival scavengers that threatened to swoop down and carry off the best pickings. In the moon of turning leaves, Indians packed up wigwams and returned to their villages. If the next season of snow was as grueling as the last, the mangy mongrels might themselves become a starving family's sustenance.

Therese's open front door invited crisp morning air to replace the odors of last night's cooking and the more subtle scent of George's illness. I knocked on the doorframe before entering.

"In here," Therese called.

Early morning was the brief time we reserved for each other, the time before the obligations of the day pressed in on us. I pulled out a worn chair and sat at the kitchen table. "Robinson's engagés are loading his bateaux this morning. I expect they will shove off before I return home."

Therese dropped into a chair across from me. She nudged the teapot my way. "It's been a mere week since he married Peemissaquotoquay,[28] and he's eager to get to his winter posts."

"Their wedding gave us a lively time."

"I suppose folks enjoyed themselves, if that's what you mean." Therese's words, squeezed through pursed lips, carried no warmth. "Food enough to feed every Indian along Misigami's shores. And the fiddlers, including Francois, were in fine form."

"I hear judgment in your voice, sister. You are not good at hiding disapproval."

"It's no secret I'd have been happier if Rix had married Peemissaquotoquay in the Catholic Church. Father Richard would have still been here if they'd moved up the wedding by a few days. It would have proven no burden."

"Peemissaquotoquay clings to tribal ways," I said. "The marriage for a hundred moons was what she wanted. And Rix holds to the Protestant faith."

"Are you saying God countenances their country union? They had the opportunity for a Christian marriage pleasing in his sight."

"I am saying that we browbeat Miskwabunokwa almost as much as John Tanner does. Perhaps we should keep our opinions about Peemissaquotoquay and Rix to ourselves."

"Saving eternal souls is hardly what I'd call browbeating. Is salvation no longer important to you?"

"I have not figured out what God wants, and do not presume to speak for him."

"Still—"

"No *still*. You will have many years to work at converting Peemissaquotoquay, and Rix too, for that matter. For now share their joy. Remember, my marriage was à la façon du pays for ten years. Your first marriage was likewise a country marriage."

"Of necessity—for lack of a priest—not choice. And Pierre[29] deserted me—left us when Marianne was but an infant…went his way as though neither of us were of any more import than an Englishman's honor."

"I married in the church when a priest was available. Joseph had thrown in the promise of a priest's blessing as part of the bargain with my uncle, but I ended up as alone as if he had cast us aside. Father Richard says there are no guarantees. Our lives prove it."

George wheezed in the next room. I waited to see if Therese would interrupt our talk to attend to him. Before she moved, we heard Marianne say, "It's okay, Papa. Take a sip." The wheezing stopped, and I picked up my tirade.

"White Ox cared nothing for my children left fatherless." The muscles of my throat pulsed. I clenched my teeth to imprison further words.

"I'm sorry. You may be right. Either way, I don't wish to argue with you. The church gives our women protection from men who would use and then abandon them like a winter-damaged bateaux."

I reached across the table and gripped Therese's wide hand. "I rejoice that Rix will take over my posts with an Odawa wife at his side. It will make the transition easier and our people more likely to trust him. Other problems do not need resolution today."

Therese looked up. Her expression softened. The tension between us drained. I relaxed. We sat for several minutes in companionable silence.

Except as an infant, for all of her forty-five years, Therese knew hard work. She picked berries from the time she toddled. She planted corn and squash and beans, then gathered those crops during the harvest moon. She helped Maman collect wild rice. She learned to clean furs, patch and paddle canoes, pitch and take down wigwams, cook meals with whatever food could be scrounged, and make maple syrup, sugar, and candy.

Many nights, as children, our stomachs growled and protested sleep. Death was no stranger to our village. Battle, starvation, and disease—small pox, typhus, influenza, whooping cough—were as common as pebbles along the beach.

I studied my sister's face. Life had etched deep furrows between her eyebrows. Downward sloping wrinkles at the edges of her mouth made her appear serious, if not sad.

We were both tall women, towering over our friends. When we were girls, our thick hair glistened like an otter's wet fur. Therese's was now flecked with more gray than mine. My black eyes were set deep and wide like my sister's. Wampeme once told me my eyes reflected what they saw. He compared them to the Sowanquesake River where a canopy of leaves blocked the sun and was mirrored on the placid water. Whatever his meaning, I took it as flattery.

Therese was broad-shouldered, built of big bones that she claimed were more suited to a hunter than a genteel lady. To me, she remained beautiful, although I heard her called plain. Now middle-aged, she complained she had become fleshy. A woman meant to bring comfort to children and grandchildren, she argued, not desire to men.

Growing up, my sister told me often that she felt cheated when our features were painted on similar oval canvases. She envied what she described as my delicate, chiseled nose and full lips. Equally often, she said, she prayed that God would forgive her such covetousness. I do not believe either of us could rightly be called vain, but even if so inclined, the passage of time made vanity hard to support.

"Will you miss the work?" she asked.

I poured myself more tea, added a teaspoon of maple sugar, and stirred. "The French may be better traders, but all I know about my Hyson tea I learned from the English." I repeated her question. "Will I miss the work? You mean the trading? The wintering?"

"Of course. This will be the first year since you were fourteen and married Joseph that you will not be a part of the business."

"If I suffer remorse, it is so little, it is no burden. It is right for younger traders to make their fortunes. I am grateful for the role we played in teaching them. Gurdon Hubbard and John Kinzie Junior bring fresh blood, and it pleases me that my posts will be in Robinson's capable hands." I looked at the elm tree outside the kitchen window. I watched a robin twist its head and peer skyward searching for signs it was time to journey south. "I should have done it sooner." *At least a year earlier.* "No, I will not miss it. I have Harriet. I hope my daughter rests easier knowing I care for her child."

"God's will is sometimes strangely timed, is it not?"

"If by 'strangely timed' you mean because I was at winter camp while you sat beside my dying daughter when she gasped her last breath—"

I pulled my hands back from Therese's, jerked up my head. Saying the words made me feel as if I had been struck hard across the face. "And this year, you will be trading in the villages, and I will stay on the island. I have trouble calling it God's will. I suppose it could be called fate."

Therese had not meant to verbally wound me, but more talk of Josette's death would deepen the gash, so I sent the question back to her. "And what of you, sister? Will you miss remaining on the island?"

"George intended to trade for a few more years, but the apoplexy leaves him too weak."

"I wish we had the secret to restore George's health." I rose and walked behind her chair, patted her hair, and laid my cheek atop her head. "I am so, so sorry."

"He's a proud man. A good man who keeps his troubles inside and puts on a strong front for the girls and me."

"You and George do not need the money. Fur has made us rich beyond anything we dreamed when we were girls living in the village."

She grinned at the good-natured competition between us. "I've not fared quite so well as you, sister, but you are right. Trading, selling maple sugar, and the little extra George earned by teaching last year…we've been blessed. No one under our roof goes hungry." She turned, looked up at me, then got to her feet. I took her hand as we walked toward the front door.

"I go because George wants to hold on to the fur business. He believes next year he'll be strong enough to get back into it. He doesn't want to lose his engagés or his territory."

"And what of your feelings? Leaving the island for winter posts and villages?"

"I'll only make short trips to L'Arbre Croche. Keeping George's hope alive brings its own reward. This winter, if God permits, he will again instruct young boys. It's a noble task and gives him purpose. I leave a fortnight hence. My outfit is ordered and packed. I'll make one trip by canoe and another in the season when ice freezes the path to the mainland."

"Oh, Therese..." I hugged my sister, smelled the faint sweet odor of crushed trillium that clung to her clothes and drifted from the direction of the bedroom.[30] "I would much prefer to have you here every day this winter, but your heart speaks with compassion and wisdom." She, too, must have heard St. Benedict. *Listen, and attend with the ear of your heart.*

"I'm not so sure it's wisdom, sister." Therese's words followed me outside. "It's living each day of my life as God hands it to me."

Therese Marcotte La Sallier Schindler, photo from Reminiscences of Early Days on Mackinac Island, by Elizabeth Baird, 1898
Public Domain

Angelique was polishing the dining room furniture with her homemade concoction of oil, turpentine, and vinegar when I walked in.

"Your shadow, Miss Harriet, is still sleeping," she said. "You tired her out yesterday letting her play with Betsy. Harriet struggles to keep up."

"And today I have promised her a picnic."

"You indulge her, but I understand." The gleam in Angelique's eyes overshadowed the gruffness with which she spoke. She could no more refuse the household darling than could I.

"How can you overindulge a child who has lost her maman?" I asked.

"And what of you when Captain Pierce returns for her? Will your heart survive?"

"I hope he will leave her with me until she is fully grown. If not, I will make sure she remembers me. I will play every game she wants to play. I will tell her every story she wants to hear. I will make her cornbread with maple syrup every day if that is what she wants."

Angelique raised her eyebrows as if to say "enough," but it just encouraged me. "I will help her choose what she wants to wear, and if we have nothing that suits her, I will exchange beaver pelts for a new frock made by a seamstress at the shop on Market Street. When Harriet scrapes her knee or bruises her elbow, I will comfort her. If she ever leaves me, I will be forced to make do with memories, and I will have a stock of plenty."

Angelique shook her head. "Lordy, I've heard enough." She set aside the sock with which she had been dusting. "I'll prepare the lunch."

Harriet and I headed toward Sugar Loaf Rock. She rode part of the distance on my back, her arms around my neck and her legs clamped about my waist. "We are almost there." I placed the basket on the ground and stooped to set her on the path. "You can walk the rest of the way." I straightened her bonnet before gathering up our lunch.

"Did Angelique make me maple sugar candy?" She scrutinized the woven basket.

"You have to wait and see." I clasped the opening tight so she could not peek.

"Tell me…tell me…please, Nookomis, tell me the truth."

"What if I cannot remember?"

"You are teasing." Harriet's words were a playful whine as she tugged on my doeskin leggings.

"Well, maybe there is the tiniest piece."

"No, I think you brought me the biggest piece of candy ever."

"You think that, do you?"

"Yes."

"And why would that be?" I took her hand and grinned down at her.

"'Cause you love me."

I picked a shaded spot within sight of Sugar Loaf, spread the shawl that had been atop the food in the basket, and set the remaining contents on it.

She eyed the candy, but patiently ate the dried venison, bread, and apple that I handed her. With only the core left, she asked, "May I have my candy now?"

"Are you sure you do not want more meat?"

"I'm sure. My mouth wants candy."

"I guess you deserve at least one small piece." I let her choose a piece from the four that Angelique had put in a leather pouch.

She carefully studied them for size and chose neither the largest nor the smallest, but one in between.

"You know the makakoon basket we keep in the kitchen?" I asked.

"The one that holds the maple sugar you use to sweeten my porridge and your tea?" She nibbled the edges of the treat, taking tiny bites.

"Yes. Those cone-shaped baskets are made of birch bark." I pointed to the rock formation ahead of us. "Sugar Loaf got its name because it looks like those makakoon baskets, just much, much bigger."

"I wish my candy was as big as that rock. I wish it was this big." She spread her arms wide.

"If you ate that much you might turn into candy. You would be too big to move and would sit forever next to the rock."

Harriet sucked in her cheeks and shook her head, sending the long ringlets below the back of her bonnet bobbing. "That wouldn't be fun."

"Maybe you should be thankful for small pieces of candy." I handed her another.

When she finished the second piece, she rested her head on my lap.

"Our people believe if you look closely at the rock you can see the face of a man that Gitchie Manitou turned to stone."

She sat up again and her eyes popped wide. "Could Gitchie Manitou really turn people to stone?"

"The story says he could."

"Tell me about the man turned to stone. Please, Nookomis?"

"You do not want to sit here quietly and watch for squirrels and deer?"

"I can watch and listen at the same time."

"I suppose you can."

Before I began I said a silent thank you to Benjamin for giving me precious time with my granddaughter. I loved telling her stories as much as she enjoyed listening to them.

"A very long time ago, long before you were here, long before your maman and papa were born, and even a long time before your great-great-grandpapa Kewanoquat lived, there was no Mackinac Island, just lots and lots of water. Our people, the Odawa, fished right on this spot where we sit, because it was not yet land. The men caught wonderful whitefish like Angelique cooks for you.

"One night a big fog settled over the water. For three days the people who lived on the mainland saw nothing." I pointed west. "On the morning of the fourth day, the sun chased away the fog. The people stood on their shore and looked toward the place where they had always paddled their canoes to fish. They saw an island with tall trees and bright red, purple, and blue flowers.

"This made no sense to them, and for many moons they did not dare venture close to the mysterious island. Finally, nine brave men loaded canoes with wampum and other treasures to offer any gods they might encounter and rowed to the strange new hump of land.

As they walked ashore they heard the voice of the Great Spirit, Gitchie Manitou. 'I have made this island, and I will dwell here among the giant rocks. Each of these tall rocks holds the spirit of a mighty Manitou who will watch and protect you—my chosen people.'" I spoke Gitchie Manitou's words in a deep voice like the Odawa storyteller at the village had done so many years ago, when he first told me the story.

Harriet covered her eyes, but peeked at me through spread fingers.

"Though there were many spirits on the island, none was as important as Gitchie Manitou," I said. "Gitchie Manitou talked to birds and animals, and they shared their wisdom with him. He was a powerful god with great magic that allowed him to grant wishes. All of the warriors wanted something, and Gitchie Manitou agreed to give each of them one wish." I handed Harriet another apple, hoping the distraction of the story caused her to forget the candy.

She took a bite of the apple. "What did they ask for?"

"Different things."

"I would ask Gitchie Manitou to give me back my maman."

"I wish you could do that. But even Gitchie Manitou would not stop death when the time came, because to do so destroyed the earth's balance. He told the warriors they could wish for anything except everlasting life. That means they could not ask to live forever."

"Tell me what they wished for."

I laid back on the shawl and propped myself on my elbow. "Well, one asked to be a war chief, strong enough to drive his enemies away."

"Did Gitchie Manitou give him his wish?"

"He did."

"What did the other men want?"

"One asked for powerful medicine so he could help his people."

"Like Dr. Beaumont?"

"Sort of. A medicine man tries to make people well, but he uses ways that are different from those of white doctors like Dr. Beaumont."

"Do they use primrose like what Angelique and Catishe collect?"

"That and other herbs and plants as well."

"Whose medicine is more powerful? The medicine men's or Dr. Beaumont's?"

"I am not sure. Maybe the Great Spirit believes that different people need different medicines."

"I don't understand."

"You are four years old. You cannot understand everything."

"I have to wait until I am old like Mrs. Mitchell?"

I laughed as I imagined Elizabeth's response to such a comment.

"Even Mrs. Mitchell cannot know everything."

"The other men, what did they ask for?"

"One wished for a commanding voice so he could speak for his people. One wanted to be a storyteller, the man who keeps our history so we never forget. One wanted to make the most seaworthy canoes. Another asked to be the fastest runner. That's all I can remember."

"Which man got turned into Sugar Loaf?"

"It was the last man. He believed that since the Gitchie Manitou promised him one wish, he had tricked the god and could now ask to live forever."

"It probably isn't good to trick a god who has magic powers."

"You see the moral of this story."

"What's a moral?"

"The lesson. Odawa stories teach lessons. Gitchie Manitou thought about the man's request. The god had made a promise and his honor did not let him go back on his word."

"What did he do?"

"Using his powerful magic he turned the young man to Sugar Loaf. He will live forever, but as a rock."

"Is the Gitchie Manitou still here?"

"No. When new people, pale-faced strangers, came to the island, Gitchie Manitou was sad. This island belonged to him. He thought the newcomers did not respect this sacred place. They used it for evil purposes. The gods, including Gitchie Manitou, could no longer dwell here in peace. Gitchie Manitou grew so unhappy that he fled to the Northern Lights."

"Is he still in the sky?"

"Yes, when you look up at night and see brilliant streaks of white light in the northern sky, you know that is where Gitchie Manitou can be found. Odawa men watch the lights to guide their way in the dark. Sometimes when Gitchie Manitou is really happy or really angry, he sends streams of green and red light across the sky to get the attention of his people."

Harriet stood and shaded her eyes with one hand and pointed with the other. "Nookomis, Nookomis, look. See? That's it. That's his face."

I turned toward where her finger aimed. "That is what people have seen for thousands of years when they look at Sugar Loaf."

We walked home through a forest of maple, cedar, and birch whose remaining leaves clung obstinately to half-naked limbs. The smell of decaying foliage mixed with the fragrance of white pine and spruce. Blue jays squawked their displeasure at approaching winter, their objections supported by the mottled red-and-orange forest floor that rustled beneath our moccasins.

"I have an idea," I said. "Since you love the maple sugar candies, maybe I should take you to sugar camp. You can watch how we get the maple syrup for such a fine treat."

"Will Auntie Schindler and Betsy and Lucy and Marianne go too?" Harriet paused to think if she had forgotten anyone. "And Angelique?"

"Angelique will stay home to tend the house. Lucy is still a baby and will stay with her. Auntie Schindler will be at L'Arbre Croche, so Marianne will take her place at sugar camp. I am sure she will bring Betsy. It will be a frolic."

Sugar Loaf
Photo courtesy of Bob Royce

14.
Sugar Camp

"With the deep snow and thick ice, came poverty and hunger. We were no longer able to take beaver in traps, or by the ordinary methods, or kill moose." **Shawshawwabenase (John Tanner, the white Indian)**

March 1822

I tucked a bag of pemmican alongside our clothes in the valise. Foolishness, I scolded myself. Francois took food aplenty to sugar camp, but old fears gnawed the edges of my logic. Dried meat was as much a talisman for dispelling uneasy thoughts as my crucifix.

I descended the stairway and from the foyer saw Harriet perched on the sitting room sofa, where she had been waiting since lunch.

"I thought you'd never be ready." She ran toward me and threw stick-thin arms around my legs. "Angelique said I had to be still and stay out of trouble until you came down."

Harriet's touch, her love and need for me—so much like that of Josette at that age—played havoc with my emotions. I still grieved my daughter's death, but at the same time enjoyed glimmerings of joy in my granddaughter's presence. "It is good you learn patience."

Harriet backed away from me and eyed the cedar-bark bag I held. "Did you remember to pack maple sugar treats?"

"We make candy at camp. No need to waste space in our satchel." I reached for her cape from the coat tree by the entry and helped her bundle up for the mile-long sleigh ride to Bois Blanc Island. "Hurry now. Francois waits."

I opened the front door and saw Francois in his red-striped blanket capote and the fringed buckskin pants I had given him for Christmas. He stood at the road by the edge of my property holding two large dogs—pure white Caribou and pitch black Nero—harnessed in tandem. He wore no hat, and his long hair, black with auburn streaks, curly on the top and straight in back, revealed a page of his family history.

"*Bonjour*, Francois." I spoke loud enough for my words to carry down the front steps and across the small picket-fenced yard.

"There is still enough snow covering the ground that I could bring the sleigh." He extended a hand to help me climb into the dark green cariole. He picked up Harriet and tossed her in the air. She squealed as he caught her and settled her next to me.

I leaned against the back of the sleigh, Harriet wedged between my knees. I tucked beaver skins around us. The sides of our sled sloped toward an open front that provided a view of the lake. Within minutes we had crossed the road in front of my house, descended the knoll to the edge of the frozen harbor, and headed southeast.

"Why does Francois run beside the dogs and switch them?" Harriet leaned forward and tried to rise. Tears welled in her eyes.

I pulled her back. "He does not hurt them, child. He barely touches them." The dogs' advancing thrust blew snow on us. I brushed it from my granddaughter's plucked beaver cap.

"Then why does he do it?" She pushed my hand away. "It's mean."

Francois urged the dogs forward, but Nero stopped to sniff a chunk of ice. It required a smack and a harsh *"Faire avance"* to get him going again.

"See that?" I said. "These dogs do not take to pulling a sled, Francois keeps them on track by showing he is boss."

"I don't like it." Harriet's voice quivered. Tears that had merely threatened moments earlier, trickled over and ran down her cheeks.

"Would you rather they veered off at the scent of other dogs and took us on a merry chase through the trees, maybe to the gate of the fort, or maybe between headstones at the cemetery?"

"Yes. Yes, for certain. I would like that." Her frown turned to giggles. "I wish Caribou and Nero lived in our yard instead of Auntie Schindler's."

"I already have plenty of work. I do not need dogs to take care of." I doubted my stern words and scowl fooled her.

She shifted her body around to face me. "But Father Richard is gone, so you don't have to talk to him all day. I could help. Please, can we get our own?"

I could not resist leaning forward and kissing her damp cheeks. "You go next door every day. You have plenty of time to play with those animals."

She must have realized her whining would get her nowhere because she grew quiet.

I was grateful for the blessings of a beautiful day and an adventure to share with my granddaughter. Sky gods had gasped sharp icy breaths and blown away the gray clouds that had blocked the sun for weeks. I loved winter, the mounds of white that cleansed Mackinac Island and buried all the quarrels and sloppiness of rendezvous. Snowdrifts softened rough edges and fashioned a serene world that reminded me of what the Great Spirit and the Father God intended for this place. My appreciation of winter, however, did not extend to continuous somber skies. This day the blue heaven dazzled more brightly than I remembered possible.

It was my first sugar camp since before the British gave up possession of Mackinac. After my papa's murder, Maman found no trader who wanted to partner with a twice-married older woman and two young, tag-along daughters. Maman, Therese, and I spent the moons of warming sun on Bois Blanc. Maple syrup was serious business, a way to earn an income when food was as scarce as a French copper. Since white sugar was hard to come by and expensive, Maman always found customers for her maple sugar. When our family ran out of corn and meat, we drank the syrup to lessen hunger pangs.

At fourteen, marriage to Joseph ended my trips with Maman to sugar camp. I became more important to the tribe as the wife of a trader who brought goods and credit to the camp. After Joseph's death, I carried on our fur business at winter posts while Therese and Maman handled sugar camp. I now had enough wealth that sugar camp was an amusement, not a necessity. Therese had taken over our family's sugar maples and had overseen construction of a large building to replace the wigwams of our childhood.

I closed my eyes and tried to imagine the old camp. I pictured the buckets, the big sugar kettles. I remembered how Maman tested trees by drilling holes on the sides that faced the morning sun. I remembered how she put her arms around the trees to measure for the number of holes to drill. I even remembered Maman telling me we could never drill the same tree the next year. But I could not remember the details of my mother's face. I recalled some of Maman's words and the song-like lilt of her speech, but not her actual voice.

Maman's bones rested in the burial ground on Bois Blanc. I would visit her gravesite while we were at sugar camp, but I would no longer see my maman's eyes or smile when I bent over that cold ground. My memories of Josette were likewise losing their sharp focus.

"Will Marianne be at the camp when we get there?" Harriet tugged on my tunic underneath the furs.

I was happy for the break in my thoughts. "Yes, Francois took her and Betsy yesterday. Then he came back for us."

"How does he know when we should go to camp?"

"He checks the trees to see if the sap is running. He lets everyone at Mackinac know when it is time. He has already begun collecting it."

"What is sap?"

"It's the tree's blood."

"We make them bleed?" The child's eyes widened. "Do we kill the trees?"

"No. We are careful not to hurt the sugar maples."

She pointed to land ahead of us. "Is that where we are going?"

"Yes. The Odawa call it Wigobiminiss."

"That's a funny name."

"It means place of the tying cord." I adjusted a fur-lined buckskin mitten that threatened to fall off Harriet's hand. "The sugar maples and their sap are not the only gift the island gives us."

"What is tying cord?" She yanked at the knit scarf around her neck as though it strangled her.

"That is what we use to lace the canoes and string snowshoes." I saw the camp through a clearing in the distance.

"Where do we pick tying cord?"

I stifled my amusement. "Tying cord is not picked. We cut it from the soft white underbark of the basswood trees." I smoothed the fringe of her loosened scarf. "From all the island gives us, you can see why the Odawa believe this is a special place."

"I like the candy trees better than tying cord."

I laughed and petted her head. The dogs climbed a snow bank that marked the island shore. Francois brought them to a halt in the middle of a stand of sugar maple and released their harnesses.

Harriet stepped onto the low side of the cariole and jumped into a snowdrift, her wool cape flying behind her. She scampered after the animals as they pranced and reveled in their freedom. When they stopped, Harriet caught up with them and laid her head on Caribou. He licked her rosy cheeks. A rabbit darted from behind a tree. Rabbit and dog tore off, leaving the child to chase after them.

Francois's eyes followed Harriet. "Don't let her go wandering off alone. There's rumor a colony of misfits took up livin' in deserted wigwams on the far end of the island. I ain't seen no sign of 'em, but it pays to be heedful."

"No truth to the story." I tried to sound like I knew what I was talking about. "It is a yarn spun by Magistrate Puthuff to explain damage caused by soldiers he hesitated to hold accountable."

I left Francois to carry our bags and headed after my granddaughter. Harriet returned to my side and gestured ahead of us toward a cedar-bark pole building about thirty feet long by eighteen feet wide. "Is that where we'll stay?"

Before I answered, Marianne and Betsy rushed to greet us.

Marianne hugged me and kissed my cheeks, first one, then the other. Betsy grabbed Harriet's hand, and I heard her say, "Follow me," as they entered the lodge ahead of us. The girls skipped to a wooden platform, eighteen inches high and four feet wide, that ran the length of the building. Harriet hoisted herself up, pulled off her gloves, cape, and hat and threw them next to her before she sat down.

"We sleep here." Betsy indicated bundles shoved against the wall. "In the morning we roll our bedding in the mats. During the day we can sit, tell stories, play games, whatever we want…when the grown-ups aren't giving us chores, or sitting here gossiping."

Harriet ran her hands over the tarpaulin that covered the walls and floors.

Betsy mimicked Harriet and her fingers drifted down the bumpy surface. "It's not pretty, but if the north wind begins howling tonight, like it did last night, you'll be mighty happy that rough canvas is here."

"What's on that side?" Harriet pointed to the opposite wall, where there was a platform identical to the one on which she sat.

"That's where we eat. At the end…that's a pantry. We keep tin dishes and food in there. The small door," Betsy pointed to the side of the closet, "leads to a room where Francois and the other men sleep." A crackling fire blazed in a long, trenched pit that had been dug midway between the platforms and ran to within six feet of either end of the building. A dancing line of three-foot flames warmed the room. The air smelled of burning oak.

Harriet's eyes skittered to the roof above the fireplace, where a huge hole provided escape for smoke.

Betsy's eyes followed my granddaughter's gaze. "When it's dark we watch the stars through that hole. Maybe tonight I'll tell you stories that your nookomis told me about the constellations."

Harriet's face lit up, but before she could get a firm promise, Marianne joined us and said, "Betsy, help me roast the partridges for dinner."

"Come. You can watch." Betsy, eight years older than Harriet, assumed an air of authority. "We skewer the birds on sticks, hold them over the fire, and make sure they don't burn or fall off."

I followed behind Harriet, Betsy, and Marianne to the center of the room.

Betsy nudged Harriet. "This is where we prepare dinner. It's also where we boil sap."

At each corner of the fire pit, five-foot posts were planted in the ground. Brass kettles hung suspended by chains from sturdy timbers anchored across these posts. The setup was many times the size of what I remembered from girlhood.

Betsy pointed at a small pot to the side of the large vessels where sap boiled. "Rabbit and squirrel are inside that one. Maman added grease drippings, onions, potatoes, water, salt, and spices." With an air of authority she added, "It will taste better than anything at home. When we finish eating dinner, the real fun begins."

"Tell me." Harriet gripped Betsy's hand.

"Ah, *non*, you must wait."

After the evening meal, women cleaned up the cooking pots. We scrubbed plates with sand from a bucket kept by the washtub, rinsed them in a container of water, and put them away. I grabbed a thick cedar-branch broom, cut evenly at the bottom, and swept the tarpaulin floor.

Betsy was assigned the task of watching Harriet. They sat on the platform where the older girl plaited my granddaughter's hair, wrapped a rawhide strip around the end of each braid, and gave them a playful tug to indicate she had finished.

When I was done sweeping, I put the broom away and grasped Harriet's hand. "You look beautiful. Now come help me." I indicated a heavy cast iron skillet next to my bag. "Can you hand that to me?" Harriet did as she was bade, and I led her closer to the fire, where Marianne heated a pan she had brought to camp.

"Stand back a ways," I said. "I want you to see, but not get burned. Our pan has to be hot enough to sizzle when I splash drops of water on it."

Harriet planted her hands on her hips and leaned forward while I demonstrated.

"It is ready for a ladle of the crepe batter we made before dinner." I handed her the scoop, and she dumped the thin liquid onto the skillet. She licked her lips as she watched the bubbling pancake.

When one side was cooked, I gave a hearty toss of the pan that launched the crepe into the air. Flames ate the misdirected pancake when it landed in the fire. "The trick is catching it, uncooked side down in the pan." Harriet threw herself to the floor and convulsed in laughter.

"What is so funny? The fire needs something to eat too. Giving it the first bite insures its favor for later tries." After my next three perfectly timed attempts, Harriet's mouth dropped open, as though Nookomis had performed a magic feat. "Do you still see something funny?"

I turned to Betsy. "You give it a try. A girl's not fit for becoming a wife until she can make crepes at sugar camp."

Henry Baird, a young lawyer on the island, had received an invitation to sugar camp. He sat within listening distance, and I surmised a romantic interest between him and my grandniece by their long, trance-like looks at each other. Betsy's face flushed. We pulled her from the platform. Marianne handed her a frying pan and a ladle of batter.

"It is time," I said, as the pancake's bubbles burst on the upper side.

Betsy gave the pan a thrust, more forward than up. The crepe flew and landed on Baird's shoulder. He snatched it and stuffed it in his mouth. Snickers and snorts filled the room.

"You have a few years before you are ready for marriage," I said.

When the revelry settled down everyone ate crepes with warm maple syrup. Harriet rubbed her stomach, groaned, and patted the top of her head. "My belly is full all the way up to here."

The next morning, after breakfast, I bundled Harriet in her winter coat and pulled her through the woods on a small oak-board sled. A woodchuck scampered across our path. I stopped, held a finger to my lips. "Shhh." I eased back, sat next to my granddaughter, and pointed. "See the snowdrift by that stand of trees?"

Harriet squinted. "The snow is wiggling. Is it a monster?" She buried her head against my shoulder.

"More likely a ruffed grouse." I drew Harriet close to keep her still. The snow erupted. A speckled brown and rust-colored bird toddled into the sun on feet that doubled as snowshoes. It took no notice of the two humans as it plucked fresh buds from newly sprouted aspen.

"It is called snow roosting," I whispered. "The bird is pretty smart. It keeps warm by burrowing in the drifts."

When Harriet tired of the show, she hopped from the sled and rushed toward the bird, flapping her arms like wings. She squealed in delight when the grouse abandoned dinner and took flight.

I caught up with her. "I have to stop someplace special before we go back. It is the place where your great-grandmaman, Thimotee,[31] is buried."

"Does she know me?"

"I am sure in the spirit world she does, but she died long before you were born."

I drew the sled through trees to a clearing a dozen rods from camp. The burial ground stood on a knoll with a view of Lake Huron. Maman would like that, I thought.

Therese had placed a small marker on Maman's grave. I stood in silence, looking down at the resting place of Maman's earthly remains. Father Richard's advice spoke to me: "Act as though you believe, and it will help your heart to follow." *Father God, she died in your presence, keep her in the joy and company of our Lord Jesus Christ until I can be reunited with her.* I slipped my hands beneath my capote and retrieved a basswood pouch from the pocket of my buckskin tunic. I took a stick of pemmican and two maple sugar candies from it, and placed them on the grave.

"You're giving the ground the candy?" Harriet's astonishment suggested displeasure.

"We make the offering because we love Thimotee."

"Maybe she only likes the pemmican..." Harriet cocked her head, then added, "and wants me to have the candy."

I withdrew another piece of maple sugar candy and handed it to Harriet.

Daffodils peeked brave heads from a clear patch of dirt in front of the sled. Harriet picked a handful. "Maybe Nookomis Thimotee would like flowers."

"Especially if they are from you."

A doe ambled into the clearing and nibbled new growth where the snow had melted. "Be still," I said. Within moments a buck poked its antlered head from behind a stand of trees. A gentle breeze carried our scent in the deer's direction, and they bounded away. In spite of my warning, Harriet squealed and threw herself onto her back in a patch of snow. An owl's *coo-coo-coo-hoo* responded from where it had been awakened in a nearby spruce.

We headed back to camp. We passed Francois and another man, each wearing a *gauje*, or yoke, on his shoulders, a bucket suspended on each side.

"What's in their buckets?" Harriet asked.

"Sap," I said.

"How do they get the sap out of the tree?"

"Let me show you." I led her to a tapped sugar maple. "This is a *gouttiere*, a spout made from the basswood I told you about yesterday. It goes in the drilled spot. The bucket hangs from it." I took her hands and put one on each side of the vessel. I gave it a gentle swish and she peered inside. "The bucket is made of birch bark, but the basswood tying cord, we call it bast, seams the sides before it's gummed over with pine pitch."

"What is pine pitch?" Harriet asked.

"Pitch is the liquid pine trees make when one of their limbs is broken. Indians gather that liquid and heat it to make a sticky substance." I waited to see if she would demand more detail. I did not remember either of my children asking so many questions.

Instead, she removed a glove, dipped a finger into the maple sap and lifted it to her tongue. "It doesn't taste as good as the candy."

"No. Collecting the sap is just the first step. It must boil for more than a day in the large copper kettles you saw inside last night. It is a delicate business. The men who help Francois make sure it never burns. If it starts to boil too hard, they tap a hemlock branch on the surface to stop it. The fire must stay hot, day and night. Maybe when you are bigger you can help tend the sap."

"Next year? I'll be almost six."

I took her hand. "Maybe." I pulled the sled behind us as we walked to the camp. "There is a story about sap—"

"Tell me."

"A long time ago," I began, "a young Odawa boy saw his bushy-tailed squirrel brother climb a tree, bite off a small limb, and lick the watery substance where it broke. The boy thought that was pretty interesting. Maybe the squirrel knew a secret. So the boy twisted off a branch and tried it himself. The taste was a little sweet, and he liked it. From that day on, when he walked through the forest, he snapped himself a twig and sucked on it. That is how we discovered the sap we use to make maple syrup and sugar. The boy told others in his tribe, and some smart men figured out how to collect great amounts of sap and boil it to get maple syrup and sugar."

"That's a good story, but it's too short."

"It's all you get today." I studied the sky. The temperature had dropped in the past few minutes. Clear blue patches gave way to ragged black clouds bashing each other for position. Crows huddled wing to wing along the low branches of an elm, their silence as telling as the clouds.

Chebbeniathon, I thought, let it be a false omen. Prickled by the guilt of Father Richard's warning about idolatry and invoking help from Odawa spirits, I apologized to the Catholic God and asked him to keep us safe.

I left the sled close to the building and took Harriet inside. She marched over to the heavy pots hanging above the fire. "How does the maple syrup turn into candy?"

I brought my thoughts back from the gathering clouds. "When the sap has boiled long enough, Francois and the others put it in oak barrels and store it. They will continue hauling in buckets of sap and making syrup until the trees stop giving it to them. During all of that time the fire must be kept roaring."

"Why do the trees stop?"

"It is Mother Earth's way. She decides when it starts and when we have enough. Since it is her gift to us, that seems fair, would you not agree?"

"Maybe." She stepped closer to the fire, and I held out a hand to stop her. "But how do we get the candy?"

"After the sap has turned into syrup, the fire is allowed to die down to a smaller flame. Then the syrup is boiled again until it is thick and gooey and sticky."

"That's candy?" She edged a few inches closer, and I again pulled her back.

"Not quite." I said. "If we stayed long enough to watch, you would see Francois take the heavier syrup and pour it into basswood boards with carved hollows shaped like bears, rabbits, turtles, otters, or squares. He puts those molds into a snow bank, and the thick sugary syrup hardens into candy."

"That's my favorite part…the candy like Angelique makes me."

"Yes, we keep plenty of syrup at the house. Otherwise, how would we satisfy your insatiable sweet tooth?"

I grinned anticipating her next questions: What does insatiable mean? And, what is a sweet tooth?

As the others slept, I watched snow spill through the roof opening into the fire, where it sizzled like the water on our crepe pans. I crawled out of my bedroll, donned moccasins and a fur-lined capote. I opened the door and was met by knee-high snowdrifts when I stepped outside.

The chill of afternoon had turned nasty and aggressive in the evening. It mocked me as I pulled the drawstring in my hood. Biting wind found chinks in my fur armor and jabbed icy daggers at my vulnerable cheeks. I coughed as frigid air gripped my lungs.

At the narrow end of the lodge, I placed a foot on a low spruce bough, put my weight on it, and broke off a sturdy, needled branch. I trudged tight against the building, reached as far as my height allowed, and with my makeshift broom began sweeping snow from the edges of the roof.

I heard a noise behind me, maybe the distance of a rod. I inched behind a nearby tree. The moonless night and heavy blowing snow obscured my vision. If I could not see, neither could the prowler. Whoever was out there made no attempt at stealth.

I grasped my broken branch, and pointed the ragged edge like a dagger. A dark figure lumbered close enough for me to make out size, but not a face. My heart pounded. I drew a slow breath, curious, but a bit unnerved. Caution served me, but not panic. Surprise gave me an advantage. I positioned my body, prepared to lunge.

"Is there someone out here?"

I recognized the voice, stepped from behind the tree's cover, and stood within arm's length of Francois. "I could have killed you," I said.

"Why were you hiding behind a tree in the thick of a snowstorm?"

"I was not hiding, but it is prudent to see who sneaks up on you in the middle of the night." I refused to admit I had been thinking about his warning of misfits on the far side of the island. "Your excuse for lurking about?"

"What do you mean, lurking? I heard a ruckus outside the men's sleeping quarters and figured I should check its source." He looked at the branch that I still wielded like a sword.

I dropped the temporary weapon to my side. "I was afraid that too much snow would cave the roof."

"*Oui*. Reasonable worry. There's a ladder in the pantry. That's the only way we can get to it." He disappeared into a cloud of white and returned a few minutes later with a shovel and a six-foot ladder that he propped against the building.

"You get on inside." He began climbing.

"I can help."

"I don't know what help you can be. The roof isn't solid enough to bear our weight and only one of us can stand on the ladder at a time. He pushed snow from the roof, and it avalanched to the ground. "Listen to me, you belong…" Before he finished the sentence he slipped and plummeted to the ground. Snow cushioned his fall, but his right foot twisted under him.

I hurried to him. "Are you hurt?" I reached for his elbow to help him up.

His howl answered my question. "It's my ankle."

"Lean on me. We will get you inside." I opened the door and directed him to sit. By firelight I saw the ankle had doubled its size. "Looks like a serious sprain. We can ice it in snow to lessen the swelling and then wrap it in strips of cotton, but I doubt it will hold your weight for a few days. Tomorrow I will fashion a crutch from a sturdy tree limb. For now, we will hobble you over to the men's quarters so you can get some rest."

I closed the door to the men's sleeping area and returned to my own bedroll. Before cocooning it around me, I covered Harriet with an extra fur blanket. I wondered how long this snow would trap us in the camp and how long our provisions would last.

Memories of childhood hunger troubled my sleep. I dreamed I had squirreled away food from the community storage sheds and hid it in my bedroll to parse out to my sisters when their bellies growled.

By morning, white drifts blocked our exit from the longhouse. The sun cooperated, the temperature climbed, and the snow began to melt. Daylight exposed my nightmares for the folly they were.

When Harriet awoke, I opened the door, scooped a bowl of fresh snow, brought it inside, drizzled it with maple syrup, and handed to her.[32] She insisted it was the best breakfast she ever tasted.

The rest of the day, the women played whist to pass long hours inside. We had not planned to return to Mackinac for two more days, so the storm did not hinder our frolic.

Harriet protested when I announced it was time to pack and return to Mackinac. "I want to see Francois make the candy."

"He will bring plenty back to Mackinac—a mocock with eighty pounds of sugar delivered to our door."

"No. I want to see him make it."

"We need to leave, Little One. The weather is unpredictable this year. First the late-season storm, and now temperatures warm enough we have no need of our gloves and coats. Soon the water will break through the ice, and it will no longer support the sled."

"Will Francois take us home?"

"Yes, but he will return to camp afterwards. Until the tree leaves unfold, he will collect sap and make syrup."

"And then candy?"

"Yes...and make candy."

"After the ice melts, how does he get to Mackinac?"

"By canoe. He will wait until the ice clears away."

"Why can't we do that?"

"We have work calling us back to Mackinac. We cannot stay away that long."

"I could come back to camp with Francois."

I shot Harriet a scowl that closed the argument. "Get your things."

I walked alongside the dogs and insisted Francois ride in the sleigh. "Better to let your ankle heal than overuse it."

The frozen path across the lake was solid until we got near shore. About five rods from the beach, water seeped through the ice. The dogs balked when the frigid water covered their feet. I heard a large cracking noise and smaller creaking sounds that signaled the ice giving way.

Francois eased himself out of the sleigh. "It can't handle the extra weight." He leaned on the crutch I had made for him. With a switch in his free hand, he urged the dogs forward.

I looked at the bay. This far from shore, water was ten feet deep. Getting caught under an ice floe was a death sentence. I crossed myself, mouthed silent words. "God who watches over his children, see our peril, guide our way."

Each step closer to Mackinac decreased our risk. It was a warm day so I was not burdened with my heavy capote.

I saw activity on shore. If we went under, I hoped someone might see and try to rescue us. Sweat broke out on my forehead. I had promised Benjamin I would take good care of his daughter and keep her safe.

My mind calculated my intended actions if the ice gave way. I needed to keep my wits about me. I would grab Harriet. The child could swim, but she would panic in the numbing water. Cold would limit the time I had to save us. I would look for light, a place already open or a spot to break through.

I was so worried about how to escape death that I stumbled when the shore reached up and told me I was home.

19th Century Canadian Cariole
Courtesy of Wikimedia Commons/Creative Commons

Native American Sugar Camp
From a watercolor by Seth Eastman 1853 Public Domain
This would have been more like the sugar camp of Magdelaine's mother. By Magdelaine's trip described in this chapter, their dwelling was a longhouse as written about by Elizabeth Therese Baird (Betsy) in her *Reminiscences*.

15.
Beaumont, Heartbreak, and Tanner Returns

"Today we are again evaluating the changing winds. May we be strong in spirit and equal to our Fathers of another day in reading the signs accurately and interpreting them wisely. May the Great Spirit look down upon us, guide us, inspire us, and give us courage and wisdom. Above all, may He look down on us and be pleased." **Red Jacket, Seneca**

June 1822

The explosion of the shotgun blast shattered the morning quiet. I dropped the wheel of cheese I had been about to purchase to the counter and dashed next door to the fur company headquarters, from where the thunderous bang had come.

Voyageur Alexis St. Martin lay crumpled on the floor. "Oh, Mother of God…Mother of God…Mother of God." His words withered into whispers. His eyes bugged wide.

Blood pooled around the dying man. Rivulets gushed down the warped planking toward the door. Samuel Abbott bent over St. Martin and attempted to stanch the flow with a blanket he had grabbed from a merchandise shelf.

"Fetch Dr. Beaumont." The trader to whom Abbott barked the order was gone before the words died behind him. Abbott turned his take-charge attitude to me. "Get me a pile of those pelts for under his head."

I handed over the furs. The stubborn set of Abbott's jaw gave away nothing. I resisted the urge to ask how the shooting had happened.

St. Martin's screams had dwindled to moans. "God it hurts." He repeated the words over and over and over, a refrain to ease his agony.

"You're Catholic, same as him," Abbott said. "Say a few words to give him comfort." It was another command, not a request.

By rote, I crossed myself. If Abbott thought it necessary, I was not going to argue. "Father God, please be with this poor man during his suffering and grant him life everlasting." Without advance notice it was the best I could offer. I doubted it made much difference to the stricken fellow.

St. Martin's eyes were unfocused by the time William Beaumont dashed to his side. The doctor knelt next to the wounded man and, less polite than I, demanded details. "What the hell happened?"

"He was checkin' a shotgun, wantin' to know if it was well made," Abbott said. He pointed to the trader who had summoned Beaumont. "This fella was trying to show him, and the confound thing went off. Poor sot was but two or three feet distant. Took the full discharge of powder and duck shot[33] in his left side. His clothes and flesh around the wound were burned crisp."

Beaumont removed the blanket. "Get me some wet cloths."

Abbott disappeared into the backroom and returned with clean rags, over which he poured a ladle of drinking water from the barrel in the corner. The last time I had seen him ladle water, he had given me a drink while I concocted lies to save Wampeme.

The doctor mumbled, but I made out, "I ain't never seen a stomach in that position. Helluva way to lose your breakfast." The sight of tangled innards and the smell they gave off—an odor that overpowered the normal rank smell of fur bales—put my own morning meal in jeopardy.

St. Martin had lost consciousness. Beaumont wiped away a top layer of blood, tissue, and partially digested food, then turned his face to his hushed audience. "There's no way this man can survive."

Beaumont eased four fingers beneath a piece of exposed lung the size of a teacup. He talked to himself as he probed. "The sixth rib is blown apart. I can't tuck things back without gettin' rid of that jagged edge."

Top teeth biting his lower lip, the doctor worked, all the while shaking his head. He clutched the base of the mangled rib with his left hand, and using a knife he extracted from his medical bag, sawed and sliced the rib back to its base. The cutting sounded like scraping fingernails over a chalkboard. Witnesses circling the spectacle looked on in fascinated horror.

When he finished, Dr. Beaumont said, "I'd guess he's got about another ten minutes before he meets his maker."

Abbott moved away from St. Martin toward where I stood next to a fur-counting table. "You best be going. There's nothing to be gained by you stayin' here watching this."

He was right, but I did not need him to tell me. Samuel Abbott was a strange one. I had seen a grimace like his before. I would have sworn it was the same as the ones Charlotte and Therese aimed at me when I misbehaved. Abbott lowered and tilted his head and matched it to a stern-set mouth, slightly lower on one side than on the other. That expression always told me my sisters were serious. They had had a right to throw me those lop-sided frowns. Samuel Abbott did not.

A week later, I strode toward a shop on Market Street and chanced upon Samuel Abbott walking from the fort. He hailed my attention.

"You might want to know St. Martin is still alive. Lucky for him he is a hearty, robust character, not yet reached his prime. A mere nineteen, he is."

On Mackinac Island news traveled as fast as a spark from a campfire in a dry July forest. I wondered why Abbott troubled himself to share widely known information. My dealings with the chief clerk convinced me he was honest and hardworking. I believed him to have a gentle heart. I had seen him play stickball with Indian children and offer counsel to their fathers. Nothing I knew of the man, however, explained his interest in me. He was never unseemly, but addressed me with more familiarity than I thought appropriate. A simple 'good morning' when we passed would have been more to my liking.

"Dr. Beaumont places poultices of flour, hot water, charcoal, and yeast on the wound. Changes it twice a day or more, and St. Martin is responding. It's a miracle."

"You consider it a mercy that he survives?" I had not meant to speak my doubt aloud—had not meant in any way to encourage conversation.

"Everything that happens is on account of God's hand. Isn't that what you Catholics preach?"

I looked toward the harbor, considered how to end our discourse. "I will continue my prayers for him." I wanted to neither argue religion nor discuss the intimacies of St. Martin with Samuel Abbott. I bade him a good day and picked up my errand where it had been interrupted.

Alexis St. Martin
Public Domain

Portrait of Dr. William Beaumont by artist Tom Jones
Public Domain

In the parlor Agatha Biddle and I partnered against Elizabeth Mitchell and Therese in a game of whist. *At least the card gods favor me.* My mild blasphemy amused me as I pulled in another trick.

A knock at the door halted the pleasantries. I rose to answer it.

Postmaster Stewart[34] smiled when I greeted him. He held out a letter to me. "This one looks worthy of personal delivery." I knew he enjoyed delivering mail. It often got him invited in for a glass of water, a short rest, and the latest gossip. Today I extended no invitation.

"Might be important," Stewart said. "It comes postage prepaid from your son-in-law."

I thanked the postmaster and returned to my guests. I resumed my chair at the table, but could not concentrate on the game. "Perhaps Benjamin is coming for a visit." I fingered the envelope. Harriet would be overjoyed to see her father. Truth be told, I wished my son, Joseph, took career signals from my son-in-law. No matter the money I had spent on Joseph's Montreal education, and no matter my words of counsel, he was determined to follow his grandpapa, papa, and me into the fur trade. I preferred that, like Benjamin, Joseph aspired to loftier pursuits.

I opened the envelope and eased out a single sheet of paper. Familiar handwriting covered a quarter page. None of the four of us playing cards could read. I called Marianne, who sat at my kitchen table making notes for the lessons she taught. I handed her the letter. "What does he say?"

Marianne's eyes tracked down the lines of tight, neat script. Her left hand reached up to cover her mouth, a gesture that did not silence her gasp.

My anticipated joy vanished. I steeled myself for whatever caused the blood to drain from my niece's cheeks.

Marianne avoided my eyes. "He is coming to Mackinac and estimates his arrival as the twenty ninth day of June, the day after tomorrow. He will stay but two days. Then he has booked passage on a steamer as far as Detroit. From there he will travel to New Hampshire before he returns to his military duties in Florida." Marianne stopped, swallowed.

I had heard only good news. "Go on."

"He will take Harriet with him on his return trip. He will entrust her care to his sister, Elizabeth McNeil. He believes his daughter will get a superior education and be taught the proper ways of a young lady. He asks you to have her things packed."

The next afternoon, I took Harriet by the hand, and we walked toward the village. Along the way we detoured to the shore. I sat on a large rock and stared out over the rippling waves, wondering where to begin. I handed her a piece of candy shaped like an otter. "Water is the source of all life."

She bit off the otter's head.

I looked at the headless candy. "The otter loves water. Maybe that is why our clan chose him as our totem."[35]

Harriet kicked off her moccasins and sat on a chunk of shale a few feet from me. She picked up a handful of pebbles and eyed them as they lay in her palm. "What is a totem?"

"A totem is the animal chosen to represent us. It is how we know who is family, our nearest relatives."

"Did you choose the otter?"

"Oh, no. It was chosen long before I was born."

One at a time, Harriet tossed the pebbles to see how far she could make them fly. "Before the Odawa came to the place where rice grew on water?"

"Maybe that long ago. It is good you remember our story. Hold it here." I touched my heart with both of my hands, one over the other. "The otter knows how important family is and puts it first, but he is also industrious and can be playful. All of those things are part of you…they are a good way to live your life."

An afternoon was short time to share history or philosophy. And pressing matters robbed me of even those hours. "Your papa is coming to Mackinac Island. He may arrive as early as tomorrow."

The child let out a squeal. "I've missed him so much. I will give him a hundred kisses."

I harnessed my emotions into submission. "He will take you on a great adventure. You will meet your Aunt McNeil and new cousins."

Harriet narrowed her eyes. "Will you come with us?"

"Not this time. You will have your papa."

"If you don't come, I'm not going on the adventure."

"It is settled, and you must go." I forced myself to be firm.

She stood, backed farther from me, eyed a large stone, and picked it up. With as much force as I believed her capable, she hurled it in my direction. Her aim was not precise, and it landed a few inches from my feet. My throat constricted, my heartbeat quickened. I rose, stepped toward her, and drew her into an embrace.

"This is a special trip for you and your papa." Before the child offered more outbursts, I pointed toward the shops. "I got word that the dresses we ordered from the seamstress last month are ready for you."

She backed away from me, her temper calmed. "From the cloth you let me choose?"

"Yes, one red with ruffles, one white for church, and the blue-and-white frock that I agreed to purchase because you stood so still when your measurements were taken. You will have pretty new clothes for your trip." *Elizabeth McNeil will see how well I have taken care of you. She will never love you better than I.*

The walk to Market Street was quiet. Harriet tried on the dresses and then, as our purchases were wrapped, I saw a carved wooden otter on a rawhide string and added it to our order.

That night, as the sun took leave of the sky to make room for its sister moon, Harriet, who had only recently gotten used to spending the night in her own bed, asked if she could sleep with me. I assented. I lay with my granddaughter until she fell asleep. I fought the urge to remain there, holding her until morning. Instead I rose and went into her room and looked at all the dolls, doll furniture, games, and other toys with which we had indulged her. I gathered dresses, petticoats, shoes, and coats, and laid them on the child-sized bed before packing them into trunks. I finger-pressed each in turn, remembering where it had last been worn, seeing Harriet's face in each reflection.

Harriet's three trunks were loaded on the borrowed postal wagon before her father arrived that morning.

"Say goodbye to your grandmother, Harriet," Benjamin said.

"I'm staying here." The child threw her arms around my neck and tightened her legs around my waist.

"Enough." Benjamin's military growl did not budge his daughter. "Enough. Do you hear me?"

"I'm not going," Harriet said. "I live with Nookomis. I don't want to go stay with Aunt McNeil. You cannot make me."

Rage consumed Benjamin's face. I feared he might strike the hysterical girl. Instead, he stepped closer. "Mother La Framboise, please put her down."

I untwisted her arms from around my neck and unwrapped her legs from about my waist. She resisted my efforts and again clutched me. Harriet's face was red and swollen. She wiped her cheeks and nose on the shoulder of my tunic. Benjamin pried his daughter away from me and set her on the ground. The child slumped into a ball and refused to stand. "Please, Nookomis. Don't make me go." Her eyes asked if she could count on me to protect her or if I, like the God that she had been told took her maman, would betray her.

I swallowed hard and swooned, fearing I would faint dead away. "Sweet girl, you will come back to visit me." I locked eyes with her father. "She will come back…?"

Benjamin bared his teeth like a wolverine ready to battle a hungry wolf, but he capitulated. "Yes, Harriet. Behave yourself and in a few years you can come back and spend a summer on the island." He ended his promise with a threat. "Continue this nonsense, and sure as I am a captain in the U.S. Army, and you are my charge, you'll never set foot on this island again."

Harriet continued whimpering, but got to her feet and followed her papa. She broke once and ran back for a last hug. I kissed her soft curls and breathed in her sweet scent. I had almost forgotten the small leather pouch filled with maple sugar candy. I handed it to her. An otter was embroidered in beads on the bag. I wanted to tell her how much I loved her. Emotion choked me, and the words stuck in my throat.

Benjamin picked up his daughter. She stiffened like a corpse against his blue waistcoat as he quickened his pace and increased the distance between us. Harriet looked over his shoulder, toward where I stood as unmoving as the warrior turned into Sugar Loaf.

"Bad things come in threes." Angelique brushed stray hair that had come loose from her braid. She finished hanging the laundry and knelt to help me pull weeds from the squash vines weaving through hills of beans and climbing stalks of corn in our backyard garden.

"I put no stock in superstitions." I rose to half-standing and moved down the row. "Do you suggest we face another tragedy this week?"

"I hope not, Madame. Already Alexis St. Martin was shot, and Harriet is gone. That should be enough to appease the spirits if we've angered them."

I loved my companion, but wondered what gave her such notions. "Harriet plucked from our midst saddens me beyond measure, but I try to see it Benjamin's way." It was easy to voice the lie, less easy for me to squelch the unchristian wish that Harriet would be returned to me because Benjamin fell overboard and drowned before they reached Detroit. I surprised myself at the violence of my imagination.

"The other…St. Martin?" I picked up where I had left off weeding. "I barely knew him—by sight perhaps, but no better. He survives. Abbott says that quite pleases Dr. Beaumont."

"It was a tragedy you witnessed the lad's misfortune." Angelique grasped a stalk of wild mustard with hands that were a trail map of her life's labor. "No lady should witness such a grisly sight."

"The hot sun affects your observations this morning. I wish the voyageur a good recovery, but thoughts of him do not trouble my days." I twisted to relieve the kinks that crouching had visited upon my back. "You and I have seen nastier, more personal events interrupt our lives." I rubbed sweat from my forehead with the back of my hand.

Before we reached the end of the row we weeded, Angelique started up again. "Captain Pierce had no reason to take Harriet."

"He is her papa. He has every right. I am only her nookomis." I turned my head toward the house, away from my slave. I again imagined Benjamin meeting his death, this time by a shotgun blast that was not as charitable to him as it had been to St. Martin. I sent a silent prayer to any god whose sensibilities might be inclined to help me. Then, as many times before, Father Richard's words, *Act as though you believe until your heart follows*, stopped my unchristian plea. I offered instead: *I'm sorry, God, for my depravity, but maybe you could figure out a way to change Benjamin's heart and bring Harriet back to me?*

"It was not as Miss Josette wished."

I offered no response. It was futile to mount a continuing argument that went against my heart. It was not Josette, nor Harriet, nor me that Benjamin worried about pleasing. If he left his daughter on Mackinac Island, she would be brought up half-squaw. No matter what success I gained, nor what wealth I accumulated, that was how he saw me.

I patted dirt around the roots of the bean plant I had disrupted by a hard yank on the thistle that choked it. Benjamin was sixth generation American by his own bragging, English before that. He might hate English soldiers but he valued his pedigree. His family did not have the Frenchmen's acceptance of Indian ways. The Pierces nurtured political ambitions. I considered my earlier wishes that Joseph follow Benjamin's example. My mixed-blood, Métis son could never enter their world.

When Maman and I married, our husbands wanted partners. Indian and mixed-blood women brought contacts and trading skills to unions. Even now, on Mackinac Island, I might be called a half-breed or squaw or savage behind my back, but my wealth guaranteed politeness to my face. Still, I watched the fur trade winding down. It no longer promised my son and granddaughter acceptance. Indians were the backbone of the fur trade. They paid for its profits with their labor, their blood and their lives. The French, the English, and the Americans, each in their turn, grew wealthy from Indian efforts.

But, God, Harriet is all I have left of Josette. I sniffed and held dirty hands against my eyes to shade the sun and hide my tears.

I picked up a flat rock and skipped it over the waves. It touched the water, jumped up again and again. I turned and saw the tepees of the Indians' summer village. *Thank you God for not bringing Wampeme to Mackinac's shore this summer.* I flung another rock. This one plunged under the water with an angry splash. "When your faith wavers," Father Richard had said, "Talk to God as though he is your friend, Magdelaine, because he is."

I know I must resist the temptation of Wampeme's strong shoulders and hungry eyes. Wampeme has two wives, and lust for him threatens my salvation. But you have taken my husband, Maman, Josette, and Benjamin Langdon. You have denied me the comfort brought by Harriet. Your ways perplex me, but I continue to abide your teachings as best I can. Father Richard says you do not send us more pain or trials than we can bear.

I imagined the fifteen-year-old Wampeme who had taken my hand, who had taught me to skip stones, and who, before I left the village, had brought me a puppy to take with me to remind me of him. The dog died before Joseph and I reached Mackinac.

I saw the Wampeme who went off to join Tecumseh's fight against the Americans. He would never accept the Catholic God. I had tried many times to explain my faith. He reminded me I was Odawa, part of a proud people with their own gods. Gods who had taken care of us for thousands of years before the white-faced strangers came. It was a debate neither of us could win. Even without two wives, Wampeme imperiled my fragile convictions.

You could send me a man more acceptable to the church. I am a woman with a woman's needs. No Frenchman. I do not want another business relationship. No unconverted Indian. I agree with you on that one. I do not need a man who tries to seduce me down old paths. Besides, I do not want someone who expects me to give up my life here to return to the villages. I have become set in my new ways. You can skip the Englishmen and Americans. They look at a mixed-blood with contempt.

I flung a skipping stone with such force that it made thirteen skips, close to my record of seventeen. *I guess you could say, God, that I have created quite a quandary for you if you set about answering this prayer.* I hoped that God not only did not mind me talking directly to him, but that he appreciated irony and had a sense of humor.

A canoe entered the harbor, and I made out one large figure, three smaller shapes. *Fine, God, we will continue this conversation later. I may not understand your ways, but I will keep trying. If you could figure out a means to get Harriet back to me, it might be easier for me to think kind thoughts of Benjamin.*

I studied the man in the canoe. As he paddled closer I recognized John Tanner. I turned and retraced my steps home. It was not a morning to tangle with the white Indian.

Another day passed before Tanner opened my front door and let himself in. Still no manners, I thought, as he walked down the hall toward me in the kitchen.

"May I have a word?" he asked.

"Seems I have no choice in the matter. Sit." I pointed to a chair. My hospitality did not include a smile. "Tea?"

"Rum would suit me better, but I don't s'pose there's much chance you'll offer any." He folded his huge hands on the table in front of him. "Tea will suffice."

I poured him a cup, took a seat across from him. "Many moons have passed since you last traveled this way. I hope your reunion with family in Kentucky went well."

"Family..." He let the word hang for a few seconds. His eyes took stock of me in a way that made me fidget.

I did nothing to fill the silence.

"Mine's in shambles," he said.

I resisted the urge to go one-on-one with him in a spitting contest of whose family heartaches deserved the prize.

"I hold you to account for that."

I shot him the look that Samuel Abbott and my sisters had perfected. Cocked my head, clenched my teeth, and scowled.

If he noticed, he ignored it. "I've come to ask you, plead with you if need be, to counsel Miskwabunokwa. Tell her it's God's will that she come with me. I leave tomorrow for Sault Ste. Marie. I'll build a house there, take care of my family. Their place is with me."

I heard controlled anger in his voice. To avoid the accusation in his eyes, I studied my fingers, the nails rough and broken from yesterday's gardening. "I cannot do that."

When I looked up again, I saw a surge of red had streamed up his neck. His hands clenched into tight fists.

"She is my wife."

"Then comply with God's command. Marry Miskwabunokwa in his church." *I hope that is your will, God. I hope it is the path you demand of this man.* I had voiced the advice so often that I could not backtrack even in the face of my own uncertainty. To do so seemed disloyal, not only to God, but to Therese.

"It makes a mockery of our life together. We are already married."

"Her eternal soul is worth more than the life you offer. Miskwabunokwa is now a devout Christian."

"Thanks be to your meddling…and your busybody sister…and that damned priest." He stood and paced away from me to the kitchen door that led to the side garden. There he stopped. Rather than leave, he turned and shuffled back to where I sat. He leaned over the table, close enough to send chills down my spine.

"I leave tomorrow, with or without my family. If Miskwabunokwa stays here, I'll be forced to abandon my children. James and John prospered poorly in Kentucky. They spoke little English. It is not easy for an Indian in a white man's world. They came this far with me rather than stay with their uncle, but I cannot watch after two boys and also do the things a man must do."

He stood tall, then backed away from me as though I had the pox. "I refuse to leave them in the care of their mother if she won't obey me. That leaves me an option only slightly less distasteful. I can place them in the school run by your brother-in-law."

"What of the girls? What of Martha and Lucy?"

"Your sister claims Lucy. You and your sister can fight over Martha. She is lost to me."

God, help me fashion a response to this man. I paused for several seconds. "You are a stubborn man, John Tanner. You turn your back on the true God. You have no one to blame for your misfortune but yourself."

He again approached me, this time with his powerful fist drawn back.

I lowered my head, ready to receive the blow. A blow to be suffered for God's honor. Or for my own hypocrisy. Maybe it would placate my unsettled conscience.

Tanner's hand smashed the table with such force that the cup and saucer from which he had been drinking bounced to the edge and crashed to the floor, sending shards in every direction. "I knew not to expect your help. You bear the fault. You cannot lay blame at the feet of your god, even if it is a vengeful, spiteful god for whom you have traded the gods of your people."

16.
The Winds of Change

"I cannot think that we are useless or God would not have created us. There is one God looking down on us all. We are all the children of one God. The sun, the darkness, the winds are all listening to what we have to say."
Geronimo, Apache

Spring 1823-Summer 1824

Rix Robinson arrived on the island for rendezvous when the ice cleared from the lake. I opened my front door to his loud knock and saw his lanky frame standing before me.

"I've come to settle accounts." He doffed his hat and followed me into the parlor. "Unless, that is, you want to resume trading."

"No. Love of the fur trade is scarce present in my blood these days." I gestured to the couch and took the chair opposite him.

He withdrew a sheet of paper from his trouser pocket. "This is the statement of our dealings as recorded by Samuel Abbott in the ledger book." He unfolded the invoice and read aloud, *"Mrs. La Framboise, Sundry merchandise, from her inventory of Grand River Outfit, 1821, and delivered to her during the summer of 1822, for ac. Of Rix Robinson, Michilimackinac, August 28, 1822."*[36]

When he finished, he passed the slip to me. "I took charge of the goods as you left word I should."

"I am grateful you were able to take my merchandise and allow me to remain here on the island with my granddaughter."

He shifted enough to extract a buckskin pouch heavy with coins from a coat pocket. He extended the payment toward me. "This should square our business."

I hefted the bag, not to weigh its contents, but to consider its import. "The note evidences the last entry bearing my name that Samuel Abbott will ever make in his ledger. And the shillings in this bag—" I held it in my hands, fondled it, "—the last money I will earn from the fur trade."

"Does that cause you sadness?" He met my eyes and then dropped his glance.

"Melancholy perhaps, but not sadness." I placed the money and note on the side table. "No. I should have done it sooner."

"I'm sorry for the circumstances. I believe Miss Josette's death caused your change of heart."

I closed my eyes, trying to see Josette's face. Every day my memory of it lost another fragment of clarity.

I aimed the conversation in a more comfortable direction. "What of Peemissaquotoquay? Why have you not brought her with you? You must both join me for dinner."

"Maybe soon, but she has invited her sister to our cabin this evening." Another slip of paper lay like a mystery on his lap. I had not seen where it came from. "I have a separate matter to discuss with you before I take my leave."

"We have further business?"

"It is not business between you and me." He picked up the document. "Two months prior to my return to Mackinac, I was given this transfer of property by the Odawa chiefs along the Grand River near your post. They asked that I pass it on to you." He did not make me ask him to read it, but began:

> *"Know all whome these may concern by these payments that whereas we the undersigned chiefs of the Indian Tribes of Grand River are connected by Blood related with Madelon La Framboise of Michilimackinac. And whereas also we are desirous of doing good unto her and her descendants or offspring to wit Joseph La Framboise and her lawful Son, Benjamin Langdon Pierce Grand Son & Josette Harriet Pierce Grand Daughter of the said Madelon La Framboise."*[37]

"The language is so formal." I shook my head, unable to make an intelligent response. "Can you summarize the gist?"

"The document is signed by ten Odawa chiefs and gives you a choice piece of property."

Years earlier, all of the land belonged to me and to every other Indian. Now I counted small parcels here and there as my own. No man or woman had the right to come upon my land without my express invitation.

Robinson interrupted my thoughts. "I can tell you the land is beautiful, I've walked it myself. I believe you are friends with the one they call Wampeme. He delivered the document to me."

My chest tightened in that way that defies control. "And how is Wampeme?"

"He does well and asks about you. This past year, however, the elder of his two wives took sick. Nothing could be done to save her from the consumption."

Robinson stayed only a short while after delivering that news. I remembered nothing of what was said in those final moments. My heart was with Wampeme.

Rix Robinson
Public Domain

A week after my meeting with Rix, Therese and I were summoned to the American Fur Company headquarters by Samuel Abbott, who sent a young boy to deliver the message.

"What do you suppose is Abbott's reason?" I asked my sister.

"The Great White Father Monroe has issued new rules for American fur traders." She picked up her step to keep abreast of my brisk stride.

"How does that affect me? I left the business."

"Maybe Abbott casts a wide net. He has no guarantee you won't take up the work again. Your merchandise remained on his books even though you instructed it be delivered to Robinson."

We reached the corner of Fort and Market streets and entered the headquarters where months earlier Alex St. Martin had been shot. Traders stood shoulder to shoulder, some puffing pipes that filled the air with blue-white smoke and a tobacco scent not altogether unpleasant.

Therese and I were the only women present. The buzz of unanswered questions stoked conversations around the room.

After several minutes, Abbott grabbed a short stool and stepped up. His eyes, though bright as the harbor on a sunny day, gave away nothing. "Good morning, friends." His voice carried no congeniality to match his words. "Robert Stuart, the American Fur Company's agent here on Mackinac Island, cannot be present this evening and asked me to address you in his stead."

I watched men shuffle from foot to foot to quiet their nerves. Abbott withdrew a folded paper from his waistcoat and cleared his throat. Before saying more, he let his eyes inspect the crowd. He seemed to make mental note of every man standing there. He did not hurry his words. I believe he wanted a sense of solemnity for what he was about to share.

Finally he spoke. "I am charged with bringing to each trader who applies for a license an edict from the government of these United States. It was signed November last, but I waited to call this meeting until rendezvous when you would all be assembled on this island. Since most of you cannot read, it is important that you pay close heed. My assistant will record the name of every man present, and you will be accountable to conform your actions to the law. Violations will be cause to revoke your trade license."

He unfolded the document, moved his fingers down the lines written there.

I whispered to Therese. "Every new government makes rules to hamper the trade and yield them more profit. Tonight we see the latest that the Americans have dreamed up."

She had no time to respond before Abbott continued. "The rules are meant to make the fur trade safer and fairer."

At least for John Jacob Astor, I thought.

He commenced reading:

"Your trade will be confined to the place to which you are licensed.

"Your transactions with the Indians will be confined to fair and friendly trade.

"You will attend no Councils held by the Indians, nor send them any talk or speech, accompanied by wampum.

"You are forbidden to take any spirituous liquors of any kind into the Indian country, or to give, sell or dispose of any to the Indians.

"Should any person attempt to trade in the Indian country without a license; or should any licensed traders carry any spirituous liquors into the Indian country; or give, sell or dispose of any to the Indians, the Indians are authorized to seize and take to their own use the goods of such traders; and the owner shall have no claim on the Indians or the United States for the same.

"Should you learn that there is any person in the Indian country, trading without a license, you will immediately report the name of such person and the place where he is trading, to some Indian agent.

"The substance of the 5th regulation you will communicate to the Indians.

"You will take all proper occasions to inculcate upon the Indians the necessity of peace; and to state to them that it is the wish of the Great

Father, the President, to live in harmony with them; and that they must shut their ears to any wild stories there may be in circulation.

"Given under my hand, at the city of Detroit this 15*th* day of November, 1822.

William Woodbridge, Secretary, And at the present vested with the powers of Superintendent of Indian Affairs therein."[58]

Abbott finished, refolded the paper into quarters. His fingers toyed with it for a few moments before he returned it to his pocket. "The government has given Indians the right to issue a complaint against any trader they believe violates these rules."

I wanted to whisper to Therese that if I were not a Christian woman with an aversion to all but friendly wagers, I would bet that the Indians' right to file complaints extended only to competitors of Astor. I remained quiet rather than risk being overheard.

"Further," Abbott said, "the government will protect no unlicensed trader, either in his person or his property, and will protect licensed traders only if they are in compliance with all of the rules."

It had the stamp of the American Fur Company all over it. I was glad to be done with the business. My son would navigate a world different from the one I had known.

"Are there questions or any part of Secretary Woodbridge's order that you want repeated?" Abbott asked.

The answer was silence.

On a hot July morning, I walked west of Mackinac Village toward Devil's Kitchen[39] where wild raspberry bushes grew. I had considered asking Therese to join me—twice as many berries and conversation, punctuated by any scolding she felt compelled to direct my way—but it was a morning I craved solitude.

Therese's love nourished me as surely as the corn and whitefish I ate. When we were young girls, traveling our yearly course between St. Joseph, Gabagouache, L'Arbre Croche, and Mackinac, my older sister watched out for me. It was no surprise that she worried as assiduously for my afterlife. I raised questions of faith and her face crumpled with misgiving. She could not bear the possibility I would stray from the one true Catholic religion. What would heaven be if we were not united in its everlasting glory, there to keep each other company for eternity? She prodded and lectured and encouraged me, to ensure I remained in that heavenly fold.

My way to God could not be carved by another. No matter how profound my love for Therese—and I did not delude myself, without Josette and Harriet, she was my rock. For me, the way to true faith was a companionless course. From failed attempts to convert her husband, I knew she understood.

Quiet suited me better that morning than Therese's judgment. I chose a spot where tall jack pines blocked telltale traces of the island's other occupants. I thought it a good place to talk to God. I had grown accustomed to heeding Father Richard's advice. I acted in accordance with the rituals of the Catholic faith so that my heart had every chance to return ever more firmly to its flock. Thrice daily I knelt with the ringing of the Angelus bells. In the morning, when I rose, I offered prayers of thanks for another day. Before meals I offered prayers of thanksgiving for the bounty I was about to receive. Before retiring at night, I offered prayers of gratitude for the day's blessings. In between, I talked to God whenever it seemed right.

I looped the basswood cord through the buckskin handle of my berry-gathering basket and tied the container around my waist.

Father God, you see the struggle that wages in my heart. I hope you are not as offended by it as my pious sister. Help me set my beliefs on the true path. Rid me of my confusion. Rid me of my doubt. I believe in a power greater than man. I am troubled sometimes, trying to understand what you expect of your earthly children. Are there limits on what you can do for them? What happens to those I love who continue to embrace the old ways? Will they suffer hell? I look about me and see your presence in every bush, every animal, every human. My heart reminds me that the Odawa believe God is present in each tree, each blade of grass, each rock along our shore. I then have to believe you are in me as surely as you are in rocks and grass. Is Odawa thinking so different than the Catholic way? Since Josette's death, these were questions I had repeatedly asked God. I still fumbled for answers.

My thoughts pulled me in so deeply that John Tanner crept within a rod before I noticed him. Even then, it was not a footfall or rustle, but the smell of his sweat and unwashed animal skins wafting on the breeze that alerted me to his presence. I had not been aware he had returned to our island, so his appearance was a double surprise. He hunkered in the shade of a maple, dangling a piece of sweetgrass from his mouth. *He reads my thoughts. He declares me a hypocrite.* I nodded a slight greeting. My veins pumped a rush of blood. Fear tingled from one of my nerves to the next, but I allowed no outward sign of faintheartedness.

He offered no return nod and said nothing. He withdrew a hunting knife from the band of his European-style trousers. Clothes could not take the backwoods out of him. Using the sharp point, he trimmed calluses from his palms, never releasing me from his stare.

You scoundrel. You swore you would depart Mackinac Island and leave Miskwabunokwa to search for God without your interference. I understand her confusion. You have forced yourself into that little shack of hers. All her clear thinking is replaced with your pigheaded ways.

I rubbed scratches on my hands, and then shoved my forearms back through the prickles to another cluster of tiny fruit. *I will not run like a spooked rabbit.* I looked directly at him, popped a perfect ripe berry into my mouth, and dropped the remainder into my basket.

When the bush had no more fruit to offer, I stepped to another shrub on the far side of the clearing, away from Tanner. He made no move to close the distance between us. *I am not your enemy, John Tanner. If Miskwabunokwa invites you back into her bed, that is her choice. My sister counsels her to obey the Catholic God, but for now I take no position other than she is allowed to find her truth without your intimidating her.*

I had no intention to turn toward home until I completed my task. With one eye on my fruit and the other on him, I picked with greater speed. *I am sorry you were yanked from your parents' homestead those long years ago. Finding your path cannot be easy, lost between two worlds as you are. I know a thing or two about that dilemma.*

Berries mounded in my basket and a last handful toppled down and landed in the sandy soil at my feet. Tanner stood between me and home. I untied the basket and gripped the handle. I took measured breaths. With long, purposeful strides, I passed within his arms' reach, close enough to show him I did not tremble at his nearness, distant enough to deny him an easy grip should he choose to grab me. I would have been surprised by the latter. His purpose was to unnerve me, not harm me. That would be no sport.

Devil's Kitchen
Photo Courtesy of Bob Royce

"You have plans this afternoon?" Angelique climbed the stairs to my bedchamber carrying a bucket of water for my washbasin. "I had hoped that today you'd offer me direction about mending your winter clothing." She watched as I leaned over and splashed my face. "I guess that waits for another time?"

"I am meeting Reverend Ferry."[40]

"Why, pray tell, would you be meeting with the Presbyterian preacher?"

"I am not quite sure." I picked up a towel and dried my face. "But he has requested a meeting."

"The mention of his name adds color to your cheeks."

"While speaking of him causes your face to twitch with disapproval." I stepped close and reached for her hand. "He preached his first service last Sunday."

"You think that's cause to celebrate?" She moved her hand away and crossed her arms.

"I do. We need a man of God on this island. I would prefer a Catholic priest, but a Presbyterian prays to the same God. He will suffice."

"You had best never repeat such blasphemy in front of Father Richard." She shook her head. I had not heard the last of her opinions on the matter.

"I believe the good father would agree. Until he can send us a priest to minister at Ste. Anne's, I welcome a religious influence, whatever the denomination. Father Richard himself preached to a Protestant congregation."

I heard footsteps on the stairway. Therese entered the room and added her opinion to what she had overheard of our conversation. "I suppose Ferry's presence could curb the rowdiness and debauchery we suffer during rendezvous."

Angelique dropped her arms to her side and her frown softened. "Pray assure me neither of you plan to attend his services?" It was a question to which she expected no answer since she had turned to leave the room.

Therese hoisted her ample body to the bed. I settled next to her and let loose a hearty laugh. "No," I sent my response trailing after Angelique, "but we can hope a rival faith on the island sparks the archdiocese in Detroit to fight for souls here."

"Nice daydream," Therese said. "I give Ferry six months before he hightails it back to Massachusetts, like those who came before him." She waved her hand dismissively. "Mackinac Islanders have too little time in the summer for preachers, and the reverend will find too few souls in the season of ice and snow for Protestants to deem staying here worthwhile. Only Catholics come to rendezvous and hope for a taste of the Holy Spirit between frolics."

"I will make you a friendly wager." I shot Therese a wink. "If you think God allows a harmless bet between sisters."

She nodded.

"Let us say my silver tea pot for your four silver tumblers. They claim this Ferry fellow is filled with fire. My silver says he stays."

"I accept your bet, if you promise no hard feelings when you lose."

I stood, pulled off my tunic, and eased a fresh one over my head. I met her eyes as soon as my face popped through.

"I've heard you are having Martha teach you to read." She effortlessly changed the subject to another matter of contention.

"You make it sound like an accusation. She is nine years old and loves her studies." I sat down beside my sister again. "Would you like to join us?"

Somber, squinted eyes buttressed her response. "Why on earth would I waste my time on such frivolity?" She inched away, but never turned me loose of her scrutiny.

"I consider it quite worthwhile."

Therese bit her top lip between her teeth. "Then you are at least glad that John Tanner lets Martha live with you."

"She has no contact with her father."

"The girl has more sense than either of her parents. They continue their sinful ways. Miskwabunokwa now waddles to her cleaning job, heavy with his bastard child."

"Whether God deems Tanner married to Miskwabunokwa or not is no reflection on the daughter. She embraces Jesus Christ as her savior. That alone should cause you and Angelique to tremble with rapture. I relay to her God's law as the Fathers taught me." Careful wording and I avoided the argument of whether my own faith wavered. "Marianne teaches Martha to read and Martha shares her lessons with me. I should think nothing in that circle would cause you offense." I tried to tease levity from my sister. "Is it so bad I wish to learn to read? Who knows, dear sister, perhaps I will find stories in books an interesting diversion…a comfort in my old age, although I concede I will never find written stories as thrilling as those of an Odawa storyteller."

"You are free to waste your time however you wish. Father Richard would undoubtedly argue that learning to read is a step up from cavorting with Presbyterians."

With my mind a jumble of questions, I hurried to meet William Ferry. My attention was redirected by a falcon that dove from its perch to the ground, where it snatched a chipmunk. The hunter crunched the rodent's tiny wriggling body in its powerful beak, and then flew to a nearby elm to enjoy a feast. The drama did not disturb the bluebird a bough below.

Maman was happy when the medicine man named me Zhaawan for the bluebird. She said bluebirds meant transition, contentment, and happiness. The Odawa welcomed these harbingers of change. Maman prayed I would help our people navigate the world of the white man while holding tight to our Odawa traditions. Maybe Reverend Ferry would offer something to help me in that endeavor.

I looked ahead as I approached the clapboard Agency House where Ferry stayed. Like most islanders, I referred to the dwelling as the Robert Stuart House because Stuart was the first clerk to move in after the building's completion. He became a seemingly permanent fixture.

I knocked on the heavy oak front doors, eager to meet William Ferry, the man who had set many tongues wagging. *I will chuckle, sister, each time I use the silver tumblers you grudgingly give me to settle our bet.*

It pleased me when Ferry, not the taciturn Stuart, opened the door and welcomed me. Ferry was a guest of the American Fur Company's chief clerk. The minister preached his first sermon from Stuart's living room.

Ferry was a slight, clean-shaven man, with a square face and a shock of brown hair combed straight back from his forehead. When he smiled, he became almost handsome in a white man's way.

"Madame La Framboise. Thank you so much for coming."

"How could I not? Your request piqued my curiosity."

Ferry stepped back and indicated an upholstered, chestnut-colored wingback chair pushed tight to the wall. In the middle of the room, several mahogany dining chairs had been arranged in short rows to accommodate religious services. The reverend took a chair identical to the one in which I sat. He leaned forward. It did not bring him much closer, but I felt the intimacy of his presence.

"Let's hope I will both satisfy your curiosity and make it worth your while."

It sounded like a business deal. I could not imagine a way it involved me. I wished he would get to the crux of the matter, but small talk was as necessary here as it was before trading furs. "Your church will grow and prosper, I pray."

He laughed. A loud, open laugh I did not associate with pious men. "Measuring growth should be an easy task when my first sermon drew only eight, and those attended more from curiosity or a love of coffee and biscuits than a calling from the Holy Spirit." His eyes were an odd gray-blue, so light in color that I believed them capable of mirroring what they beheld. I did not stare too closely for fear of seeing myself reflected. Still, his countenance took on a humor that belied the severity I had seen in his predecessors, especially Jedidiah Morse,[41] who arrived in 1820 wearing a scowl and a suit too hot for the season. When Morse departed the island a few short months later he appeared stooped and tired as well as grim.

I measured my smile, not too irreverent, not too severe. "I am glad your calling brought you to Mackinac Island."

"And yet, I don't expect you to attend my services in the near future." Again that teasing look that said he neither chided nor solicited me, but reached out in friendship. Then those haunting eyes fixed on mine and turned serious. "I came to Mackinac hoping to find a home and a partner for my other calling."

I raised my eyebrows, but turned my head—not enough that I appeared to avoid him, but enough to break the direct stare that let him read my thoughts. "Have you found it?"

"I believe I have. But I need your help. We pray differently, but have similar goals."

My brain raced, but lagged seriously behind his.

"I plan to return to Massachusetts next week."

I slumped, surprised that this news distressed me.

He quickly added, "I don't expect to be gone long. I go east to seek funds. I dream that together, you and I can open a boarding school to educate Indian children and the sons and daughters of fur traders."

"I cannot even read or write." My mouth hung open, and only conscious effort forced it shut. I had not seen the proposal advancing. "I do not understand what service I can be."

"The approval of Madame La Framboise will go a long way toward encouraging families to send their children. I pray you might help me entice Mrs. Marianne La Sallier and her stepfather, George Schindler, to teach at my—our—school." His grin widened. He picked at a loose thread of his black wool broadcloth coat, properly tailored, but its age showing. "And I wouldn't turn down any financial contribution you might care to make."

He shifted in his seat, and then stood. "I've not been a proper host. Would you care for coffee? I believe Mr. Stuart left a pot on the kitchen fire."

"Do not trouble yourself. I am more interested in your plans."

He dropped back down into the chair. A look of relief said he was happy I had declined his offer. "I hope to have a boarding school finished soon. It may take a while longer to build Mission Church, but God will provide me a way to teach children and a pulpit from which to deliver his word. I am content to share sermons from this living room, and once the boarding house is finished, I can preach from a classroom until a proper church is possible.

"I have a hunch that the education of young souls sparks your interest more than where I shall hold services, but I can't rightly say how long before we'll have a proper school." He pursed his lips, but I detected a slight nod. "I am told you have a large home that you can't fully occupy."

"I suppose that is an accurate assessment. With my granddaughter gone, it is just Angelique, Betsy, Martha Tanner, and me." I knew I forgot someone so thought for a moment. "And let me not forget little Sophia Biddle. She is three years old and her parents winter in the country. They prefer not to subject their daughter to hardship. She will be moving in with me at summer's end." I secretly wondered if the Biddles were motivated by a hope that Sophia would help fill the spaces left empty in my heart since Harriet's departure.

"Would you consider letting me the rooms you can spare? I've secured authority to hold classes in the courthouse until the school is built, but I'll need a place to board students and to instruct the girls in cooking and homemaking. I have six boys and five girls ready to start instruction in October."

"I think it could be a benefit to both of us." I reined in my emotions and tried not to appear immodestly excited. "I believe Father Richard would give his full blessing to teaching Indian children, even if he would not countenance my sitting in your pews Sunday mornings."

Mackinac Courthouse
Photo Courtesy of Bob Royce

Reverend William Montague Ferry
Photo Public Domain

Robert Stuart
Public Domain

Robert Stuart House
Photo Courtesy of Bob Royce

17.
Ferry Opens a School and Betsy Marries

"We do not want riches but we do want to train our children right." Red Cloud, **Oglala Lakota Sioux**

1824

The day after my meeting with Reverend Ferry, I awoke filled with a renewed sense of purpose. I asked St. Benedict, since he was also the patron saint of students, to intercede with God on my behalf. If idleness sought to destroy my soul, I prayed for enough labor to keep my hands set to useful task. Work alone could not save me from damnation, but if I improved the welfare of Indian children, my life had merit for its own sake.

I had long worried about the plight of my people. The Europeans—English, French, or the lesser numbers of Irish, Germans, and Scots—were not destined to sail their fancy ships back across the great sea to their earlier homes. Obwandiyag, perhaps the greatest Odawa military leader ever, failed to defeat our pale-skinned brothers. New leaders, including Black Hawk, who was unhappy with an 1804 treaty he had signed, did not seduce me with false hope. The Americans had blended all the newcomers into a country they would never abandon. They had the numbers and the weapons and the unity to make futile the Indian attempts to be rid of them. I remained on the fringes of American society, neither white nor red. The Great Spirit's children would either take the white man's road or be destroyed. I saw no alternative. Change was not a choice but a fact. Indian survival depended on our ability to adapt. We had been a people who traveled with the seasons, not a people who accumulated things that weighed us down or encouraged false values. Wampeme argued for holding to Indian ways. His reasoning sparked philosophical debate, but seemed to me unsupported by reality. If tribes moved from the life they had known for thousands of years to the American ways, they might endure. If they held to the past they would perish. Whether I was right or wrong, this I believed. Education, not guns or knives or bow and arrows, was our future. I let myself drown the sound of niggling doubt.

I slipped downstairs to the kitchen earlier than usual and watched Angelique stir batter. Her back to me, she had not heard my steps. When she sensed my presence she whirled about, bowl in hand, a startled look on her face.

"You rise early this morning, Madame. Shall I set you a place and pour your tea while we wait for the wheat cakes?"

"I suppose you should, although I have no appetite." I settled myself at the table as she bustled about preparing my breakfast. When the wheat cakes were ready, she stacked them on a plate and placed them and maple syrup in front of me, then busied herself setting the kitchen straight. She picked up a dishcloth, filled the basin with water, washed one dish, then another, and wiped them. Every few moments her eyes returned to me.

I thought about how Angelique came to me. Many years ago, my cousin,[42] Charles Langlade, captured a Pawnee girl in a raid on her village. Charles sold the abducted child to Louis Chevalier as part of a business deal. The girl grew to adulthood and gave birth to a daughter, Angelique, who was two years older than I. When I married, Louis gave Angelique to Joseph and me as a wedding gift. In spite of her history, Angelique was now family. I had an urge to declare, *You are free, go, live as you wish and have no more concern for me.* But while I had the power to fashion my future, I could not rewrite history. Turning her out, even with sufficient means, would not be the act of kindness that leaving her mother in the Indian village those many years ago might have been. "Come. Sit," I said.

"What is it, Madame? You are acting odd this morning."

"I have made a deal with Reverend Ferry."

At this her eyes opened wider, and her brows danced upward. "I worried a meeting with him would come to no good."

"Quite the contrary." I pushed away my empty breakfast plate and chuckled at her reaction. "I believe it may, with hard work, cultivate much good."

She played at grouping the salt, pepper, and sugar bowl on the center of the table. "I am listening."

"This is a big house. Upstairs there are four bedrooms. You, Martha, Betsy, and I each take one to ourselves. Soon Sophia will join us."

"*Oui.*" Her eyebrows returned to their normal position. Her fingers moved from the sugar bowl and began scratching at imaginary itches. "A three-year-old. I don't know what possessed you to agree to take her in."

"I think you very well know. That was a different discussion and has been put to rest."

"Indeed, but that sparkle in your eyes tells me I won't like what you are about to tell me anymore than I welcomed news that put us back in the child-rearing business."

Angelique's gruff exterior did not fool me. I believed that, like me, she welcomed the presence of Martha and Betsy and would be equally smitten with Sophia.

"Mr. Ferry proposes a school to teach Indian children. Those of traders as well. To that end he raises money, but it will take time to construct such a building. He offers to rent as much of my house as we can spare to serve as an interim boarding facility."

Her only expression was a stiff scowl. After a decent amount of time to allow her a response, I continued. "We can make our largest bedchamber available to Mr. Ferry's students."

"That is your room. Do you plan to sleep in a wigwam you pitch in the back yard?" She held her head, one hand on each side, as though this line of talk gave her a headache.

"Not altogether an unpleasant idea, but, no, you and I will take Betsy's room."

"And send Miss Betsy next door to her maman and grandmaman?" Her eyes narrowed, and there was no misreading the consternation reflected in those slits. "Their house is small, and she prefers staying with us."

"Betsy adores Martha and will not balk at sharing a room with her. Both will welcome little Sophia when she arrives. They will argue over who sleeps with her. Mr. Ferry has six boys and five girls signed up for a session to begin in October. My large bedroom will accommodate bunks for the girls. The reverend can take the last bedroom, and the boys will throw bedrolls in the attic. If that does not suit the Presbyterian minister, then he can leave the fourth bedroom to the boys and make his accommodations in the attic. How he uses or partitions the rooms is up to him."

Angelique was not smiling, but her scowl had grown less evident. "Who will instruct them? And where?"

"George will assist Reverend Ferry and teach the boys. A room has been made available in the courthouse for that purpose. Young gentlemen will be instructed in reading and mathematics, and blacksmithing, farming, or fishing skills as necessary. Marianne will address the girls' education. They will be taught to read and will be guided in sewing, needlecraft, and the finer points of maintaining a home. You and I cannot teach reading, but there is no reason the girls cannot learn proper housekeeping under our tutelage."

Perhaps contemplating the work that would be heaped on her, she wrung her hands and heaved a sigh. "And how about feeding such a number of children?"

"The girls will learn to cook, and their own efforts will provide their meals."

She shook her head, but a slight grin suggested she had warmed to the idea. "Finally," she said, "I'll have students other than Betsy to teach the proper way to dust."

I rose, placed my empty teacup in the washtub. "We will get the rooms arranged, furniture set up—at least temporary beds—and be ready when the students arrive."

She cleared the remaining dishes from the table. "You've had some strange ideas in the years we've been together, but this one beats all, tho' you may be right, it may serve a higher purpose."

"You may favor it more when I tell you that the funds Reverend Ferry pays will be put aside for you and your family. You will have a means of support in the event of my death."

During the summer of 1824, I received news that the Ojibwe in the northern parts were suffering a smallpox outbreak. Ahanu and his entire family had perished from the scourge. My people had endured epidemics of the white man's diseases since before my birth. Each tribe's oral history told of bodies burned in the hope of slowing the spread. Fathers and mothers, grandfathers and grandmothers, left their longhouses to prevent infecting loved ones. I remembered the plague of 1802 when Joseph and I avoided the village of Moccottiocquit to escape the disease.

The 1824 plague's devastation paralized me with guilt and anger. Guilt because I had banished Ahanu to the place of his death. Anger because there was a vaccination that prevented the disease. Indians were not given the choice to be innoculated.

William Ferry returned in the fall that year with more than funds needed for a church and school. His new bride, whom he met while in Massachusetts, was the talk of the island. Stories spread with the speed of the white man's sicknesses. It was rumored Amanda Ferry drew more men to her husband's church than God himself.

By October William Montague Ferry and I were in the education business. The same month the school opened, we faced a family calamity.

Amanda White Ferry
Public Domain

It was no mystery why my grandniece, Betsy, lived with me. My sister, Therese, nearing the age when a woman is free of child-rearing responsibilities, had adopted Lucy Tanner. Marianne, my niece, also lived with her maman and step-papa. Therese's only granddaughter, Betsy, enjoyed spending her time with Martha

Tanner, who lived with me and was like a younger sister to Betsy. It did not hurt that my grandniece received more coddling and attention from Angelique and me than she did in the busy Schindler home.

Christened Elizabeth, she was my Betsy. Not a replacement for Josette or Harriet, but a grandniece whose company eased my grief.

The lesser reason Betsy chose to live with me, and one that I was certain played into her crafty thinking, was that she counted on me to give her more freedom and scrutinize her activities less than her maman and grandmaman.

Betsy sought my counsel in matters from which dress flattered her more to which dessert she should beg Angelique to prepare for dinner. On the subject of Henry Baird, however, Betsy could not divide her family. The gentleman had set up a short-lived legal practice on our island before moving the month after sugar camp to Green Bay, where he was the first and only lawyer. In the short period of time he had enjoyed Mackinac, he had caught Betsy's eye. The attraction appeared mutual, and he had set his sights on her. Therese, Marianne, and I endured worrisome nights, but as Betsy was a mere twelve years old when her suitor struck out for Wisconsin Territory, our distress boarded the schooner and left with him.

The summer of 1824 brought Mr. Baird back into our harbor, his intentions at first no clearer than that day's hazy horizon. In retrospect, I should have considered the timing. Betsy had turned fourteen that April and was of respectable marrying age. He was twenty-four. When that fact settled into my mind, I concluded that Baird had likely paddled his canoe ashore in mid summer and not three months earlier because a legal matter held him in Green Bay those extra weeks.

Mr. Baird knocked on my door, and the screaming and yelling, the whooping and hollering, from Betsy when she opened it would have caused a sane person to seek shelter under the mistaken assumption the British again had us under siege.

Betsy invited her suitor to join us for a dinner of roast duck and Mackinac potatoes, a favorite of hers, and one I was sure she hoped would impress Baird. Angelique, always accommodating to the girls, outdid herself. When we finished the applecake with vanilla sauce and washed it down with the finest imported coffee, Betsy asked if she might speak freely.

"When have you done otherwise?" I asked. "Reticence is not a womanly charm you possess." I wanted to smile, show my grandniece I was toying with her, lighten the seriousness that crept into the dining room and settled along with the night air. I had a suspicion I should remain restrained until I understood the import of her question.

Betsy laid a hand on Mr. Baird's arm, a gesture so personal that I stiffened in anticipation of what came next.

"Mr. Baird is going to talk to Maman, Grandmaman, and Grandpapa tomorrow night. He will ask for my hand in marriage. I beg you to join us and intercede on my behalf."

I thanked God I had not given her a smile, for the change of climate in my heart, so abrupt, might have killed me. "If this were any business of mine, and I am not saying it is, for you are not—much as I love you—my child, I would refuse you."

Mr. Baird did not move or as much as murmur. His eyes remained on me, his face pleasant but noncommittal.

Betsy had too much spunk to hold her peace. "He is a good man. You cannot deny that. He is established and can provide well for me and any children we have." She turned from me to Mr. Baird and her face took on the gentle, sweet smile of the Blessed Virgin.

"Mr. Baird, pray do not think my opinions are a negative reflection of your character," I said. "I find no fault there." If I expected this to be a two-way dialogue between Mr. Baird and me, I was mistaken. He seemed unable to communicate.

"If Betsy were a few years older, if you were a few years younger, or if Green Bay was not a world away from Mackinac Island, I might give you my blessing. I would beseech her mother and grandparents to likewise consider your proposal. I would do that in spite of the fact that you would be taking our Betsy from her family sooner than I would like."

My stomach regretted the generous portion of rich duck I had consumed. "I have no magic to turn a most unattractive proposition into a situation that regales me with cheer." I stopped talking before my insides declared a full revolt.

For a moment I wondered if Mr. Baird had dropped dead. Unlike other attorneys, who offered opinions on every subject, I got no more than a wan smile from him.

Betsy unleashed more argument. "Henry is but ten years older than me. That is not so very much. Both you and Grandmaman married men much older than you." She thrummed her fingers against the table.

I swallowed several times to buy time for my queasy stomach. "We want more for you than a hasty marriage—an unbreakable bond—to which you are too young to commit."

Her eyes danced with merriment. "You know what they say, Auntie."

"I have no idea what you reference, but I'm sure you are going to enlighten me."

"About the fruit not falling far from the tree? Both you and Grandmaman were my age when you married."

A month of verbal warfare proved unsuccessful in changing Betsy's mind. Even Martha's pleas did nothing to soften my grandniece's stubbornness. Afraid the child would sneak into a canoe and leave without our blessing, we enlisted Mackinac attorney, John Bailly, to preside over a small civil ceremony in my parlor. The window shutters were thrown open to permit a view of Lake Huron, and sunshine filled the room.

Normally I disagreed with Angelique about bringing flowers inside, objecting to the disharmony that comes from cutting them from their roots to die. On this occasion, I relented, and she arranged vases of chrysanthemums, asters, and coneflowers that she cut from Mrs. Mitchell's garden. Their sweet decaying fragrance mingled with the savory odor of the pork roast drifting from the kitchen.

Betsy and Henry took their places, facing each other in front of Bailly. The bride looked radiant, a word I considered overused and inadequate, but the only way I could describe my grandniece's glow on her wedding day. In spite of my doubts, I embraced her joy.

The newly married couple sailed for Green Bay on the schooner, *Jackson*.[43] I prayed the smiles Betsy and Henry wore as they departed for their new life would never fade.

God forgive me, their happiness made me envious of a marriage entered into for a purpose other than business. I imagined Wampeme as clearly as if he stood before me with outstretched arms.

The Baird Law Office, Green Bay, Wisconsin
Register of Historic Places
Photo licensed under Creative Commons-Share All

Elizabeth Therese Fisher Baird
Photo from *Reminiscences of Early Days on Mackinac Island*
Public Domain

18.
Religious Discord and Betsy Returns

"The White People... believe we should be contented like those whose concept of happiness is materialistic and greedy, which is very different from our way."
Black Hawk, Makataimeshekiakiak, Sauk

January-September 1825

I had always favored George Schindler among my brothers-in-law, but we grew to be closer friends during a season of turning leaves when he and I helped Reverend Ferry get his school running. George had recovered from an earlier bout of debilitation and could again teach, a profession for which he proved particularly well-suited. I watched him maintain discipline and marveled at the esteem in which his pupils held him. His gentle firmness earned him even more respect from me.

We celebrated Christmas and the Day of the New Year before George suffered a second bout of apoplexy, this attack more crippling than the one he had survived three years earlier.

Therese and I were packing away holiday ornaments when we heard a loud thud, followed by Catishe's scream. We froze for a split second, then raced to the kitchen to learn the cause of the commotion. George had collapsed while pouring his morning coffee. He slumped unconscious on the floor, surrounded by broken china. My sister sent Marianne for the doctor. By the time help arrived, George had opened his eyes but remained disoriented. He regarded Therese with no sign of recognition.

During the ensuing weeks, my sister watched and thanked God for small signs of improvement. George regained halting speech, smiled when we entered his room, and welcomed our company, but he remained bedridden. The doctor said his heart was weak, and he should put his affairs in order.

I prayed for him and believed God heard my prayers. I did not try to tell God what to do, but rather asked that he be with us and help George in the way he thought best.

A letter from Father Richard came by dogsled over the frozen lake in February. The priest advised that I would have a visitor when the lake thawed. The newly ordained Reverend Francis Badin would leave Detroit on April 27, 1825, and make his first stop Mackinac Island. Reverend Edward Fenwick, bishop of an area that included Ohio, Michigan and the Wisconsin Territories, was sending Badin to determine the spiritual needs of his backcountry flock. The bishop was concerned for the souls of Indians within his diocese. Badin would stay only two days and then continue on to Drummond Island, St. Ignace, Sault Ste. Marie, Green Bay, and L'Arbre Croche.

In May, the first canoes of rendezvous arrived. Tepees sprouted on the beach, and I busied myself with the students who stayed in my home. I saw God's goodness in the young people. I appreciated St. Benedict's wisdom and stayed busy.

When I was not working with Reverend Ferry, I joined Catholics and prepared Ste. Anne's for Father Badin's visit. We repaired pews, replaced rotted floor planking, and shared our hopes that Father Badin would return to Mackinac after his travels and make the island his permanent home. If he could not do that, we hoped his report would induce Bishop Fenwick to send another priest to our community.

Father Badin's arrival, two days earlier than expected, caught me off-guard. I knelt on hands and knees on the living room floor, an apron tied about me, my backside to the door, as I showed our two female students how to properly scrub a year's worth of smoke residue from baseboards. A knotted kerchief kept my double-queued braids from getting in the way. Rolled-up rugs and furniture mounded in the middle of the room. A bucket of dirty water and dirtier rags added to the disorder. When Angelique led a man to me, the room and I presented an unholy sight.

"Madame La Framboise, I'm Father Badin." He needed no introduction. He was the first man we had seen in a priest's frock since Father Richard left the island three years earlier.

I scrambled to my feet, patting and smoothing to improve my appearance.

He extended a hand. I had no option but to offer mine after giving it a quick swipe on my apron.

"I'm pleased to finally meet you. Father Richard has told me much about you."

"I had expected to be more presentable when you arrived. Good weather must have set you on our shore in advance of schedule."

"That and my affairs ended in Detroit a day earlier than anticipated. I was eager to begin my mission." His face suggested a man my age. He had bushy eyebrows and was balding on top. A hank of thick white hair, about chin length, hung on either side of his head. Warm eyes softened an otherwise serious countenance.

I think my embarrassment amused him.

"I am sorry you found me in such disarray, but I am delighted to meet you."

He stared at the two young girls, one on either side of me. I introduced them, explaining they were students in Reverend Ferry's school, and I trained them in housekeeping. Upon hearing the name Ferry, the priest gave me a second appraisal, this time by eyes less generous. I instructed the girls to retire to the kitchen to pluck chickens for the evening meal.

Believing all priests loved their sweets, I asked Angelique to prepare a tray of pastries and serve Father Badin and me in the dining room where the house remained in better order.

"It is an honor to have you in my home."

At my gesture toward a chair, he seated himself. "I come with ulterior motives." He bit halfway into his sweet roll. "First let me apologize that I will not be here long enough this visit to offer sacraments for our spiritually hungry congregation. I have great distances to cover. The purpose of this brief stop is to determine the condition of Ste. Anne's, and to see if I can induce you to let me a room this fall. Father Richard assures me it was a pleasure to stay in your lovely home, subject to your stimulating company. We are hopeful you'll afford me the same courtesy."

I paused. I thought it would not do to have a dedicated man of God try to maintain his dignity amongst so many rowdy students. "When might you need accommodations? I currently have boarders, but I expect they will leave by the end of summer."

"Father Richard didn't mention that you regularly took in roomers." The question in his eyes invited me to explain.

I withdrew a handkerchief from the sleeve of my tunic, patted it at imagined crumbs on my mouth, folded it neatly, and put it back. Tiny efforts to buy me time. "As I mentioned, the Reverend William Ferry has started a school on the island. He is in the midst of building a boarding facility, but at this time he uses rooms in the courthouse for instruction, and his students live here."

The priest helped himself to a second pastry and placed it on his plate without inching his stern focus from me. "I suppose that such a houseful leaves little space for a temporary priest, and I'm not sure I'd feel comfortable sleeping in a room next to Presbyterians."

I repeated my previous question. "When would you need accommodation?"

"September through November." The curtness of his reply suggested that regardless of whether a room was available, he might have changed his mind about staying with me.

"Then it should work. The United States Government encourages Reverend Ferry to expand the school and has given him land for his Mission House. A carpenter from the East has drawn plans and the construction should take place this summer in time for the fall session of classes to resume."

Father Badin's mouth set a straight rigid line and his eyes lost their last trace of affability. "The Catholic Church has not met its obligation to its flock in the backwoods and on Mackinac Island. I am sorry for that. I hope we will rectify that situation soon. I will make more stops here on Mackinac until a permanent priest can be appointed. But I don't warm to the idea of you helping a Protestant when we Catholics have more than our share of spiritual needs."

His rebuke stung like I had been slapped by God himself. If his scowl was a sign, patterning my behavior after St. Benedict displeased Father Badin. "I thought the church—and God—would be happy we teach children. The work helps me move beyond my own loss and daily strengthens my faith and reaffirms God's goodness. It gives me purpose."

"You deceive yourself. Gratitude will tempt every parent of every child in Reverend Ferry's school to embrace his Protestant faith. You cannot believe your Father in heaven countenances that."

"You would rather we did not provide children with an education?"

He sipped his tea. His face relaxed. "You are right, education is a good thing. What I hope is that instead of helping Reverend Ferry, you can redirect your efforts to a Catholic school for children."

"Do you think it possible?"

"It'll be first on our list of things to talk about when I return. Until then, remember that with God, all things are possible."

One morning after picking up her mail, Marianne rushed to my house. "Sit. I have welcome news." She was flushed, and I had not seen such joy in her smile since her stepfather had taken ill. The letter in her hands fluttered like the wings of a hummingbird feeding on honeysuckle nectar.

"So read." Marianne's excitement was as infectious as typhoid.

"It is from Betsy. She is coming for a visit."

In spite of Marianne's cheer, I suffered a transient thought that my grandniece was ready to quit her marriage. I needed time to decide if I considered that good or bad. I stood, backed away to separate myself in case troublesome words followed.

"Don't distance yourself from me as though pox seeds poison the stationery." She stepped toward me, put an arm around my shoulder, and guided me back to the sofa. "Betsy comes because Papa's health fails. She wants to spend time with her grandpapa before God calls him home. Papa will cherish another chance to see her. Henry will accompany Betsy. A legal matter on the island demands his attention, the tail end of a case he started when he practiced here. But he has many more matters that require him to return to Green Bay without delay.

"Auntie, my daughter is with child and proposes to stay through her confinement. She wishes me to be nearby. During the moon of the harvest celebration, I will be blessed with a grandchild and you with your first great grandniece."

Elation replaced my earlier concern. "When will she reach Mackinac?"

"The third week of June. She and Henry will join Joseph Rolette's[44] flotilla. The man is punctual and keeps to a tight schedule."

"Punctual is not the word I have heard to describe Rolette." Betsy's news shared, I allowed myself to travel a familiar sidetrack, one that often ended with my complaints about Joseph Rolette. "Have you forgotten he is now my son's employer? I do not envy my Joseph apprenticed to a man they call Five More Rolette—"

"No matter how many furs an Indian offers, he demands five more. I have heard the disparagement of my godfather. Don't forget you and he are my godparents."

"I have counseled Joseph against working for the swindler. But a son of a certain age is deaf to his mother's advice. Joseph reached that age when I delivered him to Montreal. He was eager for an education and, if I do not delude myself, more eager to be beyond earshot of my fussing. I think when book-learning required space in his brain, he made way for it by displacing common sense."

Even as she commiserated my contempt for some of Rolette's practices, Marianne's twinkling eyes could not hide her good humor. "My poor Betsy, sister-in-law to the scoundrel."[2]

Not willing to let it go, I added, "I do not covet my grandniece's experience, sharing a trip with the man the Indian Superintendent in her parts calls the Great Indian Plague."

"Yes, Auntie. I'm familiar with that account as well." By this time her amusement had grown to giggles. My grumbling must have seemed trivial compared to the happy letter she had received. "Every dollar the Great White Father tries to get into the hands of the Menominee or Ojibwe must first pass through the slippery fingers of Rolette, where its value is halved."

"Only if the Indians are lucky. Otherwise they get a mere quarter." By this time I had caught the fever of her excitement over Betsy's return, and my grousing turned to good natured banter. "If you have time to send a letter of response, you might warn our dear Betsy to hang tight to her pocketbook during the trip."

"I think Henry knows his wife's brother-in-law well enough to exercise caution." She offered me a conciliatory nod. "If nothing else, Rolette is a cunning businessman. Your Joseph will learn much working for him. Your son is a La Framboise. Maybe with exposure to young Joseph, Mr. Rolette will become an honest man."

Humor about Rolette turned serious when Betsy did not arrive as expected. With each day that passed Marianne sought word from traders and their engagés who paddled ashore. Our worries doubled when we learned an angry storm had spewed enormous thirty-foot waves of water to frustrate those traveling from Green Bay. At least one flotilla was lost and Rolette's group remained unaccounted for.

---

[2] Betsy's father, Henry Munro Fisher, married a second time (after the marriage to Betsy's mother, Marianne La Salliere). His second marriage was to Magdelaine Gautier and they had a daughter, Jane Fisher, who married Joseph Rolette making Rolette the husband of Betsy's half sister, or her brother-in-law.

By the fifth day of our vigil, Marianne took a kitchen chair and stationed herself near enough a window overlooking the harbor so that she could keep track of any new arrival. I prayed for God's mercy. I begged for Betsy's safe arrival. My prayers covered all innocents aboard, and even a few with serious stains on their righteousness.

After six days, Rolette's bateaux floated into harbor and was greeted by loud rejoicing. Therese, Martha, Lucy, Angelique, and I all crossed ourselves and praised God. Therese dropped to her knees in an uncommon display of emotion. She threw her hands to the sky. "Thank you, Jesus, thank you, Jesus."

Betsy took great amusement in our carryings-on.

At dinner her first evening back on the island, Betsy regaled us with an account of their trip.

"The sun shone with favor on our vessels as we departed Green Bay. By our second sailing day, the gentlemen aboard appeased their restless natures by raiding our egg supply. They tossed their fragile stolen weapons at the other two canoes in our party. I hid beneath the tarpaulin protecting our fur cargo to avoid being struck and covered with a slimy mess.

"Mr. Rolette, an irritable old codger in the best of his moods, growled like a bear."

"Scolded like a blue jay," Henry added.

"No one paid the captain any heed." Betsy patted her husband's hand and nodded as if his slight interjection were pure brilliance. "The devilment halted only when fair weather turned foul. Wind-driven sheets of rain tossed our canoes as though they were of no more substance than a child's toy boats.

"I am in a delicate state and grew sick as a dog poisoned by rancid elk meat. I leaned over the side and retched. Henry held tight to me so I wouldn't fall overboard."

Henry had grinned all through Betsy's story, his eyes declaring adoration for his young wife. Clearly their love had not waned in the months since they took leave from Mackinac. I smiled, as much at their affection for one another, as at the conversation.

"Mr. Rolette searched the shore for a cove to wait out the squall," Henry said.

"By the third day the gentlemen—Mr. Baird, Mr. Kinzie and the others—again courted mischief," Betsy said. "The tempest had only temporarily stopped their tomfoolery. During a short break in the gale, the men hiked into the forest to stretch their legs. The exercise helped them contain their cockamamie antics until after dinner. Then the ceasefire was broken, and battle two of the egg wars ensued.

"One gentleman of our party wore white duck pantaloons. His pockets bulged so that his frock coat could not conceal his weapon supply. Mr. Baird and Mr. Kinzie took off after their friend and with great fleetness overtook him. They slapped his pockets until all of his eggs were broken and their contents ran down the poor fellow's pantaloons and white stockings and settled in his low shoes. The attackers dropped to the ground and rolled in the grass, laughing, gasping for air—quite exhausted.

"After a short rest, Mr. Kinzie called for more eggs, and the battle resumed. One egg veered off course and smacked Captain Rolette on the back of his balding head. He was anything but pleased."

"The war ended when the ammunition ran out," Henry said. "For the remainder of the trip, we suffered breakfasts without eggs."

"The gentlemen lamented their sad state of egglessness," Betsy said. "They struck out for another long walk. Roses and other flowers bloomed and filled the air with a pleasant fragrance. Such genteel pleasure was insufficient to dull the men's appetites for conquest. On their return to our camp, a new kind of war followed. They snuck into each other's tents, grabbed whatever they could quickly clutch—clothes, hats, bedding—and sent their ill-gotten gains flying toward the water. Mr. Kinzie's bedroll soared into the waves on its end, which made it sail remarkably well. He plunged into Lake Misigami and swam to retrieve it."

"You chuckle at my wife's story," Henry said, "but Captain Rolette was not amused. By the time we stepped on this island's shore, the captain was grateful to be rid of us."[45]

My Joseph, with his many good qualities, could not be lauded for writing often to his mother. When he lived with his aunt, Josette Ademar, in Montreal, I relied on her letters for information about him. With Joseph's departure for the Wisconsin Territory, her fount had run dry. I needed an ally who knew of my son's activities, even if that new source was a contemptible weasel. Ignoring my better judgment, I invited Rolette to dinner, eager for stories of Joseph. I decided every man had a warm spot hidden deep beneath his layers of gruff. I determined to find Rolette's.

I set six places at the table with my Star Center Spode china. I was grateful I had not rented Reverend Ferry my dining room. Angelique had fed our students early, given them a lecture about the virtue of silence, and sent them to their rooms to study. I shined the silver goblets Therese had relinquished to me when it appeared Ferry would not abandon his goals of preaching and teaching on Mackinac Island. I added baking soda imported from England to a pot of boiling water, dumped in a cup of vinegar and a handful of salt. After the goblets soaked, I removed and polished them with soft deer hide. I hoped Rolette was worth the effort.

Martha declined an invitation to join us. She retired to her room pleading a headache.

When Rolette arrived I invited him to sit at the head of the table. To his left I seated Marianne, who possessed both the wit and charm to regale the most recalcitrant guest. I took a chair on his right. No one fought me to sit closer to him. Therese, whose company I hoped would enliven conversation, sat next to her daughter, and on my side of the table I put Betsy. At the end opposite Rolette was Henry, whom I hoped to get to know better since he was now my grandniece's husband.

I opened conversation by sharing recollections of the feast we had enjoyed the day Rolette and I became Marianne's godparents.

As we talked, Angelique laid a first course of pickled beets and deviled eggs before us. Rolette, not shy about helping himself to large portions and lauding his accomplishments as he did so, treated us to an ungentlemanly summation of his exploits.

Struggling to steer the conversation in a more refined direction, I said, "Mr. Rolette, it is my understanding your parents at one time hoped priesthood would prove your calling."

He winked at me. No one else appeared to see it. Maybe I was mistaken.

"I guess you could say I've strayed a far way from the path of a priest. Celibacy and a lack of adventure didn't appeal to my more worldly sensibilities. I praise God, but not as a fulltime occupation."

I had heard from Betsy that her brother-in-law and his wife, Jane, did not enjoy a close relationship. Jane refused to follow Rolette into the country or interest herself in his business ventures. The more he talked, the more her reasoning struck me as clearheaded.

"My operation extends all the way from St. Louis to Prairie du Chien to the Red River Settlement. I have land and I raise sheep. I cut trees—or rather my men do. I have my own mills and sell lumber to farmers ready to build. The land that is cleared in the process, I offer, for a price, to new pioneers flooding our way."

His boasting exasperated me as much as his earlier wink. but less so than the feeling that crawled over my skin when he looked directly at me as though there was no one else at the table. I convinced myself it was my imagination, but still I wished to run for the washbasin to cleanse the dirty feeling from me.

"It surprises me that a woman as successful as yourself, one who remains young, sits in this house and gives up the business so readily. You could become much wealthier."

By the time Angelique served the whitefish, I had lost my appetite. "I am kept busy by Reverend Ferry's school," I said. "I visit daily." I saw no reason to add that Father Badin disapproved of my continuing efforts. I satisfied myself that I kept eyes and ears on the Presbyterians and made sure they did not convert otherwise good Catholic souls while they taught reading and writing. "I try to be part of the education of our young people, even if it is no more than cleaning a classroom after lessons. I assure you, I do not lack for opportunity to keep my hands busy."

"But a partnership of Rolette and La Framboise—and I mean the mother, not the son—would be a lucrative business venture. Together we could become John Jacob Astor's right hand. If that's not motivation enough, consider, you'd be with your son."

"My son is beyond years when he needs his maman clinging to his capote." I willed someone else at the table to pick up the conversation, and said, *thank you, God*, when Marianne piped up.

"My aunt has left behind the vulgarities of heaping money upon money. She favors a nobler calling."

My head swam with thoughts of this man, none of them flattering. But if my son found association with the braggart advantageous, I did not wish to confound his position or the favor in which Rolette held him. Further, I had not abandoned the hope of learning more about what Rolette planned as my Joseph's interest in the business. Instead of blunt honesty, I said, "Mr. Rolette, your offer overwhelms me, but my life rewards me in ways that cannot be measured by the accumulation of material goods. I understand where that would not suffice for a man astute at lining his pockets with wealth."

He smiled as though I had paid him a compliment.

"It is unfortunate that our trading endeavors did not cross paths when my husband was still alive, but my son has learned all there is to know of the business from me, and I give him to your care. I only ask that you treat him fairly, which I know a man of your honorable intentions will do. If I can beg a favor of your generous disposition, please encourage him on occasion to write a letter to his maman."

Perhaps realizing a chill behind my words, Mr. Rolette lost his tongue, a circumstance under which I found the taste of the food improved. By dessert, a subdued Rolette rejoined the conversation, complaining that there was less profit in furs than there had been during my years as a trader and that was why he was forced to diversify his holdings. It smelled as close to an apology for his boorish bragging as we were likely to get.

When he took his leave, he smiled and thanked me for a lovely evening. I expected he might kiss my hand, but that was a courtesy he could not extend because I clasped my fingers tight behind my back.

When everyone was gone, Angelique cleared away the remnants of our feast. I retired to my room and asked that she bring me a bucket of water for my washbasin. I could not climb into my bed until I washed away the experience of a dinner with Rolette.

In spite of Father Badin's criticism, I continued to help Reverend Ferry. I took seriously St. Benedict encouragement that I listen and attend with the ear of my heart. My house was crowded with students, the chaos both joyous and exhausting. Reverend Ferry's boarders had outgrown the temporary quarters of my largest bedroom and attic. Ten boys now slept in space we had arranged for six. Well-mannered as the students usually were, it was impossible to keep children quiet or prevent general rowdiness.

One night two young boys, aged eight and nine, raced chickens through the living room. The stakes were cookies they had saved from dinner. Another time, a tame raccoon they attempted to hide from me snuck into the kitchen and opened the mocock of sugar. By the time the animal's misdeed was discovered, the floor was sticky and the raccoon belligerent at being hauled away. Thin mattresses from their beds became vehicles for descending the stairs with amazing speed. One youngster knocked himself unconscious when he flew straight into the front door. Each time I stopped one prank, they found another way to test my good humor.

If all of that were not enough to fray my nerves, Father Badin, who did not approve of me aiding Presbyterians, expected to become my boarder in September. Raccoons and chickens and flying mattresses might send me to my room to hide my laughing fits from youthful offenders, but I doubted Father Badin's sense of humor stretched that far. He had left little question about how he would feel sharing a house with Presbyterians. I could bring Martha and Sophia into my room, and give the priest a bedroom of his own, but I could not rid him of the notion that close proximity to Protestants left him exposed to something more contagious than heresy.

Every day I walked to Mission Point to see how the building of the simple U-shaped Mission House progressed. The project's three-story, gabled center section, flanked by two-story, end-gable wings, was in place. A single-story square porch topped by a hipped-roof graced the front façade. The building looked near completion. Students had signed up to come from as far away as Hudson Bay and the Red River Country. With luck, the building would be finished, or close enough, to move the boys from my house before Father Badin's arrival.

I think God looked down, was not displeased with my efforts to educate children, and decided I would benefit from divine intervention. Reverend Ferry moved his students, and I got my house back before the priest arrived. I sent the boys rough bunks to Mission House, a gift from me. A sturdy four-poster bed, a goose-down mattress, and a new otter fur coverlet, all ordered at the onset of summer, arrived to ensure Father Badin's sleeping comfort. I had also purchased a desk where he could write his sermons, and a comfortable wing-backed chair like those in Mr. Stuart's house where the priest could read his Bible.

Reverend Ferry may have sensed my eagerness to help him move, but I never mentioned Father Badin's arrival as my motivation. I spent a pleasant spell helping the preacher set up the rooms in the new Mission House. He said he was sorry he had not paid me for my services teaching the girls housekeeping. I told him it had been my privilege. God gave me more than he demanded in return. Ferry nodded, and I could not avoid the traitorous thought that his countenance was more comfortable than Father Badin's.

"Well, I hope you won't be a stranger to our school," he said, and then added, "And remember, the salary was meager—or in your case—nonexistent, but you continue to have first pick of the clothes sent in charity boxes to the mission." His laughter told me he was making a small joke."[46]

Mission House and Historic Marker
Photo Courtesy of Bob Royce

Mission House
Photo Courtesy of Wikimedia Commons

Eliza Ann Baird was born on September 12, 1825. A week-long rain stopped minutes before her first lusty cry, and the sky god dressed the island in a double rainbow to celebrate her arrival. Henry had returned to Green Bay and would have to wait to meet his daughter.

Therese said the ruckus of a squalling infant would be unsettling to George. Betsy and Liza returned to my house and shared a room with Martha, who never complained of being awakened in the middle of the night by a hungry infant. Sophia, who was spending another trading season with me, had taken to crawling into my bed in a manner reminiscent of Harriet. Therese and Marianne divided their time between the Schindler home and mine. While one stayed with George, the other spent time with Betsy and Liza, then they reversed duties.

Father Badin joined our household and expressed satisfaction with his room. I noticed something I thought odd about the priest. Instead of annoyance, he smiled more when Eliza was with us, and he seemed to adore Sophia. Still, I had not warmed to the priest as I had to Father Richard. Badin's initial disapproval of my work with Reverend Ferry tainted our relationship. During the priest's stay, I avoided Mission House and Reverend Ferry, and a source of joy abandoned my spirit. I devoured Marianne's progress updates about the school.

Eliza Anne Baird
Public Domain

Two weeks after Liza's birth, I helped Betsy remove a black leather trunk from the closet and drag it near her bed. We laid out clothes, sorted and folded them for her trip back to Green Bay. While we worked, Liza slept next to us in a crib I had used for Josette and Joseph, her even breathing interrupted by soft infant sighs. I put my finger into her palm, and she clutched it without opening her eyes.

Betsy caressed the silk ribbon of a new bonnet from Paris. "I wasn't sure it would arrive before I departed." She placed the hat in its container, secured the lid, moved the box to the side of the room, and continued packing. "Grandpapa Schindler's illness renders him too weak to rise from bed. How can I leave him?" She did not wait for an answer. "Yet my own sweet child deserves to be with her father, and I promised my husband we'd return as soon as his child was born. I am tugged in the four directions of the medicine wheel." Tears welled in her eyes.

I reached over and clasped her hands. "You must content yourself knowing you brought your grandpapa joy this summer. His time is short, but the gifts you provided him—the chance to meet his great granddaughter, your reading to him in the afternoons—those memories will remain after you have gone."

"That is the point. I will be gone. I'll never see him again." She removed her hands from mine and wiped tears on the sleeve of her dress.

"Be happy when news reaches you that he is freed of his earthly tribulation." I pulled her into an embrace and whispered softly into her ear. "Your love accompanies him when he enters heaven."

Liza opened her eyes and whimpered. Betsy put the child to her breast. "Grandpapa Schindler was the only father I knew. He taught me to whittle and to fish. He taught me to play the fiddle." A short laugh escaped, and she smiled down at her daughter. "Not well, mind you, but I'd pick out notes and he would sing, '*Blow Ye Winds, Blow.*' I want Liza to know him."

I walked around to the other side of the bed, picked up cotton dresses and petticoats, and moved them closer to the chest. "Liza will have her own father. And you will tell her the stories of her Great Grandpapa Schindler."

"Maybe I should extend my visit a few months." Her eyes pleaded for approval that I did not give.

"Your maman will make the trip with you. Surely that eases your distress. Your place is with your husband."

"I miss Henry."

"I would hope so. You drove us all crazy—your insistence to marry him."

"I did, didn't I?" The devilment in her eyes suggested she savored that victory.

She turned serious again. "Maman says I'm too young to travel to Green Bay alone with a new baby. I am selfish and want her company. I won't try to change her mind. What if Grandpapa dies while she's gone? That worry is one more way I am pulled."

Between Sophia's antics, Reverend Ferry's students creating havoc, a priest moving in on the heels of Reverend Ferry's and his students' departure, and then the excitement of baby Liza's birth, that summer and early fall I dropped into bed most nights too tired for sadness. I measured my contentment by the amount of sleep I lost.

19.
Death of George Schindler

"Do not grieve. Misfortune will happen to the wisest and best of men. Death will come, always out of season. It is the command of the Great Spirit, and all nations and people must obey. What is past and what cannot be prevented should not be grieved for. Misfortunes do not flourish particularly in our lives - they grow everywhere." **Big Elk, Omaha Chief**

September-November 1825

Mrs. Mitchell had told me the secret to beautiful roses was proper pruning. The first year Joseph and I rendezvoused at Mackinac Island, I helped her trim her bushes in preparation for their winter sleep. She insisted we remove all leaves and dead wood and cut back the branches by a third. I have ever since called it Mrs. Mitchell's Rule of a Third.

As I snipped with gardening scissors, I thought what a genius that woman was when it came to growing flowers. I would never meet her exacting standards, but my roses claimed they were the second most beautiful on Mackinac.

I halted my task long enough to glance toward the village, where I saw Father Baden walking in my direction. Black robes made him easy to recognize, even at a distance. I could not tell what he held, only that his arms embraced a bundle. At first, I believed he had made purchases from the trading headquarters on his way home from his duties at Ste. Anne's, but the way he held the package, nestled against his chest, seemed wrong for merchandise.

A few rods closer and I made out a small unmoving child holding tight to a dark object.

I threw down my shears, pulled off my gloves, and hurried to meet the priest. He did not pick up his pace, rather continued a rhythmic shuffle. He had moved one hand up and patted the motionless child.

"Father Badin, whose child is this? Why do you have him?"

His voice was soft and his tone too matter-of-fact for the circumstances. "I stood at Ste. Anne's altar practicing my sermon for this Sunday. I heard a whimper, then loud crying. I opened the door and this little fella and his furry friend peered up at me from the steps." The priest touched the brown-and-tan puppy that lay snuggled to the child. It, too, was asleep. "Neither seemed happy with their situation. There were no adults, not a soul in sight. He looks about two years old, wouldn't you say?"

"It is as good a guess as I can venture." I touched the child's soft black hair, but he did not move. "Is he healthy?"

"Appears to be. Tired, and maybe hungry, but no injuries. He settled down when I picked him up."

"Do you want me to take him?" I held out my arms, but Father Baden shook his head. "No sense rousing him."

"What of the puppy?"

"He seems pretty fresh, tiny little thing."

I opened my front door. The priest headed straight for a chair and lowered himself gently, while patting the child in a manner that appeared as natural to him as delivering God's word.

"I will have Angelique prepare some cornmeal mush in case he wakes and is hungry. Then, I will see if I can locate his parents."

Finding the child's mother proved an easy task. I started with Wampeme, who camped along the shore.

"Kimama helps the child's mother search for him. They can't be far." Wampeme's anger from our last meeting apparently forgotten, he took me by the arm, a gesture with no meaning other than directing me, yet to a body starved for human touch, it stirred yearning so strong I ached with it. We headed down the beach in a southerly direction, toward a cluster of Menominee wigwams.

I did my best to ignore the flush of heat distracting me and was aided by the sight of Kimama rushing in our direction. She was accompanied by a woman unknown to me. The stranger must have understood I was there to help because she grabbed me by the shoulders. Her language had enough similar words to my Odawa[47] that I made out, "My son, my son. Gone," between breathless, choking sobs.

I smiled, raised my hands in front of me, moved them up and down slightly, to indicate she should calm herself. Her eyes remained wide and wild. Using words and gestures, I conveyed that her son was safe, and that she should follow me. She released her grip, and the tightness in her face relaxed. The four of us hastened to my house where we found Father Badin watching the child eat mush. He leaned so close to the little fellow that his priestly robes were covered with a generous portion of food that had missed its mark.

When the story of her son crawling onto the steps of Ste. Anne's was translated as best we could, the grateful mother indicated it was a sign. She promised that the following Sunday she would bring her boy for baptism.

Later that night Father Badin joined me in the living room for a cup of hot milk before he retired.

"I am guessing that is the youngest convert who ever came to you on his own," I said.

"I'll take converts any way God sends them."

His countenance brightened—positively radiated—in a way I had never seen.

"I have few regrets that I became a priest, but I would have liked children of my own." He stopped, then apologized. "I suppose that sounds impious. I think God understands. I love my calling, but bringing children into this world—creating life is a special blessing, a miracle. The innocence of children is a joy to our existence."

We sat companionably while I manipulated the conversation in the direction of my own worry. "Innocence is so easily lost. And when it is, I wonder if it can ever be reclaimed." I let my comment pass for idle musing. I had no intention of confessing the lie that saved Wampeme's life, but quite likely cost Ahanu his. Neither would I admit the weakness of my flesh when Wampeme came to my thoughts. Nor even my doubts about God since Josette's death.

"God is merciful. All sins can be forgiven." He studied my face for additional clues to my meaning. "This is a special year for forgiveness. Pope Leo XII declares it a year of Jubilee."

"It has been a long time since we have had a priest on the island to bring us Catholic news," I said. "What is Jubilee?"

"It is a unique time for remission of sins and universal pardon. The book of Leviticus promises that every fifty years shall be declared a Jubilee. God's mercies are particularly great in those years. Sins are forgiven and the sinner is restored to a state of perfect innocence."

"What must a sinner do to obtain this special forgiveness?"

"It is a gift. You must believe and open your heart to God. Then the gift is yours. That is why this year Bishop Fenwick wishes us to convert as many unbelievers as possible. They will stand before God as though without sin."

Three weeks after Betsy, Marianne, and Liza Anne departed for Green Bay, Marianne returned to Mackinac Island in time to say goodbye to her stepfather before he died.

After George's burial, Therese and I sat side by side on the couch in her living room. The sun slipped behind the horizon, and the room darkened. Neither of us suffered a pressing need to talk. Without a word, Catishe lit candles and laid two beaver-skin blankets beside us. The evening had taken on a chill, not unpleasant, but a reminder that winter would soon close in. My sister leaned over and laid her head on my shoulder. I stroked her unbound hair.

I thought back to when I met George. He and my husband became friends when Therese was married to Pierre La Sallier.

"He came as a soldier from the upper country," Therese said as though reading my thoughts, "but he met your Joseph and decided to stay."

"I still regret that misunderstanding between George and Joseph's brother—my least favorite brother-in-law—Claude."[48]

"The whole thing went away. You should never have troubled yourself over it."

"You are generous. The matter went away, but not before it caused George no end of trouble."

I heard a soft chuckle from my sister. "That proposed partnership of La Framboise and Schindler wasn't meant to be. The marriage partnership between George and me worked much better."

"I still do not know if Claude acted a scoundrel, or whether he really believed he was owed money. I can say I never fully trusted him."

"I asked George about the lawsuit once, but he insisted it was of no import."

"Your husband was a forgiving man."

"George was not one to hold grudges. He was a fair man, a decent man, and like Father Badin, a man who loved children." In the candlelight, my sister's damp cheeks glistened. "He accepted Marianne as if she were his own. When I got the idea to adopt Lucy, he went along with that too."

I leaned forward, picked up one of the blankets, and wrapped it around Therese's shoulders. Silence enveloped us. Therese's eyes closed, and I assumed she had fallen asleep until she asked, "Did you ever think of remarriage, sister?"

The question surprised me. We were as close as any two sisters could be, but some things just were. They did not urge careful reflection or probing or discussion, there being no wisdom in stirring up dissatisfaction with the temptation of what might have been.

I considered my answer. "Any woman left a widow at twenty-six thinks about it. I was fourteen when I married Joseph. He was a kind man, like your George, and for many years we had a good partnership. I repaired his canoes. I prepared his food. I warmed his bed, and I gave him children. His death saddened me, but I had no heart to enter another business arrangement given the name marriage. I preferred trading on my own."

"Were you never lonely?"

"Not in any way a marriage for mutual business benefit would cure." I did not add that when Joseph touched me—the act destined to bring me a daughter and later a son—I suffered my duty in silence. Often I closed my eyes and imagined I was with Wampeme. It was an unsatisfying escape. Joseph's hands, his arms, his mouth...no part of him was imbued with the kind of desire or love I knew Wampeme had for me. For every one of my married years, I prayed that God would wipe impure thoughts from my mind.

After my husband's death, there were unbearable nights when I longed for the heat of another human body sharing my bed, assuring me I was not alone. But just having someone, anyone, would never again have been enough.

With time, I had grown content that Joseph came to our village. Content he had asked Uncle Kinochausie for permission to marry me. Content the contract had been profitable for both Joseph and the Odawa with whom we traded. Content, most of all, because my children made up for my sacrifice. During my marriage, I had grown fond of my husband. Fondness sufficed for passion. And I had learned to respect him. Respect fashioned a substitute for love.

20.
Word from a Son

"Remember that your children are not yours to own, but are lent to you by the Creator." **Mohawk Proverb**

1826

It was always a good day that brought a letter to my home. I loved receiving news from Betsy, Father Richard, or the Widow La Framboise, my sister-in-law in Montreal.[49] This day, however, brought greater cheer than usual. The letter Postmaster Bailly placed in my hand came postage due with a return address for my son at Fort Crawford, Prairie du Chien, Wisconsin. I was thrilled to find the coins to ransom it. I fondled the missive as though running my fingers over it let me touch Joseph.

I considered rushing next door to get Marianne, but, instead, sat in the parlor holding the letter like a precious jewel, relishing its connection to my boy. I imagined his tousled, curly hair stuffed under the most recent incarnation of the bright red caps he favored, locks of it escaping confinement. I longed to reach out and touch his hands—hands I pictured chapped and blistered from hard work. When I wore thin the vision, I slipped open the envelope and extracted the sheets it held.

Marianne would stop by on her way to teach, and I anticipated the joy of her reading my son's news to me. I studied the words as I waited, a few I could now pick out and read on my own, but my reading skills had not advanced far enough that I could put together his story.

It was only a short time before my niece knocked, and walked in without waiting to be admitted.

"It is from Joseph." I held up the thin paper. "Can you spare time to read it to me?" My question was a pleasantry—a formality—because there was no way she would escape my front door without first indulging me with every sentence.

Marianne took the letter from my fingers and kissed me on the forehead. She sat beside me and began to read aloud.

"Dear Maman,

"I need to first say I am told by Betsy that Uncle Schindler has taken ill and by the time you receive this letter he may have gone to his heavenly reward. If so, please extend my condolences to Aunt Schindler and cousin Marianne. My uncle was a good man, and I know they grieve their loss. May our merciful God bring them peace.

"On a more cheerful subject, I know not the details of what transpired over a dinner I've been told took place in your lavish new house. Only do I know that I've been chastised and called an errant son, first by Rolette, and then by my dear cousin Betsy. Each hurled accusations that made failing to write one's mother seem equal to the crime of treason.

"Rolette, of course, was much less diplomatic. 'Write your maman. The dear lady languishes from lack of word from her only living child. Consider it your duty, and if it encourages you, think it an order from me.'

"Betsy, on the other hand, cajoled me as though she, herself, were my mother. 'My dear aunt,' she said, 'watches the mail delivery, ever hopeful of a few words from you. Ten minutes of your time brings her a week—nay a month—of pleasure. I've seen her beg Marianne or me to read one of your reports so many times the paper wore through.'

"After suffering their criticism, I was regaled with stories of your charm (Joseph Rolette) and love (Betsy) until I was at such a point of loneliness I had to distract myself by whitewashing the

blockhouse. When that failed the desired effect, I gave in and put this pen to paper to catch you up on my life, so you'd not have to rely so heavily on rumors packed along with the furs of traders headed to summer rendezvous. And know, dear Maman, it's better you not listen to too many rumors lest you be convinced the country has turned your gentle boy into a hard man. I swear that isn't true.

"Your only son has grown tall and even sports a beard during the cold months, but inside, my heart is little changed from the young man you delivered to Aunt La Framboise in Montreal near a decade ago.

"Of course, you've seen me in the interim, but I've enjoyed a final growth spurt that makes me near as tall as you. Considering how short I've been told Papa was, that's more than I expected. I am blessed with Papa's strong arms and shoulders, or perhaps those are attributable to the labor of the trade.

"As for my work, I know you fancied me a chief clerk at Mackinac, a lawyer like Henry, or perhaps best of all, a priest. Those pursuits were not meant to be. The rugged outdoor life suits me. I have language skills that are a valuable asset when dealing with the Sioux. Warring Sioux are our biggest barrier to trading in this corner of the wild.

"While on the matter of work, let me assure you that Joseph Rolette is not the devil he's sometimes described. He's a hard taskmaster, but at least with me, he's fair. That's the only basis on which I am qualified to judge.

"On another topic, I'm not sure what you did to impress Rolette, but he describes you in the most flattering terms, both your business prowess, which causes him to wish he could partner with you, and personally, when he speaks of your ardent spirit. The latter made me finally insist he stop lauding your charm and beauty as he was, after all, both a married man and describing my maman. If you ever decide to return to the business, I know where there are two traders, one young, one old, both named Joseph, who would be overjoyed.

"I shall be twenty on my next birthday, and my plans are to work hard and hopefully set aside enough money to support a family within the next couple of years.

"I hope this long letter buys me forgiveness if I don't write again for a few months. I am off for a four-day trip into Sioux country with Henry Sibley[50] to prepare the way for the season's trading. I carry plenty of gifts with me. When I return, I'll ready myself for winter encampment. Pray the furs are abundant this season. Remember, every pelt brings me closer to a family of my own. That in turn means grandchildren for you.

"I close by telling you that writing letters is harder than any of my physical labor. I love you and pray for your continued health. Maybe next rendezvous Rolette will let me bring the furs to Mackinac Island. Don't worry your head for a moment about me. I am in good health and good company.

"I send hugs with this letter.

"Your son,
"Joseph La Framboise"

I wanted to beg Marianne to start at the beginning and reread the letter, but she had no extra time. I secured a promise she would stop again after the lessons were taught and write a letter to Joseph from his maman. Turning the delay until then in the most favorable light, I thought about Joseph with every task of the day, considering what I would have Marianne convey. When she returned, I asked Angelique to bring us refreshments, and my niece and I sat at the dining room table, me to tell her what I wanted written, and her to do the writing.

"Dear Joseph,

"You were right in your supposition that your Uncle Schindler has passed. Your Aunt Schindler and Marianne are doing as well as can be hoped, but we all miss him. We take solace that his suffering in this

world has ended. I will extend your condolences to your aunt. Marianne received your sympathy when she read your letter to me.

"I am indebted to Joseph Rolette and Betsy for lighting a fire to your less than fervent desire to write your maman. Even with their descriptions, you cannot know the joy I find in hearing your words.

"I am not disappointed that you have gone into the trade. It is true I worry about the future of the business. My one hope, however, is for you to be happy. If neither lawyering, clerking, nor preaching the word of God would bring you satisfaction, then I rejoice that you have found a calling that does. I do not complain at how the fur trade treated me, I hope it is as generous to you.

"You are fortunate God blesses you with good health. I pray it continues. Your maman has no cause to grumble, although with each passing year I discover a new wrinkle and a few additional gray hairs. If that is the worst I suffer, I count myself fortunate. I have noted more pains this past winter season, especially in my hands, but a woman who approaches her forty-seventh year on this earth can expect a touch of rheumatism.

"Angelique prepares me poultices of boiled witch-hazel to relieve the discomfort. I try not to be a vain woman, but I have noticed of late that my fingers are becoming misshapen.[51] Forgive me, I had promised not to burden you with my minor annoyances, and yet here I am burdening you nonetheless.

"I am happy I am no longer in the business, although I seem to work as many hours as when I was. I feel more satisfaction helping educate children than I ever did trading furs. I am sure Betsy informed you we have a Presbyterian minister, Reverend William Ferry, on the island, and he has built the Mission House, a school to teach children.

"The Reverend's Mission Church remains a dream and for now, church services are held in a classroom of Mission House. Not ideal, I suppose, but arguably better than Robert Stuart's living room.

"For a while I had many boarders in my largest bedroom and attic, all students of Reverend Ferry. Marianne taught reading, and even Angelique and I did our best to contribute. Until other arrangements were secured, we instructed girls in cooking and household skills. If you *do not find a suitable wife in the back country, perhaps I can recommend one of the bright young women who attend Reverend Ferry's school.*

"I sneak daily to listen to Marianne teach reading. I say "sneak" because Father Badin, when he stayed with me, disapproved of my consorting with Presbyterians. Father Badin promises us a priest and maybe our own Catholic school soon. While Father Badin was here, a dispute arose over ownership of the land at Market and Hoban upon which Ste. Anne's sits. The good father was told the church must be moved. I have offered a piece of my property for the relocation, which I believe is imminent. I will take comfort if my house shares property with God's dwelling. Perhaps such proximity will further strengthen my faith. I do worry what will happen to the Catholic cemetery, where your father's earthly remains rest. I am told those buried there will be reinterred in a new cemetery on Garrison Road.

"Martha Tanner still lives with me. She struggles to teach me to read, but I admit I am not an apt student. With everyone's continued efforts, maybe someday when your letters arrive, I will be able to make them out for myself.

"Normally the workings of the new American government are of little concern to you and me. But word reached Mackinac of something so strange I will share it on the sheer chance its irony brings you a smile. Shortly after the island's Independence Day celebration concluded, I chanced on Samuel Abbott while in the village. He thought the oddity worth a mention. He said that of the original American revolutionaries, only John Adams and Thomas Jefferson survived until July 4th this year. Then, within hours of each other, both men died. Abbott says that the ninety-year-old Adams lay on his deathbed listening to the celebration beyond his window. His last words were, "Thomas Jefferson survives." Adams was mistaken. Jefferson had died five hours earlier at his home in Monticello. Do you think the Odawa would see a certain harmony in that sequence of events? I suppose, if asked, John Adams would be grateful he lived until his son became president. For me, the American leader is not overly important to daily life. I just pray that peace prevails.

"On Mackinac Island, politics go on as normal. The fort is quiet. No one seems to pose a significant challenge to the American government.

Lewis Cass remains our governor of the Michigan Territory, but I will not cripple Marianne's hand by telling you my feelings for the man. He makes no secret he considers Indians an inferior race, and he encourages their removal to parts of this new country where no white man would consider living.

"The new trade laws forbid providing Indians with liquor. Regardless of the law, I have come to regret my actions in that respect, and urge you never to employ ardent spirits to improve your trade advantage.

"Marianne and Martha send their love. Angelique says she will be as happy as I am when you give me grandchildren. Work hard, but do not sacrifice your soul.

"I would prattle on, but Marianne has lessons to plan. She also helps your Aunt Schindler in the care of Lucy. With Uncle Schindler gone, remaining family helps keep us going.

"I will hold you to your promise to nag Mr. Rolette for the task of bringing furs to Mackinac Island. Nothing would please my aging heart more than to lay eyes on my beloved son.

"I send hugs back to you,

"Your Maman"

21.
Dreams

"Sometimes dreams are wiser than waking." **Big Thunder, Wabanaki Algonquin**

March 9, 1827

I retired early the night Josette returned. How much my physical condition contributed to her reappearance, I cannot say, but the other-worldly experience both unnerved me, yet was strangely settling.

I suffered la grippe that evening. The meager portion of chicken soup I had eaten at dinner soured my stomach. In the middle of the night I awakened, drenched in sweat. I called for Angelique. A glimmer of light grew brighter as her near-silent footsteps padded down the hall toward my room. She entered carrying a candleholder in one hand, shielding a flame from drafts with her other. She fixed the beeswax candle on my dressing table, then laid cool fingers against my burning cheeks.

"Are you able to stand?"

I nodded.

She filled the washbasin from the pitcher standing next to it. She changed the bedding while I splashed cool water on my flushed face and donned a fresh tunic. My aching muscles protested every movement. I crawled back into the freshly made bed while Angelique soaked a square of linen and wrung it tight. She sat beside me and pressed the moist cloth to my forehead. When my fever ate up the fabric's chill, she repeated the process. After several times, she laid the cloth aside, and picked up the flickering candle. "Try to sleep, Madame," she said before she returned to her own bedchamber.

Clouds blocked out the moon and stars. Not a wisp of light crept between the closed blind slats. In darkness as complete as a burial tomb, I dropped back into a sleep that transported me to the place where I encountered my daughter.

I had known dreams before, but not like this one. I felt awake, clearheaded, my senses keener than I had ever experienced them. My surroundings came into sharp focus, my sight like that of an eagle, and my hearing as acute as the wolf stalking prey. The scent of newly budded leaves and greening bushes filled the air. I concluded it was menoukawme, the season of new life. The island should have been abuzz with the activity of rendezvous, but was deserted. I had no awareness of my feet touching the ground as I floated the familiar path that led around the point at Robinson's Folly toward Arch Rock. The sun tickled my face and head and arms as it chased away the morning chill.

Doubts had plagued me since Josette's death, but I knew in that moment—with a conviction that demanded no proof and rested on faith—that God existed. A subtler truth was equally apparent. God demanded my unflinching devotion, but it was not an affront to him if I had questions about how it all worked. He wanted, expected, maybe even demanded, that I search for my truth. I imagined a place, whether called heaven or the spirit world, where I would again see Josette, Maman, my husband Joseph, Benjamin Langdon, and all my loved ones who departed the earth before me.

My thoughts whirled as though driven by turbulent winds rearranging nature to suit their whims. I wanted only to slump to the ground and bask in the certainty of my conclusions. Before I afforded myself that indulgence, I heard soft tinkling laughter from across the waves of my great sweetwater sea. Like music it danced, gracefully gliding from sky to earth for my delight.

Mesmerized, I dropped onto a log and listened. As I sat, a tap on my shoulder distracted me. Without turning, I knew Maman stood behind me. She kissed the top of my head and then was gone. Before her departure consumed me in renewed grief, the melodic laughter I had heard seconds earlier returned and grew louder. More perfect than in life, Josette appeared, surrounded by an aura that made her seem both real and illusory. She threw her arms around me. Her flesh—if something without mass and substance can be called flesh—was cool, yet her touch filled me with warmth so comforting that I implored the moment to endure. Without my heart's bidding, tears coursed down my cheeks.

"Don't cry, Maman."

I pulled away, unsure what was happening. "I have missed you."

Unlike the Josette of real-life, she seemed completely at peace. "We will be together again. The missionary priests got it mostly right, but you must believe. And be patient. Your work here isn't finished."

So many questions confounded my brain that I did not know what to ask first. *What is it like to die? Are you in the place the priests call Heaven? Is it different from the place the Odawa call the Spirit World?*

I looked into her face—so tranquil—and was reminded of Ste. Anne's painting of the blessed Virgin Mother. I could not speak, yet there was so much I wanted to know. I thought of those who had not accepted the Catholic God. *Where are the Odawa who cling to old customs? Are Odawa gods small pieces of the Great True Catholic Father? Is there a fiery hell where non-believers suffer unimaginable horror, or is a burning inferno a figurative description of eternity exiled from God?*

I had not spoken aloud my concerns, but she said, "So much curiosity." She drew me back into an embrace. "I am not here to reveal what lies on the other side."

I laid my head against her breast. My tears soaked her silk gown. Seconds. Minutes. Time passed without meaning. As we sat, I sensed her pulling away. A space so small I could not measure it, yet I knew it was there. I clutched at and tried to hold her tight. My arms tensed. I would not be weak this time. I would not let her leave me.

Again, I held my worry inside me, but she said, "Maman, you can't keep me." Her gentle laugh taunted me, yet held such sweetness it offered no offense. I was dizzy and close to fainting.

"Maman, I came because Harriet needs you. Benjamin tries. He does. Be charitable in your judgments of him. He loves our daughter and attempts to act in her best interest."

I listened, uncommitted to granting her request, yet unwilling to speak anything that might prompt her departure.

"Harriet is but a child, confused, struggling, lost. She needs Nookomis. The Odawa part of my daughter's soul cannot survive if she loses our history." Josette dropped her gaze, but not before I saw her glistening somber eyes. "Benjamin, for all of his good qualities, does not cherish her Odawa blood. He cannot share Harriet's proud past, even if he were so inclined."

Which he is not.

"That may be true, Maman. But Benjamin is declining. If you cannot love him because he is Harriet's father and my husband, then at least pity him for the road he travels."

Husband? Within two years of your death he married the Boykin woman.[52] He is now her husband.

She looked up again, but this time if she read my thoughts, she said nothing. Her eyes held such pleading that had I responded, my only option would have been acquiescence.

She continued as though unaware of her impact on me. "His future will not follow an easy course. Already there are signs of softening of the brain, perhaps even mania. He is robbed, piece by piece, of his sanity."

For a brief second, the scowl that had consumed her face as she described Benjamin's plight faded. She grinned and patted my hands. "Of course, I see more from my current vantage point than perhaps you do from yours."

I raised my eyebrows and gave her my motherly all-knowing smile. "I do not doubt that heaven accords you a keener perspective." The light moment passed, and she returned to Benjamin's condition.

"For years my husband—"

Did she repeat the word husband to annoy me or to convince me?

"—will function without succumbing. But because I love him, nothing concerning him passes my detection."

I ignored her profession of love. "Age dulls even the most vigorous mind."

"Yes, Maman, I've seen you rise in the morning determined to tell Angelique that you wish her to clean the pantry before the new shipment of foodstuffs arrive. You go downstairs unable to remember your purpose."

"Later, during breakfast, it comes back to me."

"See? That is the difference. Benjamin is ten years younger. Already he suffers such lapses. Worse, the thoughts he chases never return. He blacks out and forgets where he is, or labors to recognize people he knows. He hides his affliction, but the malady, coupled with war and so much killing, corrupts his thinking. He struggles to raise Harriet, but her ailing, part-time papa's best attempts are insufficient. For my sake, and Harriet's, be gracious in your regard of my husband."

"It is hard to think kindly of the man who keeps my granddaughter from me."

More sweet laughter prefaced Josette's words. "Oh, you will see Harriet again. That is why I am here. To remind you that when she comes, you must be her storyteller. Not knowing her roots…not knowing who she is—" she clasped her hands over her heart—"leaves this part of her missing. You can make her whole."

She pulled farther away from me. The inches that separated us spanned the distance between our respective worlds. I reached out to my daughter, but grasped empty air.

"Oh, Maman, I didn't come to bring you pain, but rather hope."

Whatever her intention, the torment of losing her a second time doubled me over. I opened my mouth to suck air into my empty lungs.

She drew me into a last hug. "Listen to the wind," she said. "It will always carry my laughter to you. Feel the sunshine and always know the warmth of my love. Touch Harriet, and I am there."

Arch Rock
Photo Courtesy of Bob Royce

The next morning my fever broke, and I regained my vigor, but the details of the preceding night remained vivid. The Odawa believe spirits share wisdom through dreams. To my thinking, only the foolhardy ignored voices of the dead. Even as a believer in the Catholic God, I left room for the possibility that he could not reveal every tiny detail in one book. Some truths may have escaped the prophet's pen. During Father Badin's next visit, I planned to ask him a question: If the men who wrote the Bible received the message not in God's own hand but through inspiration, can we liken that to listening to dreams or voices from another world?

I felt well enough for a walk to the post office, where Postmaster Bailly handed me a letter. Later that afternoon, Marianne read the communication to me. Elizabeth McNeil had written that she suffered debility, although she offered no detail of her ailment. According to her, the doctor insisted she convalesce for a few months, which he believed would effectuate her complete recovery. She had been in contact with Benjamin, and together they had decided that Harriet would spend this summer with me. My granddaughter would arrive by steamship early in July. Until then, she would stay with a family friend.

I was weak-kneed with emotion. I cried and laughed at the same time. I dropped into a kitchen chair, fearful the joy would overcome me. I fanned myself with the letter. Marianne got me a glass of water and allowed me a sip before she pulled me up from the chair, threw her arms about me, and danced me around the kitchen. To an outsider, it would have appeared we had taken leave of our senses.

I immediately set to making plans. Harriet's room had to be redone. She was now nine-and-a-half years old and needed something more grown up than the cornhusk dolls and miniature cradleboards I had never found the heart to discard. I ordered wallpaper with rose flocking from Paris and engaged a man to hang it. I procured a delicate silken coverlet, the same shade of pink, for her bed. I purchased a slate board and a game of jackstraws from the American Fur Company headquarters, the former so she could practice her penmanship, the latter as a diversion for our evenings.

Those were easy fixes. Harder was my decision that I would take Harriet to L'Arbre Croche. If she were to understand her history, where better to hear my stories than in the longhouses where my Uncle Kinochausie now lived?

In early May 1827, John Bailly, our local barrister, knocked on my front door. Friends came to the side door. Acquaintances bearing bad news permitted themselves no such intimacy. Bailly's mouth, set gravely serious in his square jaw, did nothing to allay my dread.

"Morning, ma'am." Bailly stammered, then instead of explaining his business, he thrust a slip of paper toward me.

I shook my head. "Can you read it to me?" I clutched my arms about me and inhaled a deep breath, expecting news that might suck the air from my lungs. *Let it not be bad news concerning Harriet.*

He nodded. "It is a letter from Andrew Mitchell, Madame Elizabeth Mitchell's son."

I guessed the import of the missive without his going further. I stood like a giant oak, rooted and unable to move in any direction.

"It is dated February twenty-fifth."[53] He lowered his hand, allowing the letter to drop to his side. He did not need to see the words to relay the short message he had already read. "Mr. Mitchell mastered a vessel filled with provisions to Drummond Island. Aboard ship with him was his mother, who was enroute to visit her husband, the doctor. During the voyage, Mrs. Mitchell took ill. Her son's efforts to save her were to no avail. She is gone."

I thanked Mr. Bailly. As he turned to walk away, I slumped into a chair on the front porch. "She was a second mother to me." I doubt he heard my whisper. He had already put several steps between us. The bearer of disturbing news is not eager to witness the devastation he leaves behind.

I reached for my crucifix, but touched Wampeme's bead instead. I chastised myself for not ridding myself of the talisman, but I was weak, and it continued to hang around my neck. I pulled my fingers away as though the bauble burned with the heat of brimstone. I traced my crucifix instead. *O my Jesus, forgive me my sins. Save me from the fires of hell. Lead my soul into heaven, as I am in need of thy mercy.*

I was not ready to lose Elizabeth Mitchell. I thought of her funny way of talking, her black dresses and beaver hat, her gardens. I remembered the warm spring day of 1806, just months before Joseph's death, when he and I arrived at Mackinac, and my joy had turned instantly to sorrow. Elizabeth met us at the shore with news that my sister, Charlotte, a mere thirty-six years old, had died four months earlier on January second. My older sister and role model had been buried in the Catholic cemetery at Astor and Market Street.[54]

Elizabeth accompanied me to the cemetery and remained in her calash at the side fence, close enough for me to feel her support, but far enough away to allow me privacy.

"Elizabeth says I have to concede to God's will." I patted the dirt of my sister's grave.

I imagined Charlotte's response: "You must remain strong." I saw that lop-sided, purse-lipped grimace that she gave me when I was a child. Then I heard her soft laughter. "I'll be watching you."

I smiled and whispered back, "I know you will." No amount of happy memories, however, kept tears from spilling down my cheeks. "I hope you have found peace. Tomorrow I will light a candle for you at Ste. Anne's." I remembered the day Charles Chandonnet arrived at our village. I was twelve years old, and Charlotte's arranged marriage was an omen of my future.

When Joseph and I departed Mackinac in the fall of 1806, I found it hard to leave Elizabeth Mitchell, so great was my reliance on her mothering. I told her that I knew the next year would hold further bad news. She assured me it was grief playing with my mind. But life was fragile and my premonition was strong. Elizabeth understood as well as I did that the Odawa heeded such foreboding. She said, "I hope you are wrong. However, if more grief comes, I will be here to help you through it."

Joseph was murdered within months of that conversation. True to her word, Elizabeth greeted me when I returned for rendezvous the next spring, and she helped me through that tragedy as well.

I will sorely miss you, dear Elizabeth. Give Josette a hug for me. I look forward to the day of our reunion.

From where I sat on my front porch, I watched the gentle waves of my lake reaching like arms to comfort me until I felt calm return. Living on Mackinac Island was a sensation…an impression…a pleasure that, like the air about me, was essential but difficult to describe. God had used this plot of land as a canvas for his artistry. He painted water from which life was born and a beach sloping upward to stately pines and hardwoods that protected me. The island seemed a living thing that revealed his presence.

Grieving Elizabeth, the island was my haven and my security, my perspective from which to view the larger world. I held a deep abiding sense that man's activities were of less importance than a single pebble along the shore. Human beings were of the moment, their existence insignificant in the larger story that the land and seas told of this earth.

Mackinac Island remained anchored, steadfast in the middle of Lake Huron, taking both our transitory heartbreak and happiness in stride.

22.
Reconciliation

"A people without a history is like the wind over buffalo grass." **Sioux**

June 1827

The ship's captain took Harriet's hand to help her disembark. She stepped ashore, squinted into the sun, and frowned when her eyes seized on mine. She stood frozen, an alabaster statue gracing the harbor.

My stomach fluttered as if filled with baby birds taking their first flight. Unable to restrain myself, I rushed toward her, kissed both her cheeks, and hugged her, hoping the intimacy erased five years of separation. For a few seconds she endured the embrace, but there was no warmth in her submission. When she pulled loose, I looked at her more closely. She was slender with delicate features that foreshadowed a beautiful woman, one with little resemblance to the sobbing child Benjamin had pried from my arms when they departed the island.

"I have missed you," I said.

When she did not answer, I thanked the captain for bringing my granddaughter safely to Mackinac. His fingers clutched the narrow brim of a black felt cap he tapped against his trousers. "My pleasure, ma'am."

"I hope she was no trouble."

"Quieter than a church mouse the whole way." He gave me a nod, put his hat on his head, and turned back toward his ship. He stopped once to call out, "My men will deliver her trunk to your home."

I felt abandoned. Idle chatter with the captain had been better than the awkward silence that followed. I reached for Harriet's hand and headed us toward home. She stood nearly to my shoulders. "You have grown more than I expected." It required no response, and she offered none. A few steps farther on, she withdrew her hand from mine and adjusted her wide-brimmed bonnet. When it sat to her satisfaction, she dropped her hands to her side.

My granddaughter had changed, and not in all ways for the better. Expecting to see her face brighten, I opened the door to show her the room I had prepared.

"No one back East papers their walls in pink. Blue is the favored color." Her eyes scanned the space about her and fixed on the chalkboard.

"I thought you might practice penmanship while you are here."

"My tutors find no fault with my handwriting. Perhaps you will find another use for it."

She said it with enough innocence that I could not say for certain whether she mocked my inability to write. As I left her room she asked, "Where are Caribou and Nero?"

The dogs had both died, Caribou from old age, Nero from a sudden onset of seizures. When I relayed the grim news, her visage turned more sullen.

In a whisper I assumed was not meant for response, she said, "I should have expected it."

Over dinner the first night, she complained that Angelique's corn pudding tasted like mush.

"I could not have heard you correctly. A lady of your breeding would not offer a comment so vulgar."

Her rigid posture offered no apology. "I can't be blamed for preferring Aunt McNeil's beef roasts. The butcher cuts them special for her."

The second evening, when I brought out the jackstraws, she crossed her arms. "My friend Abigail would think this is a childish pursuit."

If my face reflected disappointment, it did nothing to stop her rant. "Don't you play checkers, or maybe you can find someone to play chess with me." She jutted her chin forward. "I can beat father when he visits."

If I saw Harriet smile at all during her first days on the island, it was only when I peeked in her room and caught her and Sophia Biddle sharing secrets. Sophia was like the summer sunshine to my granddaughter's icy winter storm. Sophia's parents, Agatha and Edward Biddle, had returned from winter camp and Sophia was spending rendezvous with them in their home on Market Street. That did not prevent the sweet child, who had brought joy to my home during their prior absences, from coming to play with Harriet. If I had hoped that Sophia's cheery disposition would rub off on my granddaughter, I was disappointed.

Often I blamed Elizabeth McNeil for spoiling the perfect four-year-old I had sent to her keeping. In more honest moments, I admitted that Elizabeth McNeil was no more indulgent than I had been. I concluded Harriet's petulance stemmed not from privilege so much as her distaste of returning to me and a past she preferred to forget. Such conviction pierced my heart more cruelly than if I had never seen her again.

Harriet and I sat side by side in the small canoe. She took advantage of the width of the plank seat to leave a foot between us. She looked away from me toward Old Fort Mackinaw as we approached the tip of the mainland, where lakes Misigami and Huron kiss. Already I missed Angelique's companionship. She had stayed behind to care for the house and keep Martha company.

Angelique's sons, Francois and Louizon, who had been my engagés in earlier years, paddled with steady hands, their voices silenced by the sour, sharp looks that accompanied Harriet's refusal to join their songs.

My granddaughter wore a robin's-egg blue cotton frock, beribboned and smocked, suitable for church and fancy celebrations. She had chosen this garment rather than wear the leggings and tunic I had laid out. For hours, my stubborn arthritic fingers had fought me as I beaded the soft buckskin yoke, trying to create a design that would please her. My effort lay folded, buried, in the bottom of our valise. I overheard her tell Angelique, "You needn't pack it. I will not dress in garments worn by savages."

On her feet my granddaughter wore hard-soled leather shoes unsuited to walking uneven trails or helping her pick her way through forests with moss and-leaf-covered floors. Moccasins, their tops decorated with fringed leather, settled beneath the tunic in our baggage.

Skimming the water's surface with my fingers, I ached to close the chasm between my granddaughter and me. I might have promised her anything if I thought she would love me again.

"My heart rejoices that you will see L'Arbre Croche."

She shrugged her shoulders.

"Your mother loved the village when she was your age."

"That was my mother."

Harriet's hostility was as tangible as the thick moist air of that summer day. My stomach sickened with the same feeling as la grippe. If I were not duty-bound to my deceased child, I might have instructed the men to turn the canoe around and return home, there to put my granddaughter on the next vessel available to carry her back to the McNeils'. At least the pain would be swift and sharp. But Josette's words—"Harriet is but a child, confused, struggling, lost"—echoed in my mind.

A breeze picked up. Francois propped our paddles in slats that held them vertical. He attached a blanket between the upright oars and let the wind propel us toward our destination. The weather deteriorated as we moved westward, and the sky darkened with rain clouds. We rounded the top of the mainland and then aimed the canoe southward. "L'Arbre Croche is summer home to hundreds of Odawa." I talked hoping that in spite of her indifference, Harriet would hear me. I talked hoping that I would break her resistance. I talked hoping to fill the silence that loomed large between us.

"The Odawa called it the Place of the Crooked Tree," I said. "The tree guides us safely ashore."

"There are many crooked trees." The sarcasm in her tone faulted my logic.

"This is the special tree that was bent by Nanabozo. At one time it was tall and perfectly straight. Taller and as straight as Nanabozo himself."

Harriet sighed, rolled her eyes. "You want to tell me the story. Go ahead."

"No. I have no stories for an unwilling listener."

We traveled several more miles and the breeze contorted into a less friendly wind. Our canoe rode up each wave and smacked back down.

Harriet's face paled. "So tell me the story, Grandmother."

I was no longer Nookomis, and *grandmother* sounded harsh on her lips. I did not delude myself that she harbored sincere interest in hearing the story. But even if she sought only a diversion to calm her burgeoning fear, I claimed the opportunity.

"Nanabozo was a respected hunter and chief. One day at L'Arbre Croche he climbed a hill, carrying on his shoulders his birch bark canoe. The canoe caught on a stately and perfectly formed tree. Nanabozo tripped. He was so angry he dropped the canoe to the ground. With a blow of his fist, he pounded the tree. All living things are our brothers. It was an unkind thing to do."

I paused, giving her ample time to chime in with questions as she had done when she was younger, but none came. She stared out at the horizon and tapped her fingers on her knees.

"A big bump rose on the side of the tree where Nanabozo struck it, and at that spot the tree bent and twisted. The angry man continued pounding the defenseless tree, and at each place he touched it, it grew off in another direction. 'That old, deformed tree is ugly and should be cut down for firewood,' said one of Nanabozo's friends. But that night at the campfire, Nanabozo's papa, a wise and respected man, told those gathered that any tree could grow with straight branches reaching for the sun, but this grotesquely twisted pine would never be mistaken for another. Its misshapen image would guide travelers ashore at a point where they met no danger from treacherous currents or rocks."

Harriet voiced no reaction. Minutes passed. Seagulls squawked overhead. The sun peeked through for a few seconds. I watched whitefish swim close enough to the surface that I could have reached out and grabbed them for the evening's dinner. But as quickly as the sun had tricked us into believing we courted its favor, it retreated behind another wall of ill-natured clouds, more vocal in their arguments with one another than those that preceded them.

Harriet began rocking side to side. "Why are we going to this place?"

"I have already told you."

"I mean really."

"When I was your age, my sisters and I considered Gabagouache the main stop on our annual migration—our home—but I spent part of my summer in Crooked Tree. We planted crops, gathered wild rice, and celebrated the moon of the harvest. You will learn Odawa customs, meet relatives, and hear the stories of your ancestors. You need to visit this place and capture it for your memory." I studied the sky with increasing concern, but hid my worry. I withdrew maple sugar candy from the pouch at my feet and laid it on the seat between us. "The village is unlike Mackinac Island or any place you have ever visited. Houses are not arranged in rows. You will see longhouses and wigwams, not homes like mine or your Aunt McNeil's."

She did not reach for the candy, but ran her tongue over her lips and frowned as though she encountered a bitter taste.

"The Odawa way is to live in harmony with Mother Earth. Indians do not displease Gitchie Manitou and cut trees to make a building site."

"We will stay in a wigwam?"

"We will stay in a longhouse with my Uncle Kinochausie. He is old and wise. You will have cousins to play with. I will teach you the games I played when I was your age."

"Like what?"

"There were many. In one, we placed large pinecones upright in a circle, then aimed a ball at them, hoping to scatter as many of the cones as possible. We also played stickball and—"

Her wide-eyed stare stopped me from going further.

"How long must we stay in this savage place?"

I was tired from the effort of placating her. "Until I decide it is time to leave."

Uncle Kinochausie's house was three miles, as Englishmen measure distance, from Wampeme's. If that worry did not fully occupy my mind, it would suffice until a more important worry came along. I resented wasting energy on a peevish child, even if she was my granddaughter.

Francois broke into my reflection. "Ma'am, I see a peek of sunshine in the far west, but between good weather and us, a storm threatens. We should high-tail it for shore." As he spoke, the wind had changed direction.

Louizon took down the blanket and grabbed the oars. "The gods take perverse pleasure in changing the weather as easily as they change a pair of moccasins." He directed his comment to Harriet, but she ignored him. The words barely cleared his mouth when raindrops pelted us like buckshot.

The next strong swell sent the candy tumbling from the seat to the bottom of the canoe. I raised a tarpaulin over Harriet and me. Within seconds waves surged to the height of a tall man and splashed over us. We took on water. I grabbed a spare set of oars and added my paddling to our effort to reach shore before capsizing.

Harriet edged closer, and in spite of the reason, her closeness delighted me.

"You are safe with Nookomis." It was a promise I might not make good, but I had no regret in making it. Lightning zigzagged the summer sky, brilliant and frightening and splendid, as it lit blackness bleaker than the devil's heart.

The roar of thunder grew deafening. A few feet from shore, Francois jumped from the canoe, lifted Harriet from the vessel, and carried her toward land. A lightning bolt struck a few rods down the beach and sheared a tree in half.

Louizon stayed with the boat. If I waited for Francois to return for me, it would leave Harriet alone, shivering on the beach while the sky unveiled its drama around her. I stepped from the canoe and waded to land.

Francois lost no time sloshing back and helping Louizon carry the canoe ashore. They scraped together a bed of pine needles, spread a tarpaulin atop of it, unloaded our baggage and belongings, and covered and secured a second tarpaulin over our possessions.

They turned the canoe on its side, drained the water from it, then propped it on oars with the bottom side to the wind. They spread a third tarpaulin under the canoe lean-to, and Harriet and I climbed under it for feeble protection.

I had little time to reflect on the safety of hunching beneath a canoe in a storm. God or Gitchie Manitou intervened and within minutes—as quickly as it had started—the violent weather spent itself. The rain stopped, clouds cleared, and the sun, ready to descend for the night, caressed the earth's western horizon.

Harriet, hair drenched and plastered to her face, looked like a drowned muskrat. Her fine dress, bedraggled and uncomely, clung to skinny legs.

"Looks as good a place to camp for the night as any other." Francois winked at Harriet. "Want to help me build a fire?" He pointed to a decaying pine stump. "Dead branches or stumps of the fir trees give us pitch wood. Even when damp, it helps us build fires."

"What is pitch wood?" Harriet asked. She had not released her grip of my fingers, and I traipsed along following Francois to the dead tree.

"I guess a child raised in New Hampshire doesn't have much reason to learn about pitch wood," he said. "A tree that is broken by high winds, or the stump of a tree chopped down, keeps making sap in the mistaken notion it can heal itself. When this sap dries it ignites as fast as a Frenchman trying to outrun a Sioux warrior."

The last thing I needed was for Francois to frighten Harriet with talk of marauding Indians. We began collecting broken fragments of wood.

To redirect conversation, I said, "Many years ago I took you to Bois Blanc for sugar camp." She did not respond, but her slight smile suggested she remembered. "On the way, I told you about the basswood tree and its gifts to the Odawa. The fir trees are likewise blessings from God. Their green boughs make excellent bedding material. Their wood can be carved into arrows. Their sap is a medicine for wounds. We can get enough of that sap to heal a scrape or burn by piercing resin blisters on young trees."

I stepped over the dead tree where we collected pitch and showed her a resin bump on a nearby living tree. "Resin has lots of uses." I punctured a bubble, ran my finger over the fresh sap, and touched it to the top of her hand. "It is sticky and makes a good glue. We use it to seal the inside of our canoes."

"I remember. You told me about the sticky pitch at Sugar Camp."

I winked, pleased with her recollection. "It might not appeal to you, but in winters when food was scarce we even boiled the tree's needles and drank the tea they made."

Harriet gathered her skirt in her left hand and used it to hold the wood she collected. She grew quiet again, but it seemed the quiet of pensiveness, not ill temper.

Francois built a roaring fire. We hung our wet clothes on a bush not far from the flames and changed into dry garments.

"Let's see if we can scavenge a few oduppeneeg." I caught her confused look. "Oduppeneeg is the Odawa word for wild potatoes, and they are sweeter than those we grow in our garden. Louizon will spear whitefish, and Francois will fix you a dinner as good as any served in the finest lodging. If that fails to fill your belly, we will sample those sweet cakes Aunt Schindler packed for us. Then, maybe I will tell you about the evil Matchie Manitou who sends the storms."

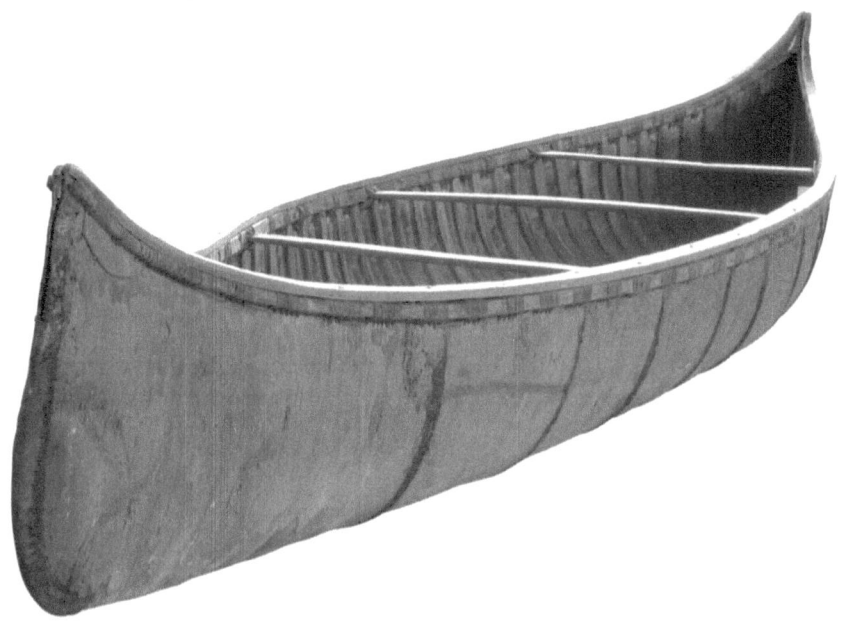

A small birch bark canoe
Photo Courtesy of the Canadian Canoe Museum/Michael Cullen
Peterborough, Ontario

Symbol for Gitchie Manitou in the Ojibwe New Testament 1988
(Wikipedia)

23.
A Storyteller

"The earth does not belong to man; man belongs to the earth. This we know. All things are connected like the blood which unites one family." **Chief Seattle**

July 1827

As we set out on day two of our journey, Louizon looked into the sun, shaded his eyes with one hand, and with his other tossed a tiny brown bundle into the waves. Soft humming accompanied the men's pull and push of the paddles. The morning was fresh with promise, and I wondered which of my granddaughter's dispositions had climbed into the canoe alongside of me: the one she possessed as a sweet child of four who loved me and sobbed at our separation, or the haughty, confused half-grown girl returned to me two short weeks ago.

"What is he doing?" Harriet's voice hinted nothing about her mood.

"He gives kinnickinnic to Matchie Manitou to secure our safe passage today."

She leaned closer to the water and watched the small mass drift away. "I don't know what that is."

"Kinnickinnic?" It reminded me of how different Odawa customs were from the traditions that filled Harriet's life. A summer seemed of insufficient duration to forge a lasting connection between two such dissimilar worlds. But I had promised Josette, and I intended to try. "It is Indian tobacco with dogwood and herbs. Tied in a small package like Francois's, it is called a carot."

Harriet looked back toward me from the spot where the lake swallowed the offering. Her eyes narrowed. "Will it really keep us from harm?"

"Louizon thinks so. He believes his token of respect appeases the spirit who sent last night's storm, and today the Manitou will not trouble our path."

"What do you think?"

Her earnestness amused me. "Ask me tonight after we have pulled ashore."

She thrust her hand into her valise and felt around. After a few seconds, she extracted the small *Grimm's Fairy Tales for Children* given to her by Marianne and began reading. Perhaps an hour passed before she looked up and said, "I fell asleep last night before you could tell me where storms come from."

I did not fancy myself a storyteller in the tradition of that respected calling, but I welcomed the opportunity to share a good tale. "The Odawa believe Matchie Manitou, son of the great hunter, Mageewemon, controls deadly weather. The father hoped his boy would become a respected chief."

"Did he?"

"No, he became more like a monster. Matchie Manitou desired a beautiful young woman who was the wife of another man. The cruel Manitou kidnapped the wife and imprisoned her on Manitou Island." I pointed downlake. "In that direction."

"Can we stop and see where he kept her?"

I was not sure if interest or restlessness motivated Harriet's request. "No, it would take us off course. And it would not matter if we did. That was many, many years ago. There would no longer be signs of Matchie Manitou's prison."

"What happened to the young woman?"

"Her heart broke. She lost the will to live."

Harriet's pale cheeks, marred by scratches where she had itched last night's mosquito bites, flushed with indignation. "She died?"

"She died. Her husband was inconsolable when he learned of her death. He rowed far out into the lake...about where we now paddle, jumped overboard, and drowned."

Harriet opened her eyes wide as an owl's and exhaled a soft gasp.

"The husband's tribe was so frightened by Matchie Manitou's powers that they held a powwow and decided they must slay the evil spirit. The bravest warriors climbed into the tribe's largest canoe and paddled toward Manitou Island. They hid until Matchie Manitou fell asleep and then crept upon him, trussed him with basswood cord, and tied a stone about his neck."

"They were going to kill him?" Harriet stared over to the island as though expecting a fearsome spirit to rise above its trees.

"They were going to try. It took all of them—I believe a dozen—to lift the huge Manitou into their canoe. He struggled, drawing on every ounce of his strength, but the ropes held tight. The warriors paddled farther out into the lake until the water under them was as deep as eight men standing on the shoulders of one another. Then they tossed the wicked Manitou overboard. He wrestled so hard to free himself that waves built to a size never before seen by humans. The canoe heaved about and finally sank. All aboard perished."

"What happened to Matchie Manitou?"

"No one knows for certain, but even today, when storms rile our lake, and waves grow so angry that men tremble, it is said that Matchie Manitou battles to get back to land."

"How does Louizon know that Matchie Manitou likes tobacco?"

She propped her small valise against her side of the canoe and laid back against it. I leaned over and handed her a stick of pemmican. She shook her head, and I returned the dried meat to the deerskin pouch at my feet. I settled opposite her, a pile of otter pelts softening the vessel's hard edge behind me. "Our tradition says that many years ago, when the Anishinaabek lived far in the direction where the sun begins its daily journey, one of our brother Bodwe'aadamiinh had a vision that something special would flourish in his garden."

Within seconds of each other, Francois and Louizon stopped their humming. Francois turned briefly in my direction and smiled without missing a stroke.

"The next day the young Bodwe'aadamiinh found strange broad green leaves sprouting from stalks next to his squash. He studied them, plucked one, put it in his mouth, and chewed. The bitter taste choked him and he spit out the foul substance. He saw nothing special about this plant and had no idea what he was expected to do with it.

"He decided to fast and ask the spirits to explain it to him. The Bodwe'aadamiinh, like the Odawa and other Indians, believe fasting clears the mind and prepares it to receive the truth. On the young man's third day without food, the Great Spirit appeared and instructed him to dry the leaves until they turned brown. The spirit said that the leaves could then be smoked in a pipe. He instructed the young man on how to make such a vessel. The spirit said the dried leaves could also be burned in the fire as incense. Most importantly, the kinnickinnic, for that is what it was called, should be used as an offering any time men wanted to gain the favor of the gods, who would smile on this gift."

"So, I guess that's a yes." She summed up my long answer, "Indian gods want tobacco."

I leaned over, patted her leg, and nodded. I allowed myself only a tiny grin, keeping a broader smile tucked in my heart.

The story ended too soon. I did not want to lose her back into the book. "There is another story about why weather changes so quickly in the Michigan Territory."

"We've got time. There isn't a lot to do in this canoe."

"Do you remember the legend I told you yesterday about Nanabozo?"

She cocked her head and wrinkled her nose. "It was only yesterday."

"Why, of course, but I was not sure you were listening."

She slouched farther down and drew both legs up onto the plank seat. For July, the weather was brisk, and she spread a Mackinac blanket over her.

"Nanabozo plays tricks and is not always perfect, but mostly he is a good spirit. He has a brother, Peepuckawis, of whom the same cannot be said. The two brothers often quarreled.

"Nanabozo, in spite of the fact that he lost his temper and twisted the tree at L'Arbre Croche, usually enjoyed a cheerful disposition. He wandered the earth, and wherever he went the birds sang. The sun directed its rays to the wildflowers, encouraging them to grow until their fragrance filled the air with delicate perfume. As Nanabozo traveled toward the North Star, he carried with him warmer weather. Sugar maples broke out in buds. Fruit and corn grew and provided food for Indians.

"Peepuckawis was jealous of the attention the tribes lavished on Nanabozo and pestered the winds to thwart his brother's journey with rain and storms, and ice and snow. At first Nanabozo ignored Peepuckawis' temper, but finally when the weather was as bad as we experienced last night…"

I sucked in a deep breath and lowered the pitch of my voice. "No, ten times worse than that, Nanabozo challenged Peepuckawis to a race. Good weather was the wager. Every time Nanabozo gained the lead, Peepuckawis called upon the winds for help. When Nanabozo dressed in furs, Peepuckawis asked the South Wind to blow heat on him. When Nanabozo shed the furs and ran in a breechclout, Peepuckawis sought the wrath of the North Wind."

Harriet pressed forward, closer to me. "Who won the race?"

"That day Nanabozo won. The sun came out and smiled on Mother Earth. But when the weather seems arbitrary, the Odawa say it is the brothers running their race."

She seemed to think about the two tales. "Which is the true story?"

"Perhaps both, or perhaps neither. They are important because they are part of who we are. It is how our people explained adversity and things they could not control."

She twisted her mouth but said nothing.

We sat companionably for a short while before she turned around on the seat, laid her head on my lap and, lulled by the paddling rhythm, fell asleep. When she awoke, I pointed at a half-circle inlet ahead.

"I see it. I see it," she said. "That's the crooked tree."

We passed three canoes as we headed toward shore. Each held a solitary man clutching a wooden pole with a sharpened stone arrowhead attached. The weapon was poised to cast at whitefish that swam into the shallow waters. We kept a respectable distance, it being impolite to disturb fishing waters. The men, in turn, nodded. It was early in the afternoon for spear-fishing. More canoes would paddle out when dusk settled. Then fishermen, two to a canoe, would join the effort to secure food. One man would hold a torch and light the water's surface while the second aimed his ready spear.

Smells of evergreen, raw earth, and smoke replaced the crisp clean air of the lake. The steady, shrill whistle of a whippoorwill called from a nearby tree. Overcome by emotion at seeing my beloved village loom ahead, I wiped my eyes, grateful that Harriet fixed on the narrow ridge of jack pines either side of the storied crooked tree rather than glance my way.

Indian villages were my home in a different way than Mackinac Island. After my father's death, Gabagouache provided a safe haven for our rudderless family. When an Odawa woman's husband deserts her, dies or, as in my father's case, is murdered, the tribe welcomes her back. If she has a brother or an uncle, they take in her and her children and support them as their own. If there is no male relative, someone in the tribe steps forward to provide. Families, especially children, are cherished, even when food is short or disease kills off the best hunters.

My Uncle Kinochausie accepted my mother, Thimotee, my sisters, and me into his already crowded dwelling. From before my second birthday until I married Joseph, my French blood meant little. I was Odawa.

A young boy, appearing small from our distance, sat on a rock and pitched a stick into the lake. A scrawny dog bounded into the waves, retrieved the stick, carried it back to the boy, and dropped it at his feet. The animal shook itself and jumped in frenzied circles around the youngster as if to say, do not stop now. The boy obliged with several tosses before he spotted us and waved his hands in our direction. He then turned and ran between the trees. I caught sight of him again as he mounted the sandy hill beyond the tree line. He remained in view until he crested the peak and descended the other side.

My uncle anticipated our homecoming, and I guessed the young boy was stationed to watch for us. He would spread the news that a canoe arrived. Word would pass from longhouse to wigwam to longhouse, and soon the entire village would be aware of our presence.

By the time Francois and Louizon carried Harriet and me ashore, and beached the canoe and our goods, my aunts and cousins streamed over the hill to welcome us.

Francois pointed north. He and his brother bid us farewell and set off toward Middle Village, where they would stay with relatives. We would see little of them until it was time to return to Mackinac.

Uncle Kinochausie lagged back from the rest of our family. The hickory cane on which he leaned spoke more to the crippling effect of advanced age than to restraint for dignity's sake.

Harriet clutched my hand. I let it go when my uncle threw his arms around me. I embraced him before I saw the stricken look in my granddaughter's eyes. I crouched, making her taller than me. "Harriet, this is your great uncle, Kinochausie."

My uncle stepped back, and in English he must have practiced for the occasion, said, "We are happy to have you with us." He handed her a necklace which she fondled, colored glass bead by colored glass bead, before putting it over her head, where it rested against her tunic. I reached for Wampeme's blue bauble around my own neck, then removed my hand when I realized what I had done.

Harriet had arisen that morning, folded her back-East dress, and tucked it away in the valise. She pulled on moccasins and the buckskin garment I had made for her. I thanked God for small blessings. She arrived at the village wearing no frills or lace. She looked up at Uncle's worn face, wrinkled and wizened with age, and returned his smile.

We walked the short distance to the knoll of Kinochausie's longhouse. "That is ours." He pointed ahead. The frame was constructed from saplings set in two parallel rows the length of the house. They curved in toward the middle, twisted and lashed to form an arc. Strips of bark fastened additional saplings to the framework and provided strength. The outside was covered with bark sheets and overlapped with rush mats. The symbol of the otter hung over the doorway.

Uncle lifted a deerskin and moved it aside so Harriet could enter. "It is a good time to visit. A longhouse is cooler during the hot season than the wigwams we use when we travel. It also provides more space."

Harriet, who was again holding my hand, said, "It looks like sugar camp."

"I'm glad you remember," I said.

She nodded, and I followed her inside.

"You can put your things there." Uncle pointed to an area with a long bench that had been cleared for our valises. The eyes of three families turned in our direction. Uncle put a hand on Harriet's shoulder. "We thank the Great Spirit you have come to us. You are our clan. You are our blood."

24.
Crooked Tree

"Like the grasses showing tender faces to each other, thus should we do, for this was the wish of the Grandfathers of the World." **Black Elk**

July 1827

That evening the men retired to the sweathouse to discuss tribal matters. The women of our longhouse settled around an outdoor fire and watched fireflies flicker in a nearby copse of trees. I had brought a mocock of maple sugar candy that Harriet passed around. She took a remaining piece for herself, nibbling the edges in a way reminiscent of our picnic many years ago. The intervening passage of time seemed less forbidding than it had two days earlier. She sat cross-legged next to me. I put my arm around her shoulders and hoped Josette watched from heaven.

We listened to night sounds of an owl and crickets. A possum ventured toward us, changed its mind, and scurried for the cover of scrub brush behind the longhouse. The crescent moon bobbed in and out between swaying branches.

Harriet put what was left of her candy in her mouth and swallowed before she broke the hush that had fallen over us. "Were you born here?"

"No. Measured by the distance a canoe travels in a day, I was born three sunsets south of here."

"Tell me about when you were born." Her voice was soft as a cloud opening to let in the sunshine.

I kissed her cheek. "I can do that." With the men gone, it was a good time to share traditions that could not be discussed in their presence. A woman's moons, pregnancy and deliveries were not matters shared with men.

"While I was growing up, Maman told me the story of my birth many times. It is part of my history."

Harriet laid her head against me and for that moment the world was perfect.

"Maman was a full-blood Odawa. Indians called her Thimotee. She married a French trader, Jean Baptiste Marcotte, and took the Christian name Marie."

I told Harriet my papa came from across the great saltwater sea and settled in Cap Santé, near Three Rivers in New France. From there he traveled the lakes to trade furs. At L'Arbre Croche he met my mother. I was born in a month of snow and ice, and he and Maman and my older sisters lived in a rugged hut in St. Joseph during that season.

"Maman was familiar with the ritual of receiving a new life. Odawa women do not make as big a fuss out of birth as white women do. For three hours, Maman had felt the rhythmic clenching that announced it was my time to enter the world. She sent my ten-year-old sister, Charlotte, to fetch Piawashe, the tribal midwife, from the nearby Bodwe'aadamiinh village. My sister also found Papa, who was trading furs at the village. She told him the joyful news and said she would return for him after the baby arrived.

"The day I was born, our hut was warm and comfortable, at least compared to outside where the frigid North wind howled. My sister Marianne, the oldest daughter still living with Maman and Papa, sat on a mat beside Maman. She prepared a cup of sage and rose hip tea with a pinch of dried, crushed winterberry bark and placed it in Maman's hands. She smoothed the heavy blankets and furs about Maman, proud she was old enough to assist with the delivery. She, too, was anxious to welcome me into the cycle of life.

"When Charlotte returned from summoning Piawashe, she kept our youngest sister, four-year-old Therese—you know her as Aunt

Schindler—quiet, so there would be no disharmony to upset me. My newborn body, mind, and spirit would appreciate peace as I entered the world. Charlotte would also stoke the fire so I would not be chilled.

"Nine-year-old Marguerite watched the sagamité simmering in the cast iron pot hung above the flame. The maple syrup-sweetened cornmeal, fat, and smoked fish would provide my family's evening meal. She added a handful of dried blackberries to mark the special occasion. She threw a small amount of dried mint into the fire to soften the fish odor. The pleasant aroma filled the air and assured me that my parents could provide for me.

"Piawashe carried a medicine bag with shells and stones and feathers, symbols of the process of creation. The pouch also contained herbs and medicine plants to minimize discomfort and control bleeding if Maman needed them. Piawashe hummed a soothing song and set to work. No words were exchanged. The old medicine woman dipped her fingers into a container of bear grease to soften Maman's skin and prevent tearing.

"Marianne refilled Maman's cup of tea. Maman managed only a couple of sips before she gasped and my tiny head emerged. Piawashe gently slid me from Maman's body. With a hunting knife, she cut the cord, preserving a piece for me to cherish for my entire lifetime; a reminder of its connection to Maman and the greater Mother Earth."

Harriet had sat spellbound, but now asked, "Do you still have it?"

"*Certainement*. I keep it in my chest of drawers along with the combs Papa gave Maman as a gift on their wedding day."

I picked up where I had left off. "From the medicine bag, Piawashe took a small rattle and laid it gently to my forehead and then dipped her gnarled fingers into a jar of sacred earth and placed a smudge where the rattle had touched."

"Why did she put dirt on you?"

"It symbolized the Odawa connection to their land.

"Piawashe handed me to Marianne. When the story was told, my sister always added that she believed God or the Great Spirit stood beside her. So perfect was the miracle of birth that it could not have happened without a spirit guiding it. My sister took me, cleaned my tiny body, and massaged bear grease on my fresh skin while Piawashe washed Maman. Marianne wrapped me tightly in a flannel blanket that Papa had brought home from rendezvous and then handed me to Maman.

"Maman used to tell me she had lost count of how many moons separated that day from the one on which she had greeted my oldest sister, named Marie after her; but she knew it had been twenty-one French years. The joy of participating in this life dance, she said, was not diminished by the births that had come between. A sixth daughter was a sign the gods, including the Catholic God who favored large families, blessed us that day.

"Maman says that when she held me for the first time, she whispered, 'I see in you the spirit of an old one come back to help our people. You are a sacred gift given to me by the Great Spirit and the Father God. I thank them for this blessing. I ask them to give me wisdom to guide you. I hope your life is filled with joy and purpose. I hope the Great Spirit allows you to serve your people, both the Odawa and the French, and that you can help them better understand one another. I hope the Catholic God showers favor on you and saves your soul.'

"By that time, Maman said, all of my sisters crowded around and ran fingers gently over my smooth cheeks and forehead. Marianne said my eyes stared back at them and looked too serious for a baby. Therese made them all laugh when she said she thought I was the color of maple sugar candy sprinkled with cinnamon. Maman told Charlotte to fetch Papa. It was time for him to come home."

The fire still blazed and the moon had a far distance to travel before disappearing.

When my story ended, Harriet stretched out on a mat, her eyes half-closed, fingers kneading the fringe of her tunic. I thought she neared sleep until she said, "That can't be your last story for the night."

The others around the circle nodded. It was not their history I recounted, but they understood the gift of her past that I was giving my granddaughter.

I considered for a moment, then said, "Maman told me about my name and my tikinagan. Both belong to the story of my birth. Time remains to tell you about them before the night calls us to rest."

I shifted my position against the birch that provided support for my tired back. "Before I came into the world, Papa told my maman that if his seventh child[55] was a girl he wanted to name her Magdelaine. He said Mary Magdelaine ministered to Christ, stayed with his body after it was taken from the cross, held vigil by the tomb, and was the first to see him after he rose from the dead.

"Papa looked forward to the day he would meet Jesus for the first time. My papa often shared his church learning with Maman because there was no priest in St. Joseph. Maman loved the story of Mary Magdelaine's redemption from a life of sin. In it, she saw hope for herself. Papa said her former idolatrous Odawa beliefs angered the real God, but he forgave her the instant she accepted him as her only true Lord."

"Don't you think the Catholic God loves the Odawa who believe in Manitous?"

Harriet's question set my right eye to twitching. I pressed it with my fingers, hoping the tic would stop. An ember had landed on her mat, and I flicked it back toward the fire. "That is a complicated question. I believe God loves all people. I try to understand what he wants." The confusion I saw in her scrunched brow made me wish for a better explanation. "I believe God expects us to embrace him as the Catholics—."

"My Aunt McNeil is Presbyterian."

"But he loves her too. And you. Certainly you."

I had no desire to wander farther down this twisted path. "I was telling you about my name. When Maman became confused about distinguishing between Mary the mother of Jesus and Mary Magdelaine, Papa pointed out that the additional name of *Magdelaine* was the way to tell them apart. He believed that Mary Magdelaine was from a place called Magdela. Papa was not positive he got every detail precise, but he was sure it was close enough that God overlooked minor errors.

"Maman agreed it was a fine name for their perfect baby. She added that when I grew older, however, she wanted a medicine man to give me an Odawa name. Otherwise I would not seem part of the tribe. Maman told me that Papa never liked the idea, but he did not argue."

Harriet turned toward me, her elbow and hand creating a prop for her head. "Did the medicine man give you the name Zhaawan?"

"Yes. But not until my second year. Maman did not ask him for a naming ceremony until she believed he could look at me and know what the right name for me would be."

"Is a naming ceremony like baptism with water splashed on you?"

"Similar. Maman held me in her arms. My closest family stood in a circle around an outdoor fire. Everyone wore their finest clothes. It was only a few months after that that my papa died. Maman said he looked proud as he handed a carot of kinnickinnic from his left hand to the left hand of the medicine man. Odawa use the left hand to transfer the gift because it is closest to the heart."

"How does the medicine man pick the right name for a baby?"

Before I could answer, one of the women rose and brought another log to the campfire. It landed with enough force that sparks shot in all directions.

I let the flames settle down, and the woman retake her place before I continued. "The name might come to the medicine man in a dream the night before the ceremony, or it might not come until he looks into the face of the child that morning."

"Which was it with your name?"

"It was like he already knew me. The medicine man lived only two longhouses from us. He had watched me growing for many moons. He later told my parents that every time he saw me, the name seemed to already be in his head. But, of course, he told no one until the naming day.

"Four of my adult relatives agreed to guide me during my lifetime. The medicine man prayed to the Great Spirit asking for his blessings on my life, and then he announced my name. He chose the name Zhaawan because it means bluebird. I was not then Zhaawan Kwe. The end of my name was added when I grew to womanhood. Zhaawan Kwe means Bluebird Woman."

"Why did he choose that name?"

"He said the bluebird is the sign of spring and love and rebirth. Indians believe that birds, because they fly, are messengers of change. He believed I would play an important role in helping my people adapt to a rapidly changing world."

Fireflies flashed close enough that I could have reached out and caught one in the palm of my hand. Two infants fell asleep on their mothers' laps. Several women soundlessly left our circle.

"Tell me about the tikinagan." Harriet said.

"Ah, yes. I am sure you have guessed that Odawa women indulge their children. My maman was no exception. She used to sing to me. '*Kwaw notchi we maw kaw te waw osk ke zheg wog quay azyas.*' When I think I hear her words, I remind myself I am really hearing her tell the stories when I was older."

"What did her song mean?"

"She called me her pretty black-eyed girl. She said that from my tikinagan, propped against a rock or hung from a tree, my eyes followed her everywhere. I learned early that smiling brought attention. My sisters and even Maman and Papa took turns making faces and dancing about for my amusement.

"One day Maman cooed at me, telling me I was her sweetest baby. That made Therese—Aunt Schindler—jealous. She had lost her place as the youngest of the sisters. She accused Maman of not loving her anymore.

"Maman set aside the basket she was weaving, drew Therese onto her lap, and told her she was now a big girl, and Maman loved all of her big girls. But I was the only sweet baby. Maman looked at me grinning from my tikinagan and told Therese that she had used the same tikinagan when she was small like me.

"As I grew up, I heard the story of the tikinagan more times than I can count. Maman told us that long ago when she realized God was going to bless her with her first child, she asked Papa to bring her the fur of several beaver kits. She sewed these into a small blanket that she laid on her sleeping mat."

"The fur wasn't for the baby?"

"It was. I am getting to that part." I swatted a sand gnat before it could bite the back of my hand. "Maman slept on the small blanket for several months to wear off the long, more bristly hairs. She wanted the softest blanket for her baby.

"She also sent Papa to find just the right black ash tree at the edge of swamp where the wild rice grew."

"There are lots of trees. What made one special?"

"Black ash will bend if it is held over steaming water. Papa cut two boards the same length. He laid them side by side. He then shaped two shorter boards that he laid across the longer boards at the top and bottom." I looked around me and picked up four sticks, two the length of my hand, two the length of my forearm, and demonstrated how it worked. "Papa held the bottom of the tikinagan over steaming water and bent it so it would rock. He rounded another board on both ends to fasten higher up on the tikinagan to hold his babies in place." I pointed to the sticks I had used and demonstrated where this board would be joined. "It took Papa a long time to get the boards the way he wanted them.

"Maman would be able to lean the tikinagan against a tree and work on her sewing or weaving, but still reach over and rock the cradleboard without picking it up."

I quieted as Harriet studied my example. When she looked back up at me, I continued. "Carved blocks of wood were attached to each side at the top of the cradleboard so if it happened to fall forward, Maman's baby would not strike its head. To these top pieces, she secured small bells. When her children were outside she wanted the gentle winds to create soothing music.

"As the time for the birth of Maman's first child came close, she beaded a feather onto the deer hide that went around the tikinagan and laced tightly up the front. The feather symbolized Maman's hope that the child she carried would be a person of honor and trust.

"Every time Maman told the story, she stopped to tell us that the baby for whom the feather was added was named Marie, but that God decided to take Marie to heaven. At that point Maman always crossed herself and asked God to watch out for Marie. One time, after she said her brief prayer, I began to cry because I would never know this sister. Maman said that was not true. Our first Marie was with God, and she was happy. Someday, Maman said, I would rejoice at meeting the sister I did not know in this world. I asked Maman if Marie would be a baby when I saw her, but Maman had no answer."

Harriet seemed to ponder this. I waited to see if she would ask questions. None came, and I picked up my story. "Maman said that for each child that God sent, she created an additional symbol. As she told the story, she always jumped ahead to the stars and moon she sewed on the tikinagan for me. I was the youngest and had not learned the virtue of patience. Even when I grew older and the story was repeated, Maman kept the order, beginning with Marie who died, then me and then the others."

"What did the moon and stars mean?" Harriet asked.

"Maman said she beaded them because the moon and stars light our way through the dark night. They would guide my journey through the difficult times the medicine man had predicted.

"After Maman satisfied my curiosity, she would point to a long curvy line of blue beads and tell me, and as many of my sisters as were listening, that Papa traded three mink pelts for those beads. They symbolized a beautiful long river and were sewn while she waited for my brother, Jean Baptiste. She wanted his life to be long and full like a river."

"Did the babies like the tikinagan?"

"Of course. All babies like it. It makes them feel secure. Like before they came into the world. Our tikinagan had a leather strap. It could hang from a tree branch. From there we watched everything around us."

"What symbols were there for the other sisters?"

"A tree was sewn on for Charlotte because Maman wanted her to grow strong and tall. An eagle was Marianne's symbol. Maman wanted her to be wise. Marguerite got a sun to encourage light to fill her life.

"For Therese, Maman sewed a rose. Therese liked the red color. She insisted Maman chose a rose because she wanted Therese to be pretty like the flower. But Maman would say she did not know Therese would be a girl when she beaded the rose. She wanted the child, boy or girl, to appreciate all of the beauty with which God created the world. Maman said it was true that after Therese arrived the rose became even more perfect because Therese was as pleasing as the flowers.

"I bragged that I got more decorations than anyone. Maman would tell me that was right. It was the family's gift to me. 'The tikinagan you used,' she said, 'became more beautiful after your brother and each of your sisters used it, just like our family became more blessed when each child joined us.'

"I asked her, 'Will you put more beads on it after me?'

"She told me it depended upon whether God gave her more children. I said I hoped he kept the rest of the babies. I remember her laughter filling the longhouse. I remember the love in her eyes. And I remember her bending down and kissing me. She said that if God agreed, she thought that was reasonable. She was running out of room on the tikinagan. I was Maman's and Papa's last child."

25.
Wild Strawberries

"Every part of this earth is sacred to my people. Every shining pine needle, every sandy shore, every mist in the dark woods, every clearing and humming insect is holy in the memory and experience of my people. The sap which courses through the trees carries the memories of the red man." **Chief Seattle**

July 1827

The next day I handed Harriet a small birch bark basket and grabbed one for myself. "Today we pick wild strawberries."

She laid aside the shells she was stringing on a thin strip of rawhide and reached for the container. "I love strawberries."

"We will slice them over skillet cake for dinner," I said.

We skirted cornfields with waist-high stalks, their fringed tassels blowing in the morning breeze. We headed close to the lakeshore, where sandy soil favored growing berries.

Along the way, Harriet hummed a song she had heard Uncle sing each morning to greet the day. She stopped and leaned close to a bush aglow with small, yellow trumpet-shaped flowers.

"Honeysuckle smells sweeter at night," I said. "When I was a girl, Maman told me it released its perfume after dark to attract hummingbird moths. A friend told me Maman was wrong. The honeysuckle saves its fragrance to enchant young lovers walking the lakeside at dusk." It had been more than three decades since Wampeme said that. He had then drawn me close and kissed me. I could still feel the warm softness of his lips on mine and the almost–innocent look on his face when I opened my eyes afterwards.

A few steps farther along, Harriet picked up a pink and black pebble. "I wouldn't mind if we stayed at L'Arbre Croche forever."

"What about your friends?" I moved closer to her as we walked.

"I would miss them, and I wish our longhouse had girls my age. Babies aren't the best companions, but I have you and Uncle. My insides feel happy here." She gave the stone a powerful throw toward the waves, but there was no hope it could reach the water from our distance. "I love Aunt McNeil. And of course, Papa. I have a big room that is all mine. Even so, I sometimes feel like I am a visitor. Here I feel I am home."

I pulled her close and hugged her. "I am glad we are here this summer. Maybe your papa and Aunt McNeil will let you spend all summers with me." If I had harbored lingering doubts, I was now sure God had given me back my granddaughter.

We had reached our destination. She picked a ripe berry and laid it on her palm for my inspection.

"It is absolutely perfect. You must throw it as far as you can so the birds can eat it."

"What?" Her eyes, soft a moment earlier, narrowed.

"If we eat that berry the plant would think it useless to make more. Out of respect, the Odawa give back the first berry picked and ask the Great Spirit, or in my case, the Catholic God, to make the plants grow more. We also offer the Great Spirit the first animal a hunter kills and the first of the rice and corn and other foods harvested."

"Does God like strawberries?"

"I never thought about it. I assume everyone loves strawberries, even God." I considered the question. "He must think they are the most delicious of all fruits."

"Why do you say that?"

"The Odawa have a story that tells me." I laughed, knowing that as surely as it was strawberry season, my declaration foretold another tale shared with my granddaughter.

Harriet gave her strawberry a mighty toss and looked at me expectantly.

"A long time ago, when our people still lived on Turtle Island, a married couple quarreled. No one remembers why they argued. Screams and angry words reached nearby wigwams. The woman ran away from her husband. When he realized she was gone, he moaned and wept. After watching the unhappy man, the Great Spirit asked him if he wanted his wife back."

Harriet pursed her lips and held up her hand to stop me. "Nookomis, was this the Great Spirit or the Father God?"

I plucked a handful of berries and dropped them into the basket I had placed on the ground. "It is an Odawa tale and therefore the Great Spirit. The Catholic God, however, would approve the lesson the story teaches."

"Did the man get his wife back?"

"Oh, yes. He promised he would never quarrel with her again, so the Great Spirit told him to go, find her, and tell her he was sorry.

"The woman had left an hour before the man and had such a head start that her husband could not catch up. The Great Spirit wanted to help the poor fellow, so he planted a large patch of blueberries on the woman's path to persuade her to halt. Her anger at her husband was so big, however, that she did not slow down to eat the blueberries."

Harriet groaned and shook her head. A red-winged blackbird swooped down, aimed at the fruit Harriet had thrown, and carried it away.

"The Great Spirit had other tricks. He enticed the wife with a bush of raspberries. That lure worked no better than the blueberries. The thorns scratched the woman's legs, but she ignored the temptation. The Great Spirit next dropped a patch of blackberries in her way, and then currants. She kept running without looking back."

The few berries Harriet had picked while listening to my story ended up in her mouth, not her container, so I put my next two handfuls into her basket.

"The Great Spirit understood it would take something very special to stop the woman. He thought hard and created a juicy new berry, all glistening and red in the bright sunlight. He planted the special fruit close to the ground. Curious about a berry she had never seen before, the woman paused to try one. It was so delicious that she stopped to pick many more.

"The man caught up with her, took her hands in his, and promised he would never raise his voice in anger against her again. She forgave him, and they made up." I picked another berry. "See how it is shaped like a heart? Some of our people call it a heartberry, and it symbolizes love. It also reminds us to forgive those with whom we argue."

I stood and stretched to loosen the stiffness in my back. "I think we have enough berries."

"Aunt McNeil's church teaches we should forgive. Maybe God could borrow your story."

We started for home and Harriet asked, "How do you say Grandpapa in Odawa?"

"Mishomis," I said. "What makes you ask?"

"Papa has told me many times about his family. We descended from Thomas Pierce who came to the Massachusetts Bay Colony in 1630. He was my great, or great great, or maybe great great great grandpapa. My Grandpapa Benjamin Pierce is a very important man. He will soon be governor of New Hampshire. Papa shares his name and says I should be proud to be his granddaughter. Grandmaman Pierce is also alive, though she doesn't favor me as much as her other grandchildren."

Harriet's words, innocent and casually spoken, wounded my heart. The wisdom of remaining silent stared me squarely in the face. Over my heart's strong objection, I refused my tongue the chance to speak. What might fall from my mouth could not help Harriet, but only deepen the hurt of being less loved.

"I wish I could have met Mishomis La Framboise." She kicked at the loose dirt on our path. "He was my maman's papa, and I will never know him."

"Do you remember last night I told you that my maman promised my sisters and me we would someday meet Marie, the sister who died before we were born?"

She nodded.

"It is like that with you and your mishomis. He will be waiting for you in the next life. You will also know him because those of us still living tell his story."

"How did he die?"

I was unprepared to share the account of how the alcohol-enraged White Ox crept into our tepee and shot Joseph.

She responded to my pause with a reprieve. "Tell me what he was like."

"Mishomis La Framboise was an honorable trader, a devoted Catholic man." The wood of cooking fires along our way smelled of burning pine and evoked fonder memories than those of my husband's death. "He traveled to L'Arbre Croche guided by the crooked tree. He traded furs here for the merchandise packed in his outfit. He came ashore exactly where we did last week, so you have walked in his footsteps."

She smiled as she contemplated that.

"Everyone rushed to meet him, all eager to see what he brought. The children bounded around him, and he pretended he had nothing for them. After a few minutes of shaking his head and saying, '*non, non*,' he would reach into the canoe and grab a handful of gewgaws, maybe candy, maybe marbles, or maybe a ball and jacks."

Harriet fondled the beads Uncle Kinochausie had given her. I unfolded the story in my own time. "When I reached the summer of my fourteenth year, your mishomis asked Uncle Kinochausie if he could marry me."

I did not tell her my value was three pieces of calico, a handful of fish hooks, and a large cast iron skillet left over from the trading season. Josette would have to be satisfied with the edited version of history that I shared with her daughter.

"Were you happy to marry him?" Harriet asked.

I looked toward the water where sunlight glistened more beautiful than any manmade bauble. Therese had asked the same question, and I felt as ill-prepared to answer it now as I had then. "We did not think about happy the way you might." I grappled with ill-fitting words. "He told the most wonderful stories." I was not sure where that came from, other than to help her see her mishomis in a favorable light without forcing me to falsehoods.

"Mishomis La Framboise told you stories? Why? You were a grown-up and his wife."

"Like the Odawa, the French love stories. It was a way your mishomis made me smile."

"Were you sad?"

"On my wedding night tears filled my eyes because marriage meant leaving my family and my village. I would miss the campfires and the tales I heard there. Your mishomis said, 'Do you think if I told you a story it would make you feel less lonesome and return cheer to your disposition?'

"At that I smiled and told him it could do no harm to try."

"What story did he tell you?"

"Oh, it has been many years. I am not sure I can remember it."

"Try."

"I remember it was about a woman who saved her husband, and your mishomis said that made it appropriate for a wedding night."

"So tell me how she did that."

Harriet was not going to be satisfied without the details so I thought back and began. "It was the tale of a poor French farmer with a sweet wife and four small children. The man was overworked and one obstacle after another tormented his days. He could barely harvest enough crops to feed his family. One afternoon, a handsome stranger happened by and made the farmer an enticing offer to resolve all of his problems. Unbeknownst to the farmer, however, the stranger was the devil. When it came time to pay, the farmer learned he had made a pact with Satan who had tricked him and would own his soul. The man's wife figured a way out of the dilemma."

When I offered no more, Harriet frowned. "That cannot be the whole story. You skipped the best parts. Start over. This time at the beginning, please."

I ran my fingers over my hair, hooking a few stray wisps behind my ear before I filled in details. When I got close to the story's end, I said, "The devil arrived to collect on the bargain. The wife sobbed and begged. 'Oh, please sir, give us a few precious minutes to set our affairs in order. I will be left to raise our children alone. Even the devil can show compassion enough to permit us a short reprieve.'

"The devil asked how much time the woman needed. As she reflected, her eyes caught sight of the half-burned candle sitting on the kitchen table. An idea sprang into her mind. 'Only until the candle burns down and dies.'

"The devil pulled out an oak-spindled kitchen chair and sat down at the table. He leaned back and smoothed his slick, black frock coat. 'That should take but a brief time. I can spare you that.' His evil laughter chilled the wife's heart, but made her even more determined to save her husband. She walked over to the candle, lifted two fingers to her tongue, and licked them before snuffing out the flame. She then grabbed the candle and clutched it close to her breast—out of reach of the devil's gloved hands 'It shall never burn down and die.'

"The devil shrieked and cursed. Smoke shot from his ears, and his unholy countenance was more fearsome than anything the woman had ever witnessed.

"There was no way to undo the agreement he had made, so the devil rose and stumbled from the house, and the husband was spared."

When the story ended, we were within steps of the longhouse. Harriet said, "Mishomis thought that story would cheer you?"

"Maybe not cheer me exactly, but your Mishomis La Framboise said that if it failed to get my mind off leaving my family, at least it proved that a good wife is the best fortune with which a man may be blessed. The wife saved her husband from the devil. Your mishomis then added that he thought he, likewise, was very blessed because God allowed him to marry me. That, of course, made me feel better."

My granddaughter was a persistent one. "So were you happy or sad with Mishomis La Framboise?"

I considered what I could fairly say. "It was a good marriage. He was a kind and fair man. He treated me well, and I helped him in every way I could. We became best friends. I respected him. Together we had two beautiful children, and now I have you. Yes, I am happy I married your mishomis."[56]

The next night Uncle Kinochausie joined us at the campfire.

"You told me the story about my Mishomis La Framboise. Tell me about my Nookomis and Mishomis Marcotte," Harriet said as we watched red-orange flames dance.

"They would be your great grandparents, my maman and papa."

"What happened to them?"

"My papa died during a wintering season." Even forty-five years later, I could not speak of it without wishing God had delayed by a day my father's course to a portage between the Fox and Wisconsin Rivers. It had been a hard winter. Indians were hungry and had no money to buy food. We heard accounts of cannibalism. The Indians stopped traders and stole or extorted goods. At one such encounter a scuffle broke out, and a Sioux named Boeuf Blanc was killed. His tribesmen felt honor bound to avenge his death, and cared little which trader they held accountable. My papa was slaughtered, his body never returned to Maman for Christian burial.

These details were repeated to me many times before I reached Harriet's age. I heard them around a campfire like the one that warmed us that night. The reason I withheld the circumstances of my husband's and my papa's deaths had more to do with the fact that their assailants were Indians than with a desire to protect my granddaughter from the truth. Harriet's family in New Hampshire already filled her head with fear and distrust of Indians.

I picked up my story, omitting the pieces I preferred not to share. "My cousin, Charles Langlade,[57] brought news of Papa's death to Maman at our winter post in Ouisconsin."[58]

"Your Nookomis Marcotte died of smallpox many years later. She was—."

"It is bad form for me to stop your story, Zhaawan Kwe, but you must tell her about Charles—Akewangeketawso—before moving on," Uncle said.

I was as hesitant to have Uncle tell his version of events as perhaps he was to have me leave my account empty of details he thought important, but it would have been more disrespectful for me to stop him than it had been for him to interrupt. "Go ahead," I said. "Tell her what you feel she must hear."

The fire reflected in Uncle's eyes as he laid his pipe aside. His face lit up bright as the moon above. "Akewangeketawso means military conqueror, and it is the name we give to my nephew, Charles Langlade."

Harriet shifted so she faced Uncle. Her eyes widened at the promise of soldierly exploits.

"He was the greatest Odawa warrior of all time, with the possible exception of Obwandiyag. Your Nookomis Marcotte, whom we called Thimotee, and I had a brother named Nissowaquet. Sometimes the white man called him Lafourche. When our nephew, Akewangeketawso, was but a year older than you are, Nissowaquet took him into battle against the Chickasaw. Akewangeketawso was protected by a great manitou, and he could not be harmed. That was Akewangeketawso's first of many battles.

"He later led a raid on Pickwillany, fought in the Battle of Monongahela, and at the Battle of the Plains of Abraham he led a group of our fiercest Odawa warriors. He fought in the American Revolution. He killed many men and counted a hundred battles to his credit. Bullets and arrows never found him. He died by the will of the Great Spirit, not man's hand." Uncle picked up his pipe again, took a huge draw, and nodded his head. He looked satisfied that he had added important history.

Uncle did not mention that Charles's first wife, Oolate, lived on the other side of this village. Harriet had met her, but her connection to the great warrior was never shared. Charles deserted Oolate and married Charlotte Bourassa, a French woman from a prosperous trading family. Charlotte was terrified of Indians and scurried to hide under the bed anytime one knocked at the Langlade home. The irony of her quirk had not escaped me. Uncle Kinochausie ignored this chapter of family history.

I loved my cousin Charles and knew that his heart held great good. He acted in accord with the times. Still, my granddaughter needed no additional tales glorifying war. "I have not yet told you about Majakwatawa, Clear Sky Woman, and Kewanoquat, Returning Cloud. They were your great great-nookomis and great great-mishomis. Kewanoquat was a famous chief who counseled his people to seek peace with the light-skinned newcomers to our land."

Uncle mumbled. "And for trusting them, he paid with his life."

During our third week at L'Arbre Croche I continued to enjoy the gossip and companionship of other women from the village. One crisp summer morning before the sun warmed the air, we pounded clothes along the lakeshore. Harriet trudged over to where I hunched at my work and introduced me to a new friend. The girl's name was Negonee. I knew from the resemblance this was a child of Wampeme.

26.
Wampeme

"We always return to our first love." Native American Proverb

July 1827

Negonee stood behind Harriet and avoided looking at me. Not yet grown in grace to match her size, her arms hung too long, her skinny legs bowed slightly, and her elbows and knees resembled the gnarly bumps on our crooked tree. She shifted her weight from foot to foot, which made her appear no less ungainly. The two neat braids hanging midway down her back spoke of a mother's love and attention. When she looked up, I saw Wampeme's eyes. They were large in proportion to her face, but there was no question she inherited their smoldering intensity from her papa.

Since our arrival at L'Arbre Croche, I had seen no sign of Wampeme. Relief and annoyance quarreled for control of my emotions. I dreaded that we would cross paths, yet was vexed that he took no steps to hurry that meeting.

"Nookomis, can I go?" Harriet asked.

Caught up in thoughts of Negonee's papa, I heard only the tail end of the question. "I am sorry. Go where?"

"Negonee wants to show me where manoomin grows on water."

Had I thought about it, I would have considered it unwise to let my granddaughter traipse off to the wild rice swamps without me to watch over her. But confounded by Wampeme's child standing in front of me, I babbled like an infant who could not yet form clear words. Finally, I managed, "The backwaters are a far distance from here."

Negonee stepped up next to Harriet. With tenacity she had also inherited from her father, she said, "I will watch out and not let harm befall her." Even her voice, though softer and less mature, bore a disconcerting similarity to Wampeme's. She spoke French, not perfect, but understandable, a fact that should not have surprised me. Most of the village spoke the language with some proficiency, and Harriet, who had been in an English-speaking home for the past five years pleased me with how much French and Odawa she retained.

"I will pack a lunch." I reached for Harriet's shoulder to direct her back into the longhouse.

Negonee tapped a leather pouch that hung at her side. "Ogawshimaw has already done so."

Both girls looked to me to answer their earlier question.

"I suppose there is no harm." My words were barely spoken before they turned to race off. "Hold on. The rice is going nowhere, at least not until fall harvest. Let me fetch a few pieces of rock candy to add to your lunch."

The girls eyed one another, then followed me inside. I knelt beside a basket where I kept the sugary treats I had purchased at the American Fur Company headquarters before I left Mackinac. "When I was a child in this village," I said, "my sisters and I helped my maman and the other women harvest manoomin."

"Before you came to Crooked Tree—the place we call Waugonawkisa[59]—my ogawshimaw let me join her and the other women as they paddled into the marshes and bound the manoomin stalks into clusters." Negonee took the candy I handed her and added it to her pouch. "We did that to make room for small canoes to pass between the stalks when harvest time comes. Wild rice plants grow about as tall as you." She eyed Harriet up and down to estimate her height.

The three of us returned outside. Negonee continued sharing her story with Harriet, a story that I had intended to tell my granddaughter. "We dig ditches along the water's edge and line them with smooth bark before we gather the rice." The girls picked up their pace and went ahead of me. "We paddle close to the stalks, grab and bend the rice clusters over our canoe, strip them of grain, and then move to the next cluster."

They ignored me as I walked behind them to the first line of trees beyond our dwelling. I felt as unimportant and useless as American paper money for trading in L'Arbre Croche. I eyed the heavens for signs of weather that might give me reason to call off their outing, but the cloudless sky refused me an ally.

Harriet reached out and took Negonee's hand as they ambled along.

"Last year was my first harvest," Negonee said. "I accidentally dropped handfuls of grain into the water."

"Was your maman vexed?"

"No. Ogawshimaw said some rice needed to escape our boat and settle to the bottom to grow more rice next year."

"Can we gather rice to bring back with us?" Harriet asked her new friend.

"It's too early. But at the harvest, we have a big celebration. You can come with me and dance on the rice."

Harriet looked back to where I lagged behind. The invitation lit up her face. "Can I go with her, Nookomis?"

"We will not stay until the celebration. I must return you to your Grandmaman McNeil before then."

The scowl Harriet gave me curved into a smile when she turned back to Negonee. "Why do you dance on rice you are going to eat?"

"To separate it from the hulls before we store it in bark chests." Negonee pulled her hand away from Harriet, stomped on one foot, then the other, and swirled around.

Harriet giggled and imitated Negonee before they resumed walking.

"Dancing on it is more fun than sorting it by hand," Negonee said.

The girls' voices trailed ever softer as the distance grew between us. "Be careful. Be back while it is still daylight." I watched until they passed from sight.

Gathering Wild Rice from a watercolor by Seth Eastman 1853 (Library of Congress Catalog Online, no restrictions to use.)

The sun crept across the sky marking time with the slow march of a messenger bearing bad news. I visited friends and spent the day in idle conversation. I headed home knowing of every child born, every marriage performed, and every illness any member of the tribe had suffered in the past year. It was late afternoon when I returned to our longhouse. Women looked up from pounding elk into pemmican strips as I passed. I was anxious to hear my granddaughter's account of the day, perhaps add a detail or two to the story that I had supposed would be mine. Uncle sat on a platform, smoking a long pipe.

"Where is Harriet?" I asked.

"I thought she'd gone off with you," he said.

"She and Negonee asked to go to the rice swamps."

Uncle's narrowed eyes called my judgment into question.

"I told them to be home by sunset."

His sharp look did not soften. "They have little time then. The sun is enjoying its final triumph."

For the next hour I busied myself sewing a second pair of leggings for Harriet. My hands twitched at every sound, my needlework uneven and as unsteady as my nerves. I tossed the leggings in a heap near my trunk. When the last glimmer of daylight faded, I said, "I am going to find them."

"Stay here," Uncle said. "I'll gather men to search."

"I am coming with you."

"Then get yourself one of my hunting knives. We'll spread out and you need to be prepared." He pointed toward his sleeping roll. "Underneath that."

By the time I retrieved a six-inch, steel-bladed hunting knife and sheath and strapped it around my waist, he was back with a dozen men.

I had walked only a few rods when I heard rustling in the forest ahead. By moonlight I saw vague movements and shadows. None that looked like two girls.

"Harriet! Negonee!" I got no response. The sounds of night creatures stalking the woods deceived my ears. I continued calling the girls' names, but walked several more rods with no sign of them. My heart lurched, beating against my ribs as though wishing to get ahead of me in the hunt. I stepped up my pace, hoping to occupy my mind with something other than visions of what tragedy might have befallen them.

Since coming to Crooked Tree I had spent time examining my faith. I taught Harriet the old ways and hoped God did not deem me blasphemous when I talked of the Great Spirit. I was about to ask God if I could strike a bargain with him in exchange for Harriet's and Negonee's safe return when I heard something that sounded like a voice far off to the edge of the wooded area.

I hastened toward it. The moon had risen round and full and bright above the trees. It painted my way in soft light. I saw two figures coming toward me. They seemed to be hugging each other.

When they got close, Negonee was the first to speak. "I'm sorry, Madame La Framboise. I failed—"

"What happened?"

The girls were alive, but my stomach was not soothed by the sight of the blood-soaked strip of buckskin tied around Negonee's thigh. By the look of it, it covered no minor scratch.

Over my interruption, she tried to explain. "On our way home we crossed the river. The one with the log bridge."

"She saved me, Nookomis. I slipped and fell in. The water was over my head. Negonee jumped in after me."

"It was a spot I knew was deep—"

"She held me tight as we went over a small waterfall. Sharp rocks gashed her leg, but she got me to shore."

"I should have watched her more closely. I promised—"

"Nookomis, she swam even when I struggled against her grip. When we climbed out of the river, there was blood everywhere."

"Harriet took my knife. She cut a piece of leather from my tunic and tied it with basswood cord I had put in my pouch to show her how we bind the manoomin into clusters."

Harriet turned to her friend. "You told me what to do."

"It has taken us a long time with many rests to get—"

I halted their account. "Negonee, we are closer to your longhouse than Uncle's. If you lean on me, do you think you can make it?"

"It is not far. I know where we are. I can walk the distance."

Her quivering voice argued otherwise. Harriet patted her friend's arm.

"Harriet was very brave. She told me she would make me a pallet of leaves and fetch help."

I wanted Negonee to be quiet. Save her strength. But I decided that letting her tell the story might distract her from the pain.

"My good intentions were of no value," Harriet said. "Negonee warned me I'd be lost at the first turn. You'd have to search for an injured girl abandoned in the forest. And for another girl wandering hopelessly, without direction."

Negonee managed a thin smile. "It is true you don't know the forest like I do." Her eyes then turned in my direction. "But I would have been in worse trouble without her."

I hugged Harriet and kissed her wet cheeks. Then I embraced Negonee. "Put your weight on me." She leaned into me. Words that had tumbled over each other as the girls told their story ceased as we hobbled the remaining distance.

I wished for a way to take back my permission for the ill-fated trip.

When we were within a stone's throw of our destination, Uncle came crashing through the forest. His search for the girls had been unsuccessful, and he had come this direction to see if perhaps they had arrived at Wampeme's longhouse. He offered to assist us the remaining steps. I assured him the situation was as much under control as it could be. I preferred he take Harriet and return home while I delivered Negonee to her parents. I did not need my granddaughter to hear the tongue-lashing I believed lay in store for me.

A moment after Uncle had turned away, Kimama rushed our way. She blanched at the sight of her daughter—the blood that oozed from the tourniquet. I stepped aside, and she helped Negonee toward the fire that burned outside their longhouse. Negonee slumped to the ground.

"Your father is hunting for you," Kimama said.

"Madame La Framboise found us."

Kimama looked at me as though seeing me for the first time.

"I am so sorry. This is my fault. I gave my permission for the girls to go to the rice swamp." I do not remember much more of my apology.

"Can you fetch me hot water?" Kimama pointed to a kettle hanging from the post over the fire. I did as she requested. She removed the dressing, touched the water to make certain it was not too hot, then poured it freely over the wound.

Ragged edges of skin splayed around the deep cut. Negonee clenched her teeth. She clutched her mother's hand tight, but did not cry out. By then everyone from inside the longhouse stood around watching our spectacle. An old woman I recognized as Kimama's aunt went inside and came back with a basket of herbs.

Kimama elevated Negonee's injured leg, rested it on a small log, and applied honey before adding a poultice of herbs.

When she finished dressing the wound, I edged toward the trees, away from the clearing. "I will leave you to your task."

Kimama shifted her glance to me. "Thank you for bringing our daughter safely home." She helped her daughter stand, and they began walking toward the longhouse. Behind her she called, "We had hoped to see you before this and under happier circumstances."

Shame is not an easy concoction to swallow, especially over the lump of guilt settled in my throat. I coveted her husband, was responsible for her daughter's injury, and had no reason to expect the gentle kindness I heard in her voice. "I will come again soon." I said it in a vague way that made no commitment.

I walked home bedeviled by my thoughts. Midway in my journey, I heard a twig snap behind me. Fearing a wolf or a bear, I gripped Uncle's knife.

"You won't need that." Wampeme strode closer. His approaching silhouette was slim and tall and straight like a man half his age. I would have preferred it if he were paunchy with critical eyes and a surly countenance.

I released the knife grip, let the weapon remain in the sheath at my side, and balled my hand into a tight fist.

"Kimama told me of the day's events. I hurried after you."

"Why?"

"You mean, other than to tell you Negonee will be fine, and you must not blame yourself?"

I nodded.

"I wanted to make sure you got home safely."

"You believe I am not capable of taking care of myself?" In spite of my harsh words, my heart beat more rapidly.

"And to invite you and Harriet to join us tomorrow night. A new storyteller has come to the village. He will be at our campfire."

I shook my head and cast about for an excuse. "Uncle promised he would tell stories tomorrow night."

"Invite him along." Wampeme matched his steps to mine. "I think Zhaawan Kwe that you avoid me. You worry about appearances. Appearances are not a problem. We are friends. We would be well-chaperoned. Maybe it is your arrogance. You peer in a mirror and it reflects a beautiful woman, so you believe I cannot resist your feminine charms?"

I flushed. It was not modesty, but embarrassment that a kernel of truth lodged in his suggestion that I believed he still desired me. Heat coursed my body and warmed my face.

He laughed, which fueled my annoyance.

"Truth has always been difficult for you, hasn't it, Zhaawan Kwe?" He stopped, but I kept moving. He caught up again. "So successful. So naïve. You take on John Jacob Astor but hide from yourself."

In the moonlight I saw his smugness, lips pressed tight, not quite a smile. I did not like being toyed with, but did not order him to leave me alone. My weakness gave him license to continue.

"Did you think my passion would not slacken with age? I am a man, and I have many pleasurable thoughts. You have no control over my thoughts."

He gave me a few seconds, perhaps baiting me. I tried to draw a mask over my countenance and offered no response.

"My mind lets me see you as often as I like, and I imagine no end of our interactions." I tasted the salty sting of his mockery. His grin turned wicked. "Desire is not a shameful thing. It is how the Great Spirit insures the continuation of our race."

He reached out and placed a hand on my arm to prevent me from colliding with a low-hanging branch. I stepped around the hazard and paused for the blink of an eye before moving away from his touch. I hoped he had not noticed my hesitation. My younger self knew both by instinct and prohibition the danger of this man. I dared not let my older self be less guarded.

"I have been on Mother Earth too long. Lust has seeped from my loins. It is all I can do to perform a man's duties with Kimama. I don't need another wife. Least of all, one with whom I'd argue every day."

"I am glad for your change of heart." My cool voice hid disappointment.

"I have no desire to feed the battle of what would be an appropriate relationship for us…who believes in the right God…or even the right way to guide our people."

I saw the light of the fire burning in front of Uncle's longhouse. "Please, I am home. I am safe. Turn before we cause gossip."

He doubled over and his laughter filled the air. "Zhaawan Kwe, we are too old to spark gossip."

He straightened and reached for my hand. "I will go, but not before I speak my mind. There was a time I wanted you more than the breath that sustained my life. It seemed important to make you return to tribal ways. It seemed important that you not forsake your people. But here you are, trying to share our history with Harriet. For that I am pleased."

"My reason has nothing to do with pleasing you." I jerked my hand from his.

"I mean no insult by saying that passion has passed." Then, as though reading my thoughts, he winked and said, "But that doesn't mean I don't hold you in the affection of an old friend."

I cringed at the way he emphasized the word *old*.

"Tomorrow night. We will see you and Harriet at our longhouse. Negonee's spirits will improve with your visit. You wouldn't deny her the healing powers brought by happiness, would you?

27.
History and Treachery

"No tribe has the right to sell land, even to each other, much less to strangers...Sell a country!? Why not sell the air, the great sea, as well as the earth? Didn't the Great Spirit make them all for the use of his children. The only way to stop this evil is for the red man to unite in claiming a common and equal right in the land, as it was first, and should be now, for it was never divided." **Tecumseh, Shawnee Leader of the Indian Confederacy**

August 1827

I awakened wishing that when I had arrived at Uncle's longhouse the previous night I had silenced my tongue. Mentioning Wampeme's invitation to Harriet was a mistake. Her excitement at the prospect of visiting Negonee's family and listening to a storyteller far surpassed my own.

I had not actually accepted Wampeme's invitation. Let him stammer when he realized his false assumption. Let him explain why those who assembled to hear Odawa tales waited for someone who would not arrive. Let him clutch his heart, believing I found it of no import that his hunger for me had dried and withered like deer strips left too long in the sun. I suppressed a smile as my imagination tortured him, but my thoughts were nonetheless pleased.

Morning crept by and afternoon tottered along. I took to my bedroll and convinced myself that my uneasy stomach came from last night's spit-roasted rabbit rather than uncomfortable memories of rendezvous the year after Joseph's death.

It had been more than twenty years since Wampeme knocked on the door of the cottage that I had shared with my husband before Joseph's murder.

"I come to express my sympathy." Wampeme's eyes reflected more than an offer of comfort. They swam with hope so intense it caused me to turn from the longing and desire pooled there. I invited him in and offered him a seat. He reached across the distance between our chairs, picked up my hand. Squeezed it in a familiar way. "Joseph is dead. I am sorry for your tragedy."

I wished his sympathy to stop there.

"I would consider it an honor to care for you and your children."

It had sounded more like a proposal than a gesture born of noble intent. My body stiffened. "Return to the village? Live with you?" I jerked my hand away and covered my mouth. "My husband is barely cold. You ask me to betray his memory with actions that suggest he was a mere substitute for you." I stood and stomped about the room.

"Wasn't he?" Wampeme, too, rose. With each of his steps toward me, I took one in the opposite direction.

"My husband is gone, but your wives are not." My emphasis on the word *wives* left no question that I disapproved of Wampeme's decision to marry Kimama.

"I set out with no intention to have two wives—I set out to marry you." He shot the accusation with a violence that wounded as surely as the gun that killed Joseph.

"My uncle arranged my marriage." I whispered, unsure my soft words reached his ears.

"You had a choice." His eyes flashed frustration, or perhaps I misread anger. "Always there remained choice."

"Choice? If I abandoned honor…duty."

He took another step toward me, but halted as though awaiting a sign. He got none. "The same honor and duty that impelled me to marry Kimama when I already had a wife?"

I did not need to hear the story again. The report that reached Mackinac was that Wampeme had traveled to the Ohio Country to join the Indian Confederacy. Instead of finding its leader, Tecumseh, the one they called Shooting Star, he stumbled on Kimama. She had been violated, beaten, a jagged wound slashed across her forehead as though her attackers considered scalping her. Instead, they turned their assault against her husband whom they tortured for sport until his heart could take no more. Kimama clung to life by a thread as thin as that spun by a spider. Wampeme pried the corpses of twin babies from her arms and attended her injuries. Her screams came from a depth so dark, so frightful, he could offer no consolation to quell them.

Wampeme nursed Kimama back to health before he returned with her to his longhouse. His first wife approved his taking a second wife.

"Life doesn't always bring us what we expect." I dropped my eyes, unwilling to let him see the resignation pooled there. I slumped back down onto the hard-backed chair and nodded toward the door. "We take what we get and live it the best way we can. That is the honor-and-duty part. You live it your way. I live it mine."

"Nookomis, you need to get up," Harriet said. "We are expected at Negonee's for the storyteller."

I started to tell her I was ill, but her eager eyes stopped me. Somehow I summoned energy and prepared myself for the ordeal ahead. I unknotted the blue bead from around my neck and slid it under my bedroll.

We needed a gift to take with us, and I gave its selection the same serious thought I would give a war-ending treaty. It had to be of more benefit to Kimama than Wampeme. It had to appear as though choosing it required no effort in spite of the anxiety it caused me. I decided upon sewing needles, a brass thimble, and several lengths of red, blue, and green ribbon.

The sky threatened a storm. By the time we arrived at our destination, clouds spat their first raindrops. The weather forced Kimama to prepare the evening meal inside the longhouse rather than over the open outdoor fire. She glanced up and greeted Harriet and me with a grin that exposed chipped front teeth. The smells of roasted venison, onions, potatoes, carrots, and summer squash filled the air. I realized I had not eaten all day and was suddenly ravenous.

Harriet rushed toward her new friend. Negonee's limp was dishearteningly apparent in her halting steps. My granddaughter thrust our gift, wrapped in a folded piece of calico, toward the young girl. In return she received a wide grin and soft "Miigwech."

The storyteller sat to the right of Wampeme in a place of honor. He looked as ancient as the rocks along our lakeshore. His wrinkled forehead made him appear wise. I presented him with a mocock of maple sugar for the stories he would share.

Wampeme thanked the Great Spirit for his generosity before we ate. Kimama filled the men's bowls, beginning with the storyteller. She pointed to a mat, and I sat with the women and children. A quick count told me there were thirty sets of ears eager for the stories.

The men ate, and after they enjoyed additional portions, Wampeme nodded to his wife. She began ladling food for the women and children. As an honor, I was the first woman served. I was flattered and smiled as I accepted the food. The silence that accompanied the meal was broken after everyone had eaten their fill.

Negonee helped her mother clear the bowls. The clouds no longer sent sprinkles, but opened wide and pelted the roof. The longhouse was warm and nurturing as a mother's embrace. My mixed feelings from earlier in the day gave way to gratitude that I could share this precious experience with Harriet, who sat between me and Negonee. We grew quiet again, waiting for the storyteller to begin.

"For hundreds of years our people, the original people of this country, have lived in harmony with Mother Earth. The Great Spirit smiled upon his people and filled their lands with sweet-water seas, clear enough to see the colorful rocks lining their depths."

Harriet leaned close to Negonee. I feared she was about to murmur a confidence to her friend. I reached over, touched her leg, and with a slight shake of my head warned that whispers would be rude.

"Whitefish swam these seas and provided nourishment for no more effort than casting a spear or dropping a net." The storyteller's soothing voice was perfect for his role. "Birch trees gave us bark for canoes. So dense were the forests that our brother squirrels traveled branch to branch for miles without touching the ground. Giant spruce, cedar, and balsam provided shelter for the animals that were our sustenance. Deer and bear and elk were our brothers. We respected them. When our arrows struck their hearts, we thanked their spirits for providing us food."

The storyteller described the Odawa ways that I wanted to share with my granddaughter. Harriet's eyes, however, were still on Negonee, who braided and unbraided ribbons on the front of her tunic.

The honored guest seemed not to notice the girls' lack of interest, but went on with his account. "Berries and squash and potatoes grew without being forced into gardens. Daisies and wild roses filled the meadows with their fragrance and beauty. We traveled with the seasons to find the plushest furs, flowing maple sap, thick sweet honey, and corn and rice ready for harvest."

The storyteller did not hurry his words, but gave his audience time to reflect on the pictures they painted. He picked up a pipe that lay alongside him, lit the tobacco in the bowl and inhaled. He closed his eyes for a moment, his face serene.

"This was before the white-skinned strangers came to our shores from across that vast salt sea that separated our world from theirs.

They came from places with harsh-sounding names: France, England, Scotland, Ireland, Germany. Their languages lacked the poetry of Indian words."

At the part about white-skinned strangers, Harriet stopped squirming and for the first time directed her attention to the unfolding story.

"The Frenchmen were the first to come in large numbers. They did not anger the Great Spirit. They honored our ways. They lived with us, married our women, and never mocked us. They did not carve our land into small parcels to be fenced and staked and protected against all save the man who claimed ownership by a document called a deed."

I wished he would quit at that point. He had agreed the French were no problem, and I could smooth over the rest of what he said. I knew he was not about to stop his story there.

"On the heels of the Frenchmen came the warriors in red coats." His voice was low, disapproval apparent in his tone. "They brought disease, took our land, and killed so many animals that we starved for want of fresh meat. We angered the Great Spirit when we adopted the newcomers' dress, their customs, their God. We lost our way. Then some of the white men said, 'This is our land. We won't answer to the French or the English kings. We are Americans.' The Long Knives were the worst of the new people."

I looked at Harriet and hoped she did not know that Long Knives was the name by which we called the Americans. If she was alarmed, her face gave no indication. All the same, I wondered if Wampeme knew the storyteller's message in advance.

"The white men write their history on papers they bind together and make their children study. Their words are not always true, yet they want our children to learn them. The most important stories they do not record."

My stomach heaved. In the short moments the storyteller had spoken, he had not only criticized my God, but also—perhaps without intent—my efforts to educate Indian children.

He looked into my eyes and, with a barely observable squint, frowned.

"Do their books tell you of our Odawa leaders like Obwandiyag, who sent a messenger asking us to take up his cause and unite the red men of all tribes? It is the shame of those of us who live at Waugonawkisa that we did not follow him. Obwandiyag listened to Neolin, the Delaware Prophet who warned us to resist the pale-skinned strangers. So great was the white man's fear of united Indians that they sent blankets, pretending them to be a gesture of friendship. The blankets were from a smallpox hospital."[60]

The storyteller looked from person to person, then settled his countenance again on me.

My neck pulsed with anger, but I locked eyes with him and refused to look away.

He picked up the story. "Other white men sent a similar gift with our great warrior, Nissowaquet. It was a box they said contained an item of huge value that would do our people much good. Nissowaquet was instructed not to open the box until he was safely within our village, or the value would be lost to his people forever. The trusting warrior believed there was something powerful inside the container. He could barely mask his eagerness for the contents to be revealed.

"He did as instructed. He reached his home and gathered his friends and family, so all could share the excitement. When the box was opened, the crowd was puzzled to find a smaller tin box. Nissowaquet removed this second box and was astounded to find a yet smaller box. This continued until he reached a box no more than an inch on any side. He opened this final box and found moldy, dust-like particles. Everyone wondered what the special power was and crowded around to inspect the treasure. Its value was not immediately apparent. Soon, however, a terrible sickness broke out among us. We realized too late the evil trick that had been played. The box contained seeds of smallpox. Even the great medicine men had no power to fight it. Lodge after lodge was empty, except for dead and rotting bodies. Death was the magic given to us by the white man.

"I tell you to beware of the white man's gifts and promises. Remember instead your own proud history.

"You come from a race of men beloved by the Great Spirit. We have heroes wiser and braver than the foreign dogs.

"Remember the name Tecumseh. You will find no praise of him on the pages of the white man's books. He lives in our hearts and stories."

I looked at my granddaughter. By firelight, she appeared very pale, very American, very confused. I wanted her to understand Odawa history, be proud of her Indian blood. But the same story can be told many ways. I looked at Wampeme. He avoided my eyes, his face passive, giving away neither guilt nor shame, nor even satisfaction.

I missed a few of the storyteller's words before I returned my attention to his message.

"Tecumseh and his younger brother, Tenskwatawa, were Shawnee who share long-ago ancestors with the Odawa. They were born in the Ohio Territory, what we call the down below, far south of where the three great sweet-water seas—Kitchi-gummi, Misigami and Karegnondi—touch one another at the Straits of Mackinaw.

"Tecumseh had not reached manhood when he and his mother found his father, bloodied and dying after an attack by white settlers. The boy bent to his father's ear and whispered, 'I will be a fire spreading over our land, seeking out and destroying our white-skinned enemies.'

"Tecumseh is like the lake that reaches our shore. It shapes our life, but is not always docile. Sometimes the sun warms the air above its tranquil, translucent waters. Blasts of cold air from the north or the west blow under the calm air. An enormous wave bursts forth as though from nowhere. It roars onto our shore in a sheet of water as high as the branches of the first row of trees. A powerful typhoon marking everything in its path. By next morning, all is serene again. There is no physical trace of the past night's violence, but the world will never be quite the same. That is how we say it was with Tecumseh."

I still read nothing in Harriet's face to tell me how the story affected her.

"Tecumseh's younger brother, Tenskwatawa, was known as the Prophet. In his youth, Tenskwatawa was slave to the white man's firewater. The Great Spirit ordered Tenskwatawa to cast away the demon rum. Thereafter Tenskwatawa had a direct connection to the Great Spirit. The Prophet preached abstinence from even a drop of alcohol and avoidance of the white man's goods, which the Great Spirit said made us lazy and took away our self-reliance. He urged a return to the customs and traditions that had been ours since the beginning of time. The white man feared Tenskwatawa's teachings. They wanted Indians dependent on them."

Harriet had inched closer to me. I took her hand, but she withdrew it from my touch.

"The white leader we called White Beaver, but whose own people called William Harrison, disputed Tenskwatawa's powers. Harrison told Indians their prophet was a fraud and issued a challenge: 'Tell the Prophet, if he is genuine, as you believe, he should command the sun to stand still or the moon and stars to alter their course. When he fails, you will know he is a liar.'

"Tenskwatawa was a holy man, but his older brother, Tecumseh, was the one revered as a great orator. Tecumseh's voice flowed smooth as honey from a pitcher onto johnnycake. When he spoke, Indians were spellbound by the music of his message.

"The brothers discussed the White Beaver's challenge, and after much reflection, they called their people to assemble. Tecumseh turned to the mass and in a speech stirring and powerful, said, 'My brothers and sisters, the white man tries to discredit us. He wants you to ignore our Great Spirit. If you do so, you will perish from the face of Mother Earth. The White Beaver wants us to prove that you can rely on Tenskwatawa. My brother should not have to reduce himself to cheap tricks. But you want proof? He will give it to you, that from thence forward, you should never question him. Listen carefully to what I say. Tenskwatawa accepts White Beaver's challenge. Fifty days from today, when the sky is clear and cloudless, when there is not so much as mist dimming the brilliant noonday rays, the Great Spirit will take the sun into his powerful hand and block its light from your eyes. The sky will be dark as a moonless night. Owls will fly, their brother birds will seek branches upon which to roost, and the red fox will begin his nightly prowl. Do not fear the darkness. It is the Great Spirit telling you to put your faith in your own people and shun the ways of the intruders.'

"And fifty days hence, in the manner Harrison challenged, Tenskwatawa predicted, and Tecumseh described, the sun was plucked from the sky."[61]

Harriet shuddered. I considered leaving, but there was no way to accomplish that without dishonor.

"The White Beaver still wanted our land. Shawnee and Odawa alike warned that pale-faced settlers should not invade lands north of the Ohio River. The white man's very own government agreed, but settlers, greedy for rich soil, found the land without recorded deed too tempting. They surged by the thousands, like flocks of pigeons that fly in such number they darken the day sky.

"Since not all Indians listened to Tecumseh's warning, Harrison found many Indians who signed away their rights for cheap fire water or trinkets. They did not own the land they sold, but that did not stop them from placing their mark on the line. Our tribes have paid for their folly.

"They should not have ignored the warnings of Tecumseh. He told us to look at what happened to our brother Delaware at Monrovia. They were called the Jesus Indians. They embraced the white man's God, befriended the white settlers who stole their land, accepted them as neighbors and brothers. They trusted the Long Knives who, in return, stunned them with mallets, scalped and murdered a hundred men, women, and children, even as they prayed in the mission. They piled the dead in front of the altar. The mission and the entire village were set afire. The white men took the Indians' horses, laden with plunder, and fled. Only two young boys, one of them scalped, survived to repeat the horror of what happened."

I squirmed where I sat. If I had been angry earlier, I now clearly believed Wampeme had used this evening to tell his version of our history to my granddaughter. I struggled to keep a civil demeanor. Fought to convince myself it was not worth making a display of my emotions. Minute by minute, my fight became harder.

"Tecumseh told his people to remember Fort Finney. Chief Moluntha believed a paper would bring peace. The Great White Father promised to protect Moluntha's tribe. If ever a white man raised a weapon against Moluntha's people, the chief was told, he should brandish the American flag like a shield, and he would be safe.

"A mob of angry white men attacked Moluntha even as he was wrapped in the useless piece of cloth the government had assured him provided protection. The chief held his copy of the treaty. Offered it to his attackers so they would see he was an honest Indian, and they should leave him and his people in peace. An American soldier repaid Moluntha's trust by chopping off his head. I say to you again, do not trust the white man." Harriet sat close enough to me that I felt the heat from her body. I whispered into her ear, "Your father is not responsible for that." Her face remained expressionless.

"Some Indians criticized Tecumseh," the storyteller said. "They argued the massacre of the Jesus Indians—even the execution of Moluntha—happened before the Treaty of Greenville. Now there was a lasting peace with the Americans. Ugly days of betrayal were behind us.

"And what did Tecumseh say back to them? 'I say to you that since the day that treaty was signed—and signed fraudulently—our people, not just Shawnee but Winnebago, Miami, Delaware, Odawa, Bodwe'aadamiinh continue to be killed. Our land continues to be stolen from us.'

"Tecumseh asked the White Beaver to rescind another treaty our brothers foolishly signed, the Treaty of Fort Wayne. Tecumseh argued: 'No man has the authority to partition and sell off land. No one had the right to do so on our behalf.'

"Harrison ignored Tecumseh's request. Tecumseh told our people that if we did not heed our history, if we did not consider the white man's betrayals, our future was clear.

"Tecumseh asked the white men a question for which they had no answer. 'When Jesus Christ came upon the earth, you killed him, the son of your own God, you drove nails through his hands and tortured him until you believed he was dead. Only after you thought you killed him did you worship him, and start slaying those who would not worship him. What kind of people is this for us to trust?'[62]

"Tecumseh traveled among the tribes, spoke to his doubters and faithful alike, urged them to join together. When the tribes were unified and all was ready for the red man to show his strength and take back his land from the pale-faced invaders, he said, there would be a sign. A sign unmistakable in its meaning. The earth would shake with such violence that dishes would fall from shelves and shatter. Waves on our lakes would dance higher than the height of our tallest sugar maple. Birch and aspen would be uprooted and fall flat on the ground. Streams would disappear from one place and spring up in another. All of these things would occur without a trace of breeze.

"On the day Tecumseh described, white settlers fell from their beds in a panic, but Indians knew the signal. It was time to join Tecumseh at Fort Detroit. There would no longer be individual tribes, but one united Indian People. Again, Tecumseh had spoken the truth.[63]

"Our brother Tecumseh fought the Long Knives. He joined the British forces, not because he loved the English, but the enemy of his enemy became his temporary ally. The saddest day in the history of our people was the day Tecumseh, our brave and honored warrior, died on the battlefield. The Long Knives—Americans—killed him. His final message to us warns us the white man will herd us onto tiny parcels of land he finds useless. He will force us to leave our homes."

When the storyteller paused, I stood as though I assumed he had come to the end of his harangue. If he planned to share more horrors, he would do so without Harriet's or my presence. I nodded to Kimama, thanked her again for her hospitality. I hugged Negonee and told her I would pray for her recovery.

"You must stay until the storm passes," Kimama said. "It is not a fit night for a dog, let alone a woman and child. We have plenty of room and extra mats and blankets."

"You are most kind, but rain will not melt us like maple sugar dropped in a cup of coffee."

I pulled back the hide that covered the entry. Kimama stepped close and whispered, "Two rods in the direction the sun rises is a small wigwam usually occupied by my brother. He is fishing on Manitou Island. It stands empty. Stay there. Do not attempt the walk to Kinochausie's longhouse." She pulled me into an embrace that felt warm and genuine.

"Miigwech. I am grateful." I avoided a look in Wampeme's direction. I harbored little doubt he had arranged the evening's treachery.

Monument bearing inscription "Here triumphed in death ninety Christian Indians, March 8, 1782." Photo released to Public Domain by photographer Kevin Myers, English Wikipedia Editor

Tecumseh
John Lossing engraving on wood, 1863
Photo Courtesy of Wikipedia Commons

28.
Death of Love

"Our Singers had warned us that a pale people would come across the Great Water and try to destroy us, but we forgot. We did not know they were evil, so we welcomed them and fed them. We taught them much of what Our Grandmother had taught us: how to hunt, grow corn and tobacco, find good things in the forest. They saw how much room we had, and wanted it...We remember our villages on fire every year and the crops slashed every fall and the children hungry every winter." **Tenskwatawa, (The Shawnee Prophet)**

August 1827

It was more than a menacing storm that threatened and chilled us as Harriet and I stepped outside. The night was so dark and the rain so raw that I took only a few steps before I recognized the imprudence of my strong-headedness. Had Kimama not offered her brother's wigwam, I would have thrust my granddaughter and me into serious danger.

I reached for Harriet's hand to prevent her stumbling along a path pitted by tree roots, rocks, and fallen branches as I steered our way toward the small dwelling two rods from Wampeme's longhouse. When my feet touched the base, I let my fingers trace the outside searching for a flap that offered entry.

How could Wampeme permit us to walk into such peril? His disregard for our welfare fueled my anger. Shivers that felt like needle-sharp accusations crawled my spine. Until tonight, in spite of our differences, Wampeme and I respected each other. Allowing the storyteller to vex Harriet's mind with stories of American barbarity was callous, a cruelty of which I never would have thought Wampeme capable.

His betrayal deadened my feelings toward him. His heartlessness accomplished what my love of God, my fear of eternal damnation, and my feeble will had been unable to achieve. I grappled with my loss, embittered and empty.

Harriet remained silent, whether because of the effort required to raise her voice above the pounding rain or because of disquieting thoughts troubling her mind, I was unsure. I found the pelt covering the entrance, lifted it, and stepped inside. I braced myself for my granddaughter's questions and pondered answers that might heal emotional gashes inflicted by the storyteller.

"What is this place?" she asked as I nudged her into the wigwam where skittering sounds greeted us.

"It belongs to Kimama's brother. In his absence, she said we can stay the night." Water soaked our hair and faces. Our buckskin tunics had kept our torsos dry. Squeaks, soft and high-pitched, announced we had company. I envisioned long naked tails and red beady eyes watching us. I smiled at a bitter thought: Wampeme should suggest the storyteller add that white men also brought us mice and rats.

Harriet stood stock still. Her voice quivered. "Do you hear that?"

"Yes…some poor creature trying to stay dry." I did not tell her that of all my brother critters, mice and rats were animals for which I least understood God's purpose. I adjusted the entry covering to leave space for the varmints to escape and breathed more easily when both the eeking and skittering stopped.

"Whatever it was, it decided not to endure our company for the comfort of a dry bed. I am sure it—or they—scampered out."

I groped my way around the small space and found two soft pelts. I guessed they were otter from the feel of them. I located a reed mat rolled against the side of the wigwam. I unfolded the mat and spread it on the hard-packed dirt floor, avoiding the dug out area around the fire pit, which had become a deep puddle. I sat, and gently tugged Harriet down next to me. "We will sleep here. It is less risky than trying to reach our longhouse in this storm." A crack of thunder supported my conclusion.

If she had any argument in her, Harriet did not express it. She crumpled against me, and I covered us with the furs. As angry as I was at the evening's turn of events, I found pleasure holding my granddaughter close.

After many minutes, Harriet's small unsteady voice asked, "Does Negonee's father hate me?"

"Of course not." My impulsive answer was reflex, without proper reflection.

"His storyteller hates Americans."

"Harriet, the Odawa respect their elders because we know they have lived long on Mother Earth. Every day they have grown in wisdom. Wisdom is a complicated thing. No one's understanding is perfect. I brought you to L'Arbre Croche because I wanted you to cherish your Odawa blood. My good intentions may have been misguided."

She snuggled closer to me, and we lay stacked like two pieces of wood piled near the fire pit. "I think Aunt McNeil would prefer I had no Odawa blood. She never speaks of it. She tells me no one wants to hear about my maman or Mackinac Island."

"I am sure your Aunt McNeil is a fine Christian woman, but on this matter she is wrong. You should never forget your maman. You must be proud of what makes you special. Special comes from Odawa, French, English, and American. All their blood runs together in you."

Her breathing was ragged. I moved my fingers across her cheeks but felt no tears.

"Why did the storyteller say those awful things tonight?"

Before I could answer, her next question tumbled out.

"Why did Negonee's papa want him to tell us about Indians who hate white people?"

I was tempted to recreate the stories in a less offensive way, or deny the truth altogether. To do so dishonored history, my people, and Harriet. "I believe Wampeme thought it important for you to hear how he views events."

"Did you know Wampeme before he married Kimama?"

I was glad she could not see my mouth drop open. "What made you ask that?"

"Negonee thinks her father once loved you. She giggled when she told me that."

"There are stories that perhaps young girls do not need to know about their nookomis."

"Did he?"

My throat constricted. I toyed with how much to tell and how the truth should be adorned. Lies might serve no one, but too much detail lacked sound judgment. "There was a time, before your Grandpapa La Framboise, when I thought Wampeme might be my husband. It was not meant to be."

"Did that sadden you?"

"Is there no end to your questions?" I hoped the tone of my voice reflected mild amusement without rebuke, yet at the same time ended her inquiry.

"Well, did it?"

"Life was different when I was your age. A girl was expected to consider marriage arranged by her papa. My papa was dead. Uncle Kinochausie was responsible for me. He was also responsible to the tribe. A good marriage benefited both a girl and her people."

"Are you sorry you brought me here? I don't want you to be sorry."

My face rested against her soft hair. The lavender smell reminded me of her maman. I inhaled several deep breaths, thankful for the memory. "No, I do not regret bringing you here. Things have turned out differently than I planned. I wanted you to keep your Odawa history in your heart. I still want that, but I did not think about how I would shelter you from disturbing tales. I never considered that you might be exposed to ugly accounts of the Americans. History's truth is told many ways."

"I am nearly grown, Nookomis. I don't need protection from the truth."

I heard the scurrying of a small animal again and hoped it stayed far to the other side of the wigwam. Harriet must have heard it too because she jerked and then wrapped the fur more tightly about her.

"Did things happen like the storyteller said?"

"He told the account as he sees it. His conclusions are reflected through his own experience. When you stand on Misigami's shore and the sun is high in the sky, you have no shadow. In early morning or when the sun wanes, your shadow is taller than you. Have you changed height?"

"No."

"But what you see is different. History is like that. Much of what we consider fact is judgment. Your papa does what his heart tells him is right. I believe that was true for the French, the English, and the Americans. Your papa fought to open new land to settlers who wanted to farm. He fought for people who came to this country to escape the rule of harsh kings. He fought to create a new country where every man would have a say in how he was governed."

"That is good?" The hesitancy in her voice made it a question seeking a desired answer.

"I am sure he believed it was right." My response did not, as I had hoped, end the discussion.

"Do you?"

I paused to consider an answer I would not regret. "It may have been right for Americans. Indians have no voice in running the new government. They are often told to move from land that has always belonged to their tribes so new people can claim it."

Her face was close enough that I felt her breath as she spoke. "And that is not right?"

"Try to understand how two people can look at the same action and conclude differently about whether it is good or bad, or even whether it is true. Indians suffered when the white men pushed them out. Suffered when the white man brought disease. And suffered yet again when the white man set himself up to rule Indians.

That is how many of the Odawa and other native people see it. They are angry."

Harriet turned to face me, moved enough that our bodies no longer touched.

"Do they hate the white people?"

"Some do."

"Do you?"

"How can you ask that? I married your grandpapa and he was French. When I was a girl in this village, I knew nights of hunger. I watched our friends die of disease and starvation. Your grandpapa La Framboise taught me to trade, took care of me, gave me children. My life was blessed."

She turned over again, leaned back in toward me, close enough that I could put my arm over her.

"Did you stop believing in the Great Spirit?"

"I listened to the priests. I believed their message. I try to let the Catholic God direct my life. There have been times when I was upset with God, but ever since I was told about him, I have believed as the Catholics do."

"Negonee doesn't believe that way."

"Each person sifts through the information they have available and chooses what is true for them."

"Are you Catholic and Odawa and French?"

"Yes. All three."

"Is Tecumseh right…will you be forced to move?"

"No. I am safe. Maybe because I am also French, maybe because I have accepted the Catholic God, and maybe because I live in a large house on Mackinac Island rather than in an Indian village."

"What of Uncle Kinochausie and Negonee?"

"I pray for them and have no choice but to put their fate in God's hands."

"The storyteller says Indians will be forced onto land that no white man wants."

"I cannot say if he is wrong. The white families will not leave. Indians will live peaceably with them, or be removed to permit the white man's progress."

"Isn't there something you can do?"

"I am just one woman. I work to educate Indian children because I think that is their best chance of a good life. Yet Indians educated the white man's way, may believe they are unwelcome in Indian villages. They may feel uncomfortable, lost between two ways of living. Your Uncle La Framboise continues to trade furs. He declares that is by choice, but some businesses or jobs, like teaching or lawyering may be closed to him."

We lay there and every time I thought Harriet was near sleep she asked another question. I filled in the details I had omitted when telling earlier stories. I told her about White Ox and the murder of her Grandpapa La Framboise. I told her of the murder of her Great Grandpapa Marcotte. I told her of Nissowaquet and Langlade—with far more detail than Uncle Kinochausie had shared. I told her of savagery, butchery, honor, and gentleness. I told her of births and deaths and marriages and survival.

As dawn approached Harriet's breathing became shallow and regular, and I knew she had drifted into sleep.

The rain stopped. The moon and a few brave stars peaked out between clouds. Dim light crept through the wigwam's smoke hole. I kissed the back of Harriet's head and whispered, "I wish in a night I could solve all of mankind's problems for you. I can only tell you one truth with certainty. You are my granddaughter, and I will always love you."

The afternoon before we departed L'Arbre Croche to return to Mackinac, I sat on a bluff staring in the direction of Manitou Island. I would never forget Wampeme's disloyalty, and yet, in some misguided way he had brought me closer to Harriet. Shielding her from every unpleasantry kept her from knowing me or her Odawa heritage. Still, I did not plan to thank him.

If I needed to look for additional benefit that came from the disaster, I had but to consider that lust for him would never again imperil my journey toward heaven.

I was lost in this reflection when something touched my shoulder, the pressure so slight I thought it might be a grasshopper. I brushed at the spot and turned.

Wampeme stood looking down at me. "I was told you leave in the morning."

I had hoped to escape an awkward last meeting. "Harriet has only two weeks before she travels east." I was grateful he could not see my heart race or my pulse quicken. I could do nothing to stop blood from rising into my face, a condition that occurred each time I found myself in his presence.

"Negonee wanted to see Harriet before she leaves, and I have unfinished business with you. I accompanied my daughter on her walk here."

"She is able to make the trip alone. She has proved that in the past." My words were so cold they could have frozen the lake in front of me. "And we have no further matters to discuss."

"I disagree. I cannot let you leave without an explanation."

"Indeed you can." I fidgeted, stood, uncomfortable with him staring down on me. "There is no need for words. The situation is clear."

"You only think so."

I considered what I had told Harriet about how two people see or experience the same thing and come away to tell different accounts. Still, I wanted to hear none of his explanation. I started to walk away.

He clasped my forearm with his age-spotted brown hand. "I've walked this distance to say my piece. When I am done, you owe me no response. Hear me out…please?"

He narrowed his eyes. Eyes that once tempted me to distraction now maddened me with desire to have this over. The muscles in his neck tensed. He stood between me and the narrow, worn path that led back to Uncle's longhouse. I twisted free of his grip and stepped around him. "We are beyond words. Let's not make it worse."

"What is worse than the death of a friendship?" He dropped his hand to his side. He did not follow after me.

I slowed my steps. In spite of my harsh response, I longed for his apology.

"The storyteller I invited is new to L'Arbre Croche. He has seen the passing of eighty years. After his wife died, he came from his village near Detroit to live out his days here with his daughter. I heard he was an esteemed and spirited master of our history. I had never heard him speak. I believed the reputation that preceded him, and asked him to come to my longhouse, my gift to you."

I said nothing, but stopped moving away. I again met his eyes and saw no deceit there, only a deep sadness that convinced me he spoke the truth.

"Zhaawan Kwe, you must believe I never would have asked him to join us if I had any notion of the stories he'd tell."

Wampeme and I stood, each fixed firmly in the spot we had stopped, neither able to move in any direction. After several long, awkward moments, I said, "Thank you for coming. Thank you for letting Negonee spend the afternoon with Harriet. Please tell Kimama how much I appreciated her kindness." I could think of no way to forget the solitary evening that had changed everything. I cursed my mind that it was not quick enough to add something eloquent, something memorable. I walked away. Left him standing alone.

Angelique had anticipated our return. The silver was polished, the furniture dusted, the carpets beaten, and a raspberry pie cooled on the table when we walked into the house.

"Where's Martha?" I asked. "I thought she would be here to greet us."

Before Angelique answered, Harriet dropped her bag and sought permission to go in search of Sophia Biddle. I nodded approval.

"It's as well that Miss Harriet's gone." Angelique closed the door behind my granddaughter.

"Pray do not burden me with trouble. I have thirteen days before my granddaughter returns to her Aunt McNeil. I intend to fill them with gaiety."

She tilted her head down so I could barely see she had closed her eyes. "I'm sorry, Madame."

I clasped her shoulders and gave her a slight shake. "What happened?" Not knowing suddenly seemed worse than anything she could tell me. Martha was not dead or grievously injured or Angelique would have sent a messenger to me in L'Arbre Croche.

"John Tanner returned to the island this summer. He flaunts a new wife and has settled into that shack near the Mitchells. Tanner insisted Martha move in with him. That was two weeks ago. Forgive me, Madame, if I should have sent word, but I figured you needed that special time with Miss Harriet. I didn't want to burden you."

"It is good…probably better that I did not know." I slumped into a chair, wiped at my eyes, and fought for composure.

"I helped Martha pack. She wept the entire time. I have not seen her since."

"Her papa likely keeps a tight hold on her."

"She is nearly a grown woman, what right does he have to dictate her life?"

"John Tanner fashions his own rights." I thought about the afternoons Martha spent teaching me to read, and how I taught her to bake the best apple pie on the island. I fell silent, wondering if God searched for pieces of my heart that had escaped prior tragedy, then poked at these healthy fragments to test my convictions.

"He made no move to take Lucy?" I asked.

"The day he came, I overheard his raised voice as he ordered Martha from our house. I will never forget it. She asked about her little sister. "Papa, by the paper you signed and the love grown in Lucy's heart, Madame Schindler is her maman.'"

"What did Tanner say?" I held my breath, fearful Angelique's next words would confirm that the brute had torn his youngest child from Therese's arms.

"He said that like her mother, Lucy was dead to him. Martha he intended to reclaim, because she could be of help to the family."

I pinched my mouth into a mirthless smile. "Does he intend to put his daughter to cleaning houses to support him as he did with Miskwabunokwa when she lived with him?"

"No. He has secured work with Colonel George Boyd."

My contempt turned to surprise. "What business does our Indian Agent have for Tanner?"

"Interpreter."

I supposed it made sense. If there was one skill Tanner could claim, it was knowledge of Indian languages.

Angelique went on, "I also hear he pours his heart out to a fellow called Edwin James, a botanist, explorer, and doctor taken with the drama of Tanner's life. This jack of all trades plans to write a book recounting the tale."

I bit my tongue but failed to curb the sarcasm forming there. "I wonder how he fashions the ending?"

As devastating as the news about Martha was, I remained committed to cherishing my last days with Harriet. Agatha Biddle agreed to let Sophia spend her afternoons with us. Harriet, Sophia, and I explored the island and picnicked at places Harriet had known when she lived with me five years earlier.

We sat on a Mackinac blanket close to Arch Rock. Sophia nibbled at fried hogmeat Angelique had prepared for our lunch. She turned toward Harriet and said, "I am going east too. Maman and Papa want me to live with my Uncle Biddle. They say I'll get educated and learn refinement."

Agatha Biddle had not mentioned to me that she was sending Sophia to live in Philadelphia with her husband's brother, an influential banker. Agatha always expressed contempt for the highfaluting ways of her wealthy in-laws. The news Sophia had blurted out was a bitter surprise. With Martha gone and Harriet leaving, I counted on Sophia to spend another winter with me and fill the house with the exuberance of youth.

I understood the importance to the Biddles of giving their daughter a superior education. I could not blame them, but the loss fractured another fragment of my heart.

The afternoon before Harriet departed, she and I sipped apple juice in the dining room and ate the plum cake Angelique had baked special for us. I wished to discuss a business matter with my granddaughter before she left. At my bidding Marianne had drafted a letter to Benjamin, and I wanted Harriet to understand the content. Although she was too young to approve the proposal I made, she would be my messenger.

I placed the envelope in her hand. "Pack this in a safe spot among your possessions and when you arrive home, make sure you give it to your papa the first time you see him." I curled her fingers around the missive. "Do you understand?"

"Yes. If that is your wish." She looked up at me with innocence and love, but her tone invited an explanation.

"The same year I was born, your Great-Grandpere Marcotte helped move Ste. Anne's church from the mainland to the corner of Market and Hoban on our island. A dispute arose and some people argued that the land upon which the church stood did not properly belong to Ste. Anne's. I invited Father Badin to move the church to my property, where we now see it from my windows."[64]

Still clutching the paper, Harriet folded her arms on the table, laid her chin on them, and looked at me. It was the attention of a dutiful, obedient child eager to please. The matter at hand failed to excite or interest her.

"Ste. Anne's Church is vital to me and all Catholics on Mackinac Island." I reached across the table and touched the document. She gave me a wan smile as though asking me to hurry on and finish this boring topic so she could be off to regale Sophia with stories of L'Arbre Croche. Maybe tell her about those awful Americans, or worse yet, that her nookomis had once been in love.

"I had three pieces of property: one given to me by the tribes of the Grand River Valley, the second the parcel where this house sits, and the third where Ste. Anne's is currently situated. I made a special request of Father Badin when I transferred the property for the church. Your maman, Benjamin Langdon, and I shall be buried under the altar."[65]

"Would that make my maman happy?"

"It would."

"Then that is what I want too."

"It is not that simple. I have sent a paper to your Uncle La Framboise asking him to relinquish any interest he may have had in the property where the church now stands. I want you to ask your father to do the same on your behalf. Upon my death, I will leave you the lot with this house. I want no confusion or difficulty for the priests about my intent or what I have given them."

"Nookomis, you worry too much. I will ask Papa about it. It won't be a problem."

Left: Current Day Ste. Anne's Church Steeple
Photo Courtesy Creative Commons Share Alike (Wikimedia Commons)
Right: Oldest known photo of Magdelaine's home on Mackinac Island,
(Pre 1900), Public Domain

29.
Mazzuchelli, Mosquitoes, and de Tocqueville

"Rather than going to church, I attend a sweat lodge; rather than accepting bread and toast from the Holy Priest, I smoke a ceremonial pipe to come into Communion with the Great Spirit; and rather than kneeling with my hands placed together in prayer, I let sweet grass be feathered over my entire being for spiritual cleansing and allow the smoke to carry my prayers into the heavens. I am a Mi'kmaq, and this is how we pray." **Noah Augustine**

1828-1833

In the last years of the 1820s, adversity closed in on me from all directions. Farmers flocked to the land around our Great Lakes, cut our trees, overhunted our animals. Beaver hats and other fur clothing lost popularity. Religious squabbles seethed below Mackinac's long-tolerant surface. Black Hawk took up the cause championed earlier by Obwandiyag, Tecumseh, and Tenskwatawa. In the face of each challenge, I counseled myself to trust God. Always when he pushed me over a spiritual cliff, he caught me before I landed, and he used my fear or grief to make my faith stronger.

My prayers for courage were liberally interspersed with thanks for God's amazing goodness. In 1828, I received word from Joseph. I could decipher parts of his current letter for myself, the remainder I had Marianne read when she dropped by with a loaf of her homemade raisin bread still warm from the oven.

My son wrote that he had married a Mdewakanton Sioux woman, daughter of Walking Dog, an important man in the tribe. Joseph described his new wife as a Christian, and said she and other converted Indians, by their hard work and honesty, made his business easier. He also said his wife—and I thought it revealing that he did not call her by name—could cook, mend traps, clean furs and shape the best snowshoes of any Indian woman within five hundred miles. In Joseph's typical irreverent way, he closed with, "She lessens my need for blankets on our sleeping platform. I hope by next year to give you a grandchild."

My son's comment must not have offended God if judged by the follow-up letter I received months later. It was too short to satisfy my hunger for details of his life, but I learned I had a grandson, named Joseph after his father and grandfather. My son described the baby as "possessed of a lusty cry, hearty appetite, and the beautiful eyes of my dear, departed sister."

The gentle back and forth of my Windsor rocker made me long to hold the child, who was hundreds of miles away on the upper St. Pierre River,[66] rather than a cold piece of paper. I praised God for his goodness, but wondered if the dwindling fur trade conspired to keep my son in the backcountry and prevent me from seeing my grandson.

Ste. Anne's, on the property I had deeded to the Catholic Church, was a fortress against a Protestant surge that struck the island in 1829. The crusade turned relentless. Protestants became religious adversaries of Catholics in the battle for souls. Robert Stuart showed the effects of earlier befriending William Ferry. The previously profane and difficult Stuart embraced a new piety and became a church elder. Each evening he held prayer sessions in his home.

Both Dr. Richard Satterlee, the new post surgeon at Fort Mackinac, and Michael Dousman, a prominent local businessman, also walked the Presbyterian path. The renewed interest in eternal salvation generated so much enthusiasm, it drove the construction of the Mission Church that had from years earlier been Reverend Ferry's dream. Dousman provided lumber, which was cut and sawn at his mill on the mainland before it was transported to the island. John Jacob Astor contributed two hundred and fifty dollars to its construction. The cornerstone was laid on August 28, 1829, and the congregation occupied its new sanctuary by the first winter snow. Sunday became a day Protestants attended church services, prayed, and rested.

Ferry's church grew. The charismatic man of God drew congregants from the garrison, the mission, the fur trade, and Indian villages. He swelled his membership rolls by thirty-three in one year, bringing the total to fifty-two. Half were Indian converts. I began to see merit in Father Baden's fear that Presbyterians would capture the hearts of Catholics if their children attended Ferry's school.

During this religious fervor, Catholics grew serious about recruiting. On Pentecost Sunday, Bishop Fenwick paid a special visit to Ste. Anne's and added sixty to our membership roster.

Seeking to ameliorate, antagonize, or perhaps avoid the religious battle, the soldiers at the garrison invited an Episcopalian chaplain, Reverend John O'Brien, to the island to serve as their spiritual leader. O'Brien soon commanded a third Christian army on our small patch of land. Like William Ferry, O'Brien came with a beautiful wife at his side. Charlotte O'Brien fancied herself a poet. I observed her walking mossy forest trails, looking wistful and melancholy, like one torn from kin and reduced to a misfit wandering spiritually marred terrain.

While the attention paid to God gladdened my heart, I regretted that friends I met on my way to market or to the fur company headquarters now offered the nod of a stranger, not the warm embrace of a fellow Christian.

The Mission Church, built in 1829 is the oldest surviving church in the state of Michigan. Ste. Anne's Catholic Church was established long before this, but the structure was replaced in 1874.
Mission Church left 1895, Public Domain
Mission Church right 2015, Courtesy of Bob Royce

Rumors floated like the sound of distant drums on a gentle summer breeze. One morning report whispered that John Tanner was packing to move his family to Sault Ste. Marie. The sun was high overhead when I headed in the direction of his ramshackle hut and found it empty. I hurried to the harbor and arrived in time to watch Tanner's new wife adjusting personal belongings in a large canoe. Tanner stood at the water's edge. He glanced in my direction, clamped his hand around Martha's wrist, and snarled at me. "This is no affair of yours."

I entertained the notion that he might be right. I had seen little of Martha in the two years since John removed her from my house. Chance meetings on the street, little more.

I remained a fair distance, perhaps a rod, from father and daughter, but spoke loud enough so he could hear. "Examine your actions, John Tanner. Look at the tears coursing Martha's cheeks."

"She belongs to me. She will do as I say."

He pushed Martha closer to the canoe, not with a gentle nudge, but with the thrust of a man intent on restraining a recalcitrant child. "Someday she will thank me."

"At fifteen she is not a child. If you leave her on the island she can earn her way providing domestic services.[67] She can live with me—"

"—so you can fill her head with more Catholic hogwash…or maybe Reverend Ferry can strengthen her religious bonds to his faith that she now accepts? Her spirit is confused and bent. I will straighten her out."

Martha stumbled and fell as her father shoved her into the vessel. She regained her balance. With the palm of her hand, she rubbed blood from her scraped shin and wiped it on her tunic.

"No, thanks." Tanner turned away from me, but the words he hurled still met their mark. "I have long held that you try to replace your lost daughter with mine."

I next saw Martha Tanner a year later when improbable circumstances returned her to Mackinac Island. John Tanner had become friends with Henry Rowe Schoolcraft,[68] the Indian Agent at Sault Ste. Marie. The cantankerous Tanner estranged those who got close to him. He suffered problems keeping Martha under his thumb. Schoolcraft grew to distrust Tanner over a dispute that raged between Schoolcraft's brother and Tanner. Details did not filter back to us, but we guessed that Martha solicited Schoolcraft to help her escape her father's servitude. Schoolcraft, likely for his own purposes, sought a way to punish Tanner. He convinced the Territory of Michigan's Legislative Council to pass a law that authorized the sheriff of Chippewa County to remove Martha Tanner from her father's custody.[69] However it happened, she was sent first to Detroit, then returned to Mackinac Island. Therese and I were happy to have our Martha back and did not pester her with questions.

At the end of 1830, while on a walk to the market, I shared news with Therese that I had received from Bishop Fenwick. "We are to receive a permanent priest."

Therese stopped short and clutched both hands over her heart. "How long have you known?"

"Early this morning. Postmaster King personally delivered the letter."

I escaped a tongue-lashing because Therese hungered more for details than an opportunity to scold me for not rushing to her door the moment the missive was handed to me.

"When will he arrive?" Before I answered, she compounded her question. "Is he a priest we know?"

"I have never heard of him. He will stay with me. He is of the Dominican Order, devoted to teaching and eradicating heresy. Both skills should serve him well. I rejoice God sends his servant to minister to our neglected faith. We can pray he discovers a way to coexist with the Protestants."

"Does this priest have a name?"

"Father Samuel Charles Mazzuchelli."[70]

Father Samuel Charles Mazzuchelli
Public Domain

Bishop Edward Dominic Fenwick, O.P.
from the Souvenir Album of American Cities:
Catholic Churches of Cincinnati and Hamilton County edition, 1896
Public Domain

Two weeks later, I welcomed a stranger who climbed the steps of my front stoop. I amended my earlier conviction that only postmasters or lawyers with bad news used the front door. Priests, fresh to the island, also chose that entry. I stared, my surprise poorly contained, at a man scarcely old enough to be an ordained priest. Only black robes confirmed his calling. Bishop Fenwick had not warned me that our new spiritual leader had yet to outgrow his youth. I was skeptical that one of such tender years could minister on God's behalf in such turbulent times.

"Expecting someone with a few more years of service, I suspect." His hearty laugh reminded me of Reverend Ferry's.

"I am sorry, Father." I stepped back and motioned him inside.

"Sorry for what? An honest reaction?" He walked past me, stopped, waited for me to show him into the parlor. "I was but seventeen when I became a Dominican novice in Italy. That was five years ago. Bishop Fenwick ordained me earlier this year. Mackinac is my first assignment."

Arithmetic came easily for me, a big advantage in my business. I played with the numbers in my head. "You are the age of my son, but look younger."

"Perhaps it is the easy life I lead."

I blushed, fearing I had been over-bold with the young priest I had just met.

He paid no heed to my awkwardness. "Does your son live close?"

"Only if you consider Fort Totten, hundreds of miles from here, close. He trades furs in the far interior."

"Then don't be surprised if I return from my travels with news of him."

Again taken aback, I asked, "You mean you will not remain on the island?"

"Oh my, no. God and Bishop Fenwick have an expansive territory for me to serve."

I said nothing. Sharing a priest with immeasurable, sparsely populated wilderness would dilute the good I expected him to do in our community.

Angelique, ghostlike as always, appeared with refreshments and provided me a few moments' respite to consider my next words. I need not have worried about conversation. The young priest spent the afternoon telling me about himself, enthusiasm riding on each revelation.

Father Mazzuchelli had been a child during the reign of Napoleon Bonaparte, the Frenchman he said had ruled his country for many years. Bonaparte was iron-fisted and power hungry. I thought the priest made the man sound much like those who alternately vied to rule my land.

Milan, a city of varied pleasures, was Father Mazzuchelli's birthplace. He described great music he called opera and said it told stories in song. He told me of dancing, known as ballet, that was performed with elegant grace, precision, and gestures. This special dancing also told stories. And he witnessed dramas acted out on theater stages by costumed men.

When I said, "All of these spectacles sound like Odawa entertainments," he laughed good-naturedly, and said, "I suppose there are similarities."

The priest said his birthplace had limestone and marble buildings filled with books. It boasted palaces with walls lined with great paintings and sculptures. Large churches, called cathedrals, glorified God and reached close to the sky. None of these could I imagine.

"How could you leave such a place?"

He again laughed that hearty laugh of a man who enjoyed life's little humors. "Bishop Fenwick traveled to Europe to raise money for his archdiocese. He filled my head with visions of America. I was at an impressionable age, when even a priest seeks adventure. The challenge of bringing God's word to multitudes living in a spiritual void appealed to me. I requested this missionary assignment."

The sparkle in the priest's eyes testified he was long on passion. "I will minister to an area bounded to the west by the Mississippi and on the east by Lake Huron, with Mackinac Island as my headquarters. I shall travel by foot throughout the Great Lakes for hundreds of miles, or in winter months by a dog-pulled sled."

All this he spoke as though he could scarce believe his good fortune. I had spent years enduring wilderness deprivations. I wondered how Father Mazzuchelli would feel about his assignment when he was my age.

In the winter of 1831, William Ferry delivered six homilies attacking Roman Catholic theology. It was as though he had never taken shelter under my roof, eaten my food, or enlisted my help to educate our children. I was forced to make a choice. As a result, friendship with the Ferrys was lost to me.

During the warm months of that year, when travel was safest, Father Mazzuchelli returned to us. Furious with Reverend Ferry's attack on Catholic doctrine, Father Mazzuchelli lashed out with fourteen of his own sermons. My heart broke for the boy-priest with lofty ideals and gentle ways. He preferred to unite men, but was caught on one side of a great divide. His efforts garnered him only three converts, but the identity of at least two of those three converts filled my heart with joy.

At Good Friday service, I was speechless to see Samuel Abbott, a long-time Anglican, present himself for sacramental confession. In front of God and the congregation he fell to his knees in the appearance of sincere repentance. He denounced his prior sins, accepted the Catholic faith, and prepared for Holy Communion. Always I had felt a strange affinity for, yet at the same time fear of, Samuel Abbott. I thanked God for his conversion of my brother in Christ.

The second convert that Sunday had a more direct impact on my life. My sister and I had tried for years to provide Martha Tanner with stability that came from the true love of the Catholic God. She would accept our arguments, declare herself one of us, then waver and turn back to Protestantism or reject God outright. The young woman was subject to melancholy and torn by many influences, yet on this day when we celebrated God's ultimate sacrifice—the crucifixion of his only son—Father Mazzuchelli accomplished what my sister and I had been unable to achieve.[71] Martha Tanner committed her life to God and the Catholic Church.

When the good Father said he worried that his efforts were not bearing sufficient fruit, I reminded him of these converts and also praised his work, which allowed us to at last open a school for Catholic children.[72]

Within a year, we had twenty-six boys and girls receiving instruction from Martha Tanner, who seemed at peace with her faith. My house hummed with excitement. When God took away one person I loved, he sent another to bring me comfort. I labored to be grateful for what I had rather than worry about when I might lose it.

Sophia had grown homesick in Philadelphia and returned to me in the winter of 1831. It was temporary. She would continue her education in the east the next year. Martha Tanner split her time between my home and Therese's, as whim suited her. Lucy stayed with me because Therese still traded during the winter season. Francois's son and Catishe, both servants of Therese, temporarily moved into my house, although they helped Marianne as needed. Marianne oversaw work being done on Therese's home and was now the only one living there.[73]

Josette was a memory I visited often, but her death no longer caused me to turn from God. Father Richard had suggested many years ago that until my faith was strong, I should act in accordance with God's commandments. I believed his advice saved both my temporal and eternal life.

I rejoined Mackinac society. I held dinner parties. Martha, Catishe, Sophia, and even Lucy grew excited every time I proposed a new guest list. We invited John Kinzie Jr. and his new bride, Juliette, to my home to celebrate their recent marriage. They were on their way by the steamship *Henry Clay* to Fort Winnebago, where John served as Indian Agent for the Americans. I included on one guest list Robert Stuart, whom I found much pleasanter since his religious conversion—even if it was the faith of Reverend Ferry. Stuart's wife Elizabeth was an angel. I often thought she could be credited equally with God for Stuart's transformation.

When I considered all of the guests who had graced my table, the Frenchman, Alexis de Tocqueville,[74] sent by his government to study American democracy, remained vivid in my mind.

De Tocqueville's concern for our social system did not stir a whit of either passion or interest in those of us assembled at my dinner party, but he never mentioned government or world leaders or even American institutions. If he studied them or us, he did so with the slyness of a fox. About a certain enemy, though, his discourse was spirited and eloquent.

Sometime between Angelique serving our guests a perfectly roasted pork loin with applesauce and a final course of coffee and cake, he said, "Madame La Framboise, dinner was superb. Better than any tavern, café, or private home I have chanced upon since in this country. An equal joy to the quality of the food, however, is that for the short time I have been your guest I have been unmolested by an insidious evil." His eyes danced with mischief, inviting questions.

Therese took the bait. "Pray, what do you mean?"

"I have not fallen casualty to a single mosquito since entering your sister's gracious home. In my country we have mosquitoes. By the standard of those you grow here, however, ours are mere gnats. Practically harmless. Requiring but a drop of blood before they move on, fully satiated. You have varmints the size of hummingbirds and hungry as wolves struggling to survive in a place barren of prey. By the time they are done sucking, I am weak and woozy. They travel in hordes. One cannot outrun them, swatting them only encourages their brethren, and the last one that bit me, looked me square in the eye, blinked…yes, I swear he did…and defied me to lay a finger on him."

"Surely you exaggerate." I suppressed a chuckle struggling to break free.

"Not in the slightest. In the past month I've tired myself more from swatting mosquitoes than hiking through forests and writing in my journal, combined." He folded his napkin and sipped coffee, waiting for someone else to take up the conversation. When no one rose to the challenge, he went on to give his only political comment of the evening.

"One thing I'll say for the pests, they are the sublime example of democracy in action. They feast on the lifeblood of Andrew Jackson with as much relish as they suck from the veins of a scoundrel like your Aaron Burr. Everyone on the moral continuum is subject to their frenzy."

I laughed but could see he was half serious. "I am pleased you find my home a refuge."

"What I want to know—what you must tell me before I leave— is how you rid yourself of the brutes?" His mouth contorted. He raised his hands and curled his fingers as if he were a monster ready to attack.

I could not remain ladylike and contain my guffaws. His display of ardor was quite the show for those of us gathered. "Mosquitoes have a refined palate," I said. "They choose only the choicest morsels." I looked him straight in the eye as he claimed the mosquito had done. "Have you ever smelled the rotting carcass of a raccoon or possum?"

"I may have had the pleasure, but if so, I've encouraged myself to forget it. Why do you ask?"

"In the backwoods, when a man or woman has little contact with human beings who might take offense, they smear their bodies with the fat of a decaying animal to discourage mosquitoes."

"It works?"

"It does, and it has certain logic. If the stink discourages human interaction, it disgusts the sensitive-nosed mosquito."

"There is no easier way?"

"Did I suggest there was not?"

"I'd like to hear my second choice. It must be more agreeable."

"Backwoodsmen also build fires and the smoke keeps away the mosquitoes."

"Less offensive than rotten grease, I suppose. But it isn't always convenient to carry a smudge pot with me. Is there a third option? Your home smells of mint and cedar and other subtle odors I can't quite identify, but which please my senses."

"You are not only an educated man, but a wise one as well. The smell of wild field mint and cedar confuse the pests. Angelique makes an essence of them. She adds chrysanthemum leaves and rosemary to the mixture when they are available. She infuses the concoction into candles that fill our house with a scent that befuddles the mosquitoes and keeps them, and chiggers, fleas, and gnats away. We use the essence in soap too. I also put cedar blocks in strategic spots throughout the house. If you look closely, you will find one under the sofa, one under each of the parlor chairs, and elsewhere hidden throughout my home. To doubly protect myself, I dab lavender on my neck. The fragrance is quite tolerable, and baffles mosquitoes. They cannot smell human blood beneath such camouflage."

"Smelling like a flower garden may cause me problems of a different sort, but still...it may be preferable to this miserable itch and my constant vigilance to avoid the beast's bite. I cannot abide another night hearing an interminable buzz inside my tent, knowing the highly-touted mosquito netting has failed again. Sleep is impossible while I track the movements of my adversary."

"I will have Angelique provide you with a package of our candles to take with you."

"You are a saint."

Bugs notwithstanding, Mackinac Island was the social hub of the wilderness.

Alex de Tocqueville
Photo Public Domain

In 1832, after nearly two decades of relative peace in the areas around Mackinac Island and L'Arbre Croche, Black Hawk's conflict erupted. The Sauk, Fox, and Kickapoo nations were angry over another broken treaty and the push to remove them from their remaining land. Every full-blood or mixed-blood Odawa, Ojibwe, and Bodwe'aadamiinh was aware of the fight Black Hawk[75] waged. Our Council of Three Fires watched to see if our tribes would be drawn into the battle.

In early May, Samuel Abbott waited in front of Ste. Anne's church before the Sunday service. He stopped Therese and me before we entered.

"I thought you would want the latest news."

Even since his Catholic baptism, Abbott made me nervous. I was about to suggest that the steps to God's house were not the proper place for gossip, but Therese spoke before I could.

"What would that news be?"

"The Illinois militia has pursued Blackhawk. A skirmish broke out at Stillman Valley. Black Hawk sent three Sauk warriors to parley, hoping to avoid further bloodshed. One of the three was killed."

"And Blackhawk retaliated?" Therese asked.

Abbott opened the door to a fellow worshiper, but then let it close as he stepped back to continue his story. "He and forty warriors attacked the military camp at dusk. The soldiers outnumbered the Sauk seven to one. But the troops were confounded by the surprise and retreated to Dixon's Ferry. Eleven militiamen were killed. They have taken to calling it Black Hawk's War."

There was no time for additional detail. I turned from Abbott and went inside. I sat in the front pew, worried more about war than the sermon. I asked God to forgive my wandering thoughts and be with Black Hawk and his men. I figured the militia had enough strength to take care of itself.

After the clash at Stillman's Run, stories drifted over fields and through forests to become the talk of Mackinac. One told of two thousand bloodthirsty savages sweeping through northern Illinois. Settlers complained the United States' militia failed to protect them. Fear rose. Rumors replaced facts. Widespread panic ensued. The government mustered five brigades of volunteers, and directed half of all federal troops from the United States Army to put down the uprising. Nine thousand soldiers from the Illinois Militia provided the majority of the force. Black Hawk never received the reinforcements he had been promised by local tribes. The lopsided war began and ended within four months.

After many clashes, seventy soldiers and settlers were dead. Black Hawk lost hundreds of his men.

I was saddened by the deaths on both sides. I asked God to help me understand the plight of my people. Black Hawk's War was a small uprising compared to earlier upheavals, but never before had my people seen the strength of the United States military aimed solely at Indians. The government seemed to be saying that Indians could only cling to cherished traditions if they could do so without frightening white neighbors. Neighbors who lived on land that Indians believed belonged to them. Many Odawa were unwilling to accept the compromise. Their plight seemed hopeless.

I watched the Cherokee and Choctaw forced from their villages. I lent my opposition voice to the American government's efforts to compel treaties and relocate Indians west. My pleas were directed to obtaining an exception in the Michigan Territory for Catholic and Christian Indians.[76]

It was not a good year for Indians. In the winter of 1832-33, another pox scourge ran through the villages.[77]

The year closed with more distressing news. Father Gabriel Richard, who so tirelessly attended my faith when it wavered, had died assisting victims of a cholera epidemic in Detroit. The night after I learned this news, I added a message for my favorite priest to my evening prayers. "Father Richard, if you can see me from your special place in the heavens, please know I am devastated by your death, but you should be happy to see, I accept God's will." I dabbed my tears with the sleeve of my tunic remembering his gentle ways, his sweet smile, and the day he came into my life. "You are on the list of people I will be eager to embrace when I get to heaven."

Chief Black Hawk, Makataimeshekiakiah
Artist Rendering Circa 1837
Public Domain

30.
Gathering Storm

"I would have been better pleased if you had never made such promises than that you should have made them and not performed them." **Shinguaconse, Little Pine**

1833-1838

In 1833, I held a dinner party to welcome the Schoolcrafts to our island. Mr. Schoolcraft assumed the center of attention. His contribution to polite dinner conversation sounded more like a monologue than a two-way discourse.

I have been accused of being too formal, stiff with my words, even long-winded. On the night I remember, however, Henry Schoolcraft made anything I had ever said seem simple and unassuming.

"It had always been my goal to explore, to the extent my modest abilities allowed, the vast interior of this continent," he said. "Whereas Meriwether and others of his ilk made a beeline for the Pacific, I indulged a simple desire to chart the heart of the country. One burning question that captured my imagination was the source of the Mississippi."

It sounded like a speech to the American congress seeking exploration funds. Although I had met Mr. Schoolcraft during his prior visits to Mackinac, I decided to reserve until I knew him better, an opinion of whether he was a braggart or an excellent raconteur. He never hesitated to regale us with stories of his acquaintance with important people or his explorations aimed at opening the country's interior to settlers. He avoided saying white settlers, but few Indians wanted to move and take up farming.

Unlike the boastful Mr. Joseph Rolette, Mr. Schoolcraft managed to portray himself in a self-effacing manner that merely skirted the edges of offensiveness. Mr. Schoolcraft looked at the ten of us seated around my dining room table that night, and studied each face. When Therese yawned, he raised his voice ever so slightly and delivered a new twist to bring her back into the conversation.

"General Lewis Cass, while governor of this territory, got it wrong." Schoolcraft smirked and gave us a knowing nod before sharing his big secret. "He and I had a rollicking good time when I joined his expedition back in 1820. But I have proven the error in my friend's declaration that the Mississippi started in Cass Lake, which he named for himself. The true source of the river is Lake Itasca, a small body of water your people—" he looked at his wife, Jane, then at Therese and me—"called Lake Omashkoozo-zaaga'igan."

Jane said, "Elk Lake."

Schoolcraft smiled at her translation. "Indeed. However, I have renamed it Lake Itasca from Latin words meaning true head. Cass did not travel far enough. His lake lies a bit downstream of the actual source."

After relinquishing the conversation to others, Schoolcraft picked up again during a perfect cherry cobbler dessert. "I expect that Jane and I will be settled soon," he said, "and we hope that my dear friend, Henry Wadsworth Longfellow,[78] will accept my invitation to live a while here on the island and draw inspiration from Mackinac's beauty and fascinating populace."

I wondered if he used the word fascinating to mean peculiar.

"Can you imagine dinner parties with Longfellow in attendance?"[79] He dropped the name Longfellow a second time, but no one seemed eager to pick up the conversation.

Schoolcraft bowed his head as though studying the coffee in his cup. He added generous portions of cream and maple syrup and stirred.

He sighed as though undertaking to educate the uncultured. "Henry is a professor at Bowdoin College. It's a marvelous school in Brunswick, Maine. Indians called the town Pejepscot for its rocky rapids. Professor Longfellow published a translation of Jorge Manrique's poetry this year."

No one picked up the conversation or seemed much interested. Schoolcraft appeared baffled, "I consider my friend a colleague since I, too, dabble in the literary arts. I'm not his equal, of course, but I gather Indian stories for a book I aim to write. Madame Schindler and Madame La Framboise, I relish hearing tales you could add to my collection."

Therese smiled, her eyes dancing at the honor. I fixed detachment to my face as others offered polite nods.

Perhaps sensing my lack of enthusiasm, Schoolcraft said, "Mark my words, the day will come that you will all be impressed by the name Henry Wadsworth Longfellow," and then he went back to accounts of his exploration.

Henry Wadsworth Longfellow, photos Public Domain
Engraving (right photo) by Wellstood and Peters

Though my assessment of Mr. Schoolcraft was incomplete, I adored his wife. Jane Johnson Schoolcraft was a Métis, like me, only her Indian blood came from our brother Ojibwe tribe. Jane, or Bamewawasgezhikaquay,[80] was the source of her husband's best tales. It would be to her credit if her husband's writing met with success.

The Schoolcrafts lived in an agency house east of the approach below the fort. It was a long structure with many gables, a piazza, and lovely gardens. Its window shutters were adorned with the iron letter S.

While at Mackinac, Mr. Schoolcraft conducted services at the Mission Church, but even during times of religious discord and separation, he and Jane socialized with everyone.

I remember a conversation with him that caused my cheeks to redden. It took place one afternoon along the beach. I had been walking among the wigwams that lined my way and happened upon an old Indian woman whose family had abandoned her more than a week earlier. I offered her bread and meat each day. She held out her leathery hand. I placed strips of pemmican on it. The weather would soon turn too cold for her to be left along the shore, and I considered when to invite her into my home.

Mr. Schoolcraft, having observed the incident, hurried to my side as I walked away from the poor soul. He thanked me profusely. "Without your help, God would have a much harder task caring for the unfortunates on this island. He counts on you for assistance."

I could not diminish the flush that bespoke my embarrassment. I turned away and stammered. "I hope Jane is well. I look forward to her joining us for cards tomorrow." Although flustered by his approval, I concluded that we shared a belief that in spite of our spiritual differences, we all worked in the service of one God.

Engraving of Henry Schoolcraft by Wellstood and Peters
Public Domain

Lucy Tanner was growing into a fine young woman. She was educated at Marianne's boarding school for children of fur traders. Therese and I expected Lucy to find an appropriate match and marry soon. Marianne thought her adopted sister was destined for a teaching career rather than raising a family.

Marianne planned to spend the winter of 1834 in Grand Haven, where she could access books to translate prayers and the Bible into Indian languages. My niece rented a small house not far from where Joseph and I had wintered. She requested that Lucy, Catishe, and Therese join her as she undertook the project. Therese intended to trade during the cold season in the Grand River Valley and thought it a splendid arrangement.

When the boat was near ready to depart Mackinac for Grand Haven, Lucy pleaded for a few additional weeks before leaving the island. The girl wished to spend time with her maman, Miskwabunokwa, who had procrastinated and never taken her long-threatened leave for Red River Country. Therese yielded to Lucy's request. My sister and Catishe departed for Grand Haven without her. Lucy would journey there a few weeks later, accompanied by Angelique's son, Francois Lacroix, and his family. Since she would be safe under Francois's watchful eye, it seemed a reasonable plan.

In November, Therese and Marianne prepared for Lucy's arrival, but the schooner carrying my adopted niece did not arrive. Initial worry hardened into dread. It was spring when word reached Grand Haven and Mackinac confirming that the vessel carrying Lucy and Francois had sunk. Everyone aboard perished.[81]

A suspicion, or even an assumption that tragedy has occurred, does not prevent its proof from inflicting further grievous wounds. Despair slammed down on me with force equal to the waves that killed our dear Lucy.

I could make no sense of the disaster. My first instinct was to challenge God. Then I remembered Father Richard's words: "Magdelaine, what do you expect from God? You wish to order his actions? See his plan and be given a say in it?"

Instead of questioning God, I prayed. His love allowed me to emerge from the darkness, battered and bruised, but whole.

Therese and Marianne returned to Mackinac Island the following month. At a memorial service for our lost loved ones, I asked God to help us heal. I thanked him for the time Lucy and Francois had enriched our lives. I pleaded with the almighty to be merciful to their souls. I asked that he allow Francois to play his fiddle for the angels.

If God had given me three opportunities in my life when I could have exercised clear foresight and rewritten history, I would first have used the gift before Josette's death. I would not have departed for winter camp, but remained on the island and held my dying daughter in my arms. I would have used the gift the second time before Lucy departed for Grand Haven to prevent her boarding the ill-fated schooner. I would have saved the last use because I knew there would come a time when I would need it.

In 1834, Reverend and Mrs. Ferry left Mackinac. I felt melancholy as I reflected on the years we had shared a dream. It was from Mr. Schoolcraft that I heard the church hierarchy in Boston questioned the value of an expensive boarding school on Mackinac Island and decided it was wiser to expand operations in the Lake Superior region. Fewer traders visited our island each summer and the number of students enrolled at the Mission School shrank.

That same year John Jacob Astor sold control of the American Fur Company to Ramsay Crooks, whose life had been dedicated to achieving American control of the fur trade. So single-minded was Crooks's pursuit that he blinded himself to the reality that the trade dwindled and would soon disappear. He worked to destroy his competition, fought every type of governmental interference, and championed private enterprise.[82] In spite of his earlier attempts to ruin me, I had survived. His fate would be less favorable.

Astor was seventy years old and in poor health. He was the better businessman of the two men and likely saw that the lucrative days of the fur trade had disappeared. Crooks jumped at the business opportunity and managed to raise $100,000. He persuaded his associates, including Joseph Rolette, my son's boss, to contribute another $200,000 to buy out Astor. Crooks became the new president of the enterprise he had steeped with his life-blood. My Joseph was now in cahoots with both Rolette and Crooks, a situation that did not favor my good disposition.

In April 1834, the final papers for the sale were signed. Crooks retained the name of the American Fur Company. What Astor understood, and Crooks may not have, was that with settlers crowding out the Great Lakes Indians, two necessities of the business—the Indians and the animals—were being pushed westward.

By letter, Joseph and I discussed his part in the fur trade. He assured me he still made a living and stayed busy working for Rolette. I think my son's mind was on other things. His wife had died shortly after their son was born. Joseph had married a second time. Tawachihaishawi was Sisseton Sioux, the daughter of Chief Sleepy Eye. From Joseph's description of the marriage, I concluded that he needed a mother for his child, and he had wedded the woman to provide one. I hoped they exchanged affection in the bargain.

He ended his letter by dashing my hope that he might visit Mackinac the next summer. It seemed that in spite of the words he wrote about making a living, he now found supporting his family a hardscrabble effort that demanded all of his time. I had a six-year-old grandson I had never met.

The next year, I again received letters that brought news my son could not make the trip to visit me. I was fifty-five years old. I wondered how much time I had left, and whether I would see little Joseph in my remaining years. Instead of telling me he was coming to Mackinac, Joseph prattled on about some artist named George Catlin[83] who wanted my son to take him to the Pipestone Quarry, a place considered sacred by the local Indians. The quarry's soft rock was used to make peace pipes. After considerable discussion and debate, Joseph convinced the local Indians to allow the visit.[84]

Another year passed and I got additional letters, but still no visit. Joseph was involved in a dispute over the rising timber industry. The Chippewa River district in Wisconsin was the source of great stands of majestic trees. New towns sprang up along the Mississippi. They needed wood to build homes and communities. The settlers' desire to avail themselves of this abundant natural resource grew overwhelming. President Andrew Jackson wanted the tribes of the region to cede their forestland to the United States government. For remaining fur traders, a transfer carried dire implications. More Indians would be moved, and the woods that provided the habitat for the remaining animals they hunted would finally disappear—not just be diminished, but gone.

The traders formed a group to protect their interests, and Joseph accompanied a delegation of Sioux to Washington for discussions. Despite their efforts, on September 29, 1836, another treaty was signed, and the American government forged ahead with its plan to relocate Indians. Joseph and those traders who had traveled to the nation's capital with him gained a major concession. The treaty set aside $90,000 to pay obligations the Indians had incurred to them. My son received money from this reserve.[85] Reading between the lines of his neat penmanship, I concluded the treaty did more to pay Indian debts than to secure their future.

Chief Sleepy Eye, Joseph La Framboise's Father-in-law
Public Domain

CHIEF SLEEPY EYES
(Ish-tak-ha-ba)

Sleepy Eyes, or Drooping Eyelids, was born about 1780 in a Sisseton Sioux Indian village at Swan Lake in Nicollet County. The Bureau of Indian Affairs commissioned him a chief in 1824. His fame was achieved not as a warrior or hunter but as a friend to explorers, traders, missionaries, and government officials.

Chief Sleepy Eyes signed several treaties - Prairie du Chien in 1825 and 1830, St. Peters (Mendota) in 1836, and finally, reluctantly, Traverse des Sioux in 1851.

Traditionally his band, often called the Swan Lake or Little Rock band, hunted over a broad area between Swan Lake and Coteau des Prairies in southwestern Minnesota and southeastern Dakota. After the Spirit Lake massacre in 1857, frightened settlers demanded that Sleepy Eyes' wandering band remain on reservation land along the Minnesota River. From 1857 to 1859 his chief village was at Sleepy Eye Lake, near this plaque.

Sleepy Eyes died about 1860 while hunting in Roberts County, South Dakota, and is not to be confused with a nephew of the same name who was implicated in the uprising in 1862. In 1898 the old chief's grave was located, and in 1902 he was re-buried on this site near his last home.

Early in 1838, religious battles became more personal. I received a letter from Harriet indicating that her Aunt Elizabeth and Uncle John McNeil would be traveling to Detroit. From there they would send her to Mackinac, but first she and I had to make an agreement. She and her father would sign off on the property I had given the church, but in exchange, they wanted a deed to my house and the parcel of land upon which it stood.

Harriet described many sad events that affected her decision to ask for my property. The first two, the death of her cousin Scott in the Seminole Wars and the loss of two aunts to consumption, seemed to me to have no bearing. Then she recounted the "serious financial reversals" suffered by her father. Finding myself at a loss for words to deny her request, I had Marianne pen a letter that issued a new invitation for Harriet to visit, but ignored the request for my property.

Months later I received another letter:

> *"I received your kind and welcome letter and feel grateful to you for the repeated invitations to visit you; but, dear Grandmother, before I can conveniently comply with your request, I must call your attention to an affair of importance.*
>
> *The summer I visited you, it was your sincere wish that I should assign a lot of land whereupon stood a Catholic Church—to the Catholics. My resolution was at once formed not to act until I had first consulted my Father. I said when I again visited you, I would settle the affair according to your request if possible. Therefore I am in duty bound to make arrangements to that purpose. My dearest Father informs me that there are three lots in Mackinac belonging to Uncle Joseph and myself and that it was understood the lot which is now occupied by you, was one set apart for my Mother, upon which my Father made improvements to a considerable amount, in building the house in which you live, and fencing the lot, etc., while my mother lived.*
>
> *Now I remember you told me the property was to be divided between Joseph and myself. I think it will be just to both of us to make a division of the property. I should in case of an agreement sign over my claims to the lot upon which the Church stands and he in turn sign quit claim to the lot on which you live. My father wishes no difficulty in the division, yet he thinks it necessary to have this business settled. He has the right of rent of the property during life, but he intends and will give me the whole of his property… You shall not want a house, but remain there as you have always lived. I shall then visit you with pleasure because I shall have all obstacles removed."*[86]

The tone screamed emotional coercion. It had been my money that built my home. When Benjamin invested his time and oversight, as family members do for one another without expectation of payment, he received my word that the property—upon my death and never a suggestion of a day earlier—would be split between Josette and Joseph.

I refused to immerse myself in tawdry bargaining, thus offered no response. The price of my decision was the loss of a granddaughter.

Harriet stood her ground. Her subsequent letters were cordial, but she insisted she would not visit until the matter of the property was resolved to her satisfaction.

In December, she tempted me with words that broke my heart yet again.

> *"I remember the affection and kindness bestowed when I visited you. If the property matter can be concluded, I shall come out and perhaps live with you a great while. But, I certainly cannot give all I possess, if I am ever to have my part I wish it now —more than any other time."*[87]

I tucked the letter into a box along with her earlier ones. To offer a response would admit my anguish.

31.
Saying Goodbye

"The President does not know the truth. He, like me, has been imposed upon. He does not know that you have made my young chiefs drunk and got their consent and pretended to get mine. He does not know that I have refused to sell my land and still refuse. He would not by force drive me from my home, the graves of my tribe, and my children who have gone to the Great Spirit, nor allow you to tell me your braves will take me tied like a dog if he knew the truth." **Chief Menominee of the Bodwe'aadamiinh before the forced march to Missouri**

1839-1840

If there was one thing I had learned from my earthly sojourn, the moment I thought life was all gingerbread and sweet tea, a slice of poisonous pokeberry pie would be slipped onto my plate. Sometimes it was one calamity after another, and about the only good I saw was that the new misery distracted me from the previous one.

That was how it was with Elizabeth Mitchell's death, Lucy's tragic demise, Harriet's demands, Joseph's struggles, and the church battles. Each in turn heaped varying measures of grief on my shoulders, but those heartaches were overshadowed when Kimama sent a messenger to deliver crushing news. Wampeme was dying of dropsy.[88] She invited me to come and spend final hours with him. It had been nearly a decade since I had seen or spoken to Wampeme though a hundred times my thoughts had patched our differences.

Held by a lone rawhide fastener, the plank entry door to Wampeme's longhouse dangled open. I stepped inside and waited as my eyes adjusted to the dim light filtering through holes in the roof. Wampeme, asleep and snoring, slumped against a bundle of furs that propped him upright on the sagging platform in front of me. The faint smell of freshly plucked chickens and sour milk—the stench of sickness and creeping death—fouled the air. I fought the urge to cover my nose with a handkerchief.

Kimama rushed to greet me. The easy openness of her embrace reminded me of how much had changed since that afternoon on Mackinac Island, twenty years ago, when she sought my counsel to save her husband's life. I stepped back from her hug and thanked her for sending the courier.

Sitting next to Wampeme was the storyteller whose account of history had caused the rift between Wampeme and me. I was less horrified to see the old man than surprised that he was still alive. He was even more shrunken and withered than I remembered, but I would have recognized him anywhere. His eyes were white with age, and I figured he must be at least ninety years old. When he spoke, I saw that the passage of time had not clouded his memory.

"It is good of you to come, Madame La Framboise. I hope the years have been kind to you."

His warm greeting addled me. I tasted my angry feelings and forced myself to swallow the bitterness. "God has been gracious, and it appears Crooked Tree agrees with you." My hostility toward him drained in equal proportion to my failing hope for Wampeme's recovery.

Kimama motioned me to a mat at Wampeme's side, across from the old man. It appeared he, Kimama, and I would share the death vigil. Over the next hours, she welcomed visitors who paid their respects to her husband as he awaited his crossing to the spirit world. Many who entered brought gifts Wampeme needed for the journey: a leather pouch, pemmican, extra arrows.

Kimama moved soundlessly around those gathered. She provided bowls of food, poured cups of water, removed dishes.

Always, out of the corner of her eye, she watched over Wampeme. She adjusted his blankets when he appeared chilled, wiped his brow if beads of sweat appeared.

During a spell while Wampeme slept, no callers came. The storyteller and I shared an uneasy quiet, broken only by Kimama's muted presence. After several minutes he said, "I regret the offense I caused you."

I turned away from him, not knowing how to respond.

"You are an influential woman. I had hoped you would see the plight of our people and offer your voice on their behalf."

"I care about my people. We each help in our own way." The thought crossed my mind that if he had wanted my assistance, he could have found a less offensive way to enlist it. I warned myself to let it go. Wampeme's ebbing life left little time to harbor grudges.

"For some things it is too late," he said. "As Tecumseh warned, Indians are driven from their homes and herded west like animals."

I nodded without energy or an argument to refute his charge.

"Our younger brothers, the Bodwe'aadamiinh, signed over their land without understanding what they gave up." He spoke softly, as though age had snuffed out the fiery oratory with which he had wounded me years earlier. Simple truth assumed its place.

I pictured hundreds of families packing scant belongings and accepting the order to relocate. I considered my treaty efforts on behalf of Catholic Indians. The concessions I gained did nothing for the Bodwe'aadamiinh to the south nor Indians, wherever they lived, if they could not prove to a white man's satisfaction that they accepted Catholic doctrine.

The grief that etched the old man's shriveled face reflected a quiet passion that remained even if his vigor had waned. "Cast out with no choice."

I lost my appetite. I set down the bowl Kimama had placed in my hands. I knew that few Bodwe'aadamiinh bands remained in the Michigan Territory. Still, I carried on my privileged life. The storyteller's trembling fingers and closed eyes shrouded me in guilt. "They left without bloodshed," I said.

"You prefer avoiding bloodshed to dying like men?" I heard no rancor, only resignation. It sounded like something Wampeme had once said.

"The treaties they signed promised areas set aside where they could continue living. Chief Menominee[89] and his people tried to remain peacefully along the north bank of Twin Lakes on that reserved land. The Chief was a wise and noble leader. He harbored no malice toward those who rushed to claim land that had belonged to his people. I suspect that in his heart he knew the white man would eventually demand the reserved land too."

"I respected the old chief, but a treaty transferred that land to the government. The tribe received payment of fourteen thousand dollars." I wished to recant my words even before they fully tumbled from my lips."

"Lesser chiefs signed that paper. They had no right to sell the land. Menominee learned from earlier betrayals that any payment would soon be gone. White traders gather after treaty signings like vultures around carrion. They sell the Indians liquor and trinkets—all at huge prices. The white governor does not care that Menominee did not sign the treaty. The chief was ordered to remove his people to a place called Kansas."[90]

Wampeme opened his eyes. I wondered if he overheard the conversation and wished to protect me from further discussion. I wanted to assure him I no longer begrudged the old man his opinion.

"You came." Wampeme's dry, cracked lips did not stop him from grinning when he saw me.

The old man reached out and touched Wampeme's shoulder, then he rose and left the longhouse. Kimama settled in the spot where he had perched, sentry-like, watching a stricken fellow warrior. I had no impression she was protecting her claim on a husband. We were far past that. Rather, I sensed she would care for Wampeme's physical needs while he and I carved out our peace.

"You left me no choice but to come to you. You and Kimama did not travel my way." I reached over and touched his cheek, knowing it would cause his wife no offense.

Wampeme winked. "You never invited us."

"Since when do friends require an invitation?"

"At our last parting, there was a question regarding our friendship."

Kimama stood and moved closer to the fire. I watched her prepare tea. The odor of foxglove leaves, ginger, and primrose wafted from the cup she handed me for Wampeme. The herbs would help him breathe and control the pain. The brew in a second cup was for me and smelled of cinnamon.

"I need to fetch wood." She stepped outside without waiting for a response.

I lowered my cup to the packed dirt floor and lifted the other vessel to Wampeme's mouth. He was thin as a deer after a hard winter. His hair had grayed. His skin had paled. Only his eyes, now peering out of pouched lids, seemed unchanged from when we were young. They retained the piercing quality that made me believe they saw more than I wanted to reveal. For several minutes only Wampeme's labored breathing broke the silence.

"My heart never let go of our friendship," I said.

"I'm glad your God permits friendship with heathens." A wry smile twisted his mouth.

"Friends? Oh, yes, we are taught to love everyone." I matched his playfulness with my own and returned the wink he had given me earlier.

"You admit you love me, just couldn't marry me?" Twisting my words brought an even broader grin to his face.

Kimama's reentry granted me a reprieve to the awkward accusation. It might not have mattered, because within seconds, Wampeme closed his eyes and drifted off again.

That afternoon Kimama answered my unspoken questions. "When you and Harriet left Crooked Tree after your visit those many years ago, Wampeme confronted the old storyteller about his affront to you. Their first heated argument didn't change either man's heart. Countless talks later, they had forged a mutual respect. The old storyteller became like an uncle to Wampeme."

I considered the many deaths that saddened Wampeme's life. Wampeme's mother died during his birth. His Shawnee father fought with Blue Jacket at the Battle of Fallen Timbers and succumbed to the bayonet of the one called Mad Anthony Wayne. In the moon when cornsilk turned brown, the Americans' year 1794, Wampeme had wandered into our village seeking his mother's brother, his closest remaining clan. Consumption raged through the village. Before the year ended, his uncle, too, was dead.

That evening the storyteller returned. I surprised myself and while Wampeme slept, I invited him to carry on the account he had started earlier that day. The old man eased himself down and sat cross-legged.

"The stories of Chief Menominee's fate reached me at Mackinac Island," I said, "but the details were never clear. The clerks had no interest in sharing particulars. Starved for news, we received insufficient scraps."

The old man's eyes appeared to see from a faraway place. "By the time the Great White Father sent troops, including your son-in-law, to battle the Seminole Indians, thirty million acres of land changed ownership. Always from Indians to the United States. The thievery did not happen overnight. Treaty after treaty claimed Indian hunting grounds...treaties like the one by which Menominee lost his tribe's land south of the Grand River.

"The Indians were ordered to leave, so white settlers could take possession. Chief Menominee held a council with his people and advised they should refuse to go. Men from the American government tried to persuade the chief that his fate was inevitable. Menominee, with words I cannot do justice, said he would never depart his home or the land that held the graves of his fathers.

"Quarrels followed and during the next fortnight a group of Indians, under the influence of ardent spirits, chopped down the door to the home of Mr. Watters, one of the settlers.

"The settlers retaliated by burning a dozen Indian cabins. Later, after soldiers arrived, other settlers who were friends to the Indians reported that Watters had entered Indian land without authority. Watters was eager to claim a hundred and sixty acres of the reservation for his use. He stirred up the passions of the Bodwe'aadamiinh—provided them alcohol so they would act crazy and give him an excuse to petition the Governor's assistance in removing them.

"I doubt there was any real threat of harm to the settlers. Chief Menominee was a religious man. He accepted your Christian God. He taught his people to shun liquor and live in peace with their white neighbors. There had been no trouble in the past."

"It is what happened afterwards that I do not understand. We were told the Indians attacked the white men." Without forethought, I smoothed the blanket that covered Wampeme.

If the old man noticed, or thought my gesture too intimate, he did not let on. "Another falsehood told by white men," he said. "The governor asked for a hundred armed soldiers to remove the Bodwe'aadamiinh. When the troops arrived, they gathered hundreds more volunteers. Everything happened so fast that the Bodwe'aadamiinh were surrounded before they had a chance to react. They assembled in their chapel. The soldiers ordered them not to leave until a peaceful resolution was reached.

Father Petit,[91] the Catholic priest for Menominee's band, reasoned with the soldiers. He insisted the entire tribe had been converted. The soldiers ignored this information. The priest broke down, sobbing, as he said a final mass. He removed the cross from above the altar, asked the Blessed Virgin Mary to look after the Indians, and begged the soldiers to take them to a place that would provide good hunting grounds."

From his words about the priest, I knew the storyteller had softened his view of Catholics, just as I had allowed warmer feelings about the old man to enter my heart.

"Father Baden built that chapel." I hoped to continue the conversation in a direction praising the Catholic Church's relationship with the Bodwe'aadamiinh.

The old man did not comment further on either Father Petit or Baden. "Groups of soldiers spread out in all directions to locate stragglers. A few managed to escape, but most surrendered and prepared to leave—close to a thousand Indians in a forced march.

"Wigwams and longhouses were torn down or destroyed. The village appeared struck by your God's wrath. Men, women, and children fell into line for the journey to their new western home. Along the way mothers held dying children, unable to do more to comfort them than caress their fevered brows and wipe their runny noses. Tribal elders died. Disease and hunger plagued the migration. Many adults lost heart."[92]

I cringed, fighting to cling to my belief that God had his reasons.

The old man rose. Getting to his feet was no small task if evidenced by his creaking bones. We talked no more that night.

Sleep eluded me. I lay that evening on a pallet Kimama made for me. Soft with beaver furs, it smelled of Wampeme's mossy woodsy scent. I listened to his gasps from across the room. He was a decent man, a kind man, a generous man, who would deny my Christian God with his last breath.

He does not accept Jesus Christ as his savior, but he believes in a power greater than himself. How can you deny him entry to heaven? He suffered during this life, yet lived honorably. I cannot bear the wrongfulness, the harshness, the unfairness of him and other virtuous people being cast out from your grace. Cast out where? To everlasting damnation as his reward for a life well-lived?

It was not the only time I had challenged God. At first no answers came. I felt abandoned at another crossroad without God pointing the direction. My stomach clenched with such violence I nearly cried out from the pain. Tears spilled from my eyes and dampened the animal pelts.

It is cruel. I argued as vehemently as I had when Josette died.

To my astonishment, I heard God answer. Not aloud, but with such authority he seized my mind, and I knew his presence. *You do not tell God what is cruel…or fair. But think, Magdelaine. Let's go over this again. What is the greatest of all commandments I give you?*

I responded. *To love you above all else.*

You have learned well.

Am I to accept that you are a loving God, yet you will condemn good people…deny them salvation? Is that a caring God?

I gave man free will.

I wondered if my bitterness would end our discourse. I was powerless to stop my raging thoughts. *Was it Wampeme's choice to be born Odawa? To be taught the Great Spirit was God?*

I thought I heard thunder. And then, *I demand much from those who would be saved. But when Wampeme prays to a higher power, whatever name by which he calls me, do you think I do not hear? Do not presume to decide for me who will merit salvation. I know the human heart. I know who lives a life according to my teachings. I know who believes he must give himself—body, mind and spirit—to a greater power. If mortals give me another name, do you think that is of critical import?*

Does that mean the Catholic Church is wrong?

The Catholic Church provides you a secure pathway to eternal salvation. For you to turn your back on it would endanger your soul. But you should not make assumptions on my behalf, assumptions that I cast out all who travel by another route.

I lay in the dark wondering if I asked questions and provided myself answers God never condoned. Was I risking my own redemption bargaining for the souls of others?

I remembered the words of St. Benedict: "Listen, and attend with the ear of your heart," and Father Richard, "Your own wisdom, given by God's mercy, will lead you from threatened darkness."

My wisdom and heart told me that I would see Wampeme in the place where I would also reunite with my maman, papa, Josette, and all the others I held dear, and who had departed this world before me.

The sun had chased the blackness from the night and scattered the storm clouds that troubled my mind. I arose and Kimama handed me a bowl of fresh water. When I finished washing my face, she offered me corn mush. My eyes never left Wampeme. Visitors would begin arriving soon. I moved close to him and watched his chest heave up and down, his heart ready to surrender.

He opened his eyes and with a vacant stare took in his surroundings. Then, as though his thoughts cleared, and he had shared my dreams, he asked, "Do you think we'll meet again in the world that comes after this one?"

He had called it neither the spirit world nor heaven. I did not tell him that during the night God had come to me and eased my burden.

He said, "I would like to think that…that we'll see each other in a place free of human trouble."

"I believe it will happen."

"Are you casting aside your God?" He looked more worried than relieved.

He coughed, and I leaned him forward and slapped his back trying to loosen whatever choked him. When he stopped gasping, I eased him back against the furs.

"I am more ardently Catholic today than I have ever been. I thank God for leading my way. But my God is merciful. I do not believe he condemns his children to hell because they address their prayers to the Great Spirit. He takes scant offense at the name by which they call him, so long as they obey his one uncompromising rule."

"What rule is that?"

I wanted to tell him to be still, the exertion tired him, and I could not bear being the source of his tiniest discomfort. Instead, I answered his question in a word. "Love."

He raised his eyebrows as though expecting more.

"Love is the Almighty's unyielding demand. Love of him and love of our fellowman. If an action would be hateful to you, do not visit it upon your brothers."

"Sounds like Odawa teaching."

"It does." I touched my hand to his forehead and brushed back his long hair. "The Catholic Church helps me stay on the path of treating all men as I myself want to be treated. The priests have studied hard and offer me a map for which I am grateful."

His eyes were shut, his voice so gentle and soft I had to lean near to hear. "And if I get there from a different direction?"

"I cannot believe my Odawa brothers and sisters who cling to the old ways will be denied salvation. That is not my God of love."

"After all the religious battles we suffered trying to change each other, we are not so far apart?" A smirk brightened his face. "That is good to know. Do you think perhaps it is my Great Spirit who accepts you because of the goodness in your soul...even if you call him God or the Almighty or Jesus Christ?"

I laughed. "Can we be happy we do not have to debate this further?"

"That is wise. My time is short."

We sat for another hour. As if by higher design, no guests arrived. It was just Wampeme and me as Kimama busied herself preparing the day's meal. I never let go of Wampeme's hand.

At some point Kimama joined us. Wampeme had been sleeping, but awakened and turned toward his wife. "I hope I have been a good husband to you."

He paused and drew a sharp breath as though gathering strength to continue. "You have eased my way through this world." His lips turned up slightly in a soft smile. He lifted his hand, touched her face—allowed his fingers to trace her cheeks—and wiped away her tears.

Then he closed his eyes and was free.

32.
Mackinac Heartbreak

"May the stars carry your sadness away, May the flowers fill your heart with beauty, May hope forever wipe away your tears, And, above all, may silence make you strong." **Chief Dan George**

1840-1845

I returned to Mackinac Island, forever leaving a piece of my heart in L'Arbre Croche. My body was too old for the rigors of canoe travel. I would never again visit the Indian village that along with Gabagouache and St. Joseph had anchored my childhood.

During the cold moons that ushered in 1840, I struggled with loss. My world, however, was not painted in the flames-of-hell red that colored it when my daughter died. Instead, grief cloaked me in life-affirming greens and calming blues that encouraged quiet reflection. I did not suck in great gasps of air and expel them with violence, but took deep rhythmic breaths that opened my soul and encouraged the wisdom of spirits.

I awoke one morning in need of cheer. In earlier days, I would have rushed to Elizabeth Mitchell's gracious and lively home on Market Street for a measure of mothering parsed out with an equal portion of her no-nonsense advice. But Elizabeth, too, had left me behind.

Instead of remaining in my parlor with the windows covered, allowing doldrums a stronger grip, I visited another friend who lived on Market Street. I had not seen Agatha Biddle since she and Edward departed for fur-trading camp the prior fall. Spring had now declared victory over winter, the sun shone warm on our Mackinac soil, and the Biddles had returned early for rendezvous.

Agatha was my living connection to times past. Since Josette's death, I had cherished relationships with younger girls and women, not replacements for my deceased child as John Tanner suggested, but as beneficiaries upon whom I lavished maternal feelings. I did it with Harriet and Betsy and Lucy. I did it with Agatha and with her daughter, Sophia.

As is the way of the world, each brought joy and tragedy to my life. Father Baden had warned me many years earlier, "It is easy to fault God for sending grief into our lives, but without it we would have no compassion. The tragedies we suffer teach us humanity, empathy for the losses of others. We believe adversity hardens our hearts, when the truth is that suffering softens our sharp edges and make us kinder souls."

My relationship with Agatha Biddle dated to 1810 when she was but a youngster, and I a young widow. Her family rendezvoused on Mackinac Island that summer. Agatha's mother, Marie La Vigne, known to Indians as Tousequa, became my friend. Agatha and my son Joseph, both six years old, played together. Josette, at fourteen, watched the two while Marie and I enjoyed afternoons of each other's company. We imagined Agatha and Joseph, grown up and married to each other, cementing forever our families' ties.

Instead, I sent my son to Montreal for an education, and little Agatha turned fourteen and married Edward Biddle.

Years later, I was grateful when Agatha's daughter, Sophia, and Harriet became friends, and I took Sophia to my heart during the winters she stayed with me.

I knocked on the door of the Biddle home, a small, well-kept dwelling, comfortable though not extravagant. Agatha, in midlife, was still lovely, with her father's wide smile and her mother's black eyes and long thick hair that glistened like a raven's wing. She opened the door and drew me into a hug.

I took two steps inside and closed the door behind me. "Where is Edward this afternoon?"

"Exactly where you'd expect. He's selling furs, looking over goods for next fall's outfit."

"And leaves you to enjoy a real kitchen. I smell cinnamon and apples."

"The few left from those I dried last harvest. The cake should be ready shortly. I have tea. Settle yourself." Her eyes danced and her face fairly glowed.

"It appears you have news to share that is better than either applecake or tea."

She walked to the cook stove, her back to me, drawing out the suspense. "Would you like tea now, or do you prefer to wait until the cake is done?"

"Pour me a cup of tea if you will, but you toy with my patience. What has happened?"

"Sophia will be home in a few weeks." She teased me with more silence as she carried the bone china cup and saucer and placed it in my hands. Then she said, "My daughter has met a young man. He will ask Edward for permission to marry her."

Agatha's words, along with her unbridled enthusiasm, spilled out. "He is a soldier who has requested transfer from his current assignment to Mackinac."

My mouth dropped open. "Oh, my dear God, she is twenty and marriage should come as no surprise, but somehow it does. I always expected to watch her courtship."

"That would have been hard to do when she has lived her courting years in Pennsylvania." Agatha removed the cake from the oven, sat it on the table to cool, and took a chair next to me. "You and I married by the time we turned fourteen."

"To men twice our age."

"At least you understood Joseph's French. Neither Edward nor I spoke more than a word or two of the other's language."

"Perhaps that promoted marital harmony. You and Edward have been married for many years and are devoted to each other."

She graciously offered a chuckle at my feeble humor.

I took a quick sip of my tea. "Enough side-stepping what I really want to hear. Give me the details of Sophia's intended. Who is the young man? What do you know of him?"

"I have only what her uncle Nicolas has shared with Edward and Edward with me. His name is Pemberton, Lieutenant John Clifford Pemberton."

"Sophia Pemberton," I said. "It has a nice sound."

Her smile made clear her pride. "He graduated from the Military Academy three years ago with a commission as a Second Lieutenant, Fourth Artillery. He served in the Florida War against the Seminole Indians during 1837 and 1838 and then found himself on the Northern Frontier during the Canada border disturbances at Detroit." She paused to catch her breath. "His family hails from Pennsylvania. His parents adore my daughter."

Agatha's face reflected a satisfaction that I understood. I remembered thinking, when I met Benjamin, what a good marriage my Josette had made. "God willing, this summer we will plan a wedding. You are welcome to my home if you need more space than you have here."

Agatha grew serious. "Do you remember my wedding?"

"Of course. How could I forget? It was only three years after Josette married Benjamin. You, your mother, Therese, and I wore those ornate ribbon skirts with silk shirts.[93] Tables were heaped with food enough for the entire island."

"My stepfather hosted the wedding in our family home. Samuel Abbott performed the ceremony."

"I have not forgotten a single detail. Shall our goal for Sophia be to outdo that grand occasion?"

"Let's wait and see what she wants."

A month later, Sophia appeared at my door. I was struck by how much she looked like Agatha. Even with lighter complexion, brown hair, and blue eyes, the resemblance was unmistakable. Sophia was indeed a good catch: beautiful, sweet dispositioned, a wealthy father, a fine education, and impressive family connections. I understood why she had her choice of eligible young men, why they stood in line seeking her favor. In one rumor that had reached Mackinac Island she was courted by Chief Black Hawk's son, Nashashuk.

I curtailed my thoughts. Sophia's red cheeks and trembling lips warned of bad news. I had barely led her into the parlor before tears gushed.

"I couldn't let Maman see me like this."

Her raspy voice faltered. I put my arm around her shoulders, guided her to the sofa.

"I have missed you, Auntie La Framboise."

Her use of the familiar *auntie* touched me. I had not been part of Sophia's life for several years. She sat down, I next to her, close enough I could clutch her trembling hands between mine.

"Maman has told you about Lieutenant Pemberton?"

"Yes. With much joy. I, too, am happy for you. I do not understand the tears. Your young man arrives on the island this month. Has he been delayed…or taken ill?"

"John arrived as scheduled. Yesterday. His first order of business, after stashing his gear and settling in, was as he promised me, to call on my parents and ask their permission for our wedding. Oh, Auntie, I was so, so happy."

I tiptoed around words, imagining some small fixable glitch, hoping Sophia's emotions spiraled beyond what the situation merited. A case of nerves was expected from a woman betrothed and excited about wedding details.

"John knocked on our door. I answered, holding my maman's hand, she dressed in her most elaborately beaded tunic, her hair perfect, that stoic smile on her face."

I pictured Agatha, standing regal, exactly as Sophia described her.

Sophia paused, her breath less ragged, but still anguished. I nodded for her to go on.

"He stood, nervous, but so handsome in his best, neatly-pressed military uniform. Medals pinned to the breast attested to his importance. I said, 'This is my maman.' He looked at me, then Maman. Confusion put a frown on his face."

I squeezed Sophia's hand, took my lace handkerchief, and wiped tears from her cheeks. I did not like where the story headed.

Sophia stopped, her choking sobs too great for words. She reached for the handkerchief that now lay on my lap and wiped her nose. After perhaps a full minute, she continued. "John's face distorted. His initial joy at seeing me dissolved, replaced with something hard-featured and loathsome. 'You joke,' he said. Said it aloud, as though Maman had no feelings."

At first I did not understand Sophia's meaning. Then the horror of it dawned on me, too awful for reply.

She voiced my worst fear. "He said, 'Your mother is a squaw?'"

I remained speechless, unable to offer more comfort than another caress of her damp cheeks.

"Maman reached out to him, and he stepped back. I dropped Maman's hand, followed him outside, and shut the door behind us.

"With a hiss like that of a poisonous snake, he said, 'Why didn't you tell me you were mothered by a squaw?'

"Before my eyes he transformed into a hideous imposter of the man I thought I loved…my beautiful, intelligent maman. I found my voice and stammered, 'I didn't think it mattered.'

"He shouted, maybe so his voice would be louder than mine. I prayed Maman wasn't standing on the other side of the door, listening. 'You were much mistaken if you thought marrying a woman with squaw blood would not matter. I suffer grievous insult by your duplicity, and now I am stuck at this godforsaken outpost—and by my own request—with nothing but half-breeds and Indians to surround me.' I heard him ask, 'How could you?' as I stepped back into our house and slammed the door behind me. I ran to comfort Maman, but she had taken to her bed and locked the door."[94]

By then, Sophia was not the only one crying. I could not undo the damage with false words that skin color or blood made no difference. That was a lie. I could tell her she was better off without

Lieutenant John C. Pemberton. She would not believe me, but that was the truth.

John C. Pemberton
Public Domain

Biddle House Historic Marker
Courtesy Bob Royce

Original Biddle House
Public Domain

Current Biddle House on Mackinac Island
2014 photo courtesy of Bob Royce

Later that month, Father Mazzuchelli visited me. He continued to minister in Prairie du Chien, Green Bay, and other outposts and returned to summer on the island. One evening he joined me for coffee at the dining room table. He had taken his meal with Samuel Abbott.

The priest regaled me with stories of lands he had seen that were so full of beauty they made his heart sing, of souls thirsting for truth, and of knowing he had found his calling. He hoped to spend the remainder of his life travelling the back country—even fighting his way through blizzards on snowshoes when necessary—to minister to his flocks. He welcomed each day's new challenge as a precious gift from God.

He told me that with a scarcity of priests in the northern outposts, we should be grateful that Father Santé Santelli, our new island priest, had been sent to minister at Mackinac. I assured him the priest's presence was a blessing for which I often thanked God.

Father Mazzuchelli and I were alone, and my home provided us silence broken only by our easy conversation and bluebirds singing outside the open window. A breeze, summery compared to the late-season storm of a fortnight ago, reached us from the open window.

The sun had disappeared, leaving a golden afterglow illuminating the side garden.

The tranquility of the evening encouraged me to share with Father Mazzuchelli my recurring fear about the souls of those who had died without embracing Jesus Christ as their savior. I described the night in Wampeme's longhouse when God came to me, and how he attempted to ease my concern.

"And God's word was not enough for you?" He frowned as though chastising an errant child.

"Of course I accept God's word, but what if I conjured an illusion to bring me peace?"

"Madame La Framboise, God appreciates your devotion and does not fault you when you sincerely search for answers to troubling questions." He spoke with such conviction, and I listened like a distressed babe yearning to hear its mother's songs of comfort.

"In my travels I meet many compassionate people. Whether they acknowledge God the way Catholics are taught, or not, they reaffirm my belief in the goodness of God's creation. They are pious, full of charity and love for their neighbor. They share their last bit of meat or bowl of soup. They, too, possess an earnest desire to know the truth about God. It is imprudent for any Catholic to take it upon herself to judge. To do so, as God warned you, usurps the omnipotent power reserved to him. It is why the Bible warns, 'Judge not, that ye be not judged.'"

"But do you think God will judge non-Catholics mercifully?"

"I do. God is merciful. If you do not accept that, it is your faith that wavers, not God's mercy." The lesson the priest taught me that night settled in my heart.

After years of hearing my prayers pleading that Rolette send Joseph to Mackinac Island, God must have decided to grant my supplication. I never intended that Rolette's death would put into motion the circumstances that returned my son for the summer. But with his boss's demise, it fell to my Joseph to bring the furs to rendezvous. I entreated God to be merciful to Rolette's soul, but his death did not dim the joy of a reunion with my son. That is not to say he caused me no consternation, but it was consternation welcomed by a mother in exchange for her child's company.

On Joseph's second day home, I accompanied him to the fur company headquarters as he negotiated prices for his bales. As the sun grew high in the sky, we ambled to the grassy knoll in front of the fort and opened the buckskin pouch that contained our lunch.

"I scarcely recognized you when you arrived at my door." I grinned at the long-haired, bearded man who sat next to me. I handed him two pieces of toast with a slab of ham between. "A mother should see her son more often than every ten years."

"You wouldn't have me a wastrel, would you?"

"Perhaps not. There must be a middle ground between a man tied to his maman's apron strings, and one who has married again, given me two more grandchildren, and buried two more wives in the space between visits. I ache for grandchildren I have not seen."[95]

"You always knew where we were." He swathed the rebuke in gentle tones and made it more tolerable by the kiss he leaned over and planted on my cheek.

"The rigors of travel are too much for this old body. Rheumatism seizes my back and sleeping on hard ground or sitting for days in a canoe is beyond what I can tolerate. My hands"—I held them up for him to inspect my disfigured fingers and knuckles—"make ordinary tasks near impossible.[96] Today is one of my good days. Sometimes breathing is the most strenuous task I dare tackle."

"I'm sorry Maman. If I find me another wife, I shall bring her to the island. You can meet both her and your grandchildren."

"I hope to live so long."

I enjoyed several summer weeks with Joseph. His company allowed my heart—broken for Sophia and mourning the death of Wampeme—to continue beating.

After a decade in the backwoods, Joseph was a man starved for stimulating discourse. The jumble of island social activities revived him like rainwater sprinkled on a parched bean plant. Unlike most of the traders who frolicked on the beach, refused baths, and lived in wigwams or small huts, Joseph stayed with me, my parlor much more agreeable for entertaining young ladies. My son's pride was stroked by the available women taken with his boyish charm and pleasing features. I assessed the latter as objectively as a maman is capable.

Joseph took a particular liking to Miss Eliza Jones, but I could not verify from what I heard that she returned his interest. I feared his love would go unrequited. He remained optimistic and somewhat philosophic about the relationship, letting me know that if Miss Jones did not recognize his worth, he would return to his fort and marry the sister of his first wife, another daughter of Chief Sleepy Eyes.

My son drank too much, caroused, and took the state of his eternal soul far too lightly to suit me. Yet I enjoyed his presence more than I had reveled in anything in recent memory. His zest for life imbued itself into those around him. I often found myself asking God to forgive him as I stifled my amusement.

One evening we took our dessert in the parlor, and I said, "Your cousin Betsy warned me the back country had turned you wild."

"What would Betsy know of it? I rarely see her." He tilted his head as if to challenge the basis for my comment.

"Word filters back to her of your misdeeds." My son could tell from my countenance that I teased him and meant no real criticism. I walked over to the desk and pulled out a bundle of letters tied into a neat stack. I loosened the blue ribbon and shuffled through the folded missives until I found the particular one for which I searched. I opened the pages and began reading. The words were beyond my skill, but I enjoyed showing off for Joseph. I did not tell him Marianne had read the letter to me several times, and I had committed it to memory. "Ah, yes, here it is…the news Elizabeth shared.

"Your dear son, and here please do not think me a gossip, has been the target of an amusing story. At least I hope you will find it more amusing than alarming:

"On a trip to Fort Snelling, he boarded a steamer and sat down to dinner. The strong smell of alcohol as well as his actions made it clear to those around him that he had been drinking. He finished dinner and promptly fell asleep at the table. Since the passengers had to be served dinner in three shifts, he awakened at the beginning of the second seating, ate again, fell asleep once more, and was still there for the third meal. Apparently he had as large an appetite for food as he did for ardent spirits and women. His fellow passengers considered the whole escapade entertaining and decided he needed to be 'punished' for his actions. A mock trial was held much to the merriment of all aboard."[97]

"In this same letter, Elizabeth told me your horse stepped in a hole and threw you. At the time she wrote, your injury had healed, and she assumed it permissible to tell me even though you had cautioned her to spare me the worry."

Sharing Elizabeth's letters with my son must have convinced him he could not keep things from me. After he left Mackinac that summer, he sent a letter telling me that his courtship of Miss Jones had soured. She married a rival suitor, Mr. Clark.

Joseph survived with what seemed minimal grieving. Perhaps that was the difference between men and women. Men moved on, women carried ancient hurts to their grave. True to his word, he wed a third time, and as he had predicted the marriage was to the sister of his first wife. He did not, however, keep his promise to bring her to Mackinac Island for my approval prior to the marriage. He told me he was saddened by marriages that produced few children. I thought it interesting that the lack of additional children hurt him more than the death of his wives, but I kept my thoughts to myself in my responding letter.

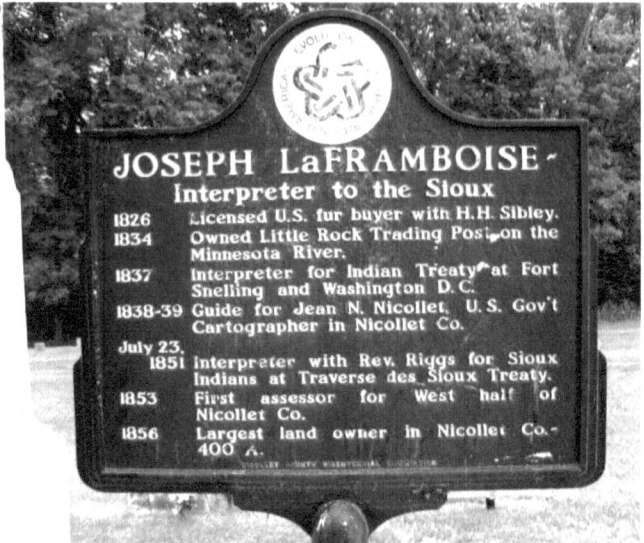

Marker at Fort Ridgely State Park

In the waning months of 1840, William Henry Harrison was elected the ninth president of the United States. He was sixty-eight years old, but if the Americans elected him to honor the wisdom they believed he gained from all those years of living, I scorned their foolhardiness. The man embodied pure evil.

On April 4, 1841, Harrison became the first American president to die in office. It had been thirty-one days since he was sworn in.

"I have no tears for him," I told Therese upon hearing the news.

Always the older sister, she scolded me. "You sound uncharitable, Sister."

"I do not mean to be unchristian. God will judge him, but I waste no precious moments mourning a man who found it sport to round up a few elderly tribal chiefs, invite them to lavish celebrations, get them drunk, and steal their land."

"I remind you, Magdelaine, you were not there."

"Yet we have heard the stories. He considered it good business to avoid paying an annuity with valuable consideration, offering instead whiskey. If you doubt the veracity of those accounts, then look to the result."

"Perhaps Tecumseh's curse has power after all."[98] Therese could not suppress her smile.

"Now that sounds unchristian. I hope the good Father Santelli never hears you say that."

"What will the Americans do for a leader now that the man they call Old Tippecanoe is dead?"

"John Tyler, the vice president, now leads this country. He must be an improvement over Harrison."

I had grown old and believed my time limited. I believed I would never see the grandchildren Joseph had given me. Harriet and I remained estranged. I could not repair or correct these situations. They were burdens I would carry to my grave.

Joseph's third wife had also died. I received word in 1845 that he married for a fourth time. His wife, Miss Jane Dickson, was the granddaughter of Colonel Dickson, who had traded at Mackinac during the war of 1812. This time my son planned to marry in the Catholic Church at Traverse Des Sioux in Minnesota. My health prevented attendance, and again Joseph did not bring his intended to Mackinac. I forgave him the broken promise and prayed this marriage, blessed by God, would bring him happiness and the larger family he wanted.[99]

Joseph had twenty-six Indians hunting for him, but made barely enough profit to feed and clothe his children. I had watched the decline of the fur trade and had hoped my son's education and connections would insure his family's survival.

My own survival vexed me less. My life drained like the last grains of sand in an hour glass. The time left to me was numbered in weeks, not years. I did not laugh in the face of death, but I believed there was little further service I could offer God or my fellow man. As daunting as crossing over was, I looked forward to standing in God's presence and experiencing, firsthand, his glory.

33.
Preparing to Go Home

"Seek to make your life long and its purpose in the service of your people. Prepare a noble death song for the day when you go over the great divide."
Tecumseh

1846

Snow had fallen each day since the new year arrived. Death masked itself somewhere in those white drifted mountains. A prowler, it lurked, sneaked close, and then whispered my name. When my heart did not stop beating, it receded to plan a stronger attack, but 1846 was the year I expected to die.[100]

Confined to bed, I pondered death. Maman, Papa, Elizabeth Mitchell, Lucy, my sister Charlotte, my husband Joseph, Wampeme. I remembered the loss of each. But Josette—her life cut short like a perfect summer stroll stopped midstride—had left my heart iced over, frozen with anger that I once believed would never thaw. My hardest challenge had been to continue living when I longed to join her.

As my passing approached, it danced with me, teased a bit. Unlike those cut down by gun or knife or childbirth, God allowed me to die at leisure. Leisure to put my affairs in order and say my goodbyes.

On the day of my sixty-sixth birthday a winter storm pelted my bedroom window with ice. I was grateful for a warm fire and a thick feather duvet.

Marianne brought a dinner tray she placed before me. Angelique baked a cake with my favorite maple sugar frosting and positioned it on my nightstand. Therese dropped into the old rocker next to my bed so she could be comfortable while we talked. They all wished me many happy returns. We smiled and for a few minutes embraced the delusion. But I knew death would claim me before plans could be made for the celebration of my sixty-seventh year.

Angelique removed the tray after I had taken a bite or two. Marianne leaned over and kissed my forehead. She told me to rest. Therese stayed to keep me company. In her lap was a tunic she beaded, and at her feet a basket of mending.

My fingers throbbed with the ache of rheumatism. My hips and legs argued they were tired of holding me upright. My body suffered less than my mind, which, under its own scrutiny, festered like a raw wound. I wondered how my earthly efforts would be judged. I reminded myself pride was a sin. Wanting to leave my mark on the world. Believing God imbued me with importance enough to change lives for the better.

If my pride was not enough for which to repent, I asked God to forgive my self-righteousness, my vainglory. Greed? I was no more free of greed and envy than any other mortal. Perhaps God would decide lust was my worst sin. I hoped he understood that one. Even on my deathbed I could not block images of a young Wampeme running along the Misigami shoreline. *Forgive me, God, these venial sins. I hope you conclude my heart was mostly right-directed. I tried to walk through the world in an upright way. I pray, let that account for something.*

My life, spent in the great forests and along the big waters, was now reduced to this box of a room. In the thirty years I had slept here, my bed—big enough for two—had never known a second warm body other than the few months Harriet joined me, and for an even shorter time, the nights that Sophia sneaked in beside me. Three pillows supported me, but I felt like a great hand squeezed and crushed my heart. Breathing was a chore. To keep away a chill, blankets swathed me like an infant on a cradleboard. A window with a view of the shoreline was my prison's finest feature. I watched a man paddle his canoe away from the protection of Mackinac Island's natural harbor, and wished I could secret my spirit in its bow to be free one last time in open space and fresh air.

"I am ready."

Therese looked up from her beading. She knew my meaning. "Don't talk silly. You'll recover from this bad spell and continue to torment me for years."

"Come, sit here beside me." I patted a spot on the bed near me. "You should be happy for me. I have lived a long time in God's paradise. Life has never been dull."

My words, rather than elicit a smile, caused her to turn away. After a short pause, she put down her needlework and moved next to me.

"Soon I shall know the joy of reunion with Maman and Josette. Joseph and Benjamin Langdon, and Elizabeth Mitchell." I said nothing of Wampeme, but my mind pleasured me with the image of his earnest eyes, his strong arms, and the sound of his sweet voice. I could not suppress a slight smile, though Wampeme was not a subject I would mention to my sister. After a few seconds that went unnoticed by Therese, I said, "I shall meet the sister we never knew." I pointed my finger. "I will tell her all about you, my bossiest older sister."

Therese offered no response to my gentle mocking. I turned serious. "There is so much of God's teaching I do not understand. I look forward to the moment it becomes clear."

"What of me? Does leaving me behind cause you no pang of remorse?"

I reached over, touched her folded hands and studied the veins prominent beneath paper thin skin. "Perhaps you should go live with Betsy and Henry. They would welcome you. I hear Green Bay is a lively place."

"I don't relish lively, and I despise change."

"Dear sister, has our life been anything if not one change after another?"

"Then in my old age, I deserve tranquility." She pouted like a two-year-old.

I chided her. "Think of it as a new adventure."

"I want nothing but peace." She snorted and sent me a scowl. "You were the one who sought adventure. Many times I wondered where you got your notions…traipsing off into the wilderness on your own after Joseph died…figuring you could play bourgeois to rowdy men…getting them to listen to you. It must have been your bad example that led me to trade when George took ill." Describing me as a bad example brought a chuckle before she again turned serious. "Our lives revolved around the fur trade, and it's gone."

"My Joseph struggles with the business. You are right, it has become near impossible to support a family on what men earn collecting furs. Not even Crooks prospers from trading peltries anymore." The thought of Ramsey Crooks struggling brought me satisfaction. I quickly asked God to forgive me the unkind musing. With inadequate time to repent, a deathbed was no place for spite.

Therese went on. "And much less so the Odawa men, unable to make a living at any work open to them."

"It troubles my heart to see our people come to Mackinac in the summer and raise their wigwams, no longer for rendezvous, but to collect annuities, their sole means to provide for families."

"They are grateful for your watchful eye."

Her words, intended to bring me comfort, had the reverse effect. "It is never enough. The problem is too big. The Odawa are hungry, without work, unable to care for their children, unable to live the old ways, unprepared to live the new."

"You can't fix everything, Magdelaine. You did what you could. Give it to God."

"You sound like Father Richard. I appreciate your words as I did his, but still, I wonder if we worsened the problems of our people."

"Nonsense." Her stern voice echoed her irritation. "I've heard you make this complaint too often. Let it go. For God's sake, do not spend the time that remains grousing over matters beyond your control. We did nothing that every other trader wasn't doing. We respected our people and tried to be fair. The Odawa invited us into their villages. They were shrewd traders. We didn't have to watch out for them as though they were children."

"I never suggested our people were childlike or without the wisdom and intelligence to make proper decisions." I considered our history before speaking again, and when I did, I smiled at my recollections. "We had brilliant leaders. Our children share a proud ancestry. They do not lack role models: Obwandiyag, Black Hawk, Menominee, Molunantha, Moccottiocquit, our grandfather Kewanoquat, and even our cousin Charles. The list is long, and I could keep you beside me until morning trying to remember them all. But there is no disputing the Odawa lacked good bargaining position, and oft times wise decisions were not open to them. Then there were the ardent spirits that befuddled the brains of so many…made them easy targets to those who stalked them as though they were prey."

"When you gave up the trade, did the Odawa not honor you with grants of land to show their regard?"

"Maybe those of us who loved and treated them the best caused the most harm of all."

She rose and began pacing. "How can you say that?" Her bowed head declared there was more truth in what I said than she cared to admit.

"The cheaters and evil-doers…Indians recognize them for what they are."

"Are you becoming addled in your old age?"

"Our people trusted us. The Odawa, the Ojibwe, the Bodwe'aadamiinh are left with no place to hunt. Many tribes have been marched west." I listened to my own voice. It sounded as weary as my body felt. "The spirits of our people are splintered, the largest pieces of their hearts left behind with the bones of their ancestors."

"We survived." She settled herself back next to me.

"We are the exception that proves the rule. The times, circumstances, and the touch of God's grace made it work for us. Others were not so fortunate."

"Unless you plan to leap from your sickbed and rewrite history, I pray you stop. God invites repentance. He does not condone mulish self-flagellation. Content yourself that God, not you—at least not any longer—will watch out for his children." Therese leaned over and adjusted the covers around me. "I have overstayed my visit. Your eyes are closing. You need sleep."

She shuffled toward the bedroom door.

I called after her. "I am ready to meet God. I hope when I stand before him, that he, like you, will be forgiving." Wheezing prevented me from saying more.

At my bidding, Angelique had summoned Samuel Abbott to draft my will. With much difficulty, she and Catishe dressed and helped me downstairs to the parlor. Mr. Abbott took careful notes for Mr. Jonathan King, an attorney from the mainland. King would craft my wishes into a legal document ready for signature. I believed there was time, but dallying at this stage might deprive me of expressing my intent.

Joseph would receive most of my estate. I hoped it made his life and that of my grandchildren easier. I lacked for nothing, yet my possessions seemed sparse. I did not know what my son might choose to keep. Moving a mahogany sideboard or bedsteads with feather mattresses hundreds of miles would prove more bother than worth. My tableware, including the four silver tumblers I got from Therese after our bet about Reverend Ferry's grit, were more easily moved. Perhaps Joseph's wife would enjoy them.

My home and the lot on which it sat would go to Harriet. It saddened me that I had been unable to satisfy Harriet's ultimatum in time to enjoy a last visit. How could I explain to my granddaughter that I did not trust her father would allow me to live in my home if I relinquished ownership?

I wanted my will to specify that both Joseph and Harriet, in order to accept their bequests, must agree to never pester the Catholic Church about the property I deeded for God's use. I hoped that would no longer be a problem. Years ago Joseph signed an agreement to that effect, and Harriet should be satisfied that she got what she had for years demanded.

I made small bequests to Therese and Marianne, set aside an amount for the poor of the island, and another to the priest who would perform my funeral service. I had taken care of Angelique years earlier, funding an account in her name with the rents Reverend Ferry paid.

Abbott finished writing, put his parchment away, but before he left, he stood in the doorway as though suppressing a matter of greater import. It is your imagination, I told myself. He probably wished to offer his condolences at my ongoing illness—my imminent demise—and as was true of many men, he struggled to find adequate words to express his sentiments.

My meeting with Mr. Abbott lasted no longer than a fine dinner from first morsel through dessert. How quickly and efficiently a life's treasures could be divided.

On March 2, Mr. King brought to my home the finished will, along with men to witness my signing. He read the bequests aloud and after each asked if I had questions. When we got to the end, I noted I had overlooked a token of affection for Agatha Biddle. Mr. King corrected the oversight by writing with blue ink in the margin a notation that she would receive one-hundred dollars. He then said, "If you agree we have now recorded the sum and substance of your desires, you may sign." He pointed to a spot on the last page. The pain in my hands was so great they trembled. I barely managed to grip the pen in a loose hold. I had learned to read a little English, but writing skills escaped me. My "X" was all I managed.

Across the room sat Samuel K. Harring, Tally O'Malley, and Samuel Abbott, silent throughout the entire proceeding. Each in turn came forward to witness. When the last had affixed his name, Mr. King said, "I declare this will signed, sealed, published, and delivered to you as your last Will and Testament."[101]

The first day of April, alone with my thoughts, I welcomed companionship. The knock on the solid pine door of my room signaled the arrival of Father Van Renterghem. A smile spread wide across my face.

"Father, how good to see you." I missed Father Mazzuchelli, who now rarely spent time on our island. Therese must have summoned our new priest to perform Extreme Unction.

"As always, it is good to see you, my child." He pulled a chair from the desk close to my bedside.

We had plenty of time to talk. Death only made overtures. It had not cast the final thrust of its sword into my bosom.

He sat down, shifted as though considering small talk. "Our church thrives. God is pleased with the work you've done in his name."

"I cling to hope that God is satisfied with my life." I coughed to clear my raspy voice. "And the children, are they learning their catechism?"

"Yes, although perhaps they would be happier to get their hands on Schoolcraft's *Literary Voyager* than the *Holy Bible*."

"It is the curse of the young, not yet worried for their eternal salvation." I smiled at our shared knowledge of fears that beset the dying.

"And you, Magdelaine? You must take comfort in the promise that you will soon be with your Savior."

"I do, Father."

"Would you like to make a confession in case God soon relieves you of your earthly burdens?"

"Yes. I would be grateful."

Father Henry, as he was often called by children who could not pronounce his difficult last name, reached into a leather bag slung over his shoulder. From it he extracted a small pouch, which he placed on the desk a few feet away. He reached in again and brought forth a glass vial that he laid next to the pouch. He turned back to me. His eyes filled with a look of compassion. "I am ready to hear it."

"Oh, my God, I am heartily sorry for the sins I have committed since my last confession. I have had doubts that are blasphemous. I ask forgiveness for my pride, lust, greed, envy. I pray forgiveness for all sins committed since my baptism into your grace, sins for which I may not even know I have blame." I stopped, not out of sins, but out of energy.

"God, the Father of mercies through the death and resurrection of his son, has reconciled the world to himself," the priest said. "He has sent the Holy Spirit among us for the forgiveness of your transgressions. Through the ministry of the Church may God give you pardon and peace. I absolve you from your sins in the name of the Father and of the Son and of the Holy Ghost." Father Henry paced back to the desk he had made our altar. He picked up a wafer, placed it on my tongue. "This is the body of Christ."

I repeated the words I had been taught. "I give thanks to God for he is good and showers his mercies on me, a wretched child of this world."

With my tongue, I pushed the Eucharist wafer around inside my mouth. When it dissolved, I struggled to swallow. On the third attempt, it was finally gone. I considered the comfort I used to take from eating. Now, even meals that should bring pleasure had lost the ability to delight my sense of taste. I could no longer distinguish the flavor of the sagamité of my childhood from the rich pastries I had served at elegant dinners in this house. Food seemed too much bother for too little joy. Yet consuming no more than a sparrow, I watched my body, once lithe and firm, swell like a loaf of bread rising on the kitchen window ledge.

Father Henry stepped back to the desk, picked up the glass vial, poured a small amount of oil into his left palm. He returned to me and dipped the middle fingers of his right hand into the liquid, touched it to my forehead, and then made the sign of the cross over parts of my infirm body. "Through this Holy Unction, and through the great goodness of his mercy, may God pardon thee whatever sins thou hast committed."

I wheezed, gasped a breath, wheezed again. The priest picked up a pitcher of water on my nightstand and filled a small glass. He lifted it to my lips. The wheezing stopped, but my eyelids were sliding closed.

"Rest, my child. Rest, and know that God stands watch over your body and your soul. I will return tomorrow." He did not add, "If you are alive." The doctor, the priest, my sister—they had given up—but I knew my body would persevere a few more days, forcing me to continue the struggle to breathe.

I slept in a seated position so the fluid in my lungs did not suffocate me. If I needed to relieve myself in the middle of the night—which happened often—I called Angelique. Without her assistance, I would drop to the floor from dizziness and there remain shivering, gulping open-mouthed for air, until someone found me.

I had energy for nothing but my thoughts, sometimes not even for them. To be embraced by heaven, I must first die. I was ready for my passing, oddly comforted that death pushed me along the same path…by the same malady…that charted the beginning of Wampeme's crossing.

34.
Startling Revelation

"Like the blood which unites one family, all things are connected." **Chief Seattle**

1846

I looked forward to one last visit from Josephine Marley. She had been stopping by my house faithfully for many weeks. Each day on her way to her teaching duties, she sat for an hour and listened to my accounts, only rarely asking a question or making a comment. I was almost out of stories, and I was growing too weak for long talks.

The preceding day after she had departed, I had another guest. That social call left me exhausted, but gave me one final tale to tell.

Yesterday had been the day I believed might be my last. Samuel Abbott came to the side door and asked Angelique for an audience with me. It seemed an unusual request. I had not seen Abbott in the month since he witnessed my will.

A creature of habit and social conformity, I was uncomfortable taking a visitor—a man, close to my age, who was neither a priest nor a doctor—in my bedchamber without the presence of another person. It was no longer reasonable for me, or those assisting me, to endure the struggle of getting me downstairs. I realized the folly of my concern, but even a few breaths away from death, I was no more able to ignore propriety than fly to heaven before God prepared my winged chariot. Angelique suggested she sit with us. Her discretion, established from our years living together, was absolute. Abbott balked at the suggestion of her presence. He shook his head, almost imperceptibly. A frown pursed his lips. But whatever troubled his mind was of such importance, it won his consent to the arrangement. He took the bedside chair offered him, and Angelique sat across the room near the door.

Foregoing small talk, Abbott asked, "Do you know the circumstances of your birth?"

"It is hard to remember one's birth." I smiled to bring levity to this strangely serious encounter. He ignored my attempt at lightheartedness.

"Surely you've been told the history of that time and how it affected your family?"

"*Certainement*. I arrived during the fourth year of the War of Independence."

"Yes, the Revolutionary War wound down, but the Americans had not yet declared victory. Your family wintered in St. Joseph the February you were born."

I wanted to ask how he knew that or why it concerned him. Instead I said, "There were eight French families and a few Bodwe'aadamiinh living there at the time."

"Patrick Sinclair was lieutenant governor and superintendent of Michilimackinac. He had moved the fort from the mainland to the island. He was a suspicious man. He believed half the Frenchmen in the territory were spies. Atop his list of worries was your family friend Louis Chevalier, who also lived at St. Joseph.[102] Sinclair called the area a den of vipers. To make him even more wary, the Spanish had stuck their noses into our war."

"Maman told me the tale many times. Sinclair sent Joseph Louis Ainsse to St. Joseph with six canoes. Ainsse who spoke several Indian languages was an interpreter for Sinclair. He was also the nephew of Louis Chevalier. Sinclair had commanded Ainsse to guide those of us wintering in St. Joseph to Mackinac Island. My papa considered it a peculiar order."

I reached to my nightstand for a cup of water, my throat dry from recounting those details. "My parents trusted Ainsse, but had no love for the Englishman, Sinclair." Another sip and I continued. "Ainsse assured Papa that Sinclair was concerned only for our safety. When we arrived on the island, the lieutenant governor arrested Mr. Chevalier and charged him with sedition."

"All French traders worried they were next."

"That was the summer Papa built our first home on Mackinac Island."

"Yes. When your father departed for winter camp in the fall of 1780, he left you, your maman, and your sisters on the island. He believed nothing untoward would happen to you here. Sinclair depended on your cousin, Charles Langlade, and your uncle, Nissowaquet, to rally Indians to fight his battles. He would never hurt you or your maman. This your father knew."

Listening to my history was not unpleasant, but fear of why Abbott retold it caused me to shiver in spite of the heat from the fireplace. *How was he privy to these details?* I summoned courage. "You know my history as well as I. What is your stake in it?"

"I'm coming to that. Believe me, Madame La Framboise, I've thought long and hard about whether we should have this conversation."

"I am not sure how many hours, or even minutes, the Lord gives me, so perhaps you should hurry the pace with which you tell your tale."

At this a smile flickered over his face. "You are right." He seemed to relax, sat back in the chair, crossed one of his long legs over the other as he had done the day I lied to him and insisted Wampeme had not killed the English trader, Wilson.

"The year your father left his family at Mackinac, he traveled during the winter to St. Joseph. He traded furs. He also checked on the welfare of friends living there."

"So—"

"Many months he was without his family. He was a good man. A devout Catholic. But the most devout man wavers in his faith and direction during a cold winter."

What was the point of his story? Why did he care about my father's faith?

"He met a Bodwe'aadamiinh woman." Abbott scrutinized my face as if he sought confirmation I could handle what he was about to confide. I refused to let my expression answer him.

"Her name is unimportant to you. Your father took up with this woman for a short while. When spring came, he left. She never expected more. He never meant to cause your family shame. No doubt he prayed for and was given God's forgiveness."

The secret broke free of its bonds. There was no way to unsay it. Before that moment, I had never heard a word that evidenced such a dalliance. My hands flew to my mouth. My gasp filled the room.

"What are you suggesting? Why trouble my deathbed with ugly rumors?" I closed my eyes and turned my head to block the sight of him. "Why disparage my papa's good name? Have you nothing better to do with your days?"

"I mean you no disrespect, but I have held your father's secret much of my life. I cannot let you pass from this world without telling you we are kin."[103]

"That is a lie."

"If you believe I am playing a perverse trick on you, I'll take my leave." He rose slowly and shuffled from his chair to the window. He paused and looked out across the harbor. In the seconds before he turned back to me, I tried to fashion a proper way to request that he leave.

Abbott broke my reflection. Gentle though his words were, they bespoke determination. I could only guess how long he had planned this visit or how often he had rehearsed his speech. He came with a piece to say, and he would not be denied the chance to say it. I was reminded of Wampeme's persistence years earlier when he apologized for inviting me to listen to the old storyteller.

"I have admired you," Abbott said, "your ardent and devoted spirit toward your God, toward those less fortunate, toward educating our young. You drew me to the Catholic Church. Everything I knew about you made me want to embrace you as family. I have longed to call you sister before we parted in this world. I have prayed you would greet me as brother when we meet in the hereafter."

I saw a tremor in his fingers before he clutched his hands together to still it. His eyes, so grave, so honest—I knew his story must be true. It explained the interest I always felt he had in me. "How did you learn of this?"

He stepped closer to my bed. "My birth mother summoned me many years ago. She was ill and not expected to survive the winter. Facing death, she unburdened her conscience. She died the spring she told me the story. By the time she delivered me, she had moved to Detroit. There, too, resided the Abbotts. They wanted a child, and my mother had no way to provide for me. When I asked them, the Abbotts confirmed her account. They treated me as their son. I loved them like natural parents."

I stopped listening. My emotions switched from denial to anger. Moments passed, each second a century. A bluebird perched on a high branch within my view. It had been a hard winter, and I had not seen one since Christmas. I wanted to hear its song one more time.

"Angelique, would you open the window? Just a little."

"But, Madame, it is cold, and you have been ill."

"A breath of fresh air will not hasten my demise."

She gave up the argument and did as I asked. The *chirwi, chitiweewidoo* that greeted me was a welcome melody and a needed respite from the disturbing conversation. The winged visitor cocked his head, eyes directed at the rigid and unmoving lot of us. I would gladly have traded places with the cheery bird.

I reached for the crucifix hanging around my neck with one hand and Wampeme's bead with the other. I fondled each, reminded that soon I would be reunited not only with my savior, but with a life-long friend whose strength and example helped me find my way.

The church bells pealed the noon Angelus. I closed my eyes and asked God to direct my next words.

When I opened my eyes again, I laughed. Laughed with more strength than I had summoned in many days. Samuel Abbott appeared amazed at my bewildering behavior. A tentative smile came to his face, as though he should join the merriment although he did not quite understand the jest. He moved toward the door.

"It is not that I receive your news with great amusement. But I do see small humor in our deceptions. For many years we each believed that good intentions excused hiding unspeakable truths from the other."

Abbott lowered his eyes. "I should have told you sooner…or not at all, Magdelaine."

"No matter." I paused to reflect on the sound of my Christian name slipping from his lips. "I believed God had no more surprises for me."

When my earlier confession struck him, he asked, "You said you deceived me. How does my secret taint you with dishonesty?"

"Not your secret. I have lived with my own unthinkable lie." I looked at Angelique and considered how she would react to the story I had hidden even from her.

Abbott raised his head, stared directly at me, waiting.

"Do you remember some twenty-six years ago…I appeared in your office on behalf of Wampeme?"

"To swear he had nothing to do with the death of that trader, Wilson?"

"Yes. That was the occasion." My tongue felt thick. It was almost as difficult to admit the lie now as it had been to utter it in the first place. My weak heart raced so fast it threatened to burst, but there would never be another occasion to unburden myself of the falsehood.

"Wampeme killed Wilson."

Now it was Abbott who smiled, and I who did not understand his reaction. Even so, speaking the truth—there in front of Samuel

Abbott and Angelique—released the damning secret I had carried within me and freed me of its judgment.

"I suspected as much," Abbott said, "but Wilson wasn't my favorite trader, and I figured he got what he deserved."

"The murder of a man is no light matter. It cannot be undone." My heart calmed, and to my surprise, I felt at peace. "I have borne the torment of Wilson's death and my lie for too long. It is time to let go of the past."

He clasped my hand, entwined his fingers with mine. I closed my eyes to bar all but our connection. I took a deep breath.

From the next world, Maman's words came back to me. *In the sacred space between inhalation and exhalation your soul receives the wisdom of spirits.*

I exhaled and thanked God for that moment of time when I chose to accept my brother.

Postscripts

"My people, some of them have run away to the hills and have no blankets, no food. No one knows where they are, perhaps freezing to death. I want to have time to look for my children and see how many of them I can find. Maybe I can find them among the dead. Hear me, my chiefs. My heart is sick and sad. From where the sun now stands I will fight no more forever.
Chief Joseph Nez Perce, statement following surrender at the battle of Bear Paw

Many of Magdelaine La Framboise's peers, friends, and loved ones outlived her, and if there is a great hereafter, it is from there that she witnessed the closing acts of each of their lives:

➤ **Samuel Abbott** died on April 26, 1851. He is buried in a crypt in the Catholic cemetery at Mackinac Island.

➤ **John Jacob Astor** died at age eighty-three in 1848. After retiring from the fur trade and his other businesses, Astor spent the remainder of his life as a patron of culture. He supported poet and writer Edgar Allan Poe and ornithologist John James Audubon, and he helped finance the presidential campaign of Henry Clay. By the time of his death, Astor was the wealthiest person in the United States, leaving an estate estimated to be worth at least twenty million. In his will, he funded the Astor Library, which was later consolidated as part of the New York Public Library. He also provided money to care for the poor in his German hometown, Walldorf. Perhaps the most bizarre provision of his will ordered that his business papers and ledgers be incinerated. Historians are left to speculate why.

➤ **Elizabeth Fisher Baird** returned to Mackinac Island for a visit in 1847, but by then her beloved Aunt, Magdelaine La Framboise, was dead. The Baird family remained prominent in Green Bay circles and Elizabeth died there in 1890. Her husband,

Henry, ran as Whig candidate for governor in 1853. He was elected Mayor of Green Bay for two terms in 1861 and 1862. He died in 1875.

➢ **Dr. William Beaumont** died on April 25, 1852, as the result of a slip on icy steps. In early 1831, while living in St. Louis, Dr. Beaumont conducted another set of experiments on Alex St. Martin's stomach. Beaumont published the account of these later experiments in 1833, as *Experiments and Observations on the Gastric Juice, and the Physiology of Digestion*. Beaumont became known as the Father of Gastric Physiology. Several schools and institutions are named in his honor.

➢ **Sophia Agatha Biddle** died of tuberculosis on July 20, 1848, at age twenty-eight. She is buried in the Catholic cemetery in the same plot as her mother, Agatha. A single rose is carved on Sophia's gravestone. One legend asserts that some years after Sophia's death, Pemberton returned to the Island and visited her grave, and that it was he who had the rose chiseled there. There is no source to substantiate this story, and it seems highly unlikely in view of Pemberton's underlying intolerance.

➢ **Ramsey Crooks** died on June 6, 1859. According to the New York Herald, "*He seemed to die of no particular disease. He quietly passed from the world as one retired to sleep.*" Ramsey Crooks was seventy-two years old.

➢ **Alexis-Charles-Henri Clérel de Tocqueville** died in Cannes, France, on April 16, 1859. The philosopher published *De la Democratie en Amerique* in 1835 after he returned from America to France, where, hopefully, he lived out his years unmolested by mosquitoes.

➢ **William Montague Ferry's** Mission House is currently on the National Register of Historic Places and operated by Mackinac

Island State Park. After leaving Mackinac Island, Ferry founded settlements in Ferrysburg and Grand Haven, both in Ottawa County, Michigan. He lived in Grand Haven and was head of the Presbyterian Church there from 1834 until his death on December 30, 1867. The interior of Mission House is not open to the public.

➢ **Gurdon Hubbard** became known as "The Father of Chicago" and wrote an account of the fur trade. In it he fondly recalls Sunday afternoons spent at the home of Magdelaine La Framboise on Mackinac Island.

➢ **Jane Dickson La Framboise,** Magdelaine's daughter-in-law, fled the family home in 1862 during the Sioux uprising. Her home in Minnesota was burned, and all family records were destroyed. Jane and Joseph's daughter, **Julia La Framboise**, later taught at a government school at Lac qui Prairie, the village of Sioux Chief, Spirit Walker.

➢ **Joseph La Framboise**, Magdelaine's son, was provided a lucrative business opportunity from the governor of Wisconsin, who was trying to secure a treaty with the Sioux. Joseph was hired to act as an interpreter at five dollars a day, a sum unheard of at that time. The result was a treaty at Traverse des Sioux, signed on July 23, 1851.

By that and a subsequent Treaty of Mendota, the Sioux traded nearly twenty-four million acres to the United States for white settlement. The Native Americans were to receive $1,665,000 in cash and annuities, but the money was subject to an exaggerated lien or debt of $400,000, known as "trader paper." Joseph submitted debts to be paid under the treaty. In part, the signing of these treaties was influenced by the outcome of Black Hawk's War, which the Native Americans saw as a detriment to their ability to negotiate favorably or remain in the area. Realizing their situation, the Wahpeton and Sisseton bands ceded their lands in southern and western Minnesota Territory, along with some lands in Iowa and Dakota Territory.

Joseph was also appointed Indian Agent at a salary of $1,200 per year and was pleased with his new position.

Joseph died on November 5, 1856. He had outlived his mother by a mere decade. Joseph was buried in the cemetery at his post of Little Rock. He was survived by his widow, Jane Dickson La Framboise. In 1915 his remains were removed to Fort Ridgley, where they rest alongside those of his children. Perhaps it is fitting that he was not buried next to his mother. She may have loved him dearly, but they were not kindred spirits. She was a woman drawn to her faith and much respected for her charitable works. Joseph was a different sort. He had his wild side and might not have been comfortable under the watchful eye of his mother and the good Catholic Fathers. Lying next to her daughter, Josette, and her grandson, Benjamin Langdon, Magdelaine is likely at peace.

- **Alexis** and **William La Framboise,** Magdelaine La Framboise's grandsons, became scouts and guides for the United States forces during the 1862 Santee Sioux uprising in Minnesota. In charge of quelling the resistance was Colonel Henry Sibley, an old friend and boss of Joseph Jr. For an account of how Henry Sibley treated Native Americans, see Dee Brown's book, *Bury My Heart at Wounded Knee.*

- **Marie Anne (Marianne) La Sallier Fisher** died on January 19, 1853, on Mackinac Island. She was sixty-three years old. She is buried next to her mother, Therese Schindler, in Ste. Anne's Catholic cemetery.

- **Angelique (Lacroix?)**, Magdelaine's faithful slave, survived to an advanced age. After Magdelaine's death Angelique was given her freedom and moved to L'Arbre Croche, where she lived with her son. Little more is known about them.

- **Father Samuel Mazzuchelli** died on February 23, 1864, after contracting an illness from a sick parishioner he had visited. He is buried at Saint Patrick's Cemetery in Benton, Wisconsin. Over the years, a case for elevating him to sainthood has been pending with the Catholic Church. In 1993, Pope John Paul II declared Father Mazzuchelli venerable—the first step in the process to sainthood. In April 2006, Italian doctors charged by the Vatican with determining the validity of miracles decided that Robert Uselmann had been miraculously cured of cancer by praying with Mazzuchelli's penance chain and asking for Mazzuchelli's intervention. Declared a miracle, this event made Mazzuchelli eligible for beatification, the next step to naming him a saint within the Church. Another verified miracle is necessary before Mazzuchelli can be canonized.

➢ **Moccottiocquit,** with whom Magdelaine had traded in the Grand River Valley, died the same year she did. He made a last visit to Grand Rapids near the time of his death. He was taken there to receive his annuity. He was said to be suffering the last stages of marasmus, a progressive wasting disease. He was described as:

> "a poor, pitiable object, without the least gleaming of intellect, and was carried back to die. He was then a noble wreck, with majesty in the skeleton look of his magnificent frame. By the people along Maple River he is remembered with much honor as one of God's noblemen."[104]

➢ **Benjamin Pierce** enjoyed a thirty-eight year career in the military. His brother, **Franklin**, was elected president in 1853. The Pierce family did not consider their political aspirations furthered by Benjamin's marriage to a woman of Indian blood; the biographies of neither Franklin nor Benjamin carry much detail of the marriage of Benjamin and Josette La Framboise. Benjamin died in New York City on April 1, 1850, at the age of fifty-nine. He remarried twice after Josette's death and had five more children. He shifted from place to place and the welfare of his motherless children and his inability to care for them added another layer of worry to the financial burdens that beset him in his later years. His cause of death was listed simply as disease of the brain. Fort Pierce, Florida, is named in his honor.

> **Harriet Pierce** inherited Magdelaine's house, but it did not insure a long happy life. She was the first wife of Major General James B. Ricketts. Harriet died young, about 1855, before she reached her fortieth birthday. Harriet and her husband had a daughter who became the wife of Lieutenant Colonel William M. Graham of the 1st United States Artillery. We do not know the name of Magdelaine's great-granddaughter, but her husband rose to the rank of Brigadier General and fought with the Union in the Second Battle of Bull Run in the Civil War. He died in Wardour, Maryland on January 16, 1916, at the home of his daughter.

Major General James B. Ricketts, husband of Harriet Pierce
Public Domain

> **Rix Robinson** made his fortune and established connections and a reputation that allowed him to become a judge and a state senator. It is believed he could have been elected governor had he not declined the nomination. He worried his second wife, Se-be-quay, would not be treated well as a governor's wife. Rix Robinson died of consumption on January 12, 1875, and is buried in Ada, Michigan.

➢ **Therese Schindler** remained on Mackinac Island for many years after Magdelaine's passing. In 1853, she moved to Green Bay, Wisconsin, where she lived until her death at age eighty-one. In compliance with her wishes, her remains were returned to the island that she and Magdelaine had loved. She is buried in the Catholic cemetery in plot 262, between Marianne Fisher and Martha Tanner.

➢ **Henry Rowe Schoolcraft** is remembered today mainly for his writing, including a six-volume study of Native Americans he penned in the 1850s. He died on December 10, 1864, and is buried in the Congressional Cemetery in Washington D.C. His papers are archived in the Library of Congress.

➢ **Alex St. Martin** parted ways with Dr. Beaumont after the doctor's second set of experiments on him in 1833. St. Martin returned to his home in Quebec province, Canada. Off and on for the next twenty years, Beaumont tried to get his prior patient to move near him in St. Louis, but the former voyager steadfastly refused. St. Martin died at St-Thomas de Joliette, Quebec, in 1880. His family, fearing the medical community might try to use the body for further experiments or perform additional autopsies, delayed burial until decomposition had set in.

➢ **John Tanner's** tragic tale deserves an ending. Perhaps Magdelaine was fortunate to be spared the details of his demise. After being found by his brother, James, John was never a happy man. James brought John back to "civilization" where John found he did not fit in. Described as sullen and possessed of a morose temperament, he was also suspicious and difficult. Lost between two worlds, he tried to reject his Indian ways, but couldn't adapt to the white man's world.

Henry Rowe Schoolcraft, the Indian Agent for Mackinac County, had become friends with John. Whether Schoolcraft befriended Tanner out of curiosity, empathy, genuine friendship, or simple pity, we cannot know. But his goodwill was cut short by bizarre turns on the contorted trail of Tanner's life. On July 5, 1846, three months after Magdelaine's death, Sault Ste. Marie was thrown into a tailspin. One of its leading citizens, James Schoolcraft, Henry's brother, fell victim to a cold-blooded assassination.

James was walking toward a field he intended to clear. Bushes stood along either side of the path he followed. From behind those bushes a killer fired at treacherously close range. An ounce ball and three buckshot caused James Schoolcraft's immediate death, knocking him with such force that he flew clean out of his shoes, which were later found by the side of the road. The shot was heard, and though the death was not witnessed, the body was quickly discovered.

Initially, suspicion turned to a Lieutenant Bryant Tilden as the culprit. Tilden served at Fort Brady and harbored grudges against James Schoolcraft. The ill-feelings stemmed from a love triangle. The cartridge and the musket involved in the murder appeared to be standard government issue.

However, it was also commonly believed that John Tanner had motive to kill James because of personal squabbles between the men, or perhaps as a way to get even with Henry Schoolcraft for instigating the legislation that removed Martha Tanner from John's home.

It was easy to imagine the antisocial and belligerent Tanner capable of the deed. Eventually Schoolcraft, always the prolific writer, reversed his fond feelings about Tanner and penned the following:

> "He is now a grey-headed, hard-featured, old man, whose feelings are at war with everyone on earth, white or red. Every attempt to meliorate his manners and Indian notions has failed. He has invariably misapprehended them, and is more suspicious, revengeful and bad tempered than any Indian I ever knew."[105]

Tanner was white only by birth, and the prejudices of the times worked against him. He was an Indian with all of the stealth and cunning his white neighbors could attribute to him. So convinced was the local community that Tanner was the guilty party in the murder of Schoolcraft that they welcomed the soldiers from Fort Brady—aggressively led by that other suspect in the matter, Lieutenant Tilden—to spearhead the search for the wanted man.

When journalist and romantic poet William Cullen Bryant arrived in the area for a visit shortly after the murder, forest fires had broken out and Bryant was told, "Tanner must have done it." So maligned was Tanner that he became the bogeyman for every evil that happened in the area.

A band of western Indians, returning to their homeland, assisted in the hunt for Tanner. When they reached John Tanner's hut they found it burned to the ground—a fact considered evidence of his guilt. There was no trace of Tanner, who was presumed to have fled.

John's disappearance was as confounding as his kidnapping had been so many years earlier. Eventually a man, searching for a lost pony, found a skeleton lying next to two gun barrels. The remainder of the gun had been destroyed when fire passed over the area. The only other evidence near the bones consisted of a few coins and other trinkets. It was assumed the bones were those of the missing Tanner, who it was believed had killed himself in a desperate final act to a bleak and lonely life.

In a further sad irony to the case, Lieutenant Tilden, on his death bed, cleared his conscience before meeting his Maker. He admitted to the murder of James Schoolcraft. The death bed confession led to speculation that Tilden had also murdered the White Indian as part of the cover-up of his original crime.

John Tanner's son James, named for his uncle, became a Unitarian missionary to the Red River Country. Another son, named John after his father and grandfather, enlisted and fought in the Civil War. He was killed in the second battle of Bull Run. If any peace ever came to John Tanner, it was only after his death.

➢ **Martha Tanner** died on July 25, 1887, at the age of seventy-four.

Taken between 1865-1870, approximately two decades after Madame La Framboise's death, this is one of the oldest pictures of Main Street, Mackinac Island.
    Photo Courtesy of Mackinac State Historic Parks

Glossary

❖ **Aanii.** *Hello,* or greeting, in Odawa language.

❖ **Ague or ague fever.** An illness marked by fever, chills, and sweating that recurs at regular intervals. Malaria was a common disease that exhibited these symptoms, but it was not the only one.

❖ **à la façon du pays.** The fur trade society developed its own marriage rite, marriage à la façon du pays (after the custom of the country). Some of these marriages were contracts for a number of moons, or months. To legitimize the children of country marriages, the Catholic Church recognized such unions, as long as the parties submitted to a church wedding when a priest became available.

❖ **Allotment.** Military pay.

❖ **Anishinaabek.** Also Anishenaabe, Anishenabe, Anishinaabeg. Native Americans of Algonquin origin.

❖ **Apoplexy.** An old-fashioned medical term referring to a stroke.

❖ **Bateaux.** Also batteaux. Shallow, flat-bottomed wooden boats of the fur trade. They ranged from 24 feet to 50 feet long and 5 feet to 8 feet wide. Birch bark canoes were also used in the fur trade. They ranged in length from 16 feet to 40 feet. Canoes were easier to portage between waterways and were favored by many French fur traders because they often could be carried by one man. By the 17th century the term canot du nord (French, canoe of the north) referenced boats constructed and adapted for speedy travel. These canots became the workhorse of the fur trade. They could carry 35 bales of fur, each weighing up to 90 pounds. They could be carried by two men and portaged in the upright position. Historical records alternately describe Magdelaine La Framboise's boats as canoes, bateaux, or canots. While the term may be imprecise, if she used canoes, they were likely large so they could carry significant cargo.

❖ **Black Robes.** Name given by Native Americans to the Catholic priests who traveled among them. It was a reference to the clothing (black cassocks) worn by the priests.

❖ **Bourgeois.** French word for boss. Bourgeois were usually of French, English, or Scottish descent, and they owned their fur trade business. They employed engagé to work for them and perform menial tasks. Bourgeois enjoyed an elevated social status in the fur trade.

❖ **Breechclout**. A strip of material—bark, cloth, leather—passed between the thighs and secured by a belt.

❖ **Calash**. From the French word calèche, a small-wheeled, open vehicle that on Mackinac Island was sometimes dog drawn.

❖ **Cariole or Carriole**. A light, toboggan-like, open sleigh pulled by dogs or horses and used in the 19th century, especially in French Canada.

❖ **Carot**. (also carotte and carrot). A cylindrical roll of tobacco. Often used as an offering to gain favor with the gods.

❖ **Certainement**. French for certainly.

❖ **Chebbeniathon**. Odawa sky god.

❖ **Chequamegon**. Fur trade settlement on the southern shore of Lake Superior.

❖ **Engagés**. Seasonal, contracted laborers who generally did not have a financial interest in the canoe or the goods. They travelled into the interior of the country and served at the posts until the next rendezvous. They did the heavy or menial work.

❖ **Frolic**. The term given to a good time of drunken excess that took place during rendezvous when traders—Indian, French, and others—tried to make up for the deprivation of winters in the lonely backwoods. The term also described an especially good time, as in "we'll make it a frolic."

❖ **Gabagouache**. A fur trading outpost where Magdelaine and Joseph La Framboise wintered and traded furs. It is pronounced ga-ba-go-wa-chay, and is current-day Grand Haven, Michigan.

❖ **Gewgaws**. A showy trifle, toy, eye-catching trinket, ornament, or decoration.

❖ **Gill**. A measurement of alcohol. Often referred to as the amount of rum allotted daily to engagés or soldiers. A gill is equal to four ounces. George Washington used the term in his General Orders.

❖ **Jambieres**. French word that during the fur trade era referred to pantaloons, or work trousers, often sewn very simply with fringe showing on the outside of the leg.

❖ **Kinnickinnic**. This is a Native American word for "to mix." Kinnickinnic is used to reference a smoking product made of leaves or barks, mixed with other plant materials available to the tribe. The Ojibwe and Odawa used a combination of red willow and spotted willow bark.

The inner bark was toasted over a fire and powdered. Bearberry and herbs were also added to the mixture, which was then kept in a cloth or leather bag.

❖ **L'Arbre Croche**. Current-day Harbor Springs. The name is French and means Crooked Tree. It was known to the Native Americans as Waganawkezee or Waugonawkisa.

❖ **La Baye**. Current-day Green Bay, Wisconsin.

❖ **La grippe**. Influenza. Symptoms included a high fever, sore throat, runny nose, muscle pains, headache, coughing, and fatigue. Sometimes la grippe was used to describe the condition of a person who was without energy and who was lethargic.

❖ **La Pointe**. Near Bayfield, Wisconsin.

❖ **Longhouse**. Structures that provided shelter for several related families. Walls were made of poles driven close together into the ground. Strips of bark, woven through the poles, formed walls. Another series of poles was bent and shaped into an arched roof, which was covered with leaves, grasses, and bark. The structure had openings at both ends, and if large enough, also in the center. These openings were covered with animal hides. A fire pit in the center offered warmth and a place for cooking. A hole, or holes, in the roof allowed smoke to escape.

Longhouse

❖ **Makakoon baskets**. Baskets generally made of birch bark.

❖ **Manoomin**. Wild rice that grows in marshes and swamps. Also *pagwadjanomin*.

❖ **Medicine wheel**. The four directions of the medicine wheel symbolize the four sacred colors of the circle of life. Man must experience each direction during life in order to honor Mother Earth.

❖ **Menoukawme**. Spring season.

- **Métis**. Mixed-blood. In the Great Lakes fur trade it generally referenced those of Native American and French blood.
- **Midewiwin**. Medicine man.
- **Miigwech**. Also migwech. *Thank you* in the Odawa language.
- **Misigami**. Lake Michigan.
- **Mocock**. Also *makuk* and *makakoon*. A birch bark container for keeping food.

- **Nookomis**. Grandmother.
- **Oduppeneeg**. Wild potatoes.
- **Ogawshimaw**. *Mother* in Odawa language.
- **Ouisconsin**. Wisconsin.
- **Outfit**. The stock of trade goods a fur trader took to exchange for furs.
- **Pagwadjanomin**. See manoomin above.
- **Pemmican**. Slices of deer or other meat (bison, moose, elk) pounded thin between stones. It incorporated melted fat and sometimes dried fruit (such as Saskatoon berries or cranberries) before it was compressed and put into skin bags. If kept dry, it could be preserved for several years. It was a staple of the fur trade. It was nutritious and provided nourishment when fresh meat or other food was not available.
- **Pipes**. In addition to being a vessel for smoking, pipe was the term for measuring the length of a journey. Voyageurs looked forward to opportunities to get out of their canoes and stretch their legs and smoke a pipe. It became common to measure the distance by the number of rest stops or "pipes" it took to get there.
- **Plucked beaver cap**. Plucking removed the long guard hair and then the under fur was shaved down to a uniform thickness. This resulted in an extremely soft pelt.
- **Portage**. Voyageurs had to stop and carry their canoes and cargoes around waterfalls and dangerous rapids. This process was known as portaging the canoe. It could involve several miles of rocky shore or thick forest and underbrush.

❖ **Rendezvous**. French term for *large gathering*. Rendezvous was the summer gathering of traders, Native Americans, and merchants on Mackinac Island. There they sold furs, conducted business transactions, purchased "outfits" (goods and merchandise) for the next season and indulged in general revelry.

❖ **Rod**. A distance of measurement commonly used by surveyors, it is equal to 16.5 feet (5.03 meters).

❖ **Sagamité**. A Native American dish made from hominy or Indian corn and animal fat, and sometimes it included vegetables and wild rice.

❖ **Sowanquesake**. The current-day Thornapple River in western Michigan.

❖ **Sulpicians**. Catholic priests who came to the United States during the French Revolution. They were the Roman Catholic Diocesan priests responsible for educating, guiding, and supporting fellow priests.

❖ **Tikinagan**. Also *tickinawgun*. A cradleboard or flat framework, usually covered with fur, to which Native Americans traditionally bound a child during the infant stage of growth. A tikinagan could be set on the ground or hung from a tree, and some were designed to be carried on a mother's back.

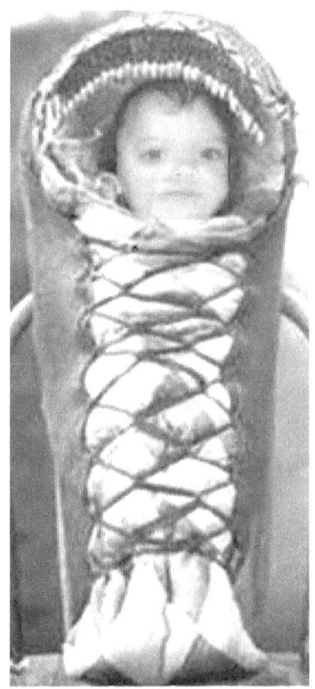

Cradleboard or Tikinagan.
Magdelaine describes a slightly different design in chapter 23.

- **Turtle Island**. In the Anishinaabek oral history the term broadly referred to North America, or more specifically to the Eastern Coast of North America from where the Anishinaabek began their travel westward.
- **Upper Country**. Canada.
- **Voyageurs**. The term comes from the French word for *traveler* and referred to French Canadians who engaged in transporting furs by canoe during the fur trade.
- **Wampeme**. White Pigeon in the Odawa language. The character named Wampeme in this novel is a fictional creation.
- **Wampum**. Traditional shell beads used by Native Americans as money. Often kept on strings and sometimes adopted by Europeans colonists as currency.

Visualizing Magdelaine

Information comes from many sources. Years ago, I was in the Hackley Library in Muskegon researching *Ardent Spirit* when a librarian told me that Benjamin Kendrick Pierce's descendent, Charles Pierce, still lived in Muskegon. Sometimes an author gets lucky.

I found an address for Mr. Pierce and sent him a letter. By return mail, he sent a newspaper article with a photo identified as Madame Madeline. On the article was handwritten in ink: "Tell you more about this. CP" (Charles Pierce).

Mr. Pierce included a phone number. I immediately called him. One sought after piece of information I had desperately coveted since beginning this project was a photo of Magdelaine La Framboise. I wanted to "see her" as I wrote the story.

Mr. Pierce was nearing one hundred years old when we had our first conversation, but his mental faculties were sharp. I told him that I had believed there were no existing photos of Magdelaine La Framboise, so I was intrigued by the article and photo.

Charlie—he insisted I call him Charlie—said he was a great-grandson of Benjamin Pierce, and his family had always claimed to be part Native American. He was fifty years old when he first sought details of what he called his connection to "the Pocahontas of Michigan."

I have been unable to confirm the details of Charlie's relationship to the Pierces, and his connection to Magdelaine La Framboise. Benjamin Pierce was survived by no sons (who would have carried the Pierce name). His only three recorded sons, Benjamin Langdon Pierce (with wife Josette), Henry Jackson Pierce, and Benjamin Kendrick Pierce Jr., all died in infancy.

Charlie Pierce died on January 3, 2011, at age 103. His only son, Buddy, preceded him in death, closing the logical avenue of further inquiry. Charlie was fascinated by history and had followed many genealogical trails that with his passing have become dead ends. His family's stories—stories he had heard since he was a child—were rich in details about Benjamin Pierce and Magdelaine La Framboise.

The photo in the newspaper article was a treasure that came from Charlie's quest for information. It had been long sequestered in his grandfather's dresser drawer. On the backside of the photograph was written Magdelaine La Framboise.

Mr. Pierce said he believed the details of the newspaper article were based on incomplete information, and that is why he had scribbled "Tell you more about this" on the copy he sent to me. From his research and his understanding of family stories, Charlie believed the photo, even though it bore the name Magdelaine La Framboise, was actually a likeness of Louise Constant (aka Cown/Cowan) Lasley, a fur trader who was several years younger than Magdelaine. Louise, according to Mr. Pierce, was related to Magdelaine, perhaps the daughter or granddaughter of one of Magdelaine's aunts. "According to the family," Pierce said, "Louise was the spitting image of Magdelaine, and that's why my grandfather wrote Magdelaine La Framboise on the back of the photo."

There was a Lasley family living on Mackinac Island at the same time as Magdelaine La Framboise. They were also fur traders, worked out of western Michigan around Grand Haven, and summered during rendezvous in their home on the island's Market Street. In spite of repeated searches, I have been unable to verify with certainty a family connection to Magdelaine.

However, I believe it is fair to give some credence to the family's persistent oral history. The photo they identified as Magdelaine La Framboise became the image I held as I wrote this book. I believe this photo may bear a reasonable similarity to what Magdelaine looked like. In fact, it may actually be a photo of her.

The picture on the cover of *Ardent Spirit* is the result of the artistic efforts of Sheila Bali, who worked with the photo of the woman Charlie Pierce believed to be Magdelaine La Framboise's doppelganger.[106] Ms. Bali modified her rendering to show double-queued braids and a shawl. The clothing and hairstyle are from a description of Magdelaine La Framboise at the wedding of her dear friend, Agatha Biddle. The details were recorded by Elizabeth Baird in her *Reminiscences of Early Days on Mackinac Island*. (pp. 44-45):

"...*a double skirt made of fine narrow broadcloth, with but one pleat on each side; no fullness in front nor in the back. The skirt reached about halfway between the ankle and the knee, and was elaborately embroidered with ribbon and beads on both the lower and upper edges. On the lower, the width of the trimming was six inches, and on the upper, five inches. The same trimming extended up the overlapping edge of the skirt. Above this horizontal trimming were rows upon rows of ribbon, four or five inches wide, placed so near together that only a narrow strip of the cloth showed, like a narrow cord. Accompanying this was a pair of leggings made of broadcloth. When the skirt is black, the leggings are of scarlet broadcloth, the embroidery about three inches from the side edge. Around the bottom the trimming is between four and five inches in width. The moccasins also were embroidered with ribbon and beads. Then we come to the blanket, as it is called, which is of fine broadcloth, either black or red, with most elaborate work of ribbon; no beads, however, are used on it. This is worn somewhat as the Spanish women wear their mantles. The waist, or sacque, is a sort of loose-fitting garment made of silk for extra occasions, but usually of calico. It is made plain, without either embroidery of ribbon or beads. The sleeves snugly fit the arm and wrist, and the neck has only a binding to finish it. Beads enough are worn around the neck to fill in and come down in front. Silver brooches are worn according to taste. The hair is worn plain, parted in the middle, braided down the back, and tied up again, making a double queue.*

Photograph that Charlie Pierce's believed was
Louise Constant Lasley

Newspaper article with photo identifed as
Madame Madeline

Ms. Bali was also provided the photo of Therese Schindler (See page 100) for possible familial facial structure. She noted that the face of Therese Schindler and the woman in Charlie's photo bore certain striking similarities, in spite of the obvious difference in age. In both photos, the left eyebrow is slightly lower than the right. The faces are of oval shape with high cheekbones. The nose and spacing of the eyes have a comparable appearance. Allowing for family likeness, the picture of Therese La Framboise lends credence to the Pierce photo as either being, or bearing a resemblance to, Magdelaine La Framboise.

From all of this information, the drawing on the cover was created. And with that drawing, I felt like I came as close as possible to seeing Magdelaine.

Rendering of Magdelaine based on available information.

Selected Bibliography and Further Reading

Allen, Robert S. "Dickson, Robert" in *Dictionary of Canadian Biography*, vol. 6 (1821-1835). University of Toronto/Université Laval-, 2003.
http://www.biographi.ca/en/bio/dickson_robert_6E.html

Ambrose, Stephen E. *Undaunted Courage: Meriwether Lewis, Thomas Jefferson, and the Opening of the American West.* New York: Simon and Shuster, 1996.

American Fur Company Employees: 1818-1819. Collections of the State Historical Society of Wisconsin, vol. xii pp.162-163.

American Fur Company Invoices: 1821-1822. Collections of the State Historical Society of Wisconsin, vol. xi pp. 370-377.

Anderson, T.G. "Papers of Captain T. G. Anderson, British Indian Agent." Wisconsin Historical Collections, vol. x (1883-1885), pp. 142-149.

Armour, David A. "Marcot, Marguerite-Magdelaine," in *Dictionary of Canadian Biography*, vol. 7, University of Toronto/Université Laval-, 2003.
http://www.biographi.ca/en/bio/marcot_marguerite_magdelaine_7E.html

———. "David and Elizabeth: the Mitchell Family of the Straits of Mackinac," Michigan History, vol. 64 no. 4 pp. 17-29.

———. "Mitchell, David," in *Dictionary of Canadian Biography*, vol. 6, University of Toronto/Université Laval-, 2003.
http://www.biographi.ca/en/bio/mitchell_david_6E.html

———. "Nissowaquet," in *Dictionary of Canadian Biography*, vol. 4, University of Toronto/Université Laval-, 2003.
http://www.biographi.ca/en/bio/nissowaquet_4E.html

——— "Who Remembers La Fourche?" Chronicle, the Membership Magazine of the Historical Society of Michigan, vol. 16 pp. 12-16 (Summer 1980).

Armour, David A., ed., *Treason? At Michilimackinac*. Mackinac Island: Mackinac Island State Park Commission, Proceedings of the General Court Martial held at Montreal in October 1768 for the Trial of Major Robert Rogers.

Armour, David A., and K. R. Widder. *At the Crossroads: Michilimackinac During the American Revolution.* Mackinac Island, Michigan: Mackinac Island State Park Commission, 1978.

Baird, Elizabeth Therese Fisher. "Indian Customs and Early Recollections." Collections of the State Historical Society of Wisconsin. Madison: Wisconsin Historical Society, 1996-2008 (from article written 1882), vol. ix pp. 303-326.

———. "Reminiscences of Early Days on Mackinac Island." Collections of the State Historical Society of Wisconsin. Madison, Wisconsin: Wisconsin Historical Society, 1996-2008 (From articles written 1886-1887), vol. xiv pp. 17-64.

———. "Reminiscences of Life in Territorial Wisconsin." Collections of the State Historical Society of Wisconsin. Madison, Wisconsin: Wisconsin Historical Society, 1996-2008 (From article written 1889), vol. xv. pp. 205-263.

Henry Baird and Elizabeth Baird Collection. Correspondence 1798-18, bx. 1, flr. 1, and Correspondence 1826-1831, bx. 1 flr 2. http://www.wisconsinhistory.org

Beaumont Papers. Notebook recording account of the Alexis St. Martin case, series 2 notebooks, 1810-1835, bx. 21, flr. 3. The Bernard Becker Medical Library Archives. becker.wustl.edu/resources/arb

Bremer, Richard G. *Indian Agent & Wilderness Scholar: The Life of Henry Rowe Schoolcraft.* Clarke Historical Library, Central Michigan University, 1987.

Berthrong, Donald J. *A Historical Report of Indian Use and Occupancy of Northern Indiana and Southwestern Michigan.* New York: Garland Publishing Inc., 1974.

Billington, Ray Allen. *Land of Savagery, Land of Promise: The European Image of the American Frontier.* New York: W.W. Norton & Company, 1981.

Blackbird, Andrew J. *History of the Ottawa and Chippewa Indians of Michigan.* Ypsilanti, Michigan: Ypsilantian Job Printing House, 1887.

Brown, Dee. *Bury My Heart at Wounded Knee: An Indian History of the American West.* New York: Henry Holt and Company, 1970.

Brown, Jennifer S.H. *Strangers in Blood: Fur Trade Company Families in Indian Country.* Norman, Oklahoma: University of Oklahoma Press, 1996.

———. *Strangers in Blood: Fur Trade Company Families in Indian Country.* Vancouver: University of British Columbia Press, 1980.

Brown, Jennifer S.H., and Jacqueline Peterson. *The New Peoples: Being and Becoming Metis in North America,* Lincoln: University of Nebraska Press, 1985.

Burby, Louis H. *Our Worthy Commander: The Life and Times of Benjamin K. Pierce in Whose Honor Fort Pierce Was Named.* Fort Pierce: IRCC Pioneer Press, 1976.

Campion, Thomas J. "Indian Removal and the Transformation of Northern Indiana." Indiana Magazine of History, vol. 107 issue 1 pp. 32-62, 2011.

Cappel, Constance. *The Smallpox Genocide of the Odawa Tribe at L'Arbre Croche, 1763.* Lewiston, New York: The Edwin Mellon Press, 2007.

Cass, Lewis. *Present State of the Indians and Their Removal to the West of the Mississippi.* New York: Arno Press, 1975.

Champney, S.W. "The Greatest Woman Pioneer of Michigan, Madame La Framboise." Detroit: Detroit News, January 10, 1932, p. 13.

Clifton, J., and J. Cornell, and G. McClurken. *People of the Three Fires: Ottawa, Potawatomi, and Ojibwe.* Grand Rapids: Michigan Indian Press, 1986.

Cleland, Charles E. *Rites of Conquest: The History and Culture of Michigan's Native Americans.* Ann Arbor: University of Michigan Press, 1992.

Davidson, Gordon Charles. *The North West Company.* Berkeley: University of California Press, 1918.

De Tocqueville, Alexis. *Journey to America.* Faber and Faber, Ltd., 1959.

De Voto, Bernard. *The Course of Empire.* Cambridge: Riverside Press, 1952.

Dobson, Pamela J., ed. *The Tree That Never Dies: Oral History of the Michigan Indians.* Grand Rapids, Michigan: Grand Rapids Public Library, 1978.

Duffy, John. "Smallpox and the Indians in the American Colonies." Bulletin of the History of Medicine 25, pp. 324-341, 1951.

Edmunds, R. David. "The Thin Red Line: Tecumseh, the Prophet and Shawnee Resistance." Timeline Magazine 4 (December 1987/January 1988), pp. 2-19.

———. *Tecumseh and the Quest for Indian Leadership.* Boston: Little Brown, 1984.

———. "Tenskwatawa," in *Dictionary of Canadian Biography*, vol. 7, University of Toronto/Université Laval-, 2003. http://www.biographi.ca/en/bio/tenskwatawa_7E.html

Epstein, Sam, and Beryl Epstein. *Dr. Beaumont and the Man with the Hole in His Stomach.* New York: Coward, McCann & Geoghegan, Inc., 1978.

Evans, Mary Ellen. "The Missing Footnote, or The Curé Who Wasn't There." Records of the American Catholic Historical Society of Philadelphia, vol. 84 no. 4 p. 199.

Everett, Franklin. Memorials of the Grand River Valley. Chicago: The Chicago Legal News Company, 1878. Republished by the Grand Rapids Historical Society, Grand Rapids, Michigan, 1984.

Fasquelle, Ethel Rowan. *When Michigan Was Young: The Story of Its Beginnings, Early Legends and Folklore.* Grand Rapids: W. B. Eerdmans Publishing Company, 1950.

Fenn, Elizabeth A. *Pox Americana: The Great Smallpox Epidemic of 1775-82.* New York: Hill and Wang, 2001.

Ferry, William M. "Extracts from Ferry Journal." American Missionary Register, vol. 5 no. 3 pp. 89-90.

Financial Record Book 1828-1838. Ste. Anne's Catholic Church, Mackinac Island, Michigan.

Frazier, Jean. *Kah-wam-da-meh (We See Each Other).* Grand Ledge, Michigan: Herman E. Cameron Memorial Foundation, 1989.

Fuller, Iola. *The Loon Feather.* New York: Harcourt Brace Jovanovich, 1940.

Fuller, Margaret. *Summer on the Lakes.* London: Ward and Lock, 1861.

Gilman, Carolyn. *Where Two Worlds Meet, The Great Lakes Fur Trade.* St. Paul: Minnesota Historical Society, 1982.

Goltz, Herbert C.W. "Tecumseh," in *Dictionary of Canadian Biography*, vol. 5, University of Toronto/Université Laval-, 2003. http://www.biographi.ca/en/bio/tecumseh_5E.html

Goodyear, Henry A. "Indians of Barry County." Pioneers and Historical Collections. Clarke Historical Library, Mt. Pleasant, Michigan: vol. 35 (1902) pp. 637-643.

Grignon, Augustin. "Seventy-two Years' Recollections." Wisconsin Historical Collections. Madison: Wisconsin Historical Society, 1996-2008, (Source creation from 1857 interview), vol. iii pp. 197-295.

Gringhuis, Dirk. *Lore of the Great Turtle: Indian Legends of Mackinac Retold.* Mackinac Island, Michigan: Mackinac State Historic Parks, 1970.

———. *Were-Wolves and Will-O-The-Wisps: French Tales of Mackinac Retold.* Mackinac Island, Michigan: Mackinac State Historic Parks, 1974.

Harrington, Steve. *Fair Shake in the Wilderness: The Life and Times of Rix Robinson,* Grand Rapids, Michigan: Maritime Press, Inc., 2001.

Hinsdale, Wilbert B. *Archaeological Atlas of Michigan.* Ann Arbor: University of Michigan Press, 2008.

Hirshfelder, A.B. and P. Molin. Foreword by Echo-Hawk, W.R. Encyclopedia of Native American Religions, New York: Checkmark Books, 2001.

Hodge, Frederick Webb. *Handbook of American Indians II.* Washington: Smithsonian Institute, Bureau of American Ethnology, 1907.

Hubbard, Gurdon Saltonstall. *The Autobiography of Gurdon Saltonstall Hubbard.* Chicago: Lakeside Press, 1911.

Jacobs, Wilbur R. *Dispossessing the American Indian.* New York: Charles Scriber's Sons, 1972.

Jameson, Anna Brownell. *Winter Studies and Summer Rambles in Canada.* Toronto: T. H. Best Printing Company Limited, 1965 reprint of 1839 edition keeping original spelling and usage.

Jarvis, Brad, D.E. "A Woman Much to Be Respected: Madeline La Framboise and the redefinition of a Métis Identity." M.A. Thesis: Department of Anthropology, Michigan State University, 1998.

Jaskowski, Helen. *A Terrible Sickness Among Them: Smallpox Stories of the Frontier,* Cambridge University Press, 1996.

Johnson, Basil H. *Anishinaubae Thesaurus.* East Lansing: Michigan State University Press, 2007.

Johnson, Ida A. *The Michigan Fur Trade.* Lansing: Michigan Historical Commission, 1919. Reprinted: Grand Rapids: Black Letter Press, 1971.

Josephy, Alvin M., ed. *The American Heritage Book of Indians.* New York: Simon and Schuster, Inc., New York, New York, (American Heritage Series) 1961.

Kane, Grace. *Myths and Legends of Mackinaw.* Cincinnati: The Editor Publishing Company, 1897.

Karamanski, Theodore J. *Blackbird's Song: Andrew J. Blackbird and the Odawa People.* East Lansing: Michigan State University Press, 2012.

Kelton, D.H. Lieutenant. *Annals of Mackinac.* Chicago: Fergus Printing Company, 1882. Reprint: Mackinac Island, Michigan, Michigan State Historic Parks, 1992.

Kelton, D.H. "Voluntary." Wisconsin Historical Collections. Madison, Wisconsin: Wisconsin Historical Society (1996-2008), vol. xxii p. 272.

Kinietz, W. Vernon. *Chippewa Village: The Story of Katikitegon.* Bloomfield Hills, Michigan: Cranbrook Institute of Science, 1947.

———. *The Indians of the Western Great Lakes 1615-1760.* Ann Arbor: University of Michigan Press, 1950.

Kinzie, Juliette. *Wau-Bun: The Early Days in the Northwest.* Philadelphia: J.B. Lippincott & Co. 1873.

Kohl, Johan G. Kitchi-Gami. *Minneapolis:* Ross & Haines, 1860.

Kubiak, William J. *Great Lakes Indians, a Pictorial Guide,* New York: Bonanza Books, 1970.

La Framboise, Magdelaine. Last Will, March 2, 1846, Probate Court Records, bk. 1 Mackinac County Court House, St. Ignace, Michigan. pp. 23-24. Inventory September 30, 1846. Probate Court Records, bk. 1 pp 29-30.

"Langlade Papers." Wisconsin Historical Collections. Madison, Wisconsin: Wisconsin Historical Society, 1996 (Article written 1877-1879), vol. viii pp. 209-223.

Lawson, Publius V. *Bravest of the Brave: Captain Charles de Langlade.* Menasha, Wisconsin: George Banta, 1904.

Lavender, David. *The Fist in the Wilderness.* Garden City, New York: Doubleday, 1964.

Long, J.C. Lord Jeffrey Amherst: *A Soldier of the King.* New York: Macmillan, 1933.

"Mackinac Register of Marriages in the Parish of Michilimackinac 1725-1821." Madison: Collections of the State Historical Society of Wisconsin, Wisconsin Historical Society, vol. xviii pp. 469-513 (1910).

"Mackinac Register, Baptisms and Interments." Collections of the State Historical Society of Wisconsin. Madison, Wisconsin: Wisconsin Historical Society, 1996-2008, vol. xix pp. 469-513 (Information collected from 1695-1821).

Madsen, Axel. *John Jacob Astor: America's First Multimillionaire.* New Jersey: John Wiley and Sons, 2001.

May, George. *War 1812: The United States and Great Britain at Mackinac, 1812-1815*. Mackinac Island, Michigan: Mackinac State Historic Parks, 1962.

Mayor, Adrienne. "The Nessus Shirt in the New World: Smallpox Blankets in History and Legend." Journal of American Folklore 108 (427) pp. 54-77, 1995.

Mazzuchelli, Samuel. *The Memoirs of Samuel Mazzuchelli*. Chicago, Illinois: Priority Press, 1967.

McDonnell, Michael. Edited by D. C. Skaggs and L. L. Nelson. *Charles-Michel Mouet de Langlade: Warrior, Soldier, and Intercultural Window in the Sixty Years War for the Great Lakes, 1754-1814*. East Lansing: Michigan State University Press, 2001.

McDowell, John E. "Madame La Framboise." Michigan History, 1972, vol. 56 no. 4 pp. 271-286.

———. "Madeline La Framboise" (Unpublished Manuscript). Clark Historical Library, Mt. Pleasant, Michigan.

———. "Therese Schindler of Mackinac: Upward Mobility in the Great Lakes Fur Trade." Wisconsin Magazine of History, vol. 61 no. 2 pp. 125-143.

McClurken, James, M. *People of the Three Fires: The Ottawa, Potawatomi, and Ojibway of Michigan*. Grand Rapids, Michigan: The Grand Rapids Intra-Tribal Council, 1986.

McKee, Irving. The Trail of Death: Letters of Benjamin Marie Petit. Kesslinger Publishing (print on demand of rare books), 2007.

Michigan Early Census Index, MIS2a985471. Michigan Pioneer and Historical Collections, vol. 10 pp. 370-371.

Nicholas, Edward. *The Chaplain's Lady*. Mackinac Island: Mackinac State Historic Parks, 1987.

Nute, Grace Lee. *Lake Superior: The American Lakes Series*. New York: The Bobbs-Merrill Company, 1944.

Parkman, Francis. *The Conspiracy of Pontiac and the Indian War after the Conquest of Canada*. Boston: Little Brown, 1886.

Petersen, Eugene T. *Mackinac Island: Its History in Pictures*. Mackinac Island: Mackinac Island State Park Commission, 1973.

Peterson, Jacqueline. "The Founders of Green Bay: A Marriage of Indian and White." Voyageur, Historical Review of Brown County and Northeast Wisconsin, Spring 1984.

Porlier, Louis B. "Capture of Mackinaw, 1763." Collections of the State Historical Society of Wisconsin, vol. xiii (1908) pp. 227-231.

http://www.wisconsinhistory.org/turningpoints/search.asp?id=47

Porter, Kenneth W. *John Jacob Astor: Business Man.* Cambridge: Harvard University Press, 1931.

Prucha, Francis Paul. *Lewis Cass and American Indian Policy.* Detroit: Published for the Detroit Historical Society, Wayne State University Press, 1967.

Quaife, Milo M. *Lake Michigan.* Indianapolis: Bobbs-Merrill Co., 1944.

Quimby, George Irving. *Indian Life in the Upper Great Lakes: 11,000 BC to 1800 AD.* Chicago: University of Chicago Press, 1960.

Randall, E.O. "Pontiac's Conspiracy." Ohio Archaeological and Historical Society Publications 12 (1903) pp. 410-437.

———. "Tecumseh, the Shawnee Chief." Ohio Archaeological and Historical Society Publications 15 (1906) pp. 418-497.

Rezek, Antoine Ivan Rev. *History of the Diocese of Sault Ste. Marie and Marquette.* Dexter, Michigan: Thomson-Shore Inc., 1907.

Richmond, Rebecca. "The Fur Traders of the Grand River Valley." Publications of the Historical Society of Grand Rapids. Grand Rapids: Historical Society of Grand Rapids, 1907.

Robertson, E.R.G. *Rotting Face: Smallpox and the American Indian.* Caldwell, Idaho. Caxton Press, 2001.

Rushforth, Brett, Bond of Alliance: *Indigenous and Atlantic Slaveries in New France,* Chapel Hill: University of North Carolina, 2012.

Scanlan, Peter L. *Prairie du Chien, French, British, American.* Menasha, Wisconsin: George Banta, 1937.

Schoolcraft, Henry R. *Information Respecting the History, Condition and Prospects of the Indian Tribes of the United States.* Philadelphia: J.B. Lippincott & Co., 1853-1856.

———. *Personal Memoirs of Thirty Years with the Indian Tribes on the American Frontiers.* Philadelphia: Lippincott & Co., 1851.

———. *The Hiawatha Legends.* Avery Color Studios, Gwinn, Michigan, 2001.

Sheldon, E.M. *The Early History of Michigan, From the First Settlement to 1815.* New York: A.S. Barnes, 1856.

Smith, Susan Sleeper. *Women, Kin, and Catholicism: New Perspectives on the Fur Trade.* Duke University Press, Ethnohistory, 47/2 (Spring 2000) pp. 423-53.

Stannard, David E. *American Holocaust: Columbus and the Conquest of the New World.* New York and Oxford: Oxford University Press, 1992.

St. John, Mrs. "Daily Life, Manners, and Customs of the Indians in Kalamazoo County." Clark Historical Library. Pioneer Historical Collections, vol. 10 (1880) pp. 166-170.

Tanner, Helen Hornbeck. *Atlas of Great Lakes Indian History.* From the Civilization of the American Indian Series. Published for the Newberry Library, Chicago: University of Oklahoma Press, 1987.

Tasse, Joseph. Translated by Sarah Fairchild Dean. "Memoir of Charles de Langlade." Wisconsin Historical Collections (1873-1876), vol. viii pp. 123-187.

Thwaites, Reuben Gold. *The Jesuit Relations and Allied Documents, Travels and Explorations of the Jesuit Missionaries in New France.* 73 vols. Cleveland: Burrows Brothers Co., 1896-1901.

Thwaites, Reuben Gold, ed. *The French Regime in Wisconsin 1634-1760.* Wisconsin Historical Collections. Madison: Wisconsin Historical Society, vols. xvii and xviii. The Society, 1906.

Thwaites, Reuben Gold. "The Fur Trade in Wisconsin. 1812-1825." Wisconsin Historical Collections, vol. xx, 1911.

Timmerman, Janet. "Joseph La Framboise: A Factor of Treaties, Trade, and Culture." A Thesis submitted to Southwest Minnesota State University, Marshall, MN, 1995, Kansas State University, 2009.

Treaty of Saginaw, 1819, between General Lewis Cass and the Chippewa Indians. Michigan Historical Library. United States Statutes at Large.

Troester, Rosalie Riegle, ed. "Historic Women of Michigan: A Sesquicentennial Celebration." Lansing: Michigan Women's Studies Association, 1987, pp. 1-13.

Van Kirk, Sylvia. *Many Tender Ties: Women in Fur Trade Society, 1670-1870.* Winnipeg, Manitoba: Watson & Dwyer Publishing Ltd., 1980.

Verrill, A. Hyatt. *The Real Americans.* New York: G.P. Putnam's Sons, 1954.

Waite, Minnie B. "Indian and Pioneer Life." Clarke Historical Library. Pioneer and Historical Collections, vol. 38 (1912) pp. 318-321.

Waldman, Carl. *Atlas of the North American Indians.* St. Paul: Wheeler Productions, 1985.

White, George H. "Alexis St. Martin of Mackinac." Clarke Historical Library. Michigan Pioneer and Historical Collections, vol. 26 pp. 646-50.

Widder, Keith R. "Magdelaine La Framboise, Fur Trader and Educator." *Historic Women of Michigan: A Sesquicentennial Celebration*. Lansing: Women's Studies Association, 1987.

———. *Reveille Till Taps: Soldier Life at Fort Mackinac, 1780-1895*. Mackinac Island: Mackinac Historic State Parks, 1972.

Wissler, C. *The American Indian*. New York: The Macmillan Co., 1938.

Wood, Edwin O. *Historic Mackinac*. New York: Macmillan Co., 1918.

Wright, John C. *The Crooked Tree: Indian Legends and a Short History of the Little Traverse Bay Region*. Harbor Springs: C. Fayette Erwin, 1917.

Genealogy Charts

"The house where we lived belonged to the widow of a French trader, an Indian by birth, and wearing the dress of her country. She spoke French fluently, and was very ladylike in her manners. She is a great character among them. They were all the time coming to pay her homage, or to get her aid and advice; for she is, I am told, a shrewd woman of business." **Margaret Fuller, feminist and contemporary of Magdelaine La Framboise, writing of La Framboise in *A Summer on the Lakes***

Tracing family connections for Magdelaine Marcotte La Framboise was fraught with complications:

1. Official governmental birth, death, and marriage records in the United States, and specifically in Mackinac County, were not kept prior to 1850, which for purposes of identifying ancestral relationships to Magdelaine La Framboise, means they are nonexistent.

2. The best records available are from Ste. Anne's Catholic Church. A copy of those records are contained in the Wisconsin Historical Collections as the Mackinac Register of Baptisms and Marriages (and a few deaths were noted). These records were handwritten in French, so when translated into English, they were subject to errors of translation.

3. The Odawa did not have a written language. French priests recorded names in the Mackinac Register without certainty of how to spell them. It is easy to see why names like Nissowaquet, Majakwatawa, and Kewanoquat had so many spelling variations. Spelling issues also plagued the writing of governmental treaties.

4. The Odawa did not reference degrees of relationship the same way Europeans did. For instance, father was not only the male parent, but might refer to all the father's brothers and the husbands of a mother's sisters. Similarly, mother was the female parent, and the term might be used to describe all the mother's sisters and all the wives of the father's brothers. Grandfathers and all of their

brothers were called grandfather. Grandmothers and all of their sisters were called grandmother.

Brothers and sisters were the children of everyone called father and mother, so this included all children of the people referred to as mother and father, paternal uncles and their wives, and maternal aunts and their husbands. There were no distinct identifiers such as uncles, aunts, great uncles, great aunts, or cousins.

Imagine an Odawa woman being asked who her father is by a French priest. We have to rely on her ability to fully understand the question since French would not likely be her first language. Then we have to assume she identifies her biological father rather than an uncle. It might seem obvious that a biological parent would be named first, but if the parent is dead, it is not a stretch to suggest the uncle might be named. We have to rely on the name given being spelled correctly by the French priest since the woman would have no ability to spell it. Finally, we have to rely on the transcriber who converted the information from French to English.

The process is rife with pitfalls and opportunities for mistakes. Still, it is interesting to try to unravel the relationships. Even if we find an Odawa name spelled several ways, we can often determine what name was intended (Kewinoquot, Kiwanoquot, or Kewanoquat).

In 1810, 4,762 people lived in the Michigan territory. No census was taken of the Native American population, but it is estimated there were a few thousand original people (fewer Odawa) in the area that is now Michigan and even fewer Frenchman. And, while first names were repeated endlessly in French families, most last names were not overly common. There were at least two lines of La Framboise and maybe only one Marcotte (spelled either Marcot or Marcotte).

The Family Charts that follow are included to help the reader visualize relationships and to document where the information originated. Research may have uncovered this information, but that doesn't always mean it is without error.

Magdelaine Marcot(te) Paternal Ancestry

Nicholas Marcotte
B. About 1579
Fecamp, France

Charles Marcot(te)
Bap 26 Feb 1599
Fecamp, France
D. 9 Oct 1678

Jacques Marcot(te)
Bap 7 Oct 1644
Moved to Canada 1667
M. 9 Sept 1670 at
Cap de la Madelaine, Canada
D. 1715

Jean Francois (Petit Jean) Marcot
B. 1685 Neuville, France
M. 6 April 1717 at Cap Santé
D. 1760

| Joseph Marcotte B. 1718 | **Jean Baptiste Marcotte** **B. 1720 at Cap Santé** **M. 24 July 1758** —Marie Neskech | Marie Anne Marcotte B. 1724 |

| Marie B. 1759 | Jean Baptiste B. 1762 | Marianne B. 1769 | Charlotte B. 1770 |

—**Jacqueline Baucher** (Boucher)

—**Elizabeth Sale**
B. 9 Sept 1670

—**Marie Anne Morrisse**

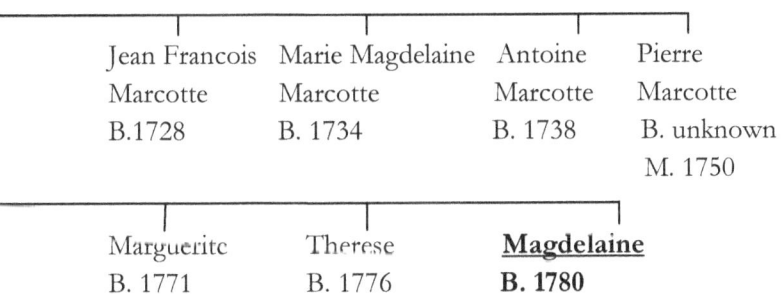

Jean Francois	Marie Magdelaine	Antoine	Pierre
Marcotte	Marcotte	Marcotte	Marcotte
B.1728	B. 1734	B. 1738	B. unknown
			M. 1750

| Marguerite | Therese | **Magdelaine** |
| B. 1771 | B. 1776 | **B. 1780** |

Much of the information for Magdelaine La Framboise's paternal ancestry was provided by Michael Marcotte, who has done extensive genealogy research, which can be seen on his website:
http://www.electroauthor.com/marcotte_genealogy/petitjean.htm.

Mr. Marcotte indicates most of the dates he used came from the *Genealogical Dictionary of the Marcotte Families*, published posthumously in 1983 by Jean Marcotte via Editions de l'echo, Montreal.

A note about the name: It is very common for the surname to be spelled "Marcot" in leases and on other notaries' registers for Jean-Baptiste's generation. His father Jean-Francois was called "Petit Jean" to distinguish him from a brother also christened Jean-Francois and called "Jannot." The grandfather, Jacques Marcotte, who arrived in Canada in 1667 with brother Nicolas, signed his name with the "Marcotte" spelling on his marriage certificate. The baptismal records for Jacques and earlier ancestors in France all used the Marcotte spelling.

The house that Jean-Baptiste was born in was demolished. The newer structure built on the same plot of land, sometime after 1761, still stands in Cap-Santé, Quebec. See photo on next page.

Jean-Baptiste's parents deeded the home in 1720 to Jean-Baptiste's brother, Francois, who by consensus of the siblings, was supposed to live there to take care of the parents in their old age. But in 1754, the mother, Marie-Anne, reclaimed the property via civil petition on the basis that Francois was neglecting her and leaving her nearly destitute. She later left all her property to Michael Marcotte's direct ancestor Antoine, another of Jean-Baptiste's brothers.

The Marcotte home of Jean Baptiste Marcotte's parents in Cap Santé
Courtesy of Michael Marcotte

Magdelaine La Framboise Parents/Siblings/Children

Claude Pelle de La Haye ——————— Marie Neskesh —
(aka Neskes, Neskeek,
Amighissen, and Thimotee)
Bapt. May 9, 1756[1]   D. Before 1804
M. Claude Pelle de La Haye May 10, 1756[2]
M. Jean Baptiste Marcotte July 24, 1758[3]
(May have married Sarrasin. See Notes)

Marie[4]	Jean Baptiste[5]	Marianne[6]
B. Sept 8, 1759	B. Jan 12, 1762	B. Sept 1769
Bapt. Sept 30, 1759	Bapt. June 13, 1762	Bapt. July 10, 1775

Therese[10]
B. about 1776   Bapt. Aug 1, 1786
M. Pierre La Salliere a la façon du pays
M. George Schindler[11] in the church July 12, 1804
D. Oct. 31, 1853[12]

Marianne La Salliere Fisher	Lucy Tanner (adopted)	Martha Tanner (adopted)
B. about 1790	B. July 20, 1820	B. about 1814
Died 1853	D. in shipwreck 1834	D. 1887

Elizabeth (Betsy) Fisher Baird
B. 1810
D. 1890

-Jean Baptiste Marcotte

Charlotte[7]
B. about 1770
M. Charles Chandonnet
a la façon du pays
M. Church July 11, 1804
D. Jan. 2, 1806 [8]

Marguerite[9]
B. August 1771
Bapt. July 10, 1775
M. Charles Wagocoucher,
aka Ougawouchen and
Agacouchin

Magdelaine[13]
B. 1780   Bapt. Aug.1, 1786
M. Joseph La Framboise[14]
a la façon du pays 1796 and in the church July 11, 1804
D. April 1846[15]

Josette
B. Sept 24, 1795
D. in childbirth 1820

Joseph   (see next page*)
B. March 1805
D. 1854

Harriet Pierce Ricketts
B. 1817
D. Jan. 17, 1854

Benjamin Langdon Pierce
B. Nov. 1820
D. Nov. 1820

Below are the wives and children of Magdelaine's son, Joseph La Framboise. There are discrepancies in the reporting of names of his first three wives, and the list of children is not complete. Some children died young and are not mentioned, but it is known that Magdelaine La Framboise had many grandchildren from her son and his four wives.

Joseph La Framboise[16]
(son of Magdelaine and
Joseph La Framboise)

Marriages
1. Daughter 1 of Chief Sleepy Eyes (M. 1827)
2. Daughter of Chief Walking Dog
3. Daughter 2 of Chief Sleepy Eyes (M. 1838)
4. Jane Dickson, Daughter of Col. Robert Dickson (M. 1845)

Children
1. Joseph B. about 1829
2. Francis
3. Alexis B. about 1840
4. Josette
5. Julia Ann B. 1842 D. 1871
6. William R. B. 1847
7. Justine B. 1849
8. Harriet
9. Eliza 1855
10. Infant sons who died at birth, dates unknown

Notes for Magdelaine Marcotte La Framboise Parents/Siblings/Children Charts

Below are the sources providing documentation for the information in the above charts. The original spellings, variations of spelling, capitalization, and punctuation from the Wisconsin translations has been retained.   *** indicate omission of repetitive phrases or illegible words from that source.

1. Wisconsin Historical Collections, Madison: State Historical Society of Wisconsin, vol. xix, p. 44. (Translations from the original French of the Mackinac Register, Baptisms, Marriages, Interments of Ste Anne's Catholic Church.)

"May 9, 1756, I solemnly baptized an outaouaise catechumen, daughter of neskes and granddaughter of kinoncharnee, sufficiently instructed and desiring holy baptism, who took the name of marie; the godfather was Mr. l'anglade, the elder and the godmother mde. Langlade, the younger ***. P. DU JAUNAY, miss. of the society of Jesus. LANGLADE; CHARLOTTE BOURASSA LANGLADE; JOSEPH BARTHELEMI BLONDEAU." *A footnote to this entry notes that Marie afterwards became the wife of Jean Baptiste Marcot. (Author Note: Outaouaise was the French name for the Odawa tribe of Native Americans. Catechumen refers to one receiving instruction in the principles of the Christian religion.)

2. ibid, vol. xviii, p. 483.

"I *** received the mutual marriage consent of Claude Pelle de la haye, voyageur; and of Marie, a young outaouais woman, Baptized yesterday, daughter of Nesxesouexite, daughter of Kinonchamee - after one publication of bans and with dispensation from two other publications *** at Michilimakina, May 10, 1756. P. DUJAUNAY miss of Society of Jesus. CLAUDE PELLE LAHAY; LANGLADE; BARTHELMI BLONDEAU; CHARLES LAPALME." (Reading the above two footnotes together it is clear they refer to the same "Marie" who is noted to have been baptized and married one day apart. This further confirms, Marie had a husband before Jean Baptiste Marcotte).

Also, Elizabeth Baird, Wisconsin Historical Collections, Madison: State Historical Society of Wisconsin, Indian Customs and Early Recollections, vol. ix, p. 323:

"Mrs. Baird, the author of those valuable and interesting papers, was born at Prairie du Chien, April 24th, 1810-the daughter of Capt. Henry Monroe Fisher, the earliest American pioneer at that place, and long a public officer and Indian trader on that frontier. Her grandmother, Madame Therese Schindler, nee Marcot, of Mackinaw, was a great granddaughter of Kewanoquat, or Returning Cloud, a distinguished Ottawa chief, and of Majakwatawa, or Clear Day Woman."

Also: Baird, Elizabeth, "Reminiscences of Early Days on Mackinac Island," Wisconsin Historical Collections, vol. xiv, p. 40: (speaking of her Aunt, Magdelaine La Framboise) "Her mother was of chiefly blood, being the daughter of Kewinaquot (Returning Cloud), one of the most powerful chiefs of the Ottawa tribe."

3. ibid, vol. xviii, pp. 484-465.

"I, *** gave the nuptial Benediction, after receiving their mutual consent, to jean Baptiste marcot and to marie Neskech, in the presence of the undersigned witnesses and others. At michilimakina July 24, 1758. M.L. LEFRANC, miss. of the society of Jesus. LANGLADE; J. JOLIETT; LA FORTUNE."

4. ibid, vol. xix, p. 59.

"September 30, 1759, I supplied the ceremonies of Baptism to marie, privately baptized by Reverend Father du jaunay, born on the 8th of the present month, legitimate daughter of jean Baptiste marcot and of marie amighissen, her father and mother. The godfather was Mr. de Langlade, and the godmother Mde. Souligni. M. L. LEFRANC, Miss of the society of Jesus. LANGLADE; AGATE LA SOULIGNI."

5. ibid, vol. xix, p. 65.

"June 13, 1762, I baptized conditionally jean Baptiste, legitimate son of jean Baptiste Marcot and of marie, his wife, born in the winter quarters at la pointe de Chagouamigoun on the twelfth of January last. The godfather was joseph St. Germain; and the godmother angelique Sejourne. P. DU JAUNAY, miss. of the society of Jesus. JOSEPH ST GERMAIN; ANGELIQUE SEJOURNE."

6. ibid, vol. xix, p. 77.

"July 10, 1776, by us, Priest and missionary, was Baptized Conditionally Marianne Marcotte, born in the month of September 1769, Of the lawful Marriage of Jean Baptiste Marcotte and of Marianne Neskeek, a savage, his wife. The godfather was hypolitte Campeau, who declared that he could not sign his name; and the godmother Marie angelique Sejourne, who signed with us. P. GIBAULT, miss. Priest. MARIE ANGELIQUE SEJOURNE."

7. *Wisconsin Historical Collections*, vol. xviii, p. 509.

"On the same day (July 16, 1804) and in the same year, after publication of two bans from the pulpit during the parochial mass, with dispensation from the third, between Charles Chandonnet, son of Andre Chandonnet and of Charlotte fisher, of the one part; and Charlotte marcot, daughter of jean Baptiste marcot and marie neskesh, of the other part;...we gave them the nuptial benediction in the presence of jean Baptiste Lamoine and Michel Lacroix, of the one part; and of joseph St. jean and Antoine guillory of the other part, all of whom signed. J. DILHET, priest. J. BTE LELMOINE; ANTOINE GUILLERY; M. LACROIX; CHANDONNETT."

8. D. H. Kelton (Lieut. U.S. Army). Annals of Fort Mackinac, Fergus Printing Company Chicago, 1882.

"Charlotte Chandonnet died January 2, 1806, and was buried in the old Roman Catholic cemetery on Astor Street."

9. *Wisconsin Historical Collections*, vol. xix, p. 77.

"July 10, 1776 by us, priest and missionary, was Baptised Conditionally Marguerite, born in the month of August, 1771 Of the Lawful Marriage of Jean Baptiste Marcotte and Of Marianne Neskeek, his wife. The Godfather was hyppolite Janis, merchant; and the godmother Agatha, wife of Sieur Cote who declared that she could not sign her name. The godfather signed with us. P. Gibault, Priest. H. JANIS."

10. ibid. vol. xix, p. 86.

August 1, 1786, I the undersigned Priest, baptized Therese, about ten years old, daughter of Sieur Jean Baptiste Marcot and of Thimotee, of the Outaois nation, his lawful wife. The Godfather was Mr. Jean Baptiste Chevalier; and the Godmother Md. Carignan, who signed with us. PAYET, Miss priest. PILLET CARIGNAN; J. BAPTE CHEVALIER.

11. ibid, vol. xviii, p. 508.

July 12, 1804, we the Undersigned priest, missionary at Michilimakina - after granting dispensation from three Bans between George Schindler, son of jean jonas Schindler and of Genevieve maranda, of the one part; and therese Marcot, daughter of jean Baptiste Marcot and of marie nesketh Sarrasin, deceased; the husband not a catholic but promising to bring up his children in the Roman catholic religion; The wife being a Catholic and preparing to make her first Communion on the day after tomorrow – received their mutual Marriage consent *** in virtue of the power Received from Monseigneur the Bishop of the United States, jean Carol; in the presence of joseph Laframboise and Louis Chevalier, of the one part; and of Charles Chandonnet and antoine guillory of the other part, all of whom signed with us. J. DILHET, missionary priest. JOSEPH LAFRAMBOISE; ANTOINE GUILLORY; GEO. SCHINDLER; LOUIS CHEVALIER, + his mark; THERESE MARCOT, + her mark; C. CHARDONNETT.

12. *Wisconsin Necrology.* Madison, Wisconsin: State Historical Society of Wisconsin, vol. 1, 1846-1958.

Obituary: "Schindler, Madame Therese was born at Old Mackinac, Mich in the year 1775. She was a lineal descendant of the principal chief of the Ottawa Nation. Most of her early life was passed at St. Joseph Michigan but she was a resident of the island of Mackinac from the year 1805 until 1853 when she came to Green Bay. During her eventful career on earth, she experienced many interesting changes and vicissitudes, and witnessed what but few persons have seen, five generations (herself the first) assembled in her late home on the Island of Mackinac at one time. Her nearest lineal descendant is her granddaughter the wife of Honorable Henry L. Baird, She possessed many amiable and ennobling traits of character without education. She was a woman of very strong, enquiring mind and with a remarkable memory. She was in her 81st year of her age. Her remains in compliance with her wishes were conveyed to Mackinac for interment."

13. *Wisconsin Historical Collections*, vol. xix, p. 86.

"August 1, 1786, I, the undersigned Priest, baptized Magdelaine, about six years old, legitimate daughter of Sieur Jean Baptiste Marcot and of Thimotee of the Outaois nation. The Godfather was Sieur Antoine Barthe; and the Godmother Madame Charles Gauthier, who declared that she could not sign her name. PAYET, Miss priest. ANTOIN BARTHE." A footnote to this entry notes that Magdelaine later married Joseph La Framboise.

14. ibid, vol. xviii, p. 507.

"July 11, 1804, we the Undersigned priest, missionary at michilimakina – after dispensation from three bans between joseph laframboise, son of jean Baptiste la framboise and of marguerite La Bissoniere, deceased, of the one part, and marguerite Magdelaine marcot, daughter of jean Baptiste marcot and of marie neskesh, of the other part – received their mutual marriage consent * * * in the presence of Michel Lacroix, of jean Baptiste lemoine, of Charles Chandonnet, and of antoine guillory who signed with us. J. DILHET, missionary priest. BTE LEMOINE; JOSEPH LAFRAMBOISE; MAGDELAINE MARCOT, + her mark; M LACROIX; ANTOINE GUILLORY; C. CHANDONNETT."

15. McDowell, Dictionary of Canadian Biography, Wikipedia, and other sources all note Magdelaine La Framboise's date of death as April 4, 1846. The gravestone that stood in Ste. Anne's churchyard noted Magdelaine's date of death as July 14, 1846, but this is clearly in error. Her will was entered into probate in June 1846. (See Magdelaine's Last Will and Testament, page 441 in notes.)

16. Online genealogies including:
https://www.geni.com/people/Joseph-La-Framboise/
the Thelen Margraf family trees,
http://michellesfamilytree.com/Ancestry.com
Detroit River Region Metis Families- Part 7, La Fontaine- La Framboise, Diane Wolford Sheppard, 2015, and Janet Timmerman (see Bibliography).

The above sources offer accounts of Joseph's marriages and children. Inconsistencies make it difficult to sort out family connections for Magdelaine La Framboise's only son. Joseph likely married four times. His first wife was the daughter of Ishahkba, or Sleepy Eye, Chief of the Sisseton-Wahpeton band of Dakota. That marriage was sometime before 1830. Joseph's first child was likely born in 1827 or 1829, and was named Joseph after his father. Joseph's first wife died soon after the marriage, and he then married the daughter of Chief Walking Dog (also reported as Chief Walking Day). This second wife quickly disappeared from the records and is also believed to have died soon after the marriage. Joseph married a third time, to another daughter of

Chief Sleepy Eye. With this wife he may have fathered Alexis, Julia Ann, and another son. Joseph's fourth and final marriage was to Jane Dickson, daughter of fur trader William Dickson. With Jane, he had several children. Two died in infancy. The remaining three were William Robert (b. 1847); Justine (b. 1849); and Eliza or Elizabeth, (b. 1855). At Joseph's death, he was said to have left a large number of children, so this list of children may be incomplete.

Joseph La Framboise's gravestone in Fort Ridgely Cemetery, Nicollet County, Minnesota.

A Langlade Connection?

Could Charles-Michel Mouet de Langlade, known as sieur de Langlade and Magdelaine Marcotte La Framboise have been first cousins, or first cousins once removed?

The author cannot say if Charles Langlade was really Magdelaine La Framboise's first cousin or first cousin once removed (in the European meaning of those relationships), nor whether La Fouche or Nissowaquet was her uncle (again in the European configuration of relationships). Both Langlade and Nissowaquet are important historical figures whose lives intersected with Magdelaine's, and it is interesting to speculate.

The chart and reference notes on the next pages support a possible conclusion that Charles Michel Langlade and Magdelaine Marcotte La Framboise could have been first cousins. This speculation cannot be verified without further information. However, various sources suggest that Domithilde Langlade (Charles's mother) and Marie Marcotte (Magdelaine's mother) were both daughters of Chief Kewanoquat and his wife Majakwatawa.

Possible Charles Langlade Connection

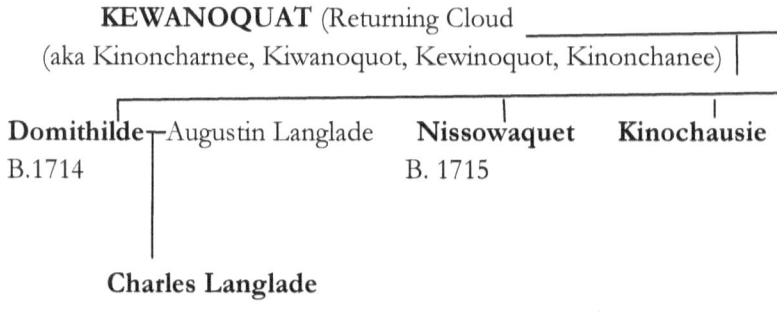

~~~~~~

There is a 26-year difference in the ages of Charles' mother (Domithilde Kewanoquat Langlade) and Magdelaine's mother (Marie Kewanoquat Marcotte), but it was not unusual during the historic time period in issue that a woman gave birth to children over a long period of years. We know the birth of Marie's children with Jean Baptiste Marcotte ranged from 1759 to 1780, or 21 years, and those children were all from her second marriage.

Marie's date of birth is approximate, so she could have been slightly older. It is also possible that Kinochausie was actually Marie's father, not her brother. If that were the case, she would be one generation further down on the chart, making Charles and Magdelaine La Framboise first cousins, once removed. *The Mackinac Register* and the *Reminiscences* of Elizabeth Baird are the best sources of information available for the times in question. The Metis History (online) and Family Genealogy charts are not always well-documented.

The use of **UNKNOWN** in the chart indicates there may have been more siblings in this generation.

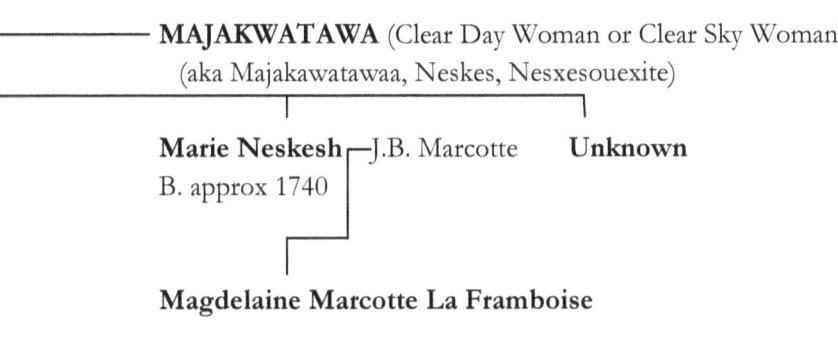

Selected Bibliography Notes for Langlade Connection Genealogy Charts

This bibliography is not likely a complete record of all the sources that exist to prove or disprove the genealogy lineage of Magdelaine Marcotte La Framboise. But they are the sources I found and reviewed.

1. Baird, Elizabeth Therese Fisher. Wisconsin Historical Collections, Madison: State Historical Society of Wisconsin, *Indian Customs and Early Recollections*, vol. ix, p. 303.

"Mrs. Baird, the author of those valuable and interesting papers, was born at Prairie du Chien, April 24th, 1810-the daughter of Capt. Henry Monroe Fisher, the earliest American pioneer at that place, and long a public officer and Indian trader on that frontier. Her grandmother, Madame Therese Schindler, nee Marcotte, of Mackinaw, was a great granddaughter of Kewanoquat, or Returning Cloud, a distinguished Ottawa chief, and of Majakwatawa, or Clear Day Woman." (Author's note: Therese Schindler was Magdelaine La Framboise's sister, so they are the same degree of relationship to Kewanoquat.)

2. Baird, Elizabeth Therese Fisher. Wisconsin Historical Collections, Madison: State Historical Society of Wisconsin, *Reminiscences of Early Days on Mackinac Island*, vol. xiv, p. 17 (footnote) and p. 40. Speaking of her

aunt, Magdelaine La Framboise: "Her mother was of chiefly blood, being the daughter of Kewanoquat (Returning Cloud), one of the most powerful chiefs of the Ottawa tribe."

3. Kelton, Dwight. Wisconsin Historical Collections, vol. xi, p. 2. (See also note 1 above).

This is a difficult note to find in the WHC. It is contained in the section on American Fur Company Invoices, which begins on page 370, but this note is tucked between pages 372 and 373, where four additional pages are inserted, seemingly out of sequence, and identified as follows: voluntary, blank page, page 2, and handwritten. The inserted page 2 contains the following information:

"Majakwatawa should be translated as Clear Sky Woman instead of Clear Day Woman as given."

(Author's note: Kelton is talking about Baird's translation for the name of Magdelaine La Framboise's grandmother.)

4. Internet genealogical notes, WikiTree, Menard Family Tree, and Ancestry.com.

Nesxesouexite (Neskes, Mijakwatawa, Otter, Nesxepuexite). Died of exposure. She was old and unable to use her legs. Her son, La Fourche, aged 18, took her outside and let her freeze to death in a snowstorm. (Author note: I have been unable to document the truth of this assertion.)

5. Skaggs, David, BLPA member and Professor Emeritus of History, Bowling Green State University,

http://users.usinternet.com/dfnels/langlade.htm, viewed 3/15/2016. "Sieur de D'Englade, as he as sometime referred to, was the son of Pierre Mouet, sieur de Moras (d. 1708 Trois-Rivieres) and Elisabeth Jutras (m. 1694 Trois Rivieres). Elisabeth was the niece of Pierre-Esprit Radisson, the early trader/explorer of the far western region. He married Domitille Oukabe dit Neveu (also known as Domithilde La Fourche or Kapiouapnonkoue) at Michilimackinac in 1728. Domitille was the daughter of Ottawa Chief Kewanoquat, sister of Ottawa Chief Nissowaquet (la Fourche) and the widow of Daniel Amiot dit Villenuve."

6. *1726-1728 Internet Metis History.*

http://home.eznet.net/~dminor/TM000122.html January 22, 2000.

"Langlade was a Métis, a half-breed, child of French trader Sieur Augustin Mouet de Langlade; his mother Domitille Villeneuve, sister of Ottawa chief La Fourche, and daughter of Chief Kewanoquat. Charles would become a trader like his father and an Indian agent, but it was his military accomplishments that most distinguished him. In 1739, when he was only ten, his uncle La Fourche had a dream, telling him that a planned expedition against the Chickasaw in Tennessee would only succeed if the boy accompanied them. Ottawa dreams are taken seriously, so with his father's permission, the boy went along with the war party. Even though the outcome of the trip was a negotiated treaty, Charles was given a native title meaning *defender of his country*."

7. *1728 Internet Metis History*, ibid.

"Michilimackinac, New France (Michigan) marriage, Augustin Mouet, sieur de Langlade a.k.a. Sieur de Langlade born 1703, died 1771/77, Green Bay, New France (Wisconsin), son of Pierre Mouet, sieur de Moras died 1708, and Elisabeth Jutras, married Domitill Oukabe dit Neve a.k.a. Domithilde La Fourche or Kapiouapnonkoue, widow Daniel Amiot dit Villeneuve and daughter of Ottawa Chief Kewanoquat."

8. *1732 Internet Metis History*, ibid.

"1732 Augustin Mouet, sieur de Langlade a.k.a. Sieur de d'Englade born 1703, died 1771/77, hired Jean Baptiste Gendon and Jean Baptiste Denot for a voyage to the Sioux (Dakota Territory)."

9. Peterson, Jacqueline. "The Founders of Green Bay: A Marriage of Indian and White." *Voyageur*, Historical Review of Brown County and Northeast Wisconsin, Spring 1984.

"Charles Langlade predictably married first an Ottawa woman of La Fourche's band. However, his fame after the destruction of Pickawillany and Braddock's defeat in 1755 secured him both a perpetual superintendency of the Indians of Green Bay and the hand of a French Creole daughter of a Detroit trader. Langlade moved permanently to Green Bay after 1763, having traded there with his father and kin from the 1740s. He carried with him an aging mother and father, his wife and two small daughters, his nephew Gauthier, and his part-Ottawa son Charles and daughter Agatha."

Peterson also wrote, "Domitille Villeneuve (her baptismal name) was the sister of the local Ottawa band chief, La Fourche, and daughter of Chief Kewanoquat."

10. ibid.
Langlade held the admiration and respect of his Ottawa kin, who named him Akewangeketawso—military conqueror. As early as age ten, he was carried into battle against the Chickasaws under the protective arm of his maternal uncle – La Fourche. (See above note 6.)

11. *Wisconsin Historical Collections*, vol. xix, p. 44.
"May 9, 1756, I solemnly baptized an outaouaise catechumen, daughter of neskes and granddaughter of kinoncharnee, sufficiently instructed and desiring holy baptism, who took the name of marie; the godfather was Mr. l'anglade, the elder and the godmother mde. Langlade, the younger ***. P. DU JAUNAY, miss. of the society of Jesus. LANGLADE; CHARLOTTE BOURASSA LANGLADE; JOSEPH BARTHELEMI BLONDEAU." *A footnote to this entry notes that Marie afterwards became the wife of Jean Baptiste Marcotte. (Author's note: The Marie referenced is Magdelaine La Framboise's mother.)

12. *Wisconsin Historical Collections*, vol. xviii, p. 483.
"I *** received the mutual marriage consent of Claude Pelle de la haye, voyageur; and of Marie, (Author note: Magdelaine La Framboise's mother) a young outaouais woman, Baptized yesterday, daughter of Nesxesouexite, daughter of Kinonchamee - after one publication of bans and with dispensation from two other publications *** at Michilimakina, May 10, 1756. P. DUJAUNAY miss of Society of Jesus. CLAUDE PELLE LAHAY; LANGLADE; BARTHELMI BLONDEAU; CHARLES LAPALME."

13. *Wisconsin Historical Collections*, vol. xix, p. 59.
"*** gave the nuptial Benediction, after receiving their mutual consent, to jean Baptiste Marcotte and to marie Neskech, in the presence of the undersigned witnesses and others. At michilimakina July 24, 1758. M.L. LEFRANC, miss. of the society of Jesus. LANGLADE; J. JOLIETT; LA FORTUNE."

14. Ancestry.com, Metis History 1754-1757.

"Charles Michel Langlade, born 1720 or 1724, died 1800, son of Augustin Mouet, sieur de Langlade and Domitille, born at Michilimackinac. He married Charlotte-Ambrose Bourassa, daughter of Rene Bourassa and Anne-Charlotte-Veronica Chevalier. Charlotte had been married previously to Jean Bte. Leduc in 1773 and in 1754 Charles had been previously married to an Ottawa woman by the name of Dourana."

15. *Dictionary of Canadian Biography*, vol. iv, 1771-1880, viewed online 3/14/2016 at

http://www.biographi.ca/en/results.php/?ft=Nissowaquet.

Nissowaquet (Nosawaguet, Sosawaket, La Fourche, Fork) "Living in proximity to Fort Michilimackinac, the band developed ties with the French. Nissowaquet's bond with his sister's son, Charles-Michel Mouet de Langlade, particularly encouraged his friendship with them and his later association with the British."

16. ibid.

"Mouet De Langlade, Charles Michel, fur-trader, officer in the colonial regular troops, and Indian Department employee; baptized 9 May 1729 at Michilimackinac (Author's note: Mackinaw City, Mich.), son of Augustin Mouet de Langlade, a prominent trader, and Domitilde, sister of Nissowaquet; m. 12 Aug. 1754 at Michilimackinac Charlotte-Ambroisine, daughter of René Bourassa, *dit* La Ronde, and they had two daughters; he also had a son Charles by an earlier liaison with an Ottawa woman; d. during the winter of 1800–1 at La Baye."

Background Notes

Along my research journey, I found many fascinating stories. Either the people, events, and places in these notes transect with Magdelaine La Framboise's life, although I didn't try to weave all of them into her story, or they provided the basis for some conclusions, such as the background of Magdelaine's slave, Angelique in note 2 below. I thought readers might find some of this background information as interesting as I did.

Readers should not assume that if the source of information is absent, the information in the novel is not true. I tried to write the story as accurately as possible, but to note the source of every minute fact, most of which are commonly known, would have become quite tedious.

("I" in these notes refers to author, J. K. Royce.)

1. Sacred Space

[1] Joseph La Framboise's murder is variously reported as taking place in western Michigan at Ada, Lowell, Grand Haven (Gabagouache), or at an encampment near the mouth of the Muskegon River.

[2] Baird, *Reminiscences*. Angelique's ghost whispers from the pages of history, but there is little definitive information about her. Probably the most reliable source is Elizabeth Baird, the grand-niece of Magdelaine La Framboise. Elizabeth spent much of her childhood with her grandmother, Therese Schindler (Magdelaine's sister), on Mackinac Island. Therese and Magdelaine lived within rods of each other. Elizabeth, or Betsy as she was called as a child, often stayed with her great aunt, Magdelaine.

As a member of the family, Elizabeth describes Magdelaine's slave, "old Angelique." In other passages, Baird refers to Angelique as a servant. It wouldn't seem unusual that a slave who has become a "devoted companion," (Baird's words) would be referred to as a servant; the reverse seems less likely (referencing a servant as a slave). In at least two places, Baird refers to Angelique and her son, Francois, as slaves. Baird says that Therese Schindler gave Francois his freedom when he came of age.

Elizabeth notes that after Magdelaine's death Angelique went to live with her son, Francois Lacroix, at Cross Village or L'Arbre Croche. If Angelique's last name was the same as that of her children, she would have been Angelique Lacroix.

Elizabeth writes that Angelique and her son, Louizon, were with Joseph and Magdelaine La Framboise on the trip when Joseph was murdered. By piecing together various nuggets of information provided by Baird, it can be assumed that Angelique had at least three children: Francois, Louizon and Catishe. This begs the question of whether Angelique married, and assuming so, did her spouse also live with Magdelaine? It is unlikely Magdelaine would have approved of out-of-wedlock children. However, I have found no documentation to clarify this issue, and I have located no mention of Angelique's husband.

McDowell, (Madame La Framboise), refers to Magdelaine's slaves, including Angelique, as colored slaves (p. 275) and then as Negro slaves (p. 278). Widder, (Magdelaine La Framboise, Fur Trader and Educator, p. 2) refers to Angelique as an Indian slave. Native American slaves were more common on Mackinac Island than slaves of African descent. Native American warfare allowed victors to take captives. There are many references to Pawnee (Panis) slaves in historical records.

One story suggests Angelique was captured by Charles Langlade in battle and given to Magdelaine's family. Another says Angelique was the daughter of a slave belonging to Louis Chevalier, a friend of Magdelaine's father. Langlade could have captured Angelique's mother and sold or given her to Chevalier who lived near the Marcottes (Magdelaine's family) at the St. Joseph post. The June 30, 1780, census, (Michigan Pioneer and Historical Collections, vol. 10, pp. 370-71) recorded every man, woman, child, and slave resident of the 149 person post at St. Joseph. In the house of M. Chevalier were:

Mr. Chevalier,
Daujinne,
Gibaut,
Pieniche,
Youtra Junior,
Mde. Chevalier,
Md. Youtra, her daughter,
Raby Tany,
Lizette, Panize, and
Angelique Panize, his child.

It is possible that Lizette was a Panis slave, and Angelique the child of Lizette and Raby Tany. Scrutiny of this entry supports this possible conclusion. Adults living in a home were likely referred to by terms of respect: Mde., Md., or Mr. Young children and slaves likely would not be given a title. It would be logical that the census taker listed all of the free persons first, slaves last. If the Angelique living with Chevalier became Magdelaine's slave, she was also a child in 1780 and possibly close in age to Magdelaine who was born four months before the census was taken.

Listed in the 1780 census, immediately after the Chevalier family, were the Marcot(te)s: "In the house of *seur* Marcot: Mde. Marcot and four children." The children would have been Magdelaine and her three sisters Therese, Charlotte, and Marguerite.

Note 101 in this section, is a copy of Magdelaine's will. There is no mention of Angelique receiving a bequest or being given her freedom upon Magdelaine's death. This may help support a conclusion that Angelique was Native American. African American slaves, if they were given their freedom, often received it in the will of their master. From a legal sense, they were chattel. Native American slavery involved war captives and wasn't as institutionalized. The captives were of the same ethnic group, and there is little proof they were considered or treated as racially inferior. Often they married within the tribe of their captor, or even replaced a dead child.

[3] Baird, *Reminiscences*, pp. 38-39. See also Kinze, Wau-Bun, p. 23, and McDowell, Madame La Framboise, p. 276. White Ox, also known by his Odawa name, Nequat, shot and killed Joseph La Framboise.

Although Baird is considered a primary authority for events relating to Magdelaine La Framboise, she placed Joseph's death in 1809, and it occurred in 1806. For a discussion detailing the date, see McDowell, Madame La Framboise, p. 277, in which two letters are cited, both dated prior to 1809, and both referencing Joseph La Framboise's death. The first letter is dated June 11, 1807, Mackinac Island, from Claude La Framboise (Joseph's brother) to John Kinzie. Claude wrote, "Having full powers to recover the Debts, etc. due to the Estate of the late deceased Joseph La Framboise..." The second letter was from George Schindler (Joseph's brother-in-law) to Solomon Sibley, dated August 22, 1807, and in it George mentions that Magdelaine was willing to turn over Joseph's papers to Claude La Framboise to help resolve a dispute that arose after Joseph's death.

3. Destiny

[4] Wampeme is a fictional character. I believed that as a beautiful, young, fourteen-year-old, Magdelaine may have had a romantic interest in a youth from her Odawa village before she married Joseph La Framboise. In the late 1700s, fourteen was an acceptable age for marriage, so my assumption seemed reasonable. Wampeme is a metaphor for tribal life and customs, and offers a perspective opposite to Magdelaine's acceptance of white culture, religion, and aspirations.

4. An Uneasy Choice

[5] Lavender, pp. 23-25. An outfit was a trader's supplies and merchandise for the trading season. It included the necessities for surviving cruel winters: food and clothing with little room left over for luxuries, although a bit of tea and brandy might find a few inches of space in the bateaux. However, it was the merchandise the trader needed to exchange for furs that was the main focus of an outfit. These trade goods were as varied as the needs of the Native Americans with whom the trader did business. An outfit included a standard unit referred to as a piece, which could be a length, or bolt of cloth, generally a heavy, coarse woolen material that came in lengths of twenty or twenty-five yards. This was the preferred cloth for Native American clothing, often having replaced animal hides. Traders also carried calicos, which had become popular, and upon occasion silk was included.

In addition to material, heavy blankets were a standard item in the outfit. For Native Americans, the blanket served many functions, first of which was warmth during the winter. A good blanket could weigh up to eight and a half pounds and measure six feet on a side.

Lesser items included axes, kettles, needles, thread, awls, looking glasses, handkerchiefs, ribbons, combs, beads, traps, knives, flints, gun powder, lead and bullet molds, short-barreled North West trade muskets, shoes, red caps, playing cards, clay pipes, and "carrots" (also spelled carots") which were twisted strands of tobacco weighing up to two pounds. Silver wristbands and earrings were popular items of trade, but originally silver was allowed only as a prestige item given to significant chiefs. In ordinary trade they were forbidden.

Of all of the items in the outfit, the one deemed most critical and most controversial was alcohol. Eight-gallon kegs containing West Indies rum were transported as an essential of the outfit. It was often watered down to double or even triple its amount. The most unscrupulous trader might simply replace the alcohol with nothing but water, and then hope he was far away when the Native Americans discovered they had been cheated.

[6] Tri-Cities Historical Museum, "An Alphabetical Directory of People from the Past Who Lived in Northwest Ottawa County: Madeline (Magdelaine) Marcotte La Framboise, Grand Haven. Published in the United States, May 1999.
"After her husband's death, Madame La Framboise assumed supervision of all 20 of the West Michigan trading posts that Joseph had managed for John Jacob Astor's American Fur Company, including a post in Crockery Township."

While it is believed Joseph and Magdelaine supervised twenty posts, it isn't necessarily true that they managed them for John Jacob Astor. In 1806, at the time of Joseph's death, Astor had not established the American Fur Company. On April 6, 1808, with permission from President Thomas Jefferson, Astor created his company. It was 1822 when he established Astor House on Mackinac Island. During Magdelaine's later years of trading on her own, she maintained posts in her individual capacity and other posts where her business was on account and risk for John Jacob Astor.

[7] Baird, *Reminiscences*, pp. 38-39. See also Kinze, Wau-Bun, p. 23. McDowell, Madame La Framboise, p. 276. The story of White Ox being brought to Magdelaine, and of her forgiving him, is contained in many accounts.

[8] McDowell, Madame La Framboise, p. 277. "In the spring following Joseph's death, Magdelaine exhumed his body and took it back to the island where she gave it a reverent, permanent burial."

5. FALSE WITNESS

[9] In my quest to learn about Magdelaine La Framboise, one piece of information continued to elude me: What was Magdelaine's Odawa name?

Magdelaine's sister, Therese, was called To-e-ak-que in the 1821 Treaty of Chicago. That same treaty mentioned Joseph La Framboise, son of Shaw-we-no-qua, but further research established this Joseph was not the son of Magdelaine Marcotte La Framboise.

Because I believed that *Ardent Spirit* benefited from an Odawa name for Magdelaine, I consulted Kenny Neganigwane Pheasant, an Odawa linguist, and asked for a translation of Bluebird Woman—the name I chose for Magdelaine—into the Odawa language. Mr. Pheasant translated Bluebird Woman as Zhaawan Kwe. The bluebird is considered an omen of change or transformation, and I believed it was a befitting symbol of Magdelaine's story.

6. JOSETTE

[10] Baird, *Reminiscences*, pp. 40-41. (Also, Widder, Kelton, and Burby) Benjamin Pierce, brother to Franklin Pierce, future president of the United States, was a captain at Fort Mackinac when he married Josette La Framboise.

[11] Therese Marcotte La Sallier Schindler, was Magdelaine's older sister. The custom of the family was to refer to aunts, uncles and grandparents by their last name, Aunt Schindler instead of Aunt Therese. Grandmaman La Framboise, not Grandmaman Magdelaine. This was a sign of respect, use of the Christian name not appropriate for children.

[12] Letter from Alex La Framboise in Montreal to Magdelaine La Framboise. Joseph La Framboise, Magdelaine's son, had been sent to Montreal for education. He was not on the island in 1820.

[13] Petersen and Van Kirk. Métis refers to mixed-blood. In the Great Lakes fur trade it generally referenced those of Native American and French blood.

7. WINTERING IN THE COUNTRY

[14] Baird, *Reminiscences*. Magdelaine La Framboise was illiterate at this time. There is debate over whether she ever learned to read and write. Letters from Madame La Framboise later cited to prove she learned these skills could as easily have been from Josette Ademar La Framboise, the widow of Alex, and sister-in-law to Magdelaine. Josette Ademar La Framboise lived in Montreal. Magdelaine's son lived with his Aunt La Framboise in

that city while attending school. The content of later letters signed from the Widow La Framboise to Marianne make it sound like the letters came from Josette Ademar La Framboise, not Magdelaine.

Baird, however, says Magdelaine did learn to read, and further claims she learned it on her own. Knowing that Elizabeth Baird spent a great deal of time with Magdelaine, it is reasonable to assume she is correct, and that Magdelaine developed some degree of ability to read. Other writers claim Magdelaine was taught by Martha Tanner, William Ferry, or Marianne La Sallier. Learning to read and write would have been difficult at the age Magdelaine is said to have acquired those skills. We have no way to know how refined her ability was, or how much was rote memorization of a catechism or other religious tracts that she learned by repetition. The fact that Magdelaine La Framboise signed her will with an "X" argues against her being able to write, although that could have been due to her "misshapen hands," as referenced in Martha Tanner letter (See note 51).

8. A Daughter's Death

[15] Betsy is Elizabeth Fisher Baird, Therese Schindler's granddaughter, Marianne La Salliere's daughter, and Magdelaine La Framboise's grandniece.

[16] Baird, *Reminiscences*. Also documented by grave marker in Catholic cemetery on Mackinac Island. Agatha Bailly Biddle was the daughter of Marie Lefevre de La Vigne (Mo-nee or Tou-se-qua) a full-blooded Native American who married Joseph Bailly. Agatha's stepfather treated her well, but she was not educated like his other children. As an adult, Agatha handled treaty money on behalf of her tribe.

[17] *Wisconsin Historical Collections*, vol. xix, p. 508. George Schindler was Therese's second husband.

[18] Burby, p. 31. Dr. William Beaumont was a friend of Benjamin Pierce, and it is almost certain he was present at Josette's death.

[19] Josette and Benjamin Pierce named Magdelaine's first grandson Benjamin Langdon Pierce. John Langdon was a founding father of the United States and a supporter of the Revolutionary War. He was a member of the Continental Congress and after twelve years, which included serving as the first president pro tempore, he became a four-time governor of New

Hampshire. He turned down his party's nomination for vice president in 1812. Langdon's family came from England in 1660 and settled in New Hampshire. The Pierces also moved from England to the United States in the mid-1600s, originally to the Massachusetts Bay Colony and then to New Hampshire. The two families had much in common, and Benjamin Pierce must have considered Langdon an honorable man and a worthy namesake for his son.

[20] George Schindler was Therese's husband. Although not a Catholic, he performed baptisms when necessity dictated. Whether George baptized Benjamin Langdon Pierce is not recorded, but a Catholic family would not have allowed the infant to die without receiving the sacrament.

9. FATHER GABRIEL RICHARD

[21] *Wisconsin Historical Collections*, vol. xix, p. 109. July 7, 1799, Father Gabriel Richard baptized Josette La Framboise.

[22] Widder, *Reveille*, pp. 3-6. Englishman Patrick Sinclair was appointed lieutenant governor and superintendent of Michilimackinac in 1775. Almost immediately, he began to move Fort Michilimackinac to Mackinac Island. Soldiers dismantled the fort and building materials. Personal property of both soldiers and civilians was transported to the island by three sloops, the *Felicity*, *Welcome*, and *Hope*. When the water froze over, efforts continued by dog sled.

Ste. Anne's and the priest's house were moved in the winter of 1780-81, and many French traders, including Jean Baptiste Marcotte, helped with the effort. On the mainland, the church had stood inside the gates of the fort. After transport to the island it was reconstructed in the village. Sinclair may have assumed that Ste. Anne's, standing close to the fort, but on its own land, showed Catholics they would enjoy religious freedom, but they were no longer in control.

By 1782, Sinclair had been promoted to major, but his expenses had come under investigation, and he returned to Quebec to untangle his finances and face charges of misconduct.

[23] The mainland city is Mackinaw, the island is Mackinac.

[24] Rezek, pp. 171-176. Father Gabriel Richard arrived in Detroit in 1798, on the Feast of Corpus Christi. After the fire of 1805, weeks before the Michigan Territory was established, he wrote, "Speramus meliora; resurget cineribus," or "We hope for better things; it will arise from the ashes." This remains Detroit's motto to current day.

While he served in Detroit, Father Richard was invited by a Protestant congregation to act as their clergyman since they had no minister. He accepted the challenge and concentrated on the common elements of all Christianity. Father Richard's service went beyond the pulpit. He established the first printing press in Detroit and published *Essais du Michigan* (in French), as well as *The Michigan Essay*, or *Impartial Observer*.

The priest was imprisoned by the British for refusing to swear an oath of allegiance after they captured Detroit during the War of 1812. Father Richard said, "I have taken an oath to support the Constitution of the United States, and I cannot take another." He was released when Tecumseh, the Shawnee chief who harbored no love for Americans, refused to fight for the British while Father Richard was imprisoned.

Father Richard became a delegate of the Michigan Territory, serving a term from 1823-1825. In 1832, he worked long hours assisting cholera victims during a wide-spread epidemic. He caught the disease and succumbed, although some accounts say he died of exhaustion. His remains were buried in a crypt in Ste. Anne's of Detroit.

11. Lucy and the Story of the White Indian

[25] Arch Rock is a natural limestone arch formed during the Nipissing postglacial period. It stands on the Lake Huron shoreline of Mackinac Island. It played an important role in many Native American legends. (See photo p. 204.)

[26] Also: Gichi Manidoo, Gitche Manitou, Gitchi Manitou, Gitchi Manidou, Gitchee Manitou, Gitchee Manito, and other variant spellings. Gitchie Manitou is the great Creator God of the Anishinaabek and many other Algonquin tribes. However, many of the details of creation were left to Nanabozo, around whom many stories were fashioned. The name Gitchie Manitou was used for God in the Ojibwe translation of the Christian Bible.

[27] WHC, Register of Baptisms.

"Lucy Tanner, born July 17, 1820, of John Tanner and of a woman savage, was baptized conditionally by the undersigned, Parish Priest of Ste. Anne du Detroit, August 4, 1821. The godfather was Etienne Dubois, and the godmother Marianne Fisher, who signed with us."

13. RIX ROBINSON TAKES OVER MAGDELAINE'S TRADE

[28] Ada Historical Society, http://www.hsmichigan.org/ada/info/ Rix Robinson married Peemissaquotoquay (Flying Cloud Woman), an Odawa, in 1821, and remained married to her for one-hundred moons. During that marriage she gave birth to Robinson's only son, John Rix Robinson. After Robinson separated from Peemissaquotoquay, he married a second Native American, Sippiquay (River Woman).

Robinson became the Supervisor for the Township of Kent in 1834, Supervisor of Ada Township in 1840, the Associate Judge of Circuit Courts for Kent County in 1844, a Michigan Senator in 1845, the State Commissioner of Internal Improvements in 1846, and a member of the State Constitutional Convention in 1850.

Robinson was also a well-known fur trader and associated himself with John Jacob Astor and the American Fur Company. Robinson negotiated with the United States Government on behalf of Native Americans and was considered a peacemaker. Rix Robinson continued to reside in Ada until his death.

[29] McDowell, *Therese Schindler*, p. 128. Pierre La Sallier married Therese in the custom of the country in 1790 and left to voyage elsewhere, sometime after their daughter Marianne was born.

[30] Native Americans used crushed trillium, also called birthroot, for a variety of medicinal purposes. In a tea it was used to stop hemorrhaging during childbirth. In a poultice it was used to cure skin irritations, treat insect bites, and relieve pain.

14. SUGAR CAMP

[31] Magdelaine's mother is referenced in various records as Amighissen, Meghissens, Migisan, Neshkeek, Neskech, Neskeek, Neskes, Sarrasin, Thimotee, Thimatee, and by the Christian name Marie. Internet Genealogical notes (Getner Family Tree, http://math.uww.edu/~mcfarlat/pictures/gentner/gentner,

viewed 3/16/2016).
Magdelaine's mother was also called Otter. The Odawa word for Otter is *nigig*. That lead me (the author) to wonder if the similarity in sound between nigig and Neshkeek, Neskech, Neskeek or Neskes may have been responsible for those names being attributed to Marie Marcotte. I also wondered if it was possible Otter or nigig was the family's totem not a given name.

[32] The Harbor Springs Museum describes this concoction from early sugar camps as the original snow cone.

15. Dr. Beaumont, Heartbreak, and Tanner Returns

[33] Myer, Jesse. *Life and Letters of Dr. William Beaumont*. Chapter vi, viewed on line at https://archive.org/details/lifelettersofdrw00myer, viewed July 2015. In his journal, Dr. Beaumont specifically calls it duck shot.

[34] Kelton, p. 16. Postmasters generally worked at a specific location. On Mackinac Island that was on Market Street. However, when a letter demanded special attention, the postal employee delivered it in person. At this time in history, mail was often mailed postage due. Important letters were prepaid.

[35] *Wisconsin Historical Collections*, vol. xviii, pp. 484-485. In her marriage record, Marie Marcotte is referenced as Marie Neskech. Nigig is the Odawa word for Otter, and this could be intended as the word Otter. (See note 31 above).

16. Winds of Change

[36] *Wisconsin Historical Collections*, vol. xi, pp. 373-374. American Fur Company Invoices 1821-1822.

[37] State Historical Society of Wisconsin, Henry and Elizabeth Baird Papers, 1787-1823, Box 6, Folder 1. Donation of Indian Chiefs to Madelon La Framboise (1823). A piece of that property is currently in the heart of Grand Rapids. (See copy of "donation," next page.)

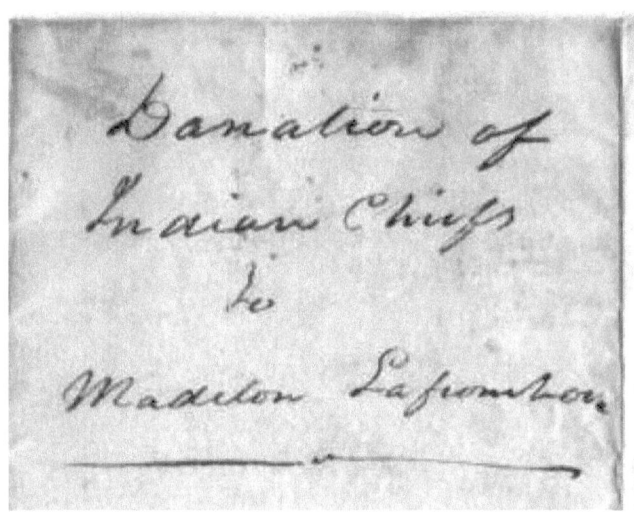

[38] Everett, p. 276-277.

[39] Devil's Kitchen is a double cave carved by the waters of Lake Huron during the Nipissing post-glacial period. It is located in the southwestern shore of Mackinac Island.

[40] *Ferry Family Papers*, Bentley Historical Library, University of Michigan, 1823 to 1904. And William Ferry's journal, American Missionary Register, vol. v, March 1824, No. 3. pp. 89-90. William Montague Ferry graduated from Union College in Brunswick, New Jersey in 1821, and was ordained as a Presbyterian minister in 1822. After graduation and ordination, he offered his services to the United Foreign Missionary Society to explore and preach among the Indian tribes of the Northwest. He was appointed to the Mackinac Mission on Mackinac Island. In 1823, he married Amanda White.

Ferry worked among the Native Americans for more than a decade. Then, because of failing health, religious controversies on the island, and a dwindling congregation, he moved downstate to Ottawa County in 1834. For the remainder of this life, he was a clergyman in Grand Haven, and for a time the postmaster of that city. Ferry died in 1868.

Ferry's journal offers a description of Magdelaine La Framboise's house during the time he rented it. "The house which I have hired is the one I had in view as mentioned before. It is situated about 1/3 mile from the village. It is a good-sized two-story building, conveniently partitioned off, but not well furnished. We have a kitchen for cooking, good-sized family room, small sleeping room for ourselves, two large sleeping rooms on the second floor, the privilege of as much of the cavereau or root house as we want, and a small part of the garden. The rest of the house, with remaining privileges, the Indian woman (with seven in her family) occupies herself. For the part I have, I pay $100 per year which is low rent in this place. Indeed, it is not half the money paid by several in the village for conveniences not as good as ours."

The original house consisted of a hipped-roof main wing. The classical portico was added at the turn of the 20th century. Changes to the interior woodwork, including the entrance hall stairway, also date to that period. In the 1990s, the home was offered for sale, and there was concern over its future. Father James Williams, then the priest at Ste. Anne's, worried that the home might lose its connection to its first illustrious owner. Father Williams discussed the situation with Dr. Michael Bacon, who operated the Mackinac Island Medical Clinic. Dr. Bacon took on the project of renovating the house and converting it to a hotel/bed-and-breakfast. Bacon was dedicated to making modifications that preserved the history of the house, but also made it a comfortable hotel. A rear addition, including a lobby and twenty guest rooms, was added. A year later another lodge building was constructed behind the original house.

[41] Father of Samuel Morse, of Morse code fame.

17. FERRY OPENS A SCHOOL AND BETSY MARRIES

[42] If Domitilde Langlade was a sister to Magdelaine's mother, Thimotee or Neskes (Marie), then Charles Langlade would be Magdelaine's first cousin, or first cousin, once removed. Records support that both Domitilde and Marie had the same parents. (See Genealogy charts, pp. 401-407).

[43] Baird, *Life in Territorial Wisconsin*, p. 205.

18. RELIGIOUS DISCORD AND BETSY RETURNS

[44] State Historical Society of Wisconsin. Dictionary of Wisconsin Biography. Madison, 1960, p. 305. Jean Joseph Rolette, often known as Joseph Rolette, was born in 1781 and died in 1842. He married Jane

Fisher, the half sister of Elizabeth Fisher Baird (Betsy). Rolette became a wealthy fur trader and was sometimes referred to as King Rolette.

He was a member of the Mackinac Company, which later reorganized as the South West Fur Company. He was a major partner in that business. Rolette eventually made an alliance with Astor's American Fur Company. Another trader, Hercules Dousman, went into business with Rolette. In time Dousman, became the dominant partner. The decline of the fur trade impacted Rolette, and he became indebted to Dousman and the American Fur Company.

In 1842 the American Fur Company was sold. Rolette and his partner then associated themselves with Henry Sibley and Pierre Chuteau and tried to create a place for their business on the upper Mississippi. A few months later, Rolette died, indebted to the new company. In a further affront to his dignity, not only was Rolette financially overpowered by his former partner, but Jane Fisher Rolette had by that time divorced her husband and married Dousman.

[45] Baird, *Reminiscences*, pp. 56-60. The spot where the canoes waited out the storm became known as Egg Harbor and remains so named today.

[46] Journal of William Ferry. The teachers at Mission school received paltry salaries, but according to the journal they got first pick of donated clothes.

19. DEATH OF GEORGE SCHINDLER

[47] Both the Menominee and Odawa languages have Algonquin roots.

[48] Letter from Claude La Framboise to Mr. John Kinzie, Mackinac, June 11, 1807, and Letter from George Schindler to Solomon Sibley, Mackinac, July 9, 1807, Detroit Public Library, Burton Historical Collections, Sibley Papers.

Claude La Framboise was Joseph La Framboise's older brother. He was born in Cape Santé and traded furs out of Montreal. He also provided traders with merchandise for their outfits. The year before Joseph's death, Joseph and George Schindler proposed going into business together as La Framboise and Schindler. They wanted to buy part of their outfit from Claude; however, Claude was unwilling to provide goods on credit to George since he was not family, so the partnership never materialized.

Somehow, in the time between the request for merchandise on account and Joseph's death, Claude must have forgotten the details. He sued George for payment of goods never delivered, and the incident ended in a nasty lawsuit that was eventually dismissed for lack of progress.

20. Word from a Son

[49] Josette Ademar La Framboise was the widow of Magdelaine's brother-in-law, Alex. Magdelaine's son, Joseph stayed with Josette La Framboise when he attended school in Montreal. There are several letters signed "The Widow La Framboise" that various authors attribute to Magdelaine La Framboise that may have actually been written by Josette Ademar La Framboise.

[50] Brown, Dee, pp. 50-61. Also, Baird papers, letters between Elizabeth Baird and Joseph La Framboise, her cousin. Henry Sibley was Joseph La Framboise's (Magdelaine's son's) boss at Little Rock Trading Post on the Minnesota River. The two men enjoyed a close relationship.

[51] Baird Papers. Correspondence dated December 2, 1844, from Martha Tanner, who was then living with Magdelaine, to Elizabeth Baird. There is mention of Magdelaine's misshapen hands. A reasonable assumption would be rheumatoid arthritis.

21. Dreams

[52] findagrave.com/Amanda Boykin, www.geni.com/people/Amanda Boykin, accessed September 8, 2016, Wikipedia, Benjamin Kendrick Pierce, accessed September 8, 2016.

Benjamin Pierce was married three times. In 1823 Pierce served in Pensacola, Florida, when he married his second wife, Amanda Boykin. The wedding took place in Alabama. Boykin was born in 1805 and died in January 1831 while her husband served at Fort Delaware. Her funeral took place in early February, and afterwards the coffin containing her remains was taken for storage to a building at the fort. The night it arrived a fire broke out, and Pierce along with four of his soldiers braved the flames to remove the remains, enabling his wife's body to be buried in the spring. Much of the post burned, but Pierce and his soldiers were able to protect the Pierce children by keeping their quarters from catching fire. It is unknown if Harriet Pierce was living with her father and stepmother at the time. In 1838, Pierce married again. His third wife, Louisa Gertrude Read, was from Delaware and the great-granddaughter of George Read, one of the signers of the Declaration of Independence.

[53] Steere Collection, Bayliss Library, Sault Ste. Marie, Michigan.
On February 25, 1827, during one of her visits to her husband on Drummond Island, Elizabeth Mitchell became ill and died. A letter from her son Andrew to John Bailey, Esq., dated April 18th, 1827 states, *"Report of a boat from Drummond Island, Andrew Mitchell master having on board the corpse of the late Mrs. Mitchell and the necessary provisions of the voyage."*

[54] Charlotte's body may have been placed in a coffin and stored for burial when the ground thawed in the spring.

24. Crooked Tree

[55] Jean Baptiste Marcotte's first child was named Marie after her mother. History shows no clear picture of what happened to this child, and she likely died as an infant. The third child born to this couple was named Marianne, and the name being so similar suggests the first Marie (or Marianne) was by then deceased and to honor her, a subsequent sister was given the name. (See Genealogy Chart, p. 392.)

25. Wild Strawberries

[56] Timmerman, pp. 1-2, and "Wisconsin Early Habitants," by Jo Bartels Alderson and Kate Alderson Reinhart. Joseph La Framboise came from a long line of fur traders who arrived in the new world from France in 1637 under the surname Fafard. They, along with numerous other traders, rebelled against laws stipulating to whom they could sell their furs. To reduce risks of apprehension, they all assumed the same surname of La Framboise, after a common bush in the area, the raspberry.

[57] I believe there is a reasonable argument that Charles Langlade was Magdelaine's first cousin. (See Genealogy, pp. 401-407).

[58] *Wisconsin Historical Collections*, vol. x, p. 350. On March 5, 1783, Charles Langlade sent his commander word of the distressing events from La Baye. His letter was addressed "Governor" and read:

"This letter is to assure you of my very humble respects and to inform you that according to the report brought by some Puants when some traders passed at the portages of Quis-consin, their nation wished to rob them, that in the tumult there was a Puant, called Boeuf Blanc killed and that, to revenge themselves, they took from Mr. Reilh five or six packets as well of liquor as other things and as they were still drunk when Mr. Blondeau passed he was also obliged to give them plunder to save his life. There were forty Saleaux, men, women, and children who were eating each other because of the famine in the La Baye des Noques. Carson, Chief of the Folles-Avoines died the 3rd of November, and one Marcotte, a trader, was killed, it is not known whether by the Sauteaux or the Sioux but that three men escaped although two were wounded.

Governor, the faithful servant of the King,
Langlade, Captain of the Indian Department"

[59] Waugonawkisa was the Odawa name for the place the French called L'Arbor Croche, or the English called Crooked Tree. It is in Northern Emett County, Michigan, somewhere close to current day Harbor Springs, although the exact location is unknown.

27. HISTORY AND TREACHERY

[60] Lord Jeffrey Amherst was commanding general of British forces in North America during the final battles of the French & Indian War (1754-1763). He enjoyed victories against the French and acquired Canada for England. He helped establish England as the world's chief colonizer at the conclusion of the Seven Years' War. Amherst's military career is tarnished by stories of smallpox-infected blankets used as germ warfare against Native Americans.

Letters between Amherst and Colonel Henry Bouquet support the allegations. The most widely known story about smallpox blankets refers to a postscript in a letter from Amherst to Bouquet wondering whether smallpox could be spread among the Native People: "Could it not be contrived to send the Small Pox among those disaffected tribes of Indians? We must on this occasion use every stratagem in our power to reduce them."

A letter from Colonel Henry Bouquet to General Amherst, dated 13 July 1763, recommends the distribution of blankets to "inoculate the Indians," and one from Amherst to Bouquet, dated 16 July 1763, approves this plan and advocates the military try "every other method that can serve to Extirpate this Execrable Race."

These letters also discuss the use of dogs to hunt the Indians, the so-called Spaniards' Method, which Amherst approved in principle, but indicated he could not implement because there were not enough dogs. In a letter dated 26 July 1763, Bouquet acknowledges Amherst's approval and writes, "all your Directions will be observed."

An additional source of information on the matter is the journal of William Trent, commander of the local militia of the townspeople of Pittsburgh, during Pontiac's siege of Fort Pitt. The journal was edited by A. T. Volwiler and printed in the *Mississippi Valley Historical Review*, 11:390-413 (1924). Trent's entry for May 24, 1763, includes the following statement: "[W]e gave them two Blankets and an Handkerchief out of the Small Pox Hospital. I hope it will have the desired effect."

Trent's journal confirms that smallpox had broken out in Fort Pitt prior to the correspondence between Bouquet and Amherst, thus he believed, making their plans reasonable.

With regard to whether the plan was actually feasible (in light of current-day scientific knowledge), see Donald A. Henderson, "Smallpox as a Biological Weapon: Medical and Public Health Management," *Journal of the American Medical Association*, vol. 281, No. 22 (June 9, 1999): A mild form of smallpox virus, Variola minor (also called alastrim), is transmitted by inhalation and is communicable for 3-7 days. The more serious smallpox virus, Variola major, is transmitted both by inhalation and by contamination; it is communicable by inhalation for 9-14 days and by contamination for several years in a dried state.

Elizabeth A. Fenn expands on this theme in her book, *Pox Americana: The Great Smallpox Epidemic of 1775-82*, (NY: Hill and Wang, 2001), discussing widespread accusations and examples of biological warfare on the American continent during this period.

Whether smallpox blankets, boxes containing scrapings from smallpox victims, or any other means of intentional spread of the disease actually worked, history is unclear. What it can assume is that there was intent to cause great harm to Native Americans in an attempt to perpetrate genocide.

⁶¹ *Solar Eclipse Newsletter*, vol. 9, Issue 6, June 2004. "June 16, 1806, Tecumseh's Eclipse. The Shawnee Chief Tecumseh believed that the only hope for tribes in east and central North America was to join together. Tecumseh's brother, Tenskwatawa, the Delaware Prophet, predicted there would be a total eclipse of the sun at noon on June 16, 1806. That eclipse would be a sign that all tribes should unite to drive out the white man. This incident is reported in: Allan W. Eckert, *A Sorrow in Our Heart, the Life of Tecumseh*. Bantam Books, 1993.

In writing *Ardent Spirit* I could not confirm an eclipse at that time. I contacted NASA and got this response from Robert M. Candey:

The page http://eclipse.gsfc.nasa.gov/SEcat5/SE1801-1900.html lists solar eclipses from 1801-1900. There was an eclipse on June 16, 1806, that crossed the United States, including what is now southern Michigan: map, http://eclipse.gsfc.nasa.gov/5MCSEmap/1801-1900/1806-06-16.gif, track on Google map:
http://eclipse.gsfc.nasa.gov/SEsearch/SEsearchmap.php?Ecl= 18060616 Besselian elements
http://eclipse.gsfc.nasa.gov/SEsearch/SEdata.php?Ecl=18060616.

⁶² Tecumseh's speech of August 11, 1810, to Governor Harrison. Indiana Historical Society, text of the speech,
http://images.indianahistory.org/cdm/ref/collection/dc007/id/19, viewed March 3, 2016.

⁶³ The New Madrid earthquake, Monday, December 16, 1811. Magnitude 6.8. (U.S. Geological Society Home Page,
http://earthquake.usgs.gov/earthquakes/states/events/1811-1812.php (HTML Document 20.47 KB)

28. DEATH OF LOVE

⁶⁴ www.steanneschurch.org/history.htm accessed 9/16/2016.
Ste. Anne's Church probably fared better under the watchful eyes of Magdelaine La Framboise than it did when it stood at the corner of Market and Hoban, where at one time the priest's house was used as a brothel. Father Gabriel Richard suggested all church icons and memorabilia be sent to Detroit to keep them safe.

[65] There are discrepancies and a few interesting, although likely fictional, tales about the path Magdelaine La Framboise's bones took on their journey to their final resting place in the basement-level museum of Ste. Anne's Church on Mackinac Island. It is documented that Magdelaine La Framboise gave the Catholic Church the property upon which Ste. Anne's Church stands. However some versions of the transaction insist that she did so in exchange for a promise that she, her daughter Josette, and her grandson Benjamin Langdon would be buried under the altar of her beloved church.

Magdelaine's will is often cited as substantiation for this alleged fact. The clause of the will that mentions burial is as follows:

> First: I commit my Soul into the hands of Almighty God and my body to the Earth, to be decently buried according to the rights and ceremonies of the Roman Catholic Church. *And it being my particular request to be buried in the lot on which Stands, the Catholic Church* [italics added] and that neither my bones or Said Church be disturbed by my heirs…"

There is no mention of burial under the altar, but merely in the lot on which the church stands. An article by V. L. Moore, ("A Pocahontas of Michigan," Mich. Hist. Magazine, 15 (1931): 71–79) included the following information about a woman who supposedly uncovered Magdelaine's grave marker under the altar:

> "The tradition that Madame La Framboise was buried under the altar of Ste. Anne's church was known to her (Mrs. Campbell) and she made a trip to Mackinac for the purpose of locating the grave. The priest in charge of Ste. Anne's disclaimed all knowledge of such an interment and was inclined to believe that the story was only a fancy of the La Framboise descendants; but Mrs. Campbell was not to be deterred by even a clerical skeptic, and finally obtained permission to explore. Since the church is somewhat elevated on its foundation, a plan to crawl beneath the floor was quite feasible, and under went Mrs. Campbell, accompanied by the astonished sexton. Nothing was to be seen but a large pile of sand which had been thrown up in excavating for a furnace, and the priest's assertions seemed to be confirmed. Mrs. Campbell, however, noted that the heap was located directly beneath the altar and ordered the sexton to dig. Grudgingly he complied and

presently, out of the sand emerged a neglected headstone, which proved to be the sought-for marker."

Church authorities confirm an understanding that burial under the altar was Magdelaine's intent.

"Magdelaine La Framboise, a prominent Mackinac Island fur trader of mixed Ottawa and French blood, provided crucial leadership and support during the first half of the nineteenth century. Her devotion is well documented in the parish register where she frequently appears as a godmother to the baptized and witness at marriages. Madame La Framboise donated the property adjacent to her home when parish leaders decided to move the church and priest's house from their original location in the village to the current site on the east side of the island harbor in the mid 1820s. In exchange for her gift of land, La Framboise asked to be buried beneath the altar at the end of her life. Father Henri Van Renterghem honored her request when she died in 1846." (http://steanneschurch.org/history.htm).

In the 1960s the church was renovated and a basement added. At that time Magdelaine's remains were moved (presumably from under the altar) to the courtyard of the church. It is possible the bones did not take a direct route, but rather spent time in a box awaiting final disposition.

A ghoulish story in online genealogy records (www.Facbook.com/TheWatkins Family Tree Project) suggests that when the bodies of Magdelaine, Josette, and Benjamin Langdon were dug up [prior to being moved to the churchyard], they were moved to a box out in the barn. Local schoolchildren would take the bones out on Halloween. The city of Mackinac forced the church to rebury them, and that is how they came to be buried in the churchyard. (Author note: I can find no verification for this story. It is doubtful there is any truth to the account.)

Another story suggests Magdelaine was not happy to be moved from under the alter to the churchyard. After the move it is alleged the steeple started to lean and the foundation started to crumble. In spite of a complete rewiring of the church, lights turned on and off without human assistance, and the blue mist of Magdelaine's ghost floated above her grave. (www.facebook.com/historyhaunted/posts/81380873197854, visited 9/19/2017).

The two ghostly tales are likely the fiction of someone's overactive imagination. What we know is that a crypt bearing Magdelaine's name and those of her daughter and grandson rested in the churchyard from 1960 until 1996, when Magdelaine's descendents asked that her remains be returned inside the church in accord with their belief that this was her original wish.

In compliance with the family's request, Magdelaine's remains were reinterred in the basement of the church, in what is now a museum. Brother Boynton is quoted in an article about the memorial held at the time, "She'll be inside, and it will be very respectful and very reverent. It will be a place of prayer and study."

By what path Magdelaine's bones got there, and regardless of where they rested along the way, it can be assumed that her ardent spirit is free, and her crypt is simply the place where we pay her our respect.

Left: The gravesite of Magdelaine Marcotte La Framboise in Ste. Anne's churchyard before it was moved inside.
Right: Magdelaine La Framboise's final resting place.
Photos Courtesy of Bob Royce

29. MAZZUCHELLI, MOSQUITOES, AND DE TOCQUEVILLE

[66] The Minnesota river was known by the French as the St. Pierre River. The name Minnesota comes from the Dakota language, *mni* meaning water

and *sóta* translated as "sky-tinted" or "cloudy-sky" water. Congress decreed a return to the aboriginal name Minnesota in 1852.

[67] Martha Tanner was indentured to Second Lieutenant John Pierce, at the fort when Tanner had earlier left her on the island. John was brother to Benjamin Pierce, Josette's husband, and Franklin Pierce, later the president of the United States. It is not a stretch to assume Martha could support herself either by housekeeping or working at the school.

[68] Henry Rowe Schoolcraft's achievements included numerous writings on Native American legends and culture, which earned him credit as the country's first ethnologist. Much of what he observed and wrote came from his wife, Jane Johnson, whom he married in 1822. She taught her husband the Ojibwe language and much about the tribe's culture. Jane (Bamewawagezhikaquay or Obahbabmwawageezhagoquay), was the daughter of prominent Scotch-Irish fur trader, John Johnson, and an Ojibwe mother, Oshauguscodawaqua. Oshauguscodawaqua was a renowned storyteller, said to possess the surest eye and fleetest foot among the women of her tribe. Much of Henry's work originated in stories told to him by his mother-in-law, who was the daughter of Ojibwe Chief Waubojeeg. Jane Johnson Schoolcraft has also been recognized as a gifted writer for her poems and stories. She has been called the first Native American literary writer in the United States.

Henry Wadsworth Longfellow visited the Schoolcrafts on Mackinac Island. While there, Longfellow lived in the Indian dormitory. He relied on information provided by the Schoolcrafts when composing his poem *Hiawatha*.

Besides collecting Ojibwe stories, Schoolcraft wrote and published a magazine called the *Literary Voyager*, which was printed as a single issue, but widely distributed in the local area. When Schoolcraft left Mackinac Island a decade after his arrival, he was in part motivated by a desire to find better publishing opportunities.

In addition to writing, Schoolcraft was a geologist, geographer, and explorer of the Lake Superior region. In 1832, he discovered the source of the Mississippi River. He served as a United States Indian agent and was elected to the legislature for the Michigan Territory. In 1836, he worked with the government and the Ojibwe to create the Treaty of Washington, wherein the Original People ceded 13 million acres to the United States. Schoolcraft, if charitable to his motives, may have believed the Ojibwe were better off turning to farming, but the subsidies promised to them to bring about their transition to a new lifestyle were underfunded. As a result, the loss of their land caused the Ojibwe great suffering.

In 1846, after Jane's death, Henry was commissioned by Congress for a major study, known as *Indian Tribes of the United States*, which was published in six volumes from 1851 to 1857. He married a second time in 1847, to Mary Howard, from a slaveholding family in South Carolina. In 1860 she published her own novel, *The Black Gauntlet*, as a defense of slavery in response to Harriet Beecher Stowe's *Uncle Tom's Cabin*. Mary Schoolcraft's book was well received, but it caused Henry's estrangement from his children who disagreed with their stepmother's politics.

[69] Text of law freeing Martha Tanner: On July 30, A.D. 1830, the legislative council of the Territory of Michigan, after mature deliberation and discussion, passed a law entitled, "An act authorizing the sheriff of Chippewa county to perform certain duties therein mentioned. That any threats of the Said John Tanner to injure the said Martha Tanner, or any person or persons with whom she may be placed...shall be deemed a misdemeanor, punishable by fine and imprisonment, at the discretion of the court."

In response to the above law, Martha Tanner was taken by the sheriff to a missionary in Detroit where she was to be cared for and educated. She soon made her way back to Mackinac Island. This is the only law ever passed in Michigan that refers to a specific individual by name.

[70] Mazzuchelli. At the end of 1830, shortly after being ordained, and while he was still in his early twenties, Father Samuel Charles Mazzuchelli arrived at Mackinac to shepherd Ste. Anne's church.

Father Mazzuchelli was born in Milan in 1806. From an early age, he felt that he was destined for the priesthood. He entered the Dominican Order and, in spite of the fact that he spoke almost no English, he immigrated to the United States where he first ministered along the Ohio River in Cincinnati.

Over the next three years Father Mazzuchelli's parish came to include much of the territory west of Lake Michigan. His headquarters became Mackinac Island and while there he resided at Madame La Framboise's home.

Magdelaine received a letter from her friend Rosalie Dousman, whose son Magdelaine godmothered, asking her to intercede and request the priest's consideration for a mission at Green Bay. Father Mazzuchelli started many back-country churches during his tenure in the area, and one answered Dousman's wish. Joseph La Framboise contributed twelve dollars to construction of the church at Green Bay, possibly at the request of his cousin Elizabeth. The priest also established Saint Gabriel's at Prairie du Chien where Joseph traded.

[71] Mazzuchelli, pp. 32-37.

[72] Mary Ellen Evans, "The Missing Footnote or, the Curé Who Wasn't There," *Records of the American Catholic Historical Society of Philadelphia*, vol. 84, No. 4, p. 199.

[73] The 1830 census cited sex and ages for those living in the La Framboise household. I have no way of knowing who they were, but drawing upon who would have been around, the following are possible: one male aged between ten and fifteen years (perhaps a grandson of Angelique or son of one of her children), two females between ten and fifteen years (Sophia and Lucy), one female between fifteen and twenty years (possibly Martha Tanner), one female between twenty and thirty years (Catishe) and one female between fifty and sixty years (Magdelaine). This speculation and the census numbers don't provide for Angelique or her husband if she had one. Because Magdelaine's home had a revolving door of priests, relatives, and young girls staying on a temporary basis, it is impossible to identify with accuracy who these people listed in the census were. It is also possible the census did not list slaves.

[74] Dictionary of Canadian Biography, Marcot, Marguerite-Magdelaine (La Framboise).
"During the 1830s and 1840s Mme. La Framboise's door was frequently opened to passing notables. Among others, Alexis de Tocqueville and Sarah Margaret Fuller, the American woman of letters, stopped to call and were amazed at this remarkable person. She was described by Juliette Augusta Kinzie as "a woman of a vast deal of energy and enterprise—of a tall and commanding figure, and most dignified deportment."

[75] Brown, p. 5, and Black Hawk, an Autobiography (1882).
Black Hawk, or Makataimeshekiakiak, was born in 1767, at Saukenuk on the Rock River. He died at a village along the banks of the Des Moines

River in 1838. He was not a civil chief of his tribe, but earned that title for his military exploits.

Black Hawk had carried out raids from the time he was fifteen. During the War of 1812, fur trader Robert Dickson recruited Black Hawk's band of about two hundred Sauk warriors to provide assistance to the British. Dickson put him in command of all the Native Americans gathered at Green Bay. Black Hawk fought in the Battle of Fort Meigs and the attack on Fort Stephenson. After the 1813 Battle of Thames and Tecumseh's death, Black Hawk grew disillusioned by the loss of so many of his band.

He blamed inferior European battle strategy and quit the war, although he rejoined the British effort in the waning days of conflict and fought in campaigns along the Mississippi River near the Illinois Territory. After the war of 1812, he returned to his village. He disagreed with the new chief and was angered by the forced removal of his people west of the Mississippi.

In 1832, late in his life, he launched Black Hawk's War, the only war in United States history officially named for an individual. He disputed the 1804 treaty that ceded the land of his birthplace to the Americans. He looked for an opportunity to drive out the Americans, and led several attacks to reclaim his homeland. He received promises of alliance from other tribes and from the British. He gathered his British Band of about five hundred warriors and a thousand old men, women and children and crossed east of the Mississippi near the mouth of the Iowa River and followed the Rock River north. During his trek he passed his birthplace, Saukenuk, and found it in ruins.

The Black Hawk War lasted less than fifteen weeks from start to finish, and its defeat of the Native Americans ended two hundred years of resistance to white encroachment on Native American lands east of the Mississippi.

After a final one-sided battle that became known as the Bad Axe Massacre, Black Hawk was captured and held at Jefferson Barracks with other leaders of his British Band. Following eight months of imprisonment, President Andrew Jackson ordered Black Hawk brought east in 1833. The journey created circus-like spectacles in many cities along the way. Curious gawkers appeared eager to see what they described as savage, bloodthirsty Indians. In Detroit a crowd burned and hanged effigies of the prisoners.

While imprisoned, Black Hawk told his story to a government interpreter who befriended him. The interpreter gave the story to a local reporter for editing. It became the first Native American autobiography published in the country, and it immediately gained popularity.

Black Hawk died in his lodge on October 3, 1837. His wife Singing Bird survived him. In his last public appearance he said: "Rock River was beautiful country. I loved my towns, my cornfields, and the home of my people. It is yours now. Keep it as we did."

Black Hawk was buried on the farm of his friend James Jordon on a bank of the Des Moines River in Davis County, Iowa. A year later his remains were stolen by James Turner, who prepared the skeleton for exhibition. Black Hawk's sons, Nashashuk and Gamesett, pleaded with Governor Robert Lucas of the Iowa Territory for a return of the remains. Eventually they were given to the Burlington Geological and Historical Society, supposedly with the sons' permission. When the Historical Society's building burned in 1855 the remains were destroyed.

[76] Campion pp. 32-62. Kappler, Charles J. *U.S. Government treaties with American Indian Tribes. Oklahoma State University Library.* Viewed online 3/19/2016.

Interest in Catholicism had grown among the Bodwe'aadamiinh in southwest Michigan in the 1820s. Chief Leopold Pokagon traveled to Detroit to seek help from Father Gabriel Richard in resisting removal. The church had been a presence in the region for one hundred and fifty years, and it had deep roots in French communities associated with the fur trade. The Pokagon band took treaty money and bought less desirable lands. Then, as Catholics with fee-simple titles to land, they remained in Michigan just north of the state line.

Magdelaine La Framboise used her diplomatic influence with white government lawmakers when the Chicago Treaty of 1832-33 was being written. She helped convince the drafters to allow Catholic Indians to remain in their camps and villages along the shorelines of the Great Lakes. According to an amendment to the 1833 treaty, status as Catholics exempted Native Americans from removal.

[77] Narrative of Andrew J. Vieau, Sr., from an interview by Reuben Thwaites, *Wisconsin Historical Collections*, vol. xi, 1888.

"In the winter of 1832-33, the small-pox scourge ran through the Indian population of the state. Father and his crew were busy throughout the winter in burying the natives, who died off like sheep with the foot-rot. With a crooked stick inserted under a dead Indian's chin they would haul the infected corpse into a shallow pit dug for its reception and give it a hasty burial. In this work, and in assisting the poor wretches who survived, my father lost much time and money; while of course none of the Indians who lived over, were capable of paying their debts to the traders. This winter ruined my father almost completely; and in 1836, aged 74 years, he removed to his homestead in Green Bay, where his father-in-law, Joseph Le Roy, still lived."

30. GATHERING STORM

[78] Samuel Longfellow, *Life of Henry Wadsworth Longfellow*. vol. ii, p. 182, Boston, 1893.

After reading Schoolcraft's works, Longfellow planned to title *The Song of Hiawatha*, his famous poem, *Manabozho* (Nanabozo) after the good spirit and sometime trickster who was part of Indian lore. However, Schoolcraft erroneously told his friend that Manabozho and Hiawatha were alternate names for the same character, and Longfellow ultimately chose the latter. Hiawatha may have been a figure of Iroquois legend. The poem references the shores of Gitchee Gumee, which is Lake Superior. Longfellow visited Mackinac Island in the 1830s and lived in the Indian Dormitory there.

The Indian Dormitory on Mackinac Island. It is not currently open to the public. Photos courtesy Bob Royce.

[80] Or Obahbabmwawageezhagoquay, which in Ojibwe means "the sound that stars make rushing through the sky."

[81] I researched vessels that perished on Lake Michigan in 1834 and contacted Valerie van Heest at Michigan Shipwreck Research Associates (MSRA). Ms. van Heest is an underwater explorer and historian, who has been involved in the discovery and archaeological documentation of numerous historic Great Lakes shipwrecks. She checked several sources and offered suggestions for further research. While records are sketchy, I was able to find a shipwreck that occurred during the time of the one that cost Lucy Tanner and Francois Lacroix and his family their lives. In November 1834, the two-masted schooner, *Prince Eugene*, was driven ashore in a gale and wrecked eight miles north of the Manistee River mouth. In the summer of 1843, a small group of adventurers salvaged a portion of the cargo by canoe. There was no mention in the records I found of the fate of the crew and any passengers.

[82] David Lavender, *A Fist in the Wilderness,* pp. 410-419.

[83] George Catlin was born in Pennsylvania in 1796. He was a writer, painter and adventurer. His art reflected primarily scenes of Native Americans and the west.

[84] Baird Papers, personal correspondence.

[85] ibid.

[86] Baird Papers. Letter dated May 14, 1838, from Harriet Pierce to Magdelaine La Framboise.

[87] ibid.

31. SAYING GOODBYE

[88] Dropsy, also anasarca, ascites, water retention, or eclampsia. Commonly known today as congestive heart failure. The term generally referred to people who were swollen with fluids. They were prone to dropping things because the brain, affected by the swelling, caused neurological side effects. Herbal medicine treated dropsy with foxglove leaves. *Digitalis purpura* or purple foxglove grows wild in the woods and is also grown as an

ornamental perennial in gardens. The herbaceous biennial self-sows and flowers every other year. The leaves, flowers, and seeds of the plant are all toxic and may prove fatal if too much is ingested.

[89] Marshall County, Indiana http://www.potawatomi-tda.org/indiana/chiefms.htm

> "Thursday, 30th Aug, 1838: Commenced collecting the Indians at Twin Lakes Encampment, Marshall County, Indiana, and succeeded in gathering by nighttime about 170. Squads of militia were sent in all directions to bring in all the Potawatomi. They continued this round up for 5 days. Travel on horseback averages about 20 miles a day. Allowing time to go and get back, this means they rounded up all the Indians within a 30 to 50 mile radius. It is about 30 miles to Chief Wamego's village on the Fulton-Cass county line. Wamego was on the Trail of Death. The militia were supposed to gather up only Potawatomi. At least one Miami, Anthony Nigo, found himself in the removal march. He told General Tipton that he was Miami, not Potawatomi, and Tipton told him to hide in the attic of Polke's trading post at Chippeway on the Tippecanoe River north of Rochester until the march had left the next morning. He did and lived the rest of his life in Indiana." [Author's note: Potawatomi is an earlier spelling of Bodwe'aadamiinh.]

[90] Kappler. August 6, 1838, was stipulated by treaty as the date by which the Indians had to emigrate.

[91] McKee. Father Benjamin Petit was the missionary priest at Twin Lakes. He was a young man with great enthusiasm, and according to all accounts devoted to his flock. By the summer of 1840, most of remaining southwestern Michigan Bodwe'aadamiinh (spelled Potawatomi in this account) were forcibly removed west of the Mississippi by the United States army commanded by General Hugh Brady. The last claims by the Original People to their homelands and hunting grounds in Indiana and southern Michigan, including that which had been reserved back to them, were extinguished.

Many avoided removal by going to Canada, although some who tried to reach Canada were intercepted by American troops. A few Catholic bands claimed specific exemption under the Treaty of 1833 (see note 76 above) and were allowed to remain. The Episcopalian mission in Allegan County, funded by provisions of the 1836 Odawa/Ojibwe treaty, offered protection to some who hoped to avoid removal.

Governor Cass, by this time, had decided against assimilation. His viewpoint had evolved to one that allowed the government to legally take Native American lands without their consent. Native American culture was incomprehensible to him. He believed that communal ownership of property led to laziness and a lack of incentive. Cass argued that the native people should not possess the land over which they roamed because allowing them to do so fated the land to non-productivity. Cass began his governorship with a willingness to try to help the Native Americans assimilate, but reluctance on their part to accept what he considered his generosity resulted in his revised plan. If they did not want to become hard-working farmers, he would resettle them elsewhere and open the Northwest Territory to those who would use the land in a manner he deemed appropriate. How he accomplished this may have been less important to him than making sure he succeeded.

[92] http://www.northcountrytrail.org/cnd/whoiscnd.htm#N_41_, accessed 3/20/2016.
President Martin Van Buren, like presidents Jefferson, Monroe, and Jackson before him, decided to "educate and civilize" the Indians. To accomplish this he involved five Christian denominations in setting up missions.

In the winter of 1836-37 the Reverend Leonard Slater led a band of Indians, numbering three hundred, from Grand Rapids to Prairieville in the vicinity of Gull Prairie and there he established an Odawa colony. Reverend Slater erected a church for them in 1840; it was also used as a schoolroom. The colony's Christianity had dual roots, going back to the earlier Baptist mission founded at Grand Rapids under the direction of Reverend Isaac McCoy. Chief Nonoquahezieh, or Noon Day, moved off with the Slater Indians. The old chief, who remained proud of his claim that he led his men in the British attack on Buffalo and set fire to that city in December 1813, died in Prairieville in 1840. He was believed to be one hundred years old.

[93] See Visualizing Magdelaine, p. 373 for description.

[94] Baird. Also, "Civil War Home Biography of Pemberton." www.civilwarhome.com. Accessed 3/20/2016, and

www.farmlib.org/mrrt/0504.docvol. lxiv, No. 5. May 2004, Accessed online 3/20/2016.

Sophia had been in Philadelphia during the religious struggles on Mackinac Island. The clash was settling down when she returned home to suffer the rejection of John Pemberton. While out East she attended an Episcopalian Church. She enjoyed friendships with both Protestants and Catholics. The young woman may have felt that her soul was tugged in many directions.

Whether caused by John's rejection or the pull of her friends, Sophia broke her remaining ties with the Catholic Church. She adopted a demeaning attitude toward her Catholic mother, Agatha, and would not be seen with her in public.

Sophia's attitude devastated Agatha. Edward Biddle was likewise distraught by his daughter's behavior. Edward loved his wife, and it pained him to watch her suffer. Sophia's attitude also troubled Magdelaine La Framboise, not just in empathy to the suffering of her friend, Agatha, but also because she feared for Sophia's soul should the young woman lose her faith.

As if the emotional turmoil was not enough, Sophia began to lose weight and energy. Her illness foreshadowed an early death at age twenty-eight. Before dying, Sophia and her family reunited, and she returned to Catholicism. She is buried in the Catholic cemetery in the same plot as her mother, Agatha.

Pemberton seemed to fare better than Sophia after their break up. He did not suffer loneliness for long. In a letter to his brother, John maligned Mackinac, complaining, "All small places are full of scandals, hot beds that find plenty of gardeners." Pemberton had no qualms about adding to the scandals and involved himself in an affair with one of the women on the island. He continued his correspondence: "I swear I love her dearly," but he confessed of one problem—"she is married." If the affair was ill-advised, it did not seem to slow John down, for his next letter indicated he broke off the relationship, but advised his brother, "It can never do harm to have a girl suppose you are in love with her, even though she is—or is about to be—married, they all love it."

Pemberton's popularity, if it could be called that, did not last forever. If his military career began with promise, it ended in disgrace.

Pemberton left Mackinac in 1841, and after a short stint at Fort Brady in Sault Ste. Marie, he was sent to Virginia. By the start of the American Civil

War in 1861, Pemberton had married a southern woman from a slave-owning family. He resigned his commission in the Union Army and fought for the Confederacy while two of his brothers fought for the Union.

Jefferson Davis ordered Pemberton to hold Vicksburg at all costs. Pemberton's immediate supervisor, Joseph E. Johnston, pressured him to abandon the city to prevent Grant from isolating nearly 30,000 soldiers inside its fortifications. Grant had driven inland to Jackson, Mississippi, and held off the threatened attack from Johnston's army to the north. Grant was able to push Pemberton's troops on the west into the defenses of Vicksburg, and after a siege, on July 4, 1863, Pemberton surrendered. The victory was one of the most decisive in the war. It eliminated a major Confederate army and cut off the trans-Mississippi states from the rest of the south. President Lincoln wrote Grant a personal letter of congratulations and nominated him major general in the Regular Army.

Pemberton resigned his commission as lieutenant general on May 18, 1864, but Jefferson Davis later appointed him a lieutenant colonel of Artillery, a position he held until the end of the War. After the Civil War, Pemberton became a farmer near Warrenton, Virginia. He returned to Pennsylvania in 1876 and died there on July 13, 1881. He is buried at Laurel Hill Cemetery in Philadelphia.

[95] Joseph La Framboise's first marriage likely took place in 1827 or 1828, and his first wife died soon thereafter. She was the daughter of Chief Sleepy Eye. Joseph then married a second time, to a daughter of Chief Walking Dog (chiefs Walking Dog and Sleepy Eyes were brothers). Magdelaine's second grandson was born in 1829 (Magdelaine's first grandson, Benjamin Langdon, son of Josette Pierce, had died days after birth). This second grandson was named Joseph, for his father and grandfather. Wife two is also believed to have died soon thereafter, perhaps in childbirth. Joseph (Magdelaine's son), married a third time. The third marriage was to a sister of wife one, another daughter of Chief Sleepy Eyes. From the third marriage were born two additional children: Alexis (1840) and Julia Ann (1842). Joseph's fourth marriage was to Jane Dickson and from that marriage there were at least five children: William Robert (born 1847), Justine (born 1849), Eliza (born 1851), Harriet (born 1852), and an infant boy who died at birth. (See Genealogy p. 394.)

[96] Baird Papers. Letter from Martha Tanner to Elizabeth Baird, December 2, 1843. "Your Aunt is not very well. Her hands look worse than ever."

97 McDowell, Unpublished manuscript, Chapter XIII, p. 24, and Baird Papers, letter from Joseph La Framboise to Elizabeth Baird, 23 August 1842, detail this incident.

98 "Harrison will die I tell you. And after him every great chief chosen every twenty years thereafter each one will die. And when they die, let everyone remember the death of my people." That is the curse allegedly hurled at Harrison by the Prophet, brother to the great Shawnee Chief Tecumseh, after Tecumseh was killed in the British Battle of the Thames. Harrison had defeated Tecumseh at the Battle of Tippecanoe so the curse is sometimes called the "Curse of Tippecanoe." The curse was first widely noted in a *Ripley's Believe It or Not* book published in 1931. The Library of Congress conducted a study in the summer of 1980 regarding the origin of the tale, and concluded that "although the story has been well-known for years, there are no documented sources and no published mentions of it." Harrison "was chosen" in 1840 and the presidents chosen every twenty years thereafter died in office: Harrison, Lincoln, Garfield, McKinley, Harding, Franklin Roosevelt and Kennedy all died in office. Ronald Reagan's survived an assassination attempt, and some believers of the curse say that broke its power.

99 Jane and Joseph had five children: William Robert, Justine, Eliza, Harriet and an infant boy who died shortly after birth. The information about this marriage and family is contained on a family tombstone in Minnesota. Magdelaine would be deprived the opportunity to know these grandchildren.

33. Preparing to Go Home

100 Magdelaine wrote to Elizabeth Baird on April 26, 1845 noting, "My health is as usual, but I am much weaker, as I am older."

101 Magdelaine La Framboise Will and Inventory: (with original spelling, capitalization, and some words indicated by a blank space because they were illegible.)

Will

At a special session of the Probate Court for the County of Michilimackinac held on the 30th day of June AD 1846. Present William Johnston Judge of Probate at Jonathon P. King's office. Samuel Abbott and Jonathon P. King appeared and presented Madaline La Framboise's Will to be approved and allowed. The Said Will being opened was read as follows to wit:

In the name of the Most holy and adorable trinity, The Father, the Son, and the Holy Ghost Amen. I, Madaline La Framboise of Mackinac in the County of Michilimackinac in the State of Michigan being in bad health, of a sound mind, memory and understanding but considering the certainty of death and the uncertainty of the time thereof, and being desirous to settle my worldly affairs, do therefore make and publish this my last will and testament in manner and form following, to wit:

First I commit my Soul into the hands of Almighty God and my body to the Earth, to be decently buried according to the rights and ceremonies of the Roman Catholic Church. And it being my particular request to be buried in the lot on which Stands, the Catholic Church and that neither my bones or Said Church be disturbed by my heirs, and after my debts and funeral charges are paid, I devise and bequeath as follows to wit:

Second I give and bequeath to my Sister Theresa Schindler One hundred Dollars.

Third I give and bequeath to Mary Ann Fisher

(Page Two)
One hundred Dollars, and

Fourth I give and bequeath to the Resident Catholic Priest for any Church services which he may perform for me after my death Fifty Dollars and one hundred dollars to Agatha Biddle. (*Author's note: There is a notation written on the will: The allowance to Agatha Biddle was introduced or added with Blue ink. Wm Johnson, Judge of Probate making this notation*).

Fifth I give and bequeath to the most Poor of the Island Fifty Dollars to be distributed by my Executors.

Sixth I give and bequeath to my Son Joseph La Framboise all the residue of my personal Estate of every description;

wishing that the piece of land on the Island which I gave for the building of the Catholic Church shall never be claimed wither by my Son Joseph La Framboise or Josette Harriet Pierce or by any of their Heirs. In Consequence of my giving and bequeathing to my Son Joseph La Framboise so much personal Estate, it is my particular wish that he relinquish to Josette Harriet Pierce or her heirs all his right, title or interest to my two story Dwelling House and lot on the Island of Mackinac.

Lastly. I do hereby constitute and appoint Samuel Abbott of Michilimackinac and Jonathon P. King to be my Sole Executors of this my last will and testament, revoking and annulling all former Wills by me made and confirming this to be my last Will and Testament.

In Testimony whereof I have hereunto set my hand and seal at Mackinac this Second day of March A.D. eighteen hundred

(Page Three)
and forty six.

Her Mark   *(Author's note: Then the name Madaline La Framboise is written in the same handwriting as the remainder of the will.)*

Signed, sealed and published and delivered by Madaline La Framboise as and for her last Will and Testament, in the presence of us, at her request, have subscribed ourselves as Witnesses thereto:
                        Samuel K. Harring
                        Tally O'Malley
                        Samuel Abbott

The Court had issued the following order for the Witnesses to appear and testify which was duly served by James C. Rice, Dept. Sherriff, State of Michigan, County of Michilimackinac, To this sheriff and Coroner.

To Samuel M. Harring, Tally O'Mally and Samuel Abbott.

You and each of you are hereby required to appear at the Jonathon P. King Offices in the village of Mackinac on the 3rd day of June at 2:00 o'clock in the afternoon to answer such questions as shall be asked touching the proving of the will of Madeline La Framboise, deceased. ____ __ ____ ____

Given under my hand this 30th day of June, AD 1846.

    William Johnston
    Judge of Probate

The Witnesses herein, duly Sworn acknowledge the making and signing of the Will by the Said Madaline La Framboise, who died that that was her last Will and Testament. ____which the following _____ __ _____ was made upon. Said Will.

    State of Michigan
    County of Michilimackinac
        At a "Special Session"

Held at the office of Jonathon P. King of the Probate County, on the 30th day of June,

(Page Four)

A.D. 1846. The Will of Madaline La Framboise was opened and presented by Samuel and Jonathon P. King, Named ___ ___ as Executors And the Said will be proved to the Satisfaction of the Judge. It is hereby allowed to be the Last Will and Testament of the Said Madaline La Framboise and upon which ____ _____ ___ ___ ____ ____ have granted to Samuel Abbott and Jonathon P. King.

    William Johnston
    Judge of Probate

The following letter Testament the same issued and to wit as filed *(Author's note: The next part is illegible.)*

    State of Michigan
    County of Michilimackinac

To all whom Presents shall come making.

Whereas by the last will and testament of Madaline La Framboise late of Mackinac which Said Will had been dully presented with all accord, ar____ and by the power in which said msrs. Samuel Abbott, Jonathon P. King and ___ as executors on the Estate of the Said Madaline La Framboise, and they having given ____ approved by the Probate Court, the Same the ____ performance of their ____ and said Executors.

        I do hereby by those ____ and this letter testamentary ____ Mrs. Ta__ Samuel Abbott and ____ Executors of the Said Estate of Madaline La Framboise deceased. First they are to ____ and one time to the Probate Court with these ____ is a true Inventory ____ this __ _____ ___ ___ __ of the testator ____ and by ____ to be administered as ____ which shall have come to the ____ by knowledge.

        Second, to administer according

(Page Five)
to the ____ and to the Will of this Testator all her goods, Chattels, rights and credits, and the proceeds of all her real estate that may be sold for the payment of her debts as legacies which shall ____ any time come to the possession of Said Executors or to the possessions of any persons for them;

Third, to render upon oath a just and true account of their administrations within one year, and at any other times when required by the Judge of Probate.

        In witness whereof I have hereunto set my hand and seal this 30th day of June in the year One Thousand Eight hundred and forty Six.

                                  William Johnston
                                  Judge of Probate

        The following Bond of Samuel Abbott and Jonathon P. King was duly presented and approved (Copy).

        Know all men by these presents, that we Samuel Abbott and Jonathon P. King, Executors on the estate of Madaline La Framboise late of Mackinac in the State of Michigan deceased, and William Scott as Security, and held and firmly bound until William Johnston Esq. Judge of Probate for the County of Michilimackinac, and to his successors in office in the sum of Seven Thousand dollars. For payment of which sum were and truly to be made, we bind ourselves, our heirs and assigned firmly by these presents if default be made in the

Conditions following to wit:
The Condition of this bond is such that where as the above bondees Samuel Abbott and Jonathon P. King having been duly appointed Executors on the Estate of the Said Madaline

(Page Six)
La Framboise, now is the Said Executors.

First, shall make and return to the probate Court within three months a true inventory of all the real estate, and all the goods, chattels, rights, and credits, which are by law to be administered and which shall have come into their possession or knowledge.

And Second, Administers according to the law, and to the will of the Said ___ his goods, chattels, rights and credits, and the proceeds of all her real estate, that may be sold for the payment of her debts and legacies, which shall at any time come to the possession of the Executors or to the possession of any person for them,

And Third: render upon oath a just and true account of their administration, within a year, and at any other times when requested by the Judge of Probate, then the above obligations to be made and paid, otherwise to remain in full force and virtue. In witness whereof we have hereunto set our hands and seals at Mackinac, this Twenty Seventh day of June in the year one thousand, Eight hundred and forty six.

Signed & Sealed & Acknowledged
in presence of:
Samuel Abbott
J. P. King
Bela Chapman
William Scott
Wm Johnston

The foregoing bond was endorsed as follows:
State of Michigan

County of Michilimackinac
I hereby approve the within bond.
William Johnston
Judge of Probate

The following order was then issued and the Court adjourned.
Mess. Samuel Abbott and J.P. Kings
Sirs,
At the Special

(Page Seven)

Sessions of the Probate Court held at the office of Jonathon P. King on the 30th day of June AD 1846. It was then ordered and decreed that Upon cause Notice of Your appointment as Executors of the Estate of Madaline La Framboise deceased to be published in some newspapers in Detroit for three weeks in succession.

Given under my hand this 30th day of June A.D. 1846.
William Johnston
Judge of Probate.

Inventory

On the 30th day of September 1846, Jonathon P. King, one of the Executors of the Estate of Madaline La Framboise presented and filed in the Probate Office an Inventory of the goods, chattels etc of Said Madaline La Framboise as follows to wit.

Inventory of the goods, Chattels, rights and Credits of Madaline La Framboise deceased as far as they have come to the possession or Knowledge of the Executors. Appraised by Smith Herrick Richard Godfrey _____ County as follows:

1 Mahogany Side Board	$20.
1 Walnut Table	$ 2.50
1 Doz Rush Bottom Chairs	$15.00
2 _____ _____	$ 4.00
1 Large Double Stove	$10.00

1 " ___ ___	$ 4.00
1 __ Cooking Stove	$15.00
1 Knife Box	$ 2.00
1 Doz Table Spoons, Silver	$18.00
3 Cooking ___	$10.00
1 Doz Lace ___ ___	$ 8.00
1 Dutch Linen + Cotton Articles	$25.00
4 Silver Tumblers	$12.00
2 Bed stands	$10.00
4 Plated Candlesticks	$12.00
2 Feather beds and bedding	$20.00
Lot cooking and Table Furniture	$12.00
1 Carpet (?)	$12.00
1 Bureau	$10.00
1 Rug	$ 3.00
1 Bedroom Stove	$10.00
1 block	$ 3.00
1 old Side Board	$10.00
1 Wash Stand, Bowl & Pitcher	$ 2.50
6 Windsor Chairs	$ 3.00
___ ___	$ 1.00
1 Rocking Chair	$ 1.25
1 lot Kitchen Furniture and Crocks	$10.00
1 Dining Table	$ 4.00
1 ___	$ 2.50
6 Chairs	$ 2.25
___ ___ ___	$ 3.00

Page Eight
Amount Brot over	App $303.00
7 Mats	$4.50
a/c of Wm Johnston Realty	$50.00
___	$75.00
do Sml K. Harring	$80.00
2 Wartins	$2.50
Amount Due from Am Fur Company	$1823.67
2 Writing Desks	$50.00
1 Spinning Wheel	$75.00

                Samuel Abbott
                J.P. King
                Executors

Sworn to in Correctness At a Special Session of the Probate Court held on the 20th day of November AD 1846.
Present William Johnston
Judge of Probate

34. STARTLING REVELATION

[102] St. Joseph had the flags of four countries fly over its soil: French, British, Spanish, and American.

[103] Kelton, Wisconsin Historical Collections, vol. xi, American Fur Company Invoices. Between pages 372 and 373, I (the author) found 4 additional pages inserted. They were captioned as follows: voluntary, [blank page], 2, and handwritten. The page captioned 2 contained a continuation of notes by Dwight Kelton. It read:

> *"Madeline, when upon her death-bed told that she was a half-sister of Samuel Abbott who had charge of the Fur Co. interests at Mackinac, and it is said they resembled each other. This may account for some of the favors she received from the Fur Co. She appointed Samuel Abbott the administrator of her estate."*

POSTSCRIPTS

[104] "Memorials of the Grand River Valley, p. 279. Old Moccottioquit.

[105] Schoolcraft, Henry R., *Thirty Years With the Indian Tribes*.

[106] Roots Web NISHNAWBE-L Archives accessed 4/18/2016. Louise "Lisette" Constant was born 15 August 1812, Muskegon, Michigan, daughter of Pierre Constant and Popamansaouekoue. She married William Lasley. They moved to Wisconsin, and Louise died there in 1907.

About the Author

J. K. Royce was born and raised in the small town of Sandusky in Michigan's Thumb. After retiring as a Michigan First Assistant Attorney General, she turned to her love of writing and authored two travel books: *Traveling Michigan's Thumb* and *Traveling Michigan's Sunset Coast*, both published by Thunder Bay Press. The Sunset Coast guide included stories about the famous and infamous with Lake Michigan ties. As she researched her travel guide, Ms. Royce asked those with whom she came in contact about people they found interesting, and who had lived along their beautiful coast. She often heard the names Carl Sandburg and Ernest Hemmingway. But another name was also repeatedly mentioned: Magdelaine La Framboise. Fascinated by the stories she heard, Ms. Royce began researching Madame La Framboise.

It took several years to finish *Ardent Spirit*. While struggling with how to make the novel as factually correct as possible with the limited information available, Ms. Royce took a two year hiatus to write a crime thriller, *PILZ*. After the publication of *PILZ*, she returned her efforts to *Ardent Spirit*, which she had by then decided to write as a fictionalized biography. For her next project, she plans to write a second legal thriller picking up where *PILZ* left off in the life of protagonist, Casey Lawrence.

Ms. Royce has authored several short stories that have appeared in magazines, anthologies, and the California Writers Club Literary Review. She and her husband Bob live in Dublin, California, but make many trips to Michigan, where a part of her heart remains.

www.ingramcontent.com/pod-product-compliance
Lightning Source LLC
Chambersburg PA
CBHW020604300426
44113CB00007B/500